THE SEAGULL READER

Essays

Second Edition

W. W. Norton & Company, Inc., also publishes

THE SEAGULL READER: POEMS, Second Edition

THE SEAGULL READER: STORIES, Second Edition

THE SEAGULL READER: PLAYS

THE SEAGULL READER: LITERATURE

THE SEAGULL READER

Essays

Second Edition

edited by Joseph Kelly

College of Charleston

W. W. Norton & Company, Inc. • New York • London

W. W. Norton & Company has been independent since its founding in 1923, when William Warder Norton and Mary D. Herter Norton first published lectures delivered at the People's Institute, the adult education division of New York City's Cooper Union. The Nortons soon expanded their program beyond the Institute, publishing books by celebrated academics from America and abroad. By mid-century, the two major pillars of Norton's publishing program—trade books and college texts—were firmly established. In the 1950s, the Norton family transferred control of the company to its employees, and today—with a staff of four hundred and a comparable number of trade, college, and professional titles published each year—W. W. Norton & Company stands as the largest and oldest publishing house owned wholly by its employees.

Since this page cannot legibly accommodate all the copyright notices,
the Permissions Acknowledgments constitute an extension of the copyright page.

Manufacturing: Haddon Craftsmen, Inc./RR Donnelley
Book design: Chris Welch.
Production manager: Jane Searle.

Library of Congress Cataloging-in-Publication Data

The seagull reader. Essays / edited by Joseph Kelly. — 2nd ed.
    p. cm.
Includes bibliographical references.
ISBN 978-0-393-93092-4 (pbk.)
    1. American essays. 2. English essays. 3. College readers. I. Kelly, Joseph, 1962–

PS682.S43 2008
808.4—dc22

                           2007019246

W. W. Norton & Company, Inc., 500 Fifth Avenue, New York, N.Y. 10110
www.wwnorton.com
W. W. Norton & Company Ltd., Castle House, 75/76 Wells Street,
London W1T 3QT

4 5 6 7 8 9 0

Contents

*

Acknowledgments

I would like to credit the help of fellow teachers who have advised me either on my own essay courses or on this manuscript, especially Susan Farrell, Julia Eichelberger, and John Ruszkiewicz. I would also like to thank my colleagues at W. W. Norton, whose steady and careful work deserves much of the credit for the Seagull Readers: Peter Simon, Conor Sullivan, Marian Johnson, Ann Kirschner. Finally, I want to acknowledge the support of Hannah and Owen Kelly, and Spencer Jones.

Along with the publisher, I am happy to thank the following for their assistance as we prepared this second edition:

Judith Allen-Leventhal (College of Southern Maryland); Amy Amendt-Raduege (Marquette University); Sonja Andrus (Collin College); Michael Antonucci (Marquette University); Janet M. Atwill (University of Tennessee); Kathleen Baca (Dona Ana Branch Community College); Nancy Barendse (Charleston Southern University); William Beaumont (Collin County Community College); Linda Bennett (Collin County Community College); Brittain A. Blair (Southeastern Illinois College); D. Brickey (Charleston Southern University); John Briggs (University of California, Riverside); Gloria Brooks (Tyler Junior College); Stuart Brown (New Mexico State University); Sean A. Brumfield (Chattahoochee Technical College); Stephen Carroll (Santa Clara University); Michele Clingman (College of the Southwest); Elizabeth L. Cobb (Chapman University): Linda Connell (New Mexico Junior College); Kathleen Davies (Ohio University, Chillicothe) Carol Bunch Davis (Texas A&M Galveston); Debra Dew (University of Colorado, Colorado Springs); Shari Dinkins (University of Southern Indiana); Patrick A.

Dolan Jr. (University of Iowa); James Drake (University of Southern Indiana); Thomas Durkin (Marquette University); Marilyn Edwards (Athens Technical College); John Farnsworth (Santa Clara University); Tyler Farrell (University of Dubuque); Susan Felch (Calvin College); Edward Geist (University of Bridgeport); Nate Gordon (Kishwaukee College): William Gorski (University of Southern California); Kathy Greenwood (New Mexico State University, Carlsbad); Susan Grimland (Collin County Community College); Bruce Gronbeck (University of Iowa); Loren Gruber (Missouri Valley College); Ann H. Guess (Alvin Community College); Judy Harris (Tomball College); J. A. Hayden (University of Tampa); Judith Hebb (Atlanta Christian College); Audrey A. Herbrich (Blinn College); Lisa Hernandez (St. Edward's University); Sharon Hileman (Sul Ross State University); Lynda James (Collin County Community College); Robert Johnson (Midwestern State University), T. R. Johnson (Tulane University); Emily Schuering Jones (John Wood Community College); Maria Keaton (Marquette University); Robert Kinsley (Ohio University); Carol Klees-Starks (Marquette University); Janna Knittel (St. Cloud State University); Katheryn Laborde (Xavier University); John Larkin (Castleton State College); Todd Lieber (Simpson College); Trudy Fortun Lohr (Marquette University); Wendy Lym (St. Edwards/Independent Scholar); Giny Brown Machann (Blinn Junior College); George Manner (Santa Fe Community College); Terry Mathias (Southeastern Illinois College); Linda Matteson (Alvin Community College); Jill McCartney (Southwest Minnesota State University); Ruth McClain (Ohio University, Chillicothe); Ryan Meany (University of Tampa); Dominic Micer (University of Southern Indiana); Joyce M. Miller (Collin College); Claudia Milstead (Missouri Valley College); Laura Moe (Ohio University, Zanesville); Bridget Moore (Tyler Junior College); Jason Nado (Marquette University); John Netland (Calvin College); Stacy Oberle (Blinn College); Chris Partida (North Harris College); David Phillips (Charleston Southern University); Dee Preteau (Southwest Minnesota State University); Stella Price (Gordon College); Mary Reilly (St. Edward's University); Donald R. Riccomini (Santa Clara University); Pam Rittof (John Wood Community College); Ray Rotella (Ohio University, Zanesville); Beverly G. Six (Sul Ross State University); Audell Shelburne (University of

Mary Hardin-Baylor); Beth Shelton (Paris Junior College); Bethany Sinnott (Catawba College); Andy Solomon (University of Tampa); Helen Strait (Southwest Texas Junior College); Jacob Stratman (Marquette University); Michael Suwak (College of Southern Maryland); Elizabeth Taylor (Brown University); David Urban (Calvin College); Martha Van Cise (Berry College); Robin Visel (Furman University); Kathleen Volk (Marquette University); Rebecca T. Watson (Midland College); Wendy Weaver (Marquette University); Jeanna White (East Texas Baptist University); Jennifer Willacker (Marquette University); Joanne Williams (Olivet College); Linda Woodson (University of Texas, San Antonio); Scott Yarbrough (Charleston Southern University); Delores Zumwalt (Collin County Community College).

THE SEAGULL READER

Essays

Second Edition

What Are Essays?

The term "essay" is related to the now-archaic verb *to essay*, which means to test something, to determine its composition (as in a metal), to discover the nature of something. The first essays were written by the Frenchman Michel de Montaigne, and published in 1580. Montaigne claimed no expertise in any area; in fact, he made a virtue of having a normal intellect and temperament. Though he was well-read and had a curious mind, he boasted no specialized knowledge in any field. His genius was to apply common sense, a tolerant attitude, and a reflective mind to the issues of his day, as he *essayed* topics as disparate as drunkenness, cannibals, and coaches. Often, all he intended to do was explore a subject, to examine it from fresh angles, to see what he might discover.

In England in the early 1600s, just about the time of the *Mayflower*, Sir Francis Bacon popularized Montaigne's form, and he brought to the genre the same respect for simple observation that he inaugurated in his new "scientific method" of reasoning. Good essayists, like good scientists, scrub all residue of cant from their eyes. They do not judge the world according to tradition and the (dubious) wisdom of the ages. The scientist, for example, does not look at the Bible or Greek philosophers to learn the laws of nature: she looks at nature. Likewise, the early essayists looked at nearly everything in the human world, and by applying common sense rather than received opinion, they made surprising discoveries—for instance, that South American "savages" were less brutal and in some ways more civilized than Europeans.

The tradition of the common intellect or common sense is still vital in modern essays. David Sedaris, for example, tells stories from his perspective as a somewhat average, middle-class, middle-aged American, but his experiences are rendered with uncommon equanimity. Thomas Lynch is an undertaker, so he confronts death far more often than most people, but he is no philosopher and he is no theologian. He observes death and ruminates on the meaning of life with the same tools that you and I might use. These traditional essayists take readers on journeys of discovery—sometimes of unexplored territory, sometimes of familiar territory approached from a refreshing angle, almost always hoping to open readers up to new ways of thinking about themselves and the world they live in.

Some modern essays make a great deal out of the writers' own experiences, telling anecdotes from their lives that illustrate some larger theme that affects us all. Bret Lott, for example, explores the nature of sin and atonement through a seemingly innocuous dust-up between him and his sons. Eudora Welty celebrates the sensory delight of childhood. Maya Angelou ponders the conjunction of race and schooling while telling the story of her own graduation. These autobiographical or **personal** essays use many of the devices of fiction, and you can read them almost the way you'd read a short story. Many have plots—stories with conflicts and resolutions—just like fiction, and because of this resemblance some people refer to them as literary essays. But typically their themes or "meanings" are more overt than you'd expect in modern fiction. They have a more obvious purpose than short stories, which generally don't announce any kind of subject or theme to be explored. Essays, by comparison, usually undertake a pretty overt exploration of their particular subject, whether it's the nature of art (Annie Dillard) or of college (James Thurber) or anything else.

Roughly a third of the selections in this volume are largely autobiographical or exploratory, and so fall into the category of personal essays. The other two-thirds of this book are made up of **rhetorical essays**. These have a definite, easily recognized persuasive purpose: they either want readers to change their minds about something, or they want readers to change what they do. Some rhetorical essays are **political**, attempting to alter the course of history by persuading people to take (or refrain from taking) action. For example, Martin Luther King's Jr. "Letter from Birmingham Jail" tried to convince moderate whites all over America that they should march arm in arm with African Americans against racists like Bull Connor, who was Birmingham's commissioner of public safety in the early 1960s.

Other persuasive essays do not try to get their readers to do anything specific—such as join the civil rights movement—as much as they attempt to change minds and attitudes. These might be called **opinion** essays because they deal more with opinions than actions. They might criticize the state of marriage in America (Judy Brady) or complain about public apathy (William F. Buckley). Some, such as Molly Ivins's essay, were first printed in the opinion-editorial (or "op-ed") section of newspapers.

These categories (exploratory, personal, political, and opinion) are not carved in stone. An opinion essay might be partially autobiographical. An exploratory essay might use the kind of logical argument you'd expect from a political speech. It is not so important that you can fit an essay into one of these categories. Ultimately, the categories are not that important. What is important is that you determine what the writer was trying to do with his or her essay.

How to Read Essays

You need to determine what you think the writer was trying to accomplish with his or her essay if you're going to analyze and evaluate it successfully. Was the writer trying to get people to do something? If so, who was his audience? What was he trying to get them to do? Or was the writer exploring a subject, perhaps in a tentative way, without really trying to prove anything at all? The key to reading any essay is to first figure out what the writer was trying to accomplish. It makes no sense to judge the logic of a personal essay—there might be little logic in it at all, but that would not be a defect. Likewise, if you read an opinion essay to open yourself up to new ways of thinking, to begin your discussion of a topic, the writer might have failed: she might have wanted to close off your opinions, narrow them down to one opinion in particular—her own. If you decide that an essay is trying to persuade you to do something or to think something, you need to be cautious. You need to be skeptical. Be on your guard. You don't want to be fooled. You don't want to be taken in by a weak or unsound argument. To properly read persuasive essays, you need to know how to argue yourself.

Knowing how to argue is particularly important in a democracy. In our society we argue about nearly everything in the public sphere—who should be president, how our schools should be run, whether we should ban smoking in restaurants. As you study political and opinion essays, you'll learn how to change the minds and behavior of people, and how others try to change your behavior and opinion. That is the essence of rhetoric, the tricks of the trade, so to speak, the tools of persuasion. They are power tools and are dangerous in the wrong hands. They are easily abused. People like Adolf Hitler and Osama bin Laden do not rule by terror alone. They were (and are) skilled in the arts of persuasion. By learning these rhetorical arts, you'll protect yourself against demagoguery. And you'll learn how to make sound decisions for your own opinions and actions, which is just as important. You'll learn how to convince others to agree with you and do what you think they ought to do.

Rhetoric, or the art of persuasion, comprises some sophisticated skills, so the bulk of this section deals with argumentation. It applies mostly (though not exclusively) to the political and opinion essays. (At the end, there's a note on how to read those essays that don't try to persuade readers, the personal essays.)

Like all arts, rhetoric involves various techniques that have proved to be effective over the years. No doubt natural talent helps the great orators and writers, but even Abraham Lincoln and Martin Luther King Jr. had to practice their art. Lincoln honed his skills in courtrooms and in legislatures, while King practiced from the pulpit. They might not have known the names of the argument forms discussed below, for many a great artist learns not from books but by imitation. But all great persuaders, no matter the level of their formal training in rhetoric, use these argument forms.

This section is divided into three parts that correspond to each type of argument: **logical**, **ethical**, and **pathetic**. The terminology may seem fairly esoteric, but learning these terms and what they mean can help you analyze an argument—that is, break it down into its parts. And only by analyzing an argument can you evaluate it. Ultimately, evaluation should be your goal in reading not only these essays but any essay. Essays often delight us, and certainly they can be read purely for the sake of enjoyment. No doubt there is pleasure in getting swept up on the wave of emotion propelled by a good rhetorician or in succumbing to the awe inspired by a noble speaker. But reading critically means carefully and artfully evaluating an argument before surrendering to anyone's opinion or bending your actions to someone's will.

So when you read essays you must be active. Fill the margins of your book with your own reactions, observations, objections, and approvals. Enter into a dialogue with the essayist. Your marginal notes will go a long way toward revealing just what strategies the essayist is using to persuade you. If the pages of this book are clean by the end of your course, you're reading too passively.

Learning to recognize valid and true arguments, and learning to resist manipulative rhetoric, takes time and hard work. You might find yourself referring back to these pages again and again before you've mastered the art of reading essays. Logical arguments are particularly difficult to analyze, especially in the often-disguised forms in which essays present them. So do not be discouraged by fitful starts and early confusion. Keep at it.

Logical Arguments

Everyone uses logic everyday. When you were in high school, you argued with your parents about whether you should be allowed to go on that overnight trip to the beach. Now when you decide whether you should go to a party or study one evening, you'll argue the matter over in your mind, just as you'll argue with friends about whether one movie is better than another, and you'll argue in your history class about what caused World War I. So you know how to argue. What you're going to learn here is what you've already been doing intuitively. But once you understand what you've been doing, once you learn how to handle the tools of rhetoric, you'll construct better arguments, and you'll be much better at identifying someone else's bad argument.

The political essays in this volume use logic more than the others. A political essay must meet a high standard of logic and evidence, because it's very hard to get people to do things they are not inclined to do. People will not change how they act unless the arguments for doing so are compelling and reasonable. Political essays, then, are excellent models to use in constructing your own logical arguments, especially the kind of writing you'll most likely be asked to do in school. Most academic writing puts a high premium on logic.

Logical arguments fall into one of two types, deductive or inductive. Roughly speaking, deductive arguments are top-down: they present general principles from which they draw a conclusion. Inductive arguments are bottom-up: they offer many examples and from these abstract a conclusion of general application.

Deduction

A deductive argument might look like this:

> Men are tall.
> Bob is a man.
> Therefore, Bob is tall.

This is the simplest type of deductive argument. Notice that the argument has three parts. The first is a statement of general applicability: "Men are tall." Rhetoricians call this the **major premise.** It applies to all things within a particular category—in this case, the category "men." The second statement, "Bob is a man," is the **minor premise**. It asserts something about a particular case, not a general category. The **conclusion** follows logically: "Bob is tall." Because Bob falls into the category "men," and because all people in that category are tall, Bob must be tall. If the conclusion follows logically from the premises, the argument is **valid.**

But a valid argument is not necessarily **sound**. It must pass another test, what we might call the **truth** test: *Do you agree with all of the premises?* In the example above, you probably objected to the major premise, "Men are tall," because you know that not all men are tall. Some men, in fact, are short. The argument might be valid (the conclusion logically follows the premises), but it is **unsound** because it is based on a **false premise**. In real life and in real arguments, very few major premises are absolutely true, so most arguments use a few qualifiers. For example, we could fix this argument with these qualifiers: "*Most* men are tall, and Bob is a man, so Bob is *probably* tall." But it would be more persuasive to change the premises altogether: "A height of six feet is tall, and Bob is six feet one inch, so Bob is tall."

When someone tries to persuade you with a deductive argument, you should break it down into its elements. Figure out what the premises and conclusion are. Only then can you properly evaluate the argument's **truth** and **validity**. Consider this famous example of deductive reasoning:

> We hold these truths to be self-evident, that all men are created equal, that they are endowed by their Creator with certain unalienable Rights, that among these are Life, Liberty, and the pursuit of Happiness. That to secure these rights, Governments are instituted among Men deriving their just powers from the consent of the governed. That whenever any Form of Government becomes destructive of these ends, it is the Right of the People to alter or to abolish it, and to institute new Government. . . . The history of the present King of Great Britain is a history of repeated injuries and usurpations, all having in direct object the establishment of an absolute Tyranny over these States. . . . We, therefore, the Representatives of the United States of America, in General Congress . . . solemnly publish and declare, That these United Colonies are, and of Right ought to be Free and Independent States.

Thomas Jefferson proposes many major premises: All men are created equal; men have the right to life, liberty, and the pursuit of happiness; governments exist to protect these rights; governments derive their legitimacy from the people; if a government is not doing its job, the people can abolish it. These statements are categorical. The first few assert truths about men in general; the others assert truths about governments in general. Jefferson expects his audience to share his belief in these truths. He calls them "self-evident" and offers no evidence or further argument to prove them. If you are a citizen of the United States, you probably believe these "truths."

Jefferson's minor premise, like all minor premises, considers a specific case: the government of Great Britain is not doing its job of securing the unalienable rights of its colonial subjects in America. To put it succinctly: King George III is a tyrant. Conclusions are usually pretty easy to identify. Any statement that you could rephrase with "therefore" in front of it is a conclusion. In the Declaration of Independence, Jefferson explicitly announces his conclusion in his last paragraph:

> We, THEREFORE . . . solemnly publish and declare, That these United Colonies are, and of Right ought to be FREE AND INDEPENDENT STATES; [etc.]

In most arguments, the conclusions won't be so obvious.

It will take some practice before you can recognize these different parts of deductive arguments, especially major and minor premises. Any statement you can rephrase with "because" in front of it is a premise:

> *Because* "whenever any Form of Government becomes destructive of [the peoples' inalienable rights], it is the Right of the People to alter or to abolish it";
> and
> *Because* King George III is destructive of American rights
> Therefore we "these United Colonies are, and of Right ought to be FREE AND INDEPENDENT STATES."

You will notice that I rephrased some of Jefferson's minor premise as I analyzed his argument; that is okay; it is often very helpful to paraphrase, so long as you retain the substance of the writer's words. The hardest part of evaluating deductive arguments is what we've just done for Jefferson's argument: **analysis**, or breaking down into parts.

Once you've properly analyzed the argument, it is relatively easy to **evaluate** it. First, apply the truth test: *Do you agree with the* *premises?* In our example, you would ask yourself, *Do I think that people should overthrow governments that don't secure their rights?* and *Do I agree that King George's government was destructive of the rights of the American colonists?* If you agree with a premise, you consider it to be **true**; if you disagree with it, you consider it to be **false**. If you identify a false premise, look to see if the writer has added a supporting argument to change your mind about that premise. For example, Jefferson clearly suspected that his readers would not agree with his minor premise, *King George is a tyrant.* So he inserted a lot of supporting evidence. Actually, the bulk of the Declaration of Independence consists of this evidence, the long list of grievances against King George. Jefferson calculated that the weight of this list would persuade his skeptical readers to agree with his minor premise, that King George's government was destructive of American rights.

If, after considering all supporting arguments, you still regard a premise as false, then you judge the argument to be unsound. If you accept the premises, then the next stop is to decide whether the argument is valid.

Philosophers use complex tests to evaluate an argument's validity, but for the purposes of rhetoric we do not need to be so precise. You can trust your own common sense to evaluate most of the arguments you'll encounter in this book and in your life. I've found with my own students that if you simply ask yourself, *Does the conclusion follow logically from the premises?* more often than not you'll judge correctly. If the answer is yes, then the argument is valid; if the answer is no, the argument is invalid. Finally, if you both agree with the premises and think the conclusion logically follows those premises, you judge the argument to be sound.

Sometimes writers leave one of their premises out. This is a common and accepted rhetorical practice, and such arguments are called **enthymemes**. For example, a few paragraphs above I reasoned that if you are a citizen of the United States, you probably believe the "self-evident" truths that Jefferson listed in the Declaration of Independence. My reasoning is a deductive argument. The minor premise is this: *You are a citizen of the United States.* (If you are not a U.S. citizen, then the premise is obviously false, but let's suppose that the minor premise is true.)

The conclusion is: *You probably believe in the self-evident "truths" espoused by the Declaration of Independence.*

I left it to you to figure out that the major premise is something like this: *Americans are raised to believe that all men are created equal, that they are endowed by their creator with certain unalienable rights, etc.* The fully analyzed argument would unfold like this:

> *Because* Americans are taught to believe all men are created equal, etc.; and *because* you are an American;
> *therefore*, you probably believe the self-evident truths of the Declaration of Independence.

As in any deductive argument, you have to lay out the pieces before you can evaluate the whole. The only difference in this case was that we had to supply the unstated major premise. Consequently, you'll never decide an enthymeme is invalid—because *you* supply the premise that will logically lead to the conclusion. You're really only testing for truth: *do you agree with the premises, both stated and un- stated?*

Once you've stated that suppressed premise for yourself, you can decide whether you think it is reasonable or not, and then you can decide whether the conclusion follows logically. But you need to state the suppressed premise before you can assess the argument.

Induction

Induction, bottom-up reasoning, is easier to grasp than deduction. It is based on this idea: If you look at a lot of specific cases, you can reasonably infer the general principle that governs them all. Rather than starting with a categorical statement, as in deduction, you use particular examples to lead you to a statement of general applicabil- ity. For example, an inductive argument might go like this:

> Kobe is tall. Shaquille is tall. Dirk is tall. Tim is tall. Carmelo is tall. Therefore, all men are tall.

The first thing you might notice is that this argument is not very **strong**. While Kobe, Shaquille, Dirk, Tim, and Carmelo might all be tall (let's suppose that we agree they are), that does not mean that *all* men are tall.

Usually you can't look at every case within a category, so a generalization is almost always an estimate. The conclusion is not going to be *definitely* true or false, but *probably* true or false. For example, proving the conclusion "Men are tall" by looking at every case is impossible. That would mean determining the height of every man on the planet. But we can take a sample of those men and draw a reasonable conclusion. Before you accept the reasonableness of any conclusion, however, you should be sure that the sample is **sufficiently large, accurate,** and **representative.**

In the inductive argument above, the sample is accurate: All the men I named are tall. But the sample is neither sufficiently large nor representative. (These two criteria often go together.) I took my sample from the National Basketball Association—clearly not representative—and I only included five men. My sample is far too narrow and small to represent men in general. A better sample would include many men selected randomly from the total population rather from the select groups you might find on basketball courts.

The Declaration of Independence is a good example of an inductive argument. Jefferson's minor premise was, to paraphrase, "King George III is a tyrant." Jefferson thought that his audience might not take this statement as self-evident, so he listed twenty-six examples of George's tyranny, from "He has refused his Assent to Laws, the most wholesome and necessary for the public good" to "He has excited domestic insurrections among us . . ." Let's see whether we are justified in inferring George III's tyranny from this sample.

Is the list accurate? If Jefferson had invented some grievances, we could dismiss the argument for being inaccurate. But they seem to be accurate enough. Is it sufficiently large? If he had listed only three or four, we might conclude that such examples constituted mistakes by the government rather than tyranny. But Jefferson has listed enough to impress most readers. Is the sample representative? If all twenty-six grievances dealt with abuses of one part of the government's powers—say, the impeding of immigration to America—they would not be representative. But the grievances touch on so many aspects of government—taxation, the support and control of the army, the judiciary, trade, immigration, etc.—that the sample's scope seems sufficiently wide. This long list of grievances, then, offers pretty persuasive support for his inductive argument. We describe such arguments as **strong**.

Note that Jefferson concludes with an assertion that is the minor premise of his deductive argument. You will find that writers commonly mix their arguments in this way. Very rarely do you find a single argument without other arguments supporting it somehow. Real-life arguments can get pretty confusing and complex. Actually, I chose the Declaration of Independence as an example because it's fairly straightforward. Jefferson was trained in rhetoric, and he laid out his argument quite clearly. Most arguments, even those you'll find in this book, are less carefully and skillfully constructed. Your task as a difficult-to-persuade, skeptical reader is to unravel those complexities and lay them out clearly so you can evaluate them.

Ethical Arguments

Ethos is the writer's or speaker's self-presentation, especially her moral standing. Within the course of a speech, certain cues will help an audience form a picture of the speaker's character. How the speaker dresses, how she carries herself on the podium, the tenor of her voice, her gestures, what she says about herself, how she treats her opponents—all contribute to the audience's view of her character. A high school student applying for a job at Wal-Mart shouldn't show up in elephant jeans sliding down his boxer shorts. Most employers would interpret such clothes as disrespectful of authority. Probably, they'd expect the high school student to be unreliable and, perhaps, even surly to customers. A candidate for the U.S. Senate who is addressing a meeting of dock workers probably does not want to come dressed like an executive because it might seem to her audience that her interests are those of management, not labor. Dress, posture, vocal tone, gestures, and the like are tools of rhetoric: They help us persuade. We call these tools **ethical arguments**.

Writers cannot persuade with the visual or aural cues that a speaker can use, because a reader cannot see or hear the writer. Even so, whether you're aware of it or not, every essay produces a picture of the writer. Personal essays, as you might expect, often do so explicitly, and opinion essays depend on such self-presentation. For example, Brent Staples presents himself to the readers of *Ms.* magazine as "a softy who is scarcely able to take a knife to a raw chicken." This self-portrait contributes to our sense of injustice when white women assume that this six-foot, bearded, bushy-haired black man is a mugger. Even his diction convinces us that Staples is an educated, respectable, unthreatening citizen. Consider this passage:

> I entered a jewelry store on the city's affluent Near North Side. The proprietor excused herself and returned with an enormous red Doberman pinscher straining at the end of a leash. . . . I took a cursory look around, nodded, and bade her goodnight.

Robbers do not *bid* people goodnight. Similarly, by whistling "sunny selections from Vivaldi's *Four Seasons*" when he walks down streets at night, Staples convinces white women that he is, like themselves, a cultured member of society, and so he's hardly likely to attack them.

Staples's essay would be much less persuasive to his white readers if he presented himself as an enraged victim of racism. This is not to say that he was never enraged. In fact, he admits that he "learned to smother the rage I felt at so often being taken for a criminal." He smothers his rage because to expose it would alienate and perhaps frighten his readers. So Staples writes in calm prose that is at times dispassionate and often funny. He comes across as a thoughtful, reasonable, likeable person. He might lose a bit of urgency in that self-presentation, but white readers are more likely to trust his story and share his sense of injustice. Instead of feeling accused, the readers of *Ms.* will identify with Staples.

Even essays that rely largely on logical arguments use ethical arguments as well. For example, Thomas Jefferson was careful to give readers a picture of the men who signed the Declaration of Independence. The very first sentence admits that "a decent respect to the opinions of mankind requires that [a people overthrowing their government] should declare the causes which impel them to the separation." In that sentence, Jefferson presents the American rebels as reflective men eager to win the approval of other governments, even monarchies, like France, who might otherwise view the rebellion as a sign of anarchy. They are not anti-authority rabble rousers, whose enthusiasm might threaten the governments of other nations. The style of the Declaration of Independence does the same thing: No maddened anarchist would begin such a declaration with a calm subordinate clause, "When in the Course of human events . . . " The signers of the Declaration of Independence present themselves as slow-to-act, prudent men who "are more disposed to suffer, while evils are sufferable, than to right themselves by abolishing the forms [of government] to which they are accustomed."

When you're evaluating someone's ethical argument, you should ask yourself questions like these:

- What authority does the writer claim?
- Does she know more about the subject than I do?
- Why should I listen to what she has to say?
- How does the writer's personal testimony affect her arguments?
- Is the writer trustworthy?
- Is she reasonable?
- Do I like the writer? Would I be happy to meet and talk with her?

The headnotes to each essay might help you answer some of these questions, and some famous writers can count on their celebrity to contribute to their ethos. But the writer who makes good use of ethos will answer these questions in the essay itself.

The good writer will also establish connections between herself and the reader. Any rhetorical situation presumes a division between writer and reader. Otherwise, there would be no need for persuasion. So a writer needs to give a reader a sense that the two of them are, despite their differences of opinion on particular issues, part of one community working toward a common goal. When you evaluate a writer's ethos, you should ask yourself whether she's established that common ground with you, and you should decide whether she is sincere.

Pathetic Arguments

Pathos refers to the emotional state of the audience. It includes their senses of pity and loathing, fear and delight, happiness and sadness, and all the emotions that can be excited by words. When you read you should be wary of your emotions. This is not to say that you should disregard them altogether. Rather, you should learn to recognize and evaluate **pathetic arguments** by asking yourself,

- At what point in the essay did I feel anger, outrage, relief, affection, and so forth?
- How did the writer elicit these emotions from me?
- Are these emotional appeals fair, or are they dishonest?

You might wonder what I mean by *honesty* when I talk of emotions. What's the difference between an honest and a dishonest emotion? Take, for example, Martin Luther King's explanation of the effects of prejudice on his young daughter:

> you suddenly find your tongue twisted and your speech stammering as you seek to explain to your six-year-old daughter why she can't go to the public amusement park that has just been advertised on television, and see tears welling up in her eyes when she is told that Funtown is closed to colored children, and see ominous clouds of inferiority beginning to form in her little mental sky, and see her beginning to distort her personality by developing an unconscious bitterness toward white people. . . .
> —then you will understand why we find it difficult to wait.

He elicits our sympathy with the father and the child so powerfully that we are tempted to suspend judgment and accept whatever proposition will end this girl's suffering. A dishonest use of pathos would ask us to do just that: substitute emotion for logic. A dispassionate evaluation might lead us to dismiss King's appeal because it is a tearjerker. After all, anyone who has a child knows that sympathy for a child's tears cannot be allowed to overcome judgment or children would eat nothing but candy. King surrounds his heartrending story with dispassionate, logical arguments, so his audience need not be swayed solely by feeling. Pathos should complement logic, not replace it.

It would also be dishonest to single out an unusual, emotionally provocative case in an attempt to sway rather than persuade. Take the example of a convicted felon who, after serving a few years in prison, is released on parole only to commit a bloody murder. Assume that this case is highly unusual: that 99 percent of convicts are successfully rehabilitated in prison, and that criminals convicted of violent crimes are rarely paroled. It would be dishonest for a candidate for district attorney to use photographs of the smiling victim or tearful interviews with the victim's parents to attack the incumbent. Such a strategy would stir up voters' emotions while not indicating just how miniscule the risk to public safety really is.

Be cautious. Be sure that when your emotions are triggered reason is not left behind. There is no formula by which you can do this. You must make yourself aware of emotional appeals and then simply use your common sense. With that caution raised, let me add that, as writers, emotions are sometimes our best aid. The vignette about King's daughter justly engages sympathy and arouses outrage; perhaps King could not over-come his readers' long-held prejudices without jerking a few tears.

A Note on Reading Personal Essays

Personal essays are often inductive because they use the method of **example**. Consider Amy Tan's essay on writing, which argues that a plain, conversational writing style is better than a learned, somewhat sophisticated writing style. I say the essay **argues** for this conclusion, but it does not lay out much in the way of logical reasoning. The argument consists of one example: Amy Tan's own experience. Once she herself started writing in a style that an unsophisticated speaker of English (her mother) could understand, Tan's career as a writer took off.

If we were to evaluate this "argument," we would apply the tests of an inductive argument. More than likely, we would decide that the argument is weak because the evidence, while accurate, is not sufficiently large and it may or may not be representative: we would probably want to see a few more cases before we could accept Tan's experience as typical of successful writers. The evidence that Tan presents us is entirely **anecdotal**: a single case, often rendered in compelling, sometimes emotionally charged language. Rhetoricians warn against being swayed by anecdotal evidence. A political candidate might make much of a "welfare queen," a lurid example of an able-bodied woman bilking working taxpayers to finance her life of leisure. But sensible voters would ask: is her case typical? is this just an outlandish, extreme example of a very unusual case? or does our public policy encourage and enable a lot of "welfare queens"? does this single anecdote fairly represent the other cases that our politician has not described? Anecdotal arguments are weak inductive arguments.

Since personal essays are often anecdotal, they usually exploit pathetic arguments. More often than not, you'll find that personal essayists appeal to your emotions—perhaps making us laugh (David Sedaris), sometimes cutting us with the razor-sharp edge of compassion (Lott). They also make ethical arguments, because personal essays depend so much on the writer's experience. Their success or failure depends, to a large degree, on whether we like the author, whether we trust the voice telling us this particular anecdote.

But it is unfair, really, to evaluate personal essays along the lines of argument. If we asked Amy Tan what she meant to do in the essay, she probably would deny any attempt to prove that a simpler style of writing is better than a sophisticated style. Possibly, she would claim to be doing no more than offering readers the benefit of her own experiences. Probably, she did not have an overt persuasive intention when she sat down to write. An opinion columnist has an overt persuasive intention. George Will, for example, wants college graduates to stop thinking about "values" and, instead, cultivate "virtues." We can evaluate his logical, ethical, and pathetic arguments to see whether we should adopt his opinion. But Eudora Welty does not have such an obvious purpose. What does she want us to think when we finish reading "Listening"? It is hard to say.

Writers of personal essays generally do not try to change our behavior or even to change our minds on some issue of public policy (a significant exception is N. Scott Momaday, who makes a definite claim in his essay). Their intentions usually are more difficult to identify, sometimes much deeper than opinion. By adopting the writer's perspective, readers are often asked to follow the writer along a path of exploratory thought or experience to a surprising conclusion. Often, they use the acid of common sense to dissolve traditional prejudices. They tempt us to see a familiar issue from an unfamiliar angle—the nature of art, for example, as manifest in the work of a stunt pilot (in Annie Dillard's essay).

How, then, should we read personal essays? Go ahead and identify their arguments—whether they are inductive, ethical, or pathetic—and even evaluate those. But your evaluations should not be the end of your reading. Nor should they be the end of your discussions. At some point, you should drop the caution you're supposed to adopt when confronted by arguments. Give yourself over to the writer's perspective, at least for a little while. Read the personal essays almost as you read fiction, suspending your disbelief, even losing yourself in the stories they relate.

Personal essays invite readers to pursue subjects themselves. Compare the anecdotal experience of the writers against your own experience and against the experiences of your classmates. Should you expand the scope of your own current perspective? Have you been too narrow and derivative in the way you've thought about the world? Have you been too dependent on grooves of thought cut for you by your parents or by teachers or by the pressures of society? Think about these things. Discuss them. Personal essays are successful not when they confirm you in a settled conclusion, but when they inspire you to further exploration.

Conclusion

With the tools of rhetoric, you should be able to analyze any essay, examine its parts, and evaluate its soundness and its strength. But you should also read these essays with an eye to their literary or aesthetic features. We have chosen these selections not only for their exemplary arguments and their historical value, but also for their beauty. There is a lot of good writing in these pages. Even the most formal, documentary prose, like that of the Declaration of Independence, resonates with a power only beauty can supply.

Abraham Lincoln closes his first inaugural address with these ringing words:

> The mystic chords of memory, stretching from every battlefield, and patriot grave, to every living heart and hearth-stone, all over

this broad land, will yet swell the chorus of the Union, when again touched, as surely they will be, by the better angels of our nature.

This quotation distinguishes itself by its stateliness, dignity, beauty. Not every essay attempts stateliness. But each does strive for aesthetic effect. Without such effects we'd find reading essays a dreary business. So while you'll need to analyze the arguments these essays contain, don't forget to enjoy them.

Maya Angelou

b. 1928

"Graduation" is an excerpt from Angelou's autobiography, I Know
Why the Caged Bird Sings *(1970). The title of that book is a quo-
tation from the 1899 poem "Sympathy" by African American poet
Paul Laurence Dunbar, which concludes with these lines:*

I know why the caged bird sings, ah me,
When his wing is bruised and his bosom sore,—
When he beats his bars and he would be free;
It is not a carol of joy or glee,
But a prayer that he sends from his heart's deep core,
But a plea, that upward to Heaven he flings—
I know why the caged bird sings!

*At least one of Angelou's intentions was to expose the bars con-
straining black Americans (and in particular black women) in
America and to number herself among the poets, preachers, musicians, and blues singers of "the wonderful, beautiful Negro race."*

Graduation

The children in Stamps[1] trembled visibly with anticipation.
Some adults were excited too, but to be certain the whole
young population had come down with graduation epi-
demic. Large classes were graduating from both the grammar school
and the high school. Even those who were years removed from their
own day of glorious release were anxious to help with preparations
as a kind of dry run. The junior students who were moving into the
vacating classes' chairs were tradition-bound to show their talents
for leadership and management. They strutted through the school
and around the campus exerting pressure on the lower grades. Their
authority was so new that occasionally if they pressed a little too
hard it had to be overlooked. After all, next term was coming, and it

---

1. A small, rural town in Arkansas.

never hurt a sixth grader to have a play sister in the eighth grade, or a tenth-year student to be able to call a twelfth grader Bubba.[2] So all was endured in a spirit of shared understanding. But the graduating classes themselves were the nobility. Like travelers with exotic destinations on their minds, the graduates were remarkably forgetful. They came to school without their books, or tablets or even pencils. Volunteers fell over themselves to secure replacements for the missing equipment. When accepted, the willing workers might or might not be thanked, and it was of no importance to the pregraduation rites. Even teachers were respectful of the now quiet and aging seniors, and tended to speak to them, if not as equals, as beings only slightly lower than themselves. After tests were returned and grades given, the student body, which acted like an extended family, knew who did well, who excelled, and what piteous ones had failed.

Unlike the white high school,[3] Lafayette County Training School distinguished itself by having neither lawn, nor hedges, nor tennis court, nor climbing ivy. Its two buildings (main classrooms, the grade school and home economics) were set on a dirt hill with no fence to limit either its boundaries or those of bordering farms. There was a large expanse to the left of the school which was used alternately as a baseball diamond or a basketball court. Rusty hoops on the swaying poles represented the permanent recreational equipment, although bats and balls could be borrowed from the P. E. teacher if the borrower was qualified and if the diamond wasn't occupied.

Over this rocky area relieved by a few shady tall persimmon trees the graduating class walked. The girls often held hands and no longer bothered to speak to the lower students. There was a sadness about them, as if this old world was not their home and they were bound for higher ground. The boys, on the other hand, had become more friendly, more outgoing. A decided change from the closed attitude they projected while studying for finals. Now they seemed not ready to give up the old school, the familiar paths and

2. Slang for "Brother."
3. Prior to the 1954 Supreme Court decision *Brown v. Board of Education of Topeka,* *Kansas,* many public schools in America were racially segregated.

classrooms. Only a small percentage would be continuing on to college—one of the South's A & M (agricultural and mechanical) schools, which trained Negro youths to be carpenters, farmers, handymen, masons, maids, cooks and baby nurses. Their future rode heavily on their shoulders, and blinded them to the collective joy that had pervaded the lives of the boys and girls in the grammar school graduating class.

Parents who could afford it had ordered new shoes and ready-made clothes for themselves from Sears and Roebuck or Montgomery Ward. They also engaged the best seamstresses to make the floating graduating dresses and to cut down second-hand pants which would be pressed to a military slickness for the important event.

Oh, it was important, all right. Whitefolks would attend the ceremony, and two or three would speak of God and home, and the Southern way of life, and Mrs. Parsons, the principal's wife, would play the graduation march while the lower-grade graduates paraded down the aisles and took their seats below the platform. The high school seniors would wait in empty classrooms to make their dramatic entrance.

In the Store I was the person of the moment. The birthday girl. The center. Bailey[4] had graduated the year before, although to do so he had had to forfeit all pleasures to make up for his time lost in Baton Rouge.

My class was wearing butter-yellow piqué dresses, and Momma launched out on mine. She smocked the yoke into tiny crisscrossing puckers, then shirred the rest of the bodice. Her dark fingers ducked in and out of the lemony cloth as she embroidered raised daisies around the hem. Before she considered herself finished she had added a crocheted cuff on the puff sleeves, and a pointy crocheted collar.

I was going to be lovely. A walking model of all the various styles of fine hand sewing and it didn't worry me that I was only twelve years old and merely graduating from the eighth grade. Besides, many teachers in Arkansas Negro schools had only that diploma and were licensed to impart wisdom.

---

4. Angelou's brother.

The days had become longer and more noticeable. The faded beige of former times had been replaced with strong and sure colors. I began to see my classmates' clothes, their skin tones, and the dust that waved off pussy willows. Clouds that lazed across the sky were objects of great concern to me. Their shiftier shapes might have held a message that in my new happiness and with a little bit of time I'd soon decipher. During that period I looked at the arch of heaven so religiously my neck kept a steady ache. I had taken to smiling more often, and my jaws hurt from the unaccustomed activity. Between the two physical sore spots, I suppose I could have been uncomfortable, but that was not the case. As a member of the winning team (the graduating class of 1940) I had outdistanced unpleasant sensations by miles. I was headed for the freedom of open fields.

Youth and social approval allied themselves with me and we trammeled memories of slights and insults. The wind of our swift passage remodeled my features. Lost tears were pounded to mud and then to dust. Years of withdrawal were brushed aside and left behind, as hanging ropes of parasitic moss.

My work alone had awarded me a top place and I was going to be one of the first called in the graduating ceremonies. On the classroom blackboard, as well as on the bulletin board in the auditorium, there were blue stars and white stars and red stars. No absences, no tardinesses, and my academic work was among the best of the year. I could say the preamble to the Constitution even faster than Bailey. We timed ourselves often: "Wethepeopleofthe-UnitedStatesinordertoformamoreperfectunion . . ." I had memorized the Presidents of the United States from Washington to Roosevelt in chronological as well as alphabetical order.

My hair pleased me too. Gradually the black mass had lengthened and thickened, so that it kept at last to its braided pattern, and I didn't have to yank my scalp off when I tried to comb it.

Louise and I had rehearsed the exercises until we tired out ourselves. Henry Reed was class valedictorian. He was a small, very black boy with hooded eyes, and long, broad nose and an oddly shaped head. I had admired him for years because each term he and I vied for the best grades in our class. Most often he bested me, but instead of being disappointed I was pleased that we shared top places between us. Like many Southern Black children, he lived with his grandmother, who was as strict as Momma and as kind as she knew how to be. He was courteous, respectful and soft-spoken to elders, but on the playground he chose to play the roughest games. I admired him. Anyone, I reckoned, sufficiently afraid or sufficiently dull could be polite. But to be able to operate at a top level with both adults and children was admirable.

His valedictory speech was entitled "To Be or Not to Be." The rigid tenth-grade teacher had helped him write it. He'd been working on the dramatic stresses for months.

The weeks until graduation were filled with heady activities. A group of small children were to be presented in a play about buttercups and daisies and bunny rabbits. They could be heard throughout the building practicing their hops and their little songs that sounded like silver bells. The older girls (nongraduates, of course) were assigned the task of making refreshments for the night's festivities. A tangy scent of ginger, cinnamon, nutmeg and chocolate wafted around the home economics building as the budding cooks made samples for themselves and their teachers.

In every corner of the workshop, axes and saws split fresh timber as the woodshop boys made sets and stage scenery. Only the graduates were left out of the general bustle. We were free to sit in the library at the back of the building or look in quite detachedly, naturally, on the measures being taken for our event.

Even the minister preached on graduation the Sunday before. His subject was, "Let your light so shine that men will see your good works and praise your Father, Who is in Heaven." Although the sermon was purported to be addressed to us, he used the occasion to speak to backsliders, gamblers and general ne'er-do-wells. But since he had called our names at the beginning of the service we were mollified.

Among Negroes the tradition was to give presents to children going only from one grade to another. How much more important this was when the person was graduating at the top of the class. Uncle Willie and Momma had sent away for a Mickey Mouse watch like Bailey's. Louise gave me four embroidered handkerchiefs. (I gave her three crocheted doilies.) Mrs. Sneed, the minister's wife, made me an underskirt to wear for graduation, and nearly every customer gave me a nickel or maybe even a dime with the instruction "Keep on moving to higher ground," or some such encouragement.

Amazingly the great day finally dawned and I was out of bed before I knew it. I threw open the back door to see it more clearly, but Momma said, "Sister, come away from that door and put your robe on."

I hoped the memory of that morning would never leave me. Sunlight was itself still young, and the day had none of the insistence maturity would bring it in a few hours. In my robe and barefoot in the backyard, under cover of going to see about my new beans, I gave myself up to the gentle warmth and thanked God that no matter what evil I had done in my life He had allowed me to live to see this day. Somewhere in my fatalism I had expected to die, accidentally, and never have the chance to walk up the stairs in the auditorium and gracefully receive my hard-earned diploma. Out of God's merciful bosom I had won reprieve.

Bailey came out in his robe and gave me a box wrapped in Christmas paper. He said he had saved his money for months to pay for it. It felt like a box of chocolates, but I knew Bailey wouldn't save money to buy candy when we had all we could want under our noses.

He was as proud of the gift as I. It was a soft-leather-bound copy of a collection of poems by Edgar Allan Poe, or, as Bailey and I called him, "Eap." I turned to "Annabel Lee" and we walked up and down the garden rows, the cool dirt between our toes, reciting the beautifully sad lines.

Momma made a Sunday breakfast although it was only Friday. After we finished the blessing, I opened my eyes to find the watch on my plate. It was a dream of a day. Everything went smoothly and to my credit. I didn't have to be reminded or scolded for anything. Near evening I was too jittery to attend to chores, so Bailey volunteered to do all before his bath.

Days before, we had made a sign for the Store, and as we turned out the lights Momma hung the cardboard over the doorknob. It read clearly: CLOSED. GRADUATION.

My dress fitted perfectly and everyone said that I looked like a sunbeam in it. On the hill, going toward the school, Bailey walked behind with Uncle Willie, who muttered, "Go on, Ju." He wanted him to walk ahead with us because it embarrassed him to have to walk so slowly. Bailey said he'd let the ladies walk together, and the men would bring up the rear. We all laughed, nicely.

Little children dashed by out of the dark like fireflies. Their crepe-paper dresses and butterfly wings were not made for running and we heard more than one rip, dryly, and the regretful "uh uh" that followed.

The school blazed without gaiety. The windows seemed cold and unfriendly from the lower hill. A sense of ill-fated timing crept over me, and if Momma hadn't reached for my hand I would have drifted back to Bailey and Uncle Willie, and possibly beyond. She made a few slow jokes about my feet getting cold, and tugged me along to the now-strange building.

Around the front steps, assurance came back. There were my fellow "greats," the graduating class. Hair brushed back, legs oiled, new dresses and pressed pleats, fresh pocket handkerchiefs and little handbags, all homesewn. Oh, we were up to snuff, all right. I joined my comrades and didn't even see my family go in to find seats in the crowded auditorium.

The school band struck up a march and all classes filed in as had been rehearsed. We stood in front of our seats, as assigned, and on a signal from the choir director, we sat. No sooner had this been accomplished than the band started to play the national anthem. We rose again and sang the song, after which we recited the pledge of allegiance. We remained standing for a brief minute before the choir director and the principal signaled to us, rather desperately I thought, to take our seats. The command was so unusual that our carefully rehearsed and smooth-running machine was thrown off. For a full minute we fumbled for our chairs and bumped into each other awkwardly. Habits change or solidify under pressure, so in our state of nervous tension we had been ready to follow our usual assembly pattern: the American national anthem, then the pledge of allegiance, then the song every Black person I knew called the Negro National Anthem. All done in the same key, with the same passion and most often standing on the same foot.

Finding my seat at least, I was overcome with a presentiment of worse things to come. Something unrehearsed, unplanned, was going to happen, and we were going to be made to look bad. I distinctly remember being explicit in the choice of pronoun. It was "we," the graduating class, the unit, that concerned me then.

The principal welcomed "parents and friends" and asked the Baptist minister to lead us in prayer. His invocation was brief and punchy, and for a second I thought we were getting back on the high road to right action. When the principal came back to the dais, however, his voice had changed. Sounds always affected me profoundly and the principal's voice was one of my favorites. During assembly it melted and lowed weakly into the audience. It had not been in my plan to listen to him, but my curiosity was piqued and I straightened up to give him my attention.

He was talking about Booker T. Washington, our "late great leader," who said we can be as close as the fingers on the hand,[5] etc. . . . Then he said a few vague things about friendship and the friendship of kindly people to those less fortunate than themselves. With that his voice nearly faded, thin, away. Like a river diminishing to a stream and then to a trickle. But he cleared his throat and said, "Our speaker tonight, who is also our friend, came from Texarkana to deliver the commencement address, but due to the irregularity of the train schedule, he's going to, as they say, 'speak and run.' " He said that we understood and wanted the man to know that we were most grateful for the time he was able to give us and then something about how we were willing always to adjust to another's program, and without more ado—"I give you Mr. Edward Donleavy."

Not one but two white men came through the door off-stage. The shorter one walked to the speaker's platform, and the tall one moved over to the center seat and sat down. But that was our principal's seat, and already occupied. The dislodged gentleman bounced around for a long breath or two before the Baptist minister gave him his chair, then with more dignity than the situation deserved, the minister walked off the stage.

Donleavy looked at the audience once (on reflection, I'm sure that he wanted only to reassure himself that we were really there), adjusted his glasses and began to read from a sheaf of papers.

---

5. From Washington's Atlanta Compromise speech (September 18, 1895), in which he accepted racial segregation in exchange for economic advancement: "In all things that are purely social we can be as separate as the fingers, yet one as the hand in all things essential to mutual progress."

He was glad "to be here and to see the work going on just as it was in the other schools."

At the first "Amen" from the audience I willed the offender to immediate death by choking on the word. But Amens and Yes, sir's began to fall around the room like rain through a ragged umbrella.

He told us of the wonderful changes we children in Stamps had in store. The Central School (naturally, the white school was Central) had already been granted improvements that would be in use in the fall. A well-known artist was coming from Little Rock to teach art to them. They were going to have the newest microscopes and chemistry equipment for their laboratory. Mr. Donleavy didn't leave us long in the dark over who made these improvements available to Central High. Nor were we to be ignored in the general betterment scheme he had in mind.

He said that he had pointed out to people at a very high level that one of the first-line football tacklers at Arkansas Agricultural and Mechanical College had graduated from good old Lafayette County Training School. Here fewer Amen's were heard. Those few that did break through lay dully in the air with the heaviness of habit.

He went on to praise us. He went on to say how he had bragged that "one of the best basketball players at Fisk sank his first ball right here at Lafayette County Training School."

The white kids were going to have a chance to become Galileos and Madame Curies and Edisons and Gauguins, and our boys (the girls weren't even in on it) would try to be Jesse Owenses and Joe Louises.

Owens and the Brown Bomber were great heroes in our world, but what school official in the white-goddom of Little Rock had the right to decide that those two men must be our only heroes? Who decided that for Henry Reed to become a scientist he had to work like George Washington Carver, as a bootblack, to buy a lousy microscope? Bailey was obviously always going to be too small to be an athlete, so which concrete angel glued to what county seat had decided that if my brother wanted to become a lawyer he had to first pay penance for his skin by picking cotton and hoeing corn and studying correspondence books at night for twenty years?

The man's dead words fell like bricks around the auditorium and too many settled in my belly. Constrained by hard-learned manners I couldn't look behind me, but to my left and right the proud graduating class of 1940 had dropped their heads. Every girl in my row had found something new to do with her handkerchief. Some folded the tiny squares into love knots, some into triangles, but most were wadding them, then pressing them flat on their yellow laps.

On the dais, the ancient tragedy was being replayed. Professor Parsons sat, a sculptor's reject, rigid. His large, heavy body seemed devoid of will or willingness, and his eyes said he was no longer with us. The other teachers examined the flag (which was draped stage right) or their notes, or the windows which opened on our now-famous playing diamond.

Graduation, the hush-hush magic time of frills and gifts and congratulations and diplomas, was finished for me before my name was called. The accomplishment was nothing. The meticulous maps, drawn in three colors of ink, learning and spelling decasyllabic words, memorizing the whole of *The Rape of Lucrece*[6]—it was for nothing. Donleavy had exposed us.

We were maids and farmers, handymen and washerwomen, and anything higher that we aspired to was farcical and presumptuous.

Then I wished that Gabriel Prosser and Nat Turner had killed all whitefolks in their beds[7] and that Abraham Lincoln had been assassinated before the signing of the Emancipation Proclamation, and that Harriet Tubman[8] had been killed by that blow on her head and Christopher Columbus had drowned in the *Santa María.*

It was awful to be Negro and have no control over my life. It was brutal to be young and already trained to sit quietly and listen to charges brought against my color with no chance of defense. We should all be dead. I thought I should like to see us all dead, one on top of the other. A pyramid of flesh with the whitefolks on the bottom, as the broad base, then the Indians with their silly tomahawks and teepees and wigwams and treaties, the Negroes with their mops and recipes and cotton sacks and spirituals sticking out of their

6. A long narrative poem by William Shakespeare.

7. Prosser and Turner both led rebellions in which the slaves killed their "masters."

8. African American abolitionist (c. 1820–1913) who led slaves to freedom on the Underground Railroad.

mouths. The Dutch children should all stumble in their wooden shoes and break their necks. The French should choke to death on the Louisiana Purchase (1803) while silkworms ate all the Chinese with their stupid pigtails. As a species, we were an abomination. All of us.

Donleavy was running for election, and assured our parents that if he won we could count on having the only colored paved playing field in that part of Arkansas. Also—he never looked up to acknowledge the grunts of acceptance—also, we were bound to get some new equipment for the home economics building and the workshop.

He finished, and since there was no need to give any more than the most perfunctory thank-you's, he nodded to the men on the stage, and the tall white man who was never introduced joined him at the door. They left with the attitude that now they were off to something really important. (The graduation ceremonies at Lafayette County Training School had been a mere preliminary.)

The ugliness they left was palpable. An uninvited guest who wouldn't leave. The choir was summoned and sang a modern arrangement of "Onward, Christian Soldiers," with new words pertaining to graduates seeking their place in the world. But it didn't work. Elouise, the daughter of the Baptist minister, recited "Invictus,"[9] and I could have cried at the impertinence of "I am the master of my fate, I am the captain of my soul."

My name had lost its ring of familiarity and I had to be nudged to go and receive my diploma. All my preparations had fled. I neither marched up to the stage like a conquering Amazon, nor did I look in the audience for Bailey's nod of approval. Marguerite Johnson,[1] I heard the name again, my honors were read, there were noises in the audience of appreciation, and I took my place on the stage as rehearsed.

I thought about colors I hated: ecru, puce, lavender, beige and black.

There was shuffling and rustling around me, then Henry Reed

9. An inspirational poem by William Ernst Henley (1849–1903).
1. Angelou's given name; Bailey nick- named her "Maya," and "Angelou" is a variation of her first husband's last name— "Angelo."

was giving his valedictory address, "To Be or Not to Be." Hadn't he heard the whitefolks? We couldn't *be*, so the question was a waste of time. Henry's voice came out clear and strong. I feared to look at him. Hadn't he got the message? There was no "nobler in the mind" for Negroes because the world didn't think we had minds, and they let us know it. "Outrageous fortune"? Now, that was a joke. When the ceremony was over I had to tell Henry Reed some things. That is, if I still cared. Not "rub," Henry, "erase." "Ah, there's the erase." Us.

Henry had been a good student in elocution. His voice rose on tides of promise and fell on waves of warnings. The English teacher had helped him to create a sermon winging through Hamlet's soliloquy. To be a man, a doer, a builder, a leader, or to be a tool, an unfunny joke, a crusher of funky toadstools. I marveled that Henry could go through with the speech as if we had a choice.

I had been listening and silently rebutting each sentence with my eyes closed; then there was a hush, which in an audience warns that something unplanned is happening. I looked up and saw Henry Reed, the conservative, the proper, the A student, turn his back to the audience and turn to us (the proud graduating class of 1940) and sing, nearly speaking,

"Lift ev'ry voice and sing
Till earth and heaven ring
Ring with the harmonies of Liberty . . ."

It was the poem written by James Weldon Johnson. It was the music composed by J. Rosamond Johnson. It was the Negro national anthem. Out of habit we were singing it.

Our mothers and fathers stood in the dark hall and joined the hymn of encouragement. A kindergarten teacher led the small children onto the stage and the buttercups and daisies and bunny rabbits marked time and tried to follow:

"Stony the road we trod
Bitter the chastening rod
Felt in the days when hope, unborn, had died.
Yet with a steady beat

Have not our weary feet
Come to the place for which our fathers sighed?"

Every child I knew had learned that song with his ABC's and along
with "Jesus Loves Me This I know." But I personally had never
heard it before. Never heard the words, despite the thousands of
times I had sung them. Never thought they had anything to do with
me.

On the other hand, the words of Patrick Henry had made such
an impression on me that I had been able to stretch myself tall and
trembling and say, "I know not what course others may take, but as
for me, give me liberty or give me death."

And now I heard, really for the first time:

"We have come over a way that with tears
has been watered,
We have come, treading our path through
the blood of the slaughtered."

While echoes of the song shivered in the air, Henry Reed bowed his
head, said "Thank you," and returned to his place in the line. The
tears that slipped down many faces were not wiped away in shame.

We were on top again. As always, again. We survived. The depths
had been icy and dark, but now a bright sun spoke to our souls. I
was no longer simply a member of the proud graduating class of
1940; I was a proud member of the wonderful, beautiful Negro race.

Oh, Black known and unknown poets, how often have your auc-
tioned pains sustained us? Who will compute the lonely nights
made less lonely by your songs, or by the empty pots made less
tragic by your tales?

If we were a people much given to revealing secrets, we might
raise monuments and sacrifice to the memories of our poets, but
slavery cured us of that weakness. It may be enough, however, to
have it said that we survive in exact relationship to the dedication of
our poets (include preachers, musicians and blues singers).

1970

Anne Applebaum
b. 1964

> *Shortly after 9/11, George W. Bush declared that the United States would wage a war against terrorism. Because terrorist groups like Al-Qaeda do not fight in uniforms or on battlefields, and because they generally operate underground, independent of any established nation, the United States determined that it had to pursue methods that violated accepted rules of war. For example, based on the advice of Alberto Gonzales, then a White House attorney, President Bush decided that the Geneva Conventions, which govern how nations must treat prisoners of war, did not apply to America's prisoners in the war on terror. Even more controversial were a series of legal opinions and tacit policy positions that sanctioned the torture of suspected terrorists. The debate became acute in November 2004, when Bush nominated Gonzales to replace John Ashcroft as the U.S. Attorney General. Such nominations require confirmation by the Senate, and many Democrats opposed Gonzales because, in the words of* USA Today, *"while at the White House," Gonzales wrote legal memos arguing that "President Bush's wartime powers superseded anti-torture laws and treaties." Applebaum published this essay in the* Washington Post *shortly before the Senate began debating Gonzales's nomination. In February 2005, the Senate confirmed Gonzales in a vote of 60 to 36.*

The Torture Myth

Just for a moment, let's pretend that there is no moral, legal, or constitutional problem with torture. Let's also imagine a clear-cut case: a terrorist who knows where bombs are about to explode in Iraq. To stop him, it seems that a wide range of Americans would be prepared to endorse "cruel and unusual" methods. In advance of confirmation hearings for Attorney General–designate Alberto Gonzales last week, the *Wall Street Journal* argued that such scenarios must be debated, since "what's at stake in this controversy is nothing less than the ability of U.S. forces to interrogate enemies who want to murder innocent civilians." Alan Dershowitz, the liberal legal scholar, has argued in the past that interrogators in such a case should get a "torture warrant" from a judge. Both of these arguments rest on an assumption: that torture—defined as physical pressure during interrogation—can be used to extract useful information.

But does torture work? The question has been asked many times since September 11, 2001. I'm repeating it, however, because the Gonzales hearings inspired more articles about our lax methods ("Too Nice for Our Own Good" was one headline), because similar comments may follow this week's trial of Spec. Charles Graner, the alleged Abu Ghraib ringleader, and because I still cannot find a positive answer. I've heard it said that the Syrians and the Egyptians "really know how to get these things done." I've heard the Israelis mentioned, without proof. I've heard Algeria mentioned, too, but Darius Rejali, an academic who recently trolled through French archives, found no clear examples of how torture helped the French in Algeria—and they lost that war anyway. "Liberals," argued an article in the liberal online magazine *Slate* a few months ago, "have a tendency to accept, all too eagerly, the argument that torture is ineffective." But it's also true that "realists," whether liberal or conservative, have a tendency to accept, all too eagerly, fictitious accounts of effective torture carried out by someone else.

By contrast, it is easy to find experienced U.S. officers who argue precisely the opposite. Meet, for example, retired Air Force Col. John Rothrock, who, as a young captain, headed a combat interrogation team in Vietnam. More than once he was faced with a ticking time-bomb scenario: a captured Vietcong guerrilla who knew of plans to kill Americans. What was done in such cases was "not nice," he says. "But we did not physically abuse them." Rothrock used psychology, the shock of capture and of the unexpected. Once, he let a prisoner see a wounded comrade die. Yet—as he remembers saying to the "desperate and honorable officers" who wanted him to move faster— "if I take a Bunsen burner to the guy's genitals, he's going to tell you just about anything," which would be pointless. Rothrock, who is no squishy liberal, says that he doesn't know "any professional intelligence officers of my generation who would think this is a good idea."

Or listen to Army Col. Stuart Herrington, a military intelligence specialist who conducted interrogations in Vietnam, Panama, and Iraq during Desert Storm, and who was sent by the Pentagon in

2003—long before Abu Ghraib—to assess interrogations in Iraq. Aside from its immorality and its illegality, says Herrington, torture is simply "not a good way to get information." In his experience, nine out of ten people can be persuaded to talk with no "stress methods" at all, let alone cruel and unusual ones. Asked whether that would be true of religiously motivated fanatics, he says that the "batting average" might be lower: "perhaps six out of ten." And if you beat up the remaining four? "They'll just tell you anything to get you to stop."

Worse, you'll have the other side effects of torture. It "endangers our soldiers on the battlefield by encouraging reciprocity." It does "damage to our country's image" and undermines our credibility in Iraq. That, in the long run, outweighs any theoretical benefit. Herrington's confidential Pentagon report, which he won't discuss but which was leaked to *The Post* a month ago, goes farther. In that document, he warned that members of an elite military and CIA task force were abusing detainees in Iraq, that their activities could be "making gratuitous enemies" and that prisoner abuse "is counterproductive to the Coalition's efforts to win the cooperation of the Iraqi citizenry." Far from rescuing Americans, in other words, the use of "special methods" might help explain why the war is going so badly.

An up-to-date illustration of the colonel's point appeared in recently released FBI documents from the naval base at Guantanamo Bay, Cuba. These show, among other things, that some military intelligence officers wanted to use harsher interrogation methods than the FBI did. As a result, complained one inspector, "every time the FBI established a rapport with a detainee, the military would step in and the detainee would stop being cooperative." So much for the utility of torture.

Given the overwhelmingly negative evidence, the really interesting question is not whether torture works but why so many people in our society want to believe that it works. At the moment, there is a myth in circulation, a fable that goes something like this: Radical terrorists will take advantage of our fussy legality, so we may have to suspend it to beat them. Radical terrorists mock our namby-pamby prisons, so we must make them tougher. Radical terrorists are nasty, so to defeat them we have to be nastier.

Perhaps it's reassuring to tell ourselves tales about the new forms of "toughness" we need, or to talk about the special rules we will create to defeat this special enemy. Unfortunately, that toughness is self-deceptive and self-destructive. Ultimately it will be self-defeating as well.

2005

Nicholson Baker
b. 1957

> Baker is best known as a novelist, and his novels are as strange as this essay. They tend to delve into the consciousness, so that in one novel, for example, the entire "action" takes place within the space of few minutes while a father feeds his infant child. His focus is always on the minutiae of life and the sparkle of language. This piece was published in his collection The Size of Thoughts, alongside other strange works, such as a long, comical discussion of nail clippers. Here he takes a familiar "genre" of writing, the recipe, and plays with its conventions to make something memorable and pleasing to read. This is not persuasion in the usual sense. It is, rather, a way of making readers reconsider the minutiae of their own lives.

Recipe

The Monroe County Library System, of Monroe, Michigan, asked for a recipe to include in a collection of "Favorite Recipes by Favorite Authors," entitled Read 'em and Eat.

Take one ingot of unsweetened Baker's chocolate, remove the paper, and drop it in a tiny saucepan settled over an adjustable heat-source. Then unfold one end of a brand-new silver bar of unsalted Land O Lakes butter and cut a chunk off roughly comparable to the piece of Baker's chocolate, which has by this time begun to smear slightly. (An old stick of butter has too much refrigerator flavor in its exposed end.) The butter will melt faster than the chocolate. Entertain yourself by breaking the ingot of chocolate into its two halves and pushing the halves and the subsiding chunk of butter around with the tip of the butter knife. Then abandon the butter knife and switch to a spoon. When the unmelted chocolate is no more than a small soft shape difficult to locate in the larger velouté, shake some drifts of confectioners' sugar into the liquid. You're aiming for a bittersweet taste, a taste quite a bit less sweet than ice cream—so sprinkle accordingly. But you'll find that a surprising amount of sugar is necessary. Stir idly. If the mixture becomes thick and paste-like, add another three-eighth-inch sliver of butter; to your relief, all will effortlessly reliquefy. Avoid bubbling or burning the mixture, which can now be called sauce. Turn off the heat, or turn it down so low that you don't have to worry about it. Spoon out some premium plain vanilla ice cream. Lately this has become hard to find—crowded out by low-fat premiums and Fragonard flavors. But you want the very best vanilla ice cream available in your area; you have to have that high butterfat content for it to be compatible with the chocolate sauce. Spoon the sauce over the ice cream. It will harden. This is what you have been working for. Once cooled, it will make a nice sound when you tap it with a spoon. If you want more tappable chocolate sauce and you have already covered your scoop or scoops of ice cream with a complete trelliswork, simply turn over one of the scoops and dribble more over the exposed underside. Eat with haste, because premium vanilla ice cream melts fast. Refrigerate the unused sauce right in the original saucepan, covered with tinfoil, with the spoon resting in it; that way, when you put it back on the hear-source, you'll be able to brandish the whole solidified disk of chocolate merely by lifting the spoon. It looks like a metal detector.

1991

James Baldwin
1924–1987

> *Baldwin was writing his novel* Go Tell It on the Mountain *(1953) in Paris when his lover, Lucien Happersberger, began to suspect that the writer was headed for a nervous breakdown. Happersberger took Baldwin to his family's chalet in Loèche-les-Bains, a remote mountain village in Switzerland. Baldwin spent two weeks there in the summer of 1951 and again that winter. His treatment in Switzerland led Baldwin to the insights he expresses in "Stranger in the Village" on the relation between blacks and whites in America, an issue he'd been thinking about for a long time. He published this essay in* Harper's *magazine, whose readers would have been familiar, even as early as 1953, with the civil rights debate. They would have been mostly well-educated white men and women sympathetic to the difficulties faced by blacks in America. Baldwin does not try to persuade these readers to any particular action or even to modify their political ideology. Instead, he tries to reveal to them certain aspects of their own character.*

Stranger in the Village

From all available evidence no black man had ever set foot in this tiny Swiss village before I came. I was told before arriving that I would probably be a "sight" for the village; I took this to mean that people of my complexion were rarely seen in Switzerland, and also that city people are always something of a "sight" outside of the city. It did not occur to me—possibly because I am an American—that there could be people anywhere who had never seen a Negro.

It is a fact that cannot be explained on the basis of the inaccessibility of the village. The village is very high, but it is only four hours from Milan and three hours from Lausanne. It is true that it is virtually unknown. Few people making plans for a holiday would elect to come here. On the other hand, the villagers are able, presumably, to come and go as they please—which they do: to another town at the foot of the mountain, with a population of approximately five thousand, the nearest place to see a movie or go to the bank. In the village there is no movie house, no bank, no library, no theater; very few radios, one jeep, one station wagon; and, at the moment, one typewriter, mine, an invention which the woman next door to me here had never seen. There are about six hundred people living here, all Catholic—I conclude this from the fact that the Catholic church is open all year round, whereas the Protestant chapel, set off on a hill a little removed from the village, is open only in the summertime when the tourists arrive. There are four or five hotels, all closed now, and four or five *bistros*, of which, however, only two do any business during the winter. These two do not do a great deal, for life in the village seems to end around nine or ten o'clock. There are a few stores, butcher, baker, *épicerie*,[1] a hardware store, and a money-changer— who cannot change travelers' checks, but must send them down to the bank, an operation which takes two or three days. There is something called the *Ballet Haus*, closed in the winter and used for God knows what, certainly not ballet, during the summer. There seems to be only one schoolhouse in the village, and this for the quite young children; I suppose this to mean that their older brothers and sisters at some point descend from these mountains in order to complete their education—possibly, again, to the town just below. The landscape is absolutely forbidding, mountains towering on all four sides, ice and snow as far as the eye can reach. In this white wilderness, men and women and children move all day, carrying washing, wood, buckets of milk or water, sometimes skiing on Sunday afternoons. All week long boys and young men are to be seen shoveling snow off the rooftops, or dragging wood down from the forest in sleds.

The village's only real attraction, which explains the tourist season, is the hot spring water. A disquietingly high proportion of these tourists are cripples, or semicripples, who come year after year—from other parts of Switzerland, usually—to take the waters. This lends the village, at the height of the season, a rather terrifying air of sanctity, as though it were a lesser Lourdes.[2] There is often something beautiful, there is always something awful, in the specta-

---

1. Grocery (French).

2. Town in southwestern France famous for the miraculous cures attributed to its waters and for the purported appearances there of the Virgin Mary.

cle of a person who has lost one of his faculties, a faculty he never questioned until it was gone, and who struggles to recover it. Yet people remain people, on crutches or indeed on deathbeds; and wherever I passed, the first summer I was here, among the native villagers or among the lame, a wind passed with me—of astonishment, curiosity, amusement, and outrage. That first summer I stayed two weeks and never intended to return. But I did return in the winter, to work; the village offers, obviously, no distractions whatever and has the further advantage of being extremely cheap. Now it is winter again, a year later, and I am here again. Everyone in the village knows my name, though they scarcely ever use it, knows that I come from America—though, this, apparently, they will never really believe: black men come from Africa—and everyone knows that I am the friend of the son of a woman who was born here, and that I am staying in their chalet. But I remain as much a stranger today as I was the first day I arrived, and the children shout *Neger! Neger!* as I walk along the streets.

It must be admitted that in the beginning I was far too shocked to have any real reaction. In so far as I reacted at all, I reacted by trying to be pleasant—it being a great part of the American Negro's education (long before he goes to school) that he must make people "like" him. This smile-and-the-world-smiles-with-you routine worked about as well in this situation as it had in the situation for which it was designed, which is to say that it did not work at all. No one, after all, can be liked whose human weight and complexity cannot be, or has not been, admitted. My smile was simply another unheard-of phenomenon which allowed them to see my teeth— they did not, really, see my smile and I began to think that, should I take to snarling, no one would notice any difference. All of the physical characteristics of the Negro which had caused me, in America, a very different and almost forgotten pain were nothing less than miraculous—or infernal—in the eyes of the village people. Some thought my hair was the color of tar, that it had the texture of wire, or the texture of cotton. It was jocularly suggested that I might let it all grow long and make myself a winter coat. If I sat in the sun for more than five minutes some daring creature was certain to come along and gingerly put his fingers on my hair, as though he were afraid of an electric shock, or put his hand on my hand, astonished that the color did not rub off. In all of this, in which it must be conceded there was the charm of genuine wonder and in which there was certainly no element of intentional unkindness, there was yet no suggestion that I was human: I was simply a living wonder.

I knew that they did not mean to be unkind, and I know it now; it is necessary, nevertheless, for me to repeat this to myself each time that I walk out of the chalet. The children who shout *Neger!* have no way of knowing the echoes this sound raises in me. They are brimming with good humor and the more daring swell with pride when I stop to speak with them. Just the same, there are days when I cannot pause and smile, when I have no heart to play with them; when, indeed, I mutter sourly to myself, exactly as I muttered on the streets of a city these children have never seen, when I was no bigger than these children are now: *Your* mother *was a nigger.* Joyce[3] is right about history being a nightmare—but it may be the nightmare from which no one *can* awaken. People are trapped in history and history is trapped in them.

There is a custom in the village—I am told it is repeated in many villages—of "buying" African natives for the purpose of converting them to Christianity. There stands in the church all year round a small box with a slot for money, decorated with a black figurine, and into this box the villagers drop their francs. During the *carnaval*[4] which precedes Lent, two village children have their faces blackened—out of which bloodless darkness their blue eyes shine like ice—and fantastic horsehair wigs are placed on their blond heads; thus disguised, they solicit among the villagers for money for the missionaries in Africa. Between the box in the church and the blackened children, the village "bought" last year six or eight African natives. This was reported to me with pride by the wife of one of the *bistro* owners and I was careful to express astonishment and pleasure at the solicitude shown by the village for the souls of black folk. The *bistro* owner's wife beamed with a pleasure far more genuine than my own and seemed to feel that I might now breathe more easily concerning the souls of at least six of my kinsmen.

---

3. James Joyce (1882–1941), Irish novelist; Baldwin is referring here to a line from Joyce's novel *Ulysses*: "History is a night-mare from which I am trying to awake."

4. A period of exuberance before Lent's abstinence; Mardi Gras.

I tried not to think of these so lately baptized kinsmen, of the price paid for them, or the peculiar price they themselves would pay, and said nothing about my father, who having taken his own conversion too literally never, at bottom, forgave the white world (which he described as heathen) for having saddled him with a Christ in whom, to judge at least from their treatment of him, they themselves no longer believed. I thought of white men arriving for the first time in an African village, strangers there, as I am a stranger here, and tried to imagine the astounded populace touching their hair and marveling at the color of their skin. But there is a great difference between being the first white man to be seen by Africans and being the first black man to be seen by whites. The white man takes the astonishment as tribute, for he arrives to conquer and to convert the natives, whose inferiority in relation to himself is not even to be questioned; whereas I, without a thought of conquest, find myself among a people whose culture controls me, has even, in a sense, created me, people who have cost me more in anguish and rage than they will ever know, who yet do not even know of my existence. The astonishment with which I might have greeted them, should they have stumbled into my African village a few hundred years ago, might have rejoiced their hearts. But the astonishment with which they greet me today can only poison mine.

And this is so despite everything I may do to feel differently, despite my friendly conversations with the *bistro* owner's wife, despite their three-year-old son who has at last become my friend, despite the *saluts* and *bonsoirs* which I exchange with people as I walk, despite the fact that I know that no individual can be taken to task for what history is doing, or has done. I say that the culture of these people controls me—but they can scarcely be held responsible for European culture. America comes out of Europe, but these people have never seen America, nor have most of them seen more of Europe than the hamlet at the foot of their mountain. Yet they move with an authority which I shall never have; and they regard me, quite rightly, not only as a stranger in their village but as a suspect latecomer, bearing no credentials, to everything they have—however unconsciously—inherited.

For this village, even were it incomparably more remote and incredibly more primitive, is the West, the West onto which I have been so strangely grafted. These people cannot be, from the point of view of power, strangers anywhere in the world; they have made the modern world, in effect, even if they do not know it. The most illiterate among them is related, in a way that I am not, to Dante, Shakespeare, Michelangelo, Aeschylus, Da Vinci, Rembrandt, and Racine; the cathedral at Chartres says something to them which it cannot say to me, as indeed would New York's Empire State Building, should anyone here ever see it. Out of their hymns and dances come Beethoven and Bach. Go back a few centuries and they are in their full glory—but I am in Africa, watching the conquerors arrive.

The rage of the disesteemed is personally fruitless, but it is also absolutely inevitable; this rage, so generally discounted, so little understood even among the people whose daily bread it is, is one of the things that makes history. Rage can only with difficulty, and never entirely, be brought under the domination of the intelligence and is therefore not susceptible to any arguments whatever. This is a fact which ordinary representatives of the *Herrenvolk*,[5] having never felt this rage and being unable to imagine it, quite fail to understand. Also, rage cannot be hidden, it can only be dissembled. This dissembling deludes the thoughtless, and strengthens rage and adds, to rage, contempt. There are, no doubt, as many ways of coping with the resulting complex of tensions as there are black men in the world, but no black man can hope ever to be entirely liberated from this internal warfare—rage, dissembling, and contempt having inevitably accompanied his first realization of the power of white men. What is crucial here is that, since white men represent in the black man's world so heavy a weight, white men have for black men a reality which is far from being reciprocal; and hence all black men have toward all white men an attitude which is designed, really, either to rob the white man of the jewel of his naïveté, or else to make it cost him dear.

The black man insists, by whatever means he finds at his disposal, that the white man cease to regard him as an exotic rarity and recognize him as a human being. This is a very charged and difficult moment, for there is a great deal of will power involved in the white man's naïveté. Most people are not naturally reflective any more

5. Master race (German).

than they are naturally malicious, and the white man prefers to keep the black man at a certain human remove because it is easier for him thus to preserve his simplicity and avoid being called to account for crimes committed by his forefathers, or his neighbors. He is inescapably aware, nevertheless, that he is in a better position in the world than black men are, nor can he quite put to death the suspicion that he is hated by black men therefore. He does not wish to be hated, neither does he wish to change places, and at this point in his uneasiness he can scarcely avoid having recourse to those legends which white men have created about black men, the most usual effect of which is that the white man finds himself enmeshed, so to speak, in his own language which describes hell, as well as the attributes which lead one to hell, as being as black as night.

Every legend, moreover, contains its residuum of truth, and the root function of language is to control the universe by describing it. It is of quite considerable significance that black men remain, in the imagination, and in overwhelming numbers in fact, beyond the disciplines of salvation; and this despite the fact that the West has been "buying" African natives for centuries. There is, I should hazard, an instantaneous necessity to be divorced from this so visibly unsaved stranger, in whose heart, moreover, one cannot guess what dreams of vengeance are being nourished; and, at the same time, there are few things on earth more attractive than the idea of the unspeakable liberty which is allowed the unredeemed. When, beneath the black mask, a human being begins to make himself felt one cannot escape a certain awful wonder as to what kind of human being it is. What one's imagination makes of other people is dictated, of course, by the laws of one's own personality and it is one of the ironies of black-white relations that, by means of what the white man imagines the black man to be, the black man is enabled to know who the white man is.

I have said, for example, that I am as much a stranger in this village today as I was the first summer I arrived, but this is not quite true. The villagers wonder less about the texture of my hair than they did then, and wonder rather more about me. And the fact that their wonder now exists on another level is reflected in their attitudes and in their eyes. There are the children who make those delightful, hilarious, sometimes astonishingly grave overtures of friendship in the unpredictable fashion of children; other children, having been taught that the devil is a black man, scream in genuine anguish as I approach. Some of the older women never pass without a friendly greeting, never pass, indeed, if it seems that they will be able to engage me in conversation; other women look down or look away or rather contemptuously smirk. Some of the men drink with me and suggest that I learn how to ski—partly, I gather, because they cannot imagine what I would look like on skis—and want to know if I am married, and ask questions about my *métier*.[6] But some of the men have accused *le sale nègre*[7]—behind my back—of stealing wood and there is already in the eyes of some of them that peculiar, intent, paranoiac malevolence which one sometimes surprises in the eyes of American white men when, out walking with their Sunday girl, they see a Negro male approach.

There is a dreadful abyss between the streets of this village and the streets of the city in which I was born, between the children who shout *Neger!* today and those who shouted *Nigger!* yesterday— the abyss is experience, the American experience. The syllable hurled behind me today expresses, above all, wonder: I am a stranger here. But I am not a stranger in America and the same syllable riding on the American air expresses the war my presence has occasioned in the American soul.

For this village brings home to me this fact: that there was a day, and not really a very distant day, when Americans were scarcely Americans at all but discontented Europeans, facing a great unconquered continent and strolling, say, into a marketplace and seeing black men for the first time. The shock this spectacle afforded is suggested, surely, by the promptness with which they decided that these black men were not really men but cattle. It is true that the necessity on the part of the settlers of the New World of reconciling their moral assumptions with the fact—and the necessity—of slavery enhanced immensely the charm of this idea, and it is also true that this idea expresses, with a truly American bluntness, the atti-

6. Business (French).
7. Derogatory term, literally "dirty black" (French).

tude which to varying extents all masters have had toward all slaves.

But between all former slaves and slave-owners and the drama which begins for Americans over three hundred years ago at Jamestown, there are at least two differences to be observed. The American Negro slave could not suppose, for one thing, as slaves in past epochs had supposed and often done, that he would ever be able to wrest the power from his master's hands. This was a supposition which the modern era, which was to bring about such vast changes in the aims and dimensions of power, put to death; it only begins, in unprecedented fashion, and with dreadful implications, to be resurrected today. But even had this supposition persisted with undiminished force, the American Negro slave could not have used it to lend his condition dignity, for the reason that this supposition rests on another: that the slave in exile yet remains related to his past, has some means—if only in memory—of revering and sustaining the forms of his former life, is able, in short, to maintain his identity.

This was not the case with the American Negro slave. He is unique among the black men of the world in that his past was taken from him, almost literally, at one blow. One wonders what on earth the first slave found to say to the first dark child he bore. I am told that there are Haitians able to trace their ancestry back to African kings, but any American Negro wishing to go back so far will find his journey through time abruptly arrested by the signature on the bill of sale which served as the entrance paper for his ancestor. At the time—to say nothing of the circumstances—of the enslavement of the captive black man who was to become the American Negro, there was not the remotest possibility that he would ever take power from his master's hands. There was no reason to suppose that his situation would ever change, nor was there, shortly, anything to indicate that his situation had ever been different. It was his necessity, in the words of E. Franklin Frazier,[8] to find a "motive for living under American culture or die." The identity of the American Negro comes out of this extreme situation, and the evolution of this identity was a source of the most intolerable anxiety in the minds and the lives of his masters.

8. African American intellectual (1894–1962) and author of *Bourgeoisie noire* (1955) (The Black Bourgeoisie).

For the history of the American Negro is unique also in this: that the question of his humanity, and of his rights therefore as a human being, became a burning one for several generations of Americans, so burning a question that it ultimately became one of those used to divide the nation. It is out of this argument that the venom of the epithet *Nigger!* is derived. It is an argument which Europe has never had, and hence Europe quite sincerely fails to understand how or why the argument arose in the first place, why its effects are so frequently disastrous and always so unpredictable, why it refuses until today to be entirely settled. Europe's black possessions remained—and do remain—in Europe's colonies, at which remove they represented no threat whatever to European identity. If they posed any problem at all for the European conscience, it was a problem which remained comfortingly abstract: in effect, the black man, *as a man*, did not exist for Europe. But in America, even as a slave, he was an inescapable part of the general social fabric and no American could escape having an attitude toward him. Americans attempt until today to make an abstraction of the Negro, but the very nature of these abstractions reveals the tremendous effects the presence of the Negro has had on the American character.

When one considers the history of the Negro in America it is of the greatest importance to recognize that the moral beliefs of a person, or a people, are never really as tenuous as life—which is not moral—very often causes them to appear; these create for them a frame of reference and a necessary hope, the hope being that when life has done its worst they will be enabled to rise above themselves and to triumph over life. Life would scarcely be bearable if this hope did not exist. Again, even when the worst has been said, to betray a belief is not by any means to have put oneself beyond its power; the betrayal of a belief is not the same thing as ceasing to believe. If this were not so there would be no moral standards in the world at all. Yet one must also recognize that morality is based on ideas and that all ideas are dangerous—dangerous because ideas can only lead to action and where the action leads no man can say. And dangerous in this respect: that confronted with the impossibility of remaining faithful to one's beliefs, and the equal impossibility of becoming free of them, one can be driven to the most inhuman excesses. The ideas on which American beliefs are based are not, though Americans often seem to think so, ideas which originated in America. They came out of Europe. And the establishment of democracy on the American continent was scarcely as radical a break with the past as was the necessity, which Americans faced, of broadening this concept to include black men.

This was, literally, a hard necessity. It was impossible, for one thing, for Americans to abandon their beliefs, not only because these beliefs alone seemed able to justify the sacrifices they had endured and the blood that they had spilled, but also because these beliefs afforded them their only bulwark against a moral chaos as absolute as the physical chaos of the continent it was their destiny to conquer. But in the situation in which Americans found themselves, these beliefs threatened an idea which, whether or not one likes to think so, is the very warp and woof of the heritage of the West, the idea of white supremacy.

Americans have made themselves notorious by the shrillness and the brutality with which they have insisted on this idea, but they did not invent it; and it has escaped the world's notice that those very excesses of which Americans have been guilty imply a certain, unprecedented uneasiness over the idea's life and power, if not, indeed, the idea's validity. The idea of white supremacy rests simply on the fact that white men are the creators of civilization (the present civilization, which is the only one that matters; all previous civilizations are simply "contributions" to our own) and are therefore civilization's guardians and defenders. Thus it was impossible for Americans to accept the black man as one of themselves, for to do so was to jeopardize their status as white men. But not so to accept him was to deny his human reality, his human weight and complexity, and the strain of denying the overwhelmingly undeniable forced Americans into rationalizations so fantastic that they approached the pathological.

At the root of the American Negro problem is the necessity of the American white man to find a way of living with the Negro in order to be able to live with himself. And the history of this problem can be reduced to the means used by Americans—lynch law and law, segregation and legal acceptance, terrorization and concession—either to come to terms with this necessity, or to find a way around it, or (most usually) to find a way of doing both these things at once. The resulting spectacle, at once foolish and dreadful, led someone to make the quite accurate observation that "the Negro-in-America is a form of insanity which overtakes white men."

In this long battle, a battle by no means finished, the unforeseeable effects of which will be felt by many future generations, the white man's motive was the protection of his identity; the black man was motivated by the need to establish an identity. And despite the terrorization which the Negro in America endured and endures sporadically until today, despite the cruel and totally inescapable ambivalence of his status in his country, the battle for his identity has long ago been won. He is not a visitor to the West, but a citizen there, an American; as American as the Americans who despise him, the Americans who fear him, the Americans who love him—the Americans who became less than themselves, or rose to be greater than themselves by virtue of the fact that the challenge he represented was inescapable. He is perhaps the only black man in the world whose relationship to white men is more terrible, more subtle, and more meaningful than the relationship of bitter possessed to uncertain possessor. His survival depended, and his development depends, on his ability to turn his peculiar status in the Western world to his own advantage and, it may be, to the very great advantage of that world. It remains for him to fashion out of his experience that which will give him sustenance, and a voice.

The cathedral at Chartres, I have said, says something to the people of this village which it cannot say to me; but it is important to understand that this cathedral says something to me which it cannot say to them. Perhaps they are struck by the power of the spires, the glory of the windows; but they have known God, after all, longer than I have known him, and in a different way, and I am terrified by the slippery bottomless well to be found in the crypt, down which heretics were hurled to death, and by the obscene, inescapable gargoyles jutting out of the stone and seeming to say that God and the devil can never be divorced. I doubt that the villagers think of the devil when they face a cathedral because they have never been identified with the devil. But I must accept the status which myth, if nothing else, gives me in the West before I can hope to change the myth.

Yet, if the American Negro has arrived at his identity by virtue of the absoluteness of his estrangement from his past, American white men still nourish the illusion that there is some means of recovering the European innocence, of returning to a state in which black men do not exist. This is one of the greatest errors Americans can make. The identity they fought so hard to protect has, by virtue of that battle, undergone a change: Americans are as unlike any other white people in the world as it is possible to be. I do not think, for example, that it is too much to suggest that the American vision of the world—which allows so little reality, generally speaking, for any of the darker forces in human life, which tends until today to paint moral issues in glaring black and white—owes a great deal to the battle waged by Americans to maintain between themselves and black men a human separation which could not be bridged. It is only now beginning to be borne in on us—very faintly, it must be admitted, very slowly, and very much against our will—that this vision of the world is dangerously inaccurate, and perfectly useless. For it protects our moral high-mindedness at the terrible expense of weakening our grasp of reality. People who shut their eyes to reality simply invite their own destruction, and anyone who insists on remaining in a state of innocence long after that innocence is dead turns himself into a monster.

The time has come to realize that the interracial drama acted out on the American continent has not only created a new black man, it has created a new white man, too. No road whatever will lead Americans back to the simplicity of this European village where white men still have the luxury of looking on me as a stranger. I am not, really, a stranger any longer for any American alive. One of the things that distinguishes Americans from other people is that no other people has ever been so deeply involved in the lives of black men, and vice versa. This fact faced, with all its implications, it can be seen that the history of the American Negro problem is not merely shameful, it is also something of an achievement. For even when the worst has been said, it must also be added that the perpetual challenge posed by this problem was always, somehow, perpetually met. It is precisely this black-white experience which may prove of indispensable value to us in the world we face today. This world is white no longer, and it will never be white again.

1953

Michael Bérubé

b. 1961

Since the 1960s, so-called "culture wars" have been waged along many fronts in the United States. One of these battlefields is the college classroom. In his 1987 book The Closing of the American Mind, *Allan Bloom attacked what he saw as a dangerous cultural relativism being taught on American campuses, and he advocated a frank adjudication of values, a way of discerning which cultures were superior and which inferior. His view was a reaction against the multicultural trend of tolerance in American universities, which was itself a reaction against the smug sense of racial and cultural superiority generated by imperialism. Bloom's book triggered a general conservative assault on the liberal ideology that dominated American colleges, and behind this vanguard were public debaters like Rush Limbaugh and Dinesh D'Souza. The conservatives were so effective that "liberal" became a bad word in American culture, something avoided even by Democratic politicians. This essay is part of Bérubé's 2006 book,* What's Liberal about the Liberal Arts? Classroom Politics and "Bias" in Higher Education, *which attempts to reclaim the word and persuade readers to fight for what it denominates.*

Paying for Freedom

What is it we believe, we stubborn ones who continue to call ourselves liberals and progressives? First and foremost, we believe that a person's prospects and life chances should not depend on accidents of birth. We think it is a good idea to wriggle free of long-conventional beliefs about class and caste, Pharaoh and slave, lord and serf, and to imagine that each of us has an equal moral claim on the rest of us. But we think we haven't yet wriggled free enough, because even today too many humans' life chances depend far too heavily on whether one is born man or woman, dark-skinned or light-skinned, Alabaman or Angolan or Afghan, a resident of a comfy exurban collar county or a denizen of a polluted and ravaged industrial pit. That's why we believe in progressive taxation on both incomes and investments as a way of trying to compensate or ameliorate some of those accidents of birth. We advocate progressive taxation not because we resent the rich—on the contrary, a fortunate few of us are among the rich—but because we fear that the concentration of great wealth in few hands effectively undermines the project of democracy, and (on our happy days) we do not want to believe that the American experiment in democracy, which has included African-Americans only in the past forty years (and hardly satisfactorily at that) and has yet to be extended to gay men and lesbians, has already degenerated into a foul combination of oligarchy and plutocracy. And we advocate progressive taxation not because we like government and bureaucracy—on the contrary, most of us distrust the IRS and don't like dealing with the Department of Motor Vehicles, either, even as we know these things are necessary—but because we know that the state is the very last resort for the weak, the disabled, and the impoverished. It's not necessarily the best resort—far from it. Liberals know this well, having worked for decades to reform everything from labor laws to mental institutions. But we think it's immoral (yes, *immoral*) for free-market conservatives to leave our weakest citizens to depend on the whims of private charities, and to leave our wealthiest and most powerful citizens with the mere option of deciding whether or not to contribute to the common weal today or tomorrow or the next day. When liberals say we're all in this together, or that we should be, we mean that we have obligations to one another—and that we should collectively, democratically devise the means for realizing those obligations. That this is not broadly understood as a moral position says a great deal about the poverty of our public discourses of morality.

Some of us like to say that taxation is the price you pay for living in a civilized society. That's true as far as it goes, but it doesn't go nearly far enough. Rather, we should say that taxation is the price you pay for living in a free society, because this strikes more directly at the heart of libertarian economic mythologies. The reason a successful American entrepreneur should contribute to the common weal is that even if (as happens only rarely) her success is due only to her own individual talents, she couldn't have achieved that success in Saudi Arabia or Namibia or Kazakhstan. Americans who strike it rich—bless their clever hearts—do so in part because they live in a society that makes such things possible. It is in their long-term interests, and the interests of their associates and descendants, that the free society that enabled their success remain stable and secure, lest it turn slowly into a North American banana republic in which a constellation of overlords and apparatchiks live in gated communities with armed sentries overlooking the *favelas* below. Liberals like me tend to see George W. Bush's economic policies, with their massive public deficits and massive shifts of taxation from investment to income, as the force that will not only undo the American social contract but will eat away at the very idea of a social contract. We know that conservative anti-tax crusaders and political organizers like Grover Norquist say as much in so many words when they speak of shrinking government to the size at which it can be drowned in the bathtub, and we pay Norquist and his Norquistas the compliment of believing them. But when the Norquista version of the United States actually plays out in practice, we liberals don't see a government drowned in a bathtub; we see hundreds of poor and disabled Americans drowned in the streets of New Orleans.

In response, conservatives and libertarians typically complain that raising marginal tax rates will stifle growth, because if a multimillionaire entrepreneur or investor thinks that he's only going to see 50 cents from the next dollar he makes, he won't bother making the dollar. That's possible, though I have trouble imagining the scenario at work here—not merely because I have no personal experience with it, but more seriously because I find it hard to imagine a Clever Entrepreneur who thinks, "Well, I've made ten million this year, but if I make another two million I only get to keep one million of it, so I'm going to stop developing and promoting my product right about now." This sounds to me more like a rational-choice-theory textbook exercise than like actual human behavior, but even if it isn't, I am surprised that liberals and progressives haven't made a more forceful case that it might in fact be a good thing to have a tax system that does discourage the ultrawealthy from becoming ultra-ultra-ultrawealthy. Conservatives and libertarians claim that progressive-tax "disincentives" will lead entrepreneurs to create fewer jobs than they might otherwise, but that clearly wasn't the case in the bad old days of the 1950s and 1960s, when the top tax rate for individuals was 70 percent. If indeed such "disincentives" are a problem for exceptionally high wage earners, then perhaps some clever tax attorneys could devise very steep rates for very high income levels along with tax credits and cuts for very wealthy people who actually create jobs with their money instead of hoarding it, moving it into offshore tax shelters, or donating it to electoral campaigns and political action committees (just to name three other popular avenues for significant wealth). I'm a literature professor, not a tax specialist. But the arguments I've heard from the right against progressive income and investment taxes just don't add up; they sound to me like the rationalizations of people who have already decided they don't like the idea of "social welfare" or the "common weal" or "obligations to one's fellow citizens," and are looking for convenient excuses to opt out of public systems altogether. Liberals and progressives, by contrast, sound to me like people who still care about our social infrastructure—our transportation systems, our disability services, our schools, our hospitals, our parks, our air, our water, our food industry—but who still haven't figured out ways of preventing the public good from being misadministered and subverted by inefficient or corrupt government bureaucracies (though we have learned that fully nationalized economies give rise to behemoth state apparatuses which function efficiently only when it comes to political repression). But when it comes to the actual conduct of the state and its many agencies, I'll take the flawed but fixable attempts of liberals any day over the deliberate malice of conservatives, who serve in the offices of the Department of Energy, the Environmental Protection Agency, or the Equal Employment Opportunity Commission chiefly in order to make sure that the foxes run the henhouse.

2006

Judy Brady
b. 1937

Brady wrote "I Want a Wife" for the premier issue of Ms. *maga-zine, which was published first as an insert in* New York *magazine in December 1971 and then on its own in July 1972. Feminist ac-tivists and New York businesswomen working in the magazine business collaborated on the venture that would, in the words of one of its founding editors, concern "how a woman can change her life and . . . [her] relationship with husbands, lovers, children, other women, [her] job and the community in which [she] lives." Three hundred thousand copies of the insert issue were printed, and it sold out in eight days. Although Gloria Steinem pitched* Ms. *to all women regardless of race or class or marital status, its main au-dience was the white, middle-class women who read other national magazines, like* Good Housekeeping *and* Cosmopolitan. *The cover story in the first issue— "The Housewife's Moment of Truth"— described the "click of recognition" when a housewife realizes that she is oppressed. Brady's essay would also have been designed to raise the consciousness of readers who were being introduced to feminism in the pages of this glossy, national magazine. Like Jonathan Swift, Brady persuades through irony: What she says is not what she wants.*

I Want a Wife

I belong to that classification of people known as wives. I am A Wife. And, not altogether incidentally, I am a mother.

Not too long ago a male friend of mine appeared on the scene fresh from a recent divorce. He had one child, who is, of course, with his ex-wife. He is obviously looking for another wife. As I thought about him while I was ironing one evening, it sud-denly occurred to me that I, too, would like to have a wife. Why do I want a wife?

I would like to go back to school so that I can become economi-cally independent, support myself, and, if need be, support those dependent upon me. I want a wife who will work and send me to school. And while I am going to school I want a wife to take care of my children. I want a wife to keep track of the children's doctor and dentist appointments. And to keep track of mine, too. I want a wife to make sure my children eat properly and are kept clean. I want a wife who will wash the children's clothes and keep them mended. I want a wife who is a good nurturant attendant to my children, who arranges for their schooling, makes sure that they have an adequate social life with their peers, takes them to the park, the zoo, etc. I want a wife who takes care of the children when they are sick, a wife who arranges to be around when the children need special care, because, of course, I cannot miss classes at school. My wife must arrange to lose time at work and not lose the job. It may mean a small cut in my wife's income from time to time, but I guess I can tolerate that. Needless to say, my wife will arrange and pay for the care of the children while my wife is working.

I want a wife who will take care of *my* physical needs. I want a wife who will keep my house clean. A wife who will pick up after me. I want a wife who will keep my clothes clean, ironed, mended, replaced when need be, and who will see to it that my personal things are kept in their proper place so that I can find what I need the minute I need it. I want a wife who cooks the meals, a wife who is a *good* cook. I want a wife who will plan the menus, do the necessary grocery shopping, prepare the meals, serve them pleasantly, and then do the cleaning up while I do my studying. I want a wife who will care for me when I am sick and sympathize with my pain and loss of time from school. I want a wife to go along when our family takes a vacation so that someone can continue to care for me and my children when I need a rest and change of scene.

I want a wife who will not bother me with rambling complaints about a wife's duties. But I want a wife who will listen to me when I feel the need to explain a rather difficult point I have come across in my course of studies. And I want a wife who will type my papers for me when I have written them.

I want a wife who will take care of the details of my social life. When my wife and I are invited out by my friends, I want a wife who will take care of the babysitting arrangements. When I meet people at school that I like and want to entertain, I want a wife who will have the house clean, will prepare a special meal, serve it to me and my friends, and not interrupt when I talk about the things that interest me and my friends. I want a wife who will have arranged that the children are fed and ready for bed before my guests arrive so that the children do not bother us.

And I want a wife who knows that sometimes I need a night out by myself.

I want a wife who is sensitive to my sexual needs, a wife who makes love passionately and eagerly when I feel like it, a wife who makes sure that I am satisfied. And, of course, I want a wife who will not demand sexual attention when I am not in the mood for it. I want a wife who assumes the complete responsibility for birth control, because I do not want more children. I want a wife who will remain sexually faithful to me so that I do not have to clutter up my intellectual life with jealousies. And I want a wife who understands that *my* sexual needs may entail more than strict adherence to monogamy. I must, after all, be able to relate to people as fully as possible.

If, by chance, I find another person more suitable as a wife than the wife I already have, I want the liberty to replace my present wife with another one. Naturally, I will expect a fresh, new life; my wife will take the children and be solely responsible for them so that I am left free.

When I am through with school and have a job, I want my wife to quit working and remain at home so that my wife can more fully and completely take care of a wife's duties.

My God, who *wouldn't* want a wife?

1971

William F. Buckley Jr.
b. 1925

> *Buckley, editor of the* National Review *from 1955 until 1990 and host of the PBS talk show* Firing Line *for its entire run, 1966 to 1999, is one of the leading voices of conservative politics in America. His syndicated column, "On the Right," brought his opinions to millions of newspaper readers across the country. This selection from his column—"Why Don't We Complain?"—is a good example of the personal essay: Reflecting on his own experience leads Buckley to some insights that he can then widely apply. In this case, Buckley uses his experiences on a train and in a movie theater to support claims about the political apathy of Americans in general. The essayist does not expect the anecdotes he uses as evidence to persuade readers fully; rather, they are meant to prompt readers to examine their own experience and decide whether it confirms his insights. The essay was first published in* Esquire, *an upscale men's magazine ("esquire" used to be a title of respect claimed by men sufficiently wealthy or well bred to consider themselves "gentlemen"). Buckley certainly means for the "we" in the essay's title to refer to all Americans, but in the context of* Esquire *that pronoun refers to a narrower class of people.*

Why Don't We Complain?

It was the very last coach and the only empty seat on the entire train, so there was no turning back. The problem was to breathe. Outside the temperature was below freezing. Inside the railroad car, the temperature must have been about 85 degrees. I took off my overcoat, and a few minutes later my jacket, and noticed that the car was flecked with the white shirts of passengers. I soon found my hand moving to loosen my tie. From one end of the car to the other, as we rattled through Westchester County, we sweated; but we did not moan.

I watched the train conductor appear at the head of the car. "Tickets, all tickets, please!" In a more virile age, I thought, the passengers would seize the conductor and strap him down on a seat over the radiator to share the fate of his patrons. He shuffled down the aisle, picking up tickets, punching commutation cards. *No one addressed a word to him.* He approached my seat, and I drew a deep breath of resolution. "Conductor," I began with a considerable edge to my voice. . . . Instantly the doleful eyes of my seatmate turned tiredly from his newspaper to fix me with a resentful stare: what question could be so important as to justify my sibilant intrusion into his stupor? I was shaken by those eyes. I am incapable of making a discreet fuss, so I mumbled a question about what time were we due in Stamford (I didn't even ask whether it would be before or after dehydration could be expected to set in), got my reply, and went back to my newspaper and to wiping my brow.

The conductor had nonchalantly walked down the gauntlet of eighty sweating American freemen, and not one of them had asked him to explain why the passengers in that car had been consigned to suffer. There is nothing to be done when the temperature *outdoors* is 85 degrees, and indoors the air conditioner has broken down; obviously when that happens there is nothing to do, except perhaps curse the day that one was born. But when the temperature outdoors is below freezing, it takes a positive act of will on somebody's part to set the temperature *indoors* at 85. Somewhere a valve was turned too far, a furnace overstoked, a thermostat maladjusted: something that could easily be remedied by turning off the heat and allowing the great outdoors to come indoors. All this is so obvious. What is not obvious is what has happened to the American people.

It isn't just the commuters, whom we have come to visualize as a supine breed who have got onto the trick of suspending their sensory faculties twice a day while they submit to the creeping dissolution of the railroad industry. It isn't just they who have given up trying to rectify irrational vexations. It is the American people everywhere.

A few weeks ago at a large movie theatre I turned to my wife and said, "The picture is out of focus." "Be quiet," she answered. I obeyed. But a few minutes later I raised the point again, with mounting impatience. "It will be all right in a minute," she said apprehensively. (She would rather lose her eyesight than be around when I make one of my infrequent scenes.) I waited. It was *just* out of focus—not glaringly out, but out. My vision is 20-20, and I assume that is the vision, adjusted, of most people in the movie house. So, after hectoring my wife throughout the first reel, I finally prevailed upon her to admit that it *was* off, and very annoying. We then settled down, coming to rest on the presumption that: a) someone connected with the management of the theatre must soon notice the blur and make the correction; or b) that someone seated near the rear of the house would make the complaint in behalf of those of us up front; or c) that—any minute now—the entire house would explode into catcalls and foot stamping, calling dramatic attention to the irksome distortion.

What happened was nothing. The movie ended, as it had begun, just out of focus, and as we trooped out, we stretched our faces in a variety of contortions to accustom the eye to the shock of normal focus.

I think it is safe to say that everybody suffered on that occasion. And I think it is safe to assume that everyone was expecting someone else to take the initiative in going back to speak to the manager. And it is probably true even that if we had supposed the movie would run right through with the blurred image, someone surely would have summoned up the purposive indignation to get up out of his seat and file his complaint.

But notice that no one did. And the reason no one did is because we are all increasingly anxious in America to be unobtrusive, we are reluctant to make our voices heard, hesitant about claiming our rights; we are afraid that our cause is unjust, or that if it is not unjust, that it is ambiguous; or if not even that, that it is too trivial to justify the horrors of a confrontation with Authority; we will sit in an oven or endure a racking headache before undertaking a head-on, I'm-here-to-tell-you complaint. That tendency to passive compliance, to a heedless endurance is something to keep one's eyes on—in sharp focus.

I myself can occasionally summon the courage to complain, but I cannot, as I have intimated, complain softly. My own instinct is so strong to let the thing ride, to forget about it—to expect that someone will take the matter up, when the grievance is collective, in my behalf—that it is only when the provocation is at a very special key, whose vibrations touch simultaneously a complexus of nerves, allergies, and passions, that I catch fire and find the reserves of courage and assertiveness to speak up. When that happens, I get quite carried away. My blood gets hot, my brow wet, I become unbearably and unconscionably sarcastic and bellicose: I am girded for a total showdown.

Why should that be? Why could not I (or anyone else) on that railroad coach have said simply to the conductor, "Sir,"—I take that back: that sounds sarcastic—"Conductor, would you be good enough to turn down the heat? I am extremely hot. In fact, I tend to get hot every time the temperature reaches 85 degr—" Strike that last sentence. Just end it with the simple statement that you are extremely hot, and let the conductor infer the cause.

Every New Year's Eve I resolve to do something about the Milquetoast[1] in me and vow to speak up, calmly, for my rights, and for the betterment of our society, on every appropriate occasion. Entering last New Year's Eve I was fortified in my resolve because that morning at breakfast I had had to ask the waitress three times for a glass of milk. She finally brought it—after I had finished my eggs, which is when I don't want it any more. I did not have the manliness to order her to take the milk back, but settled instead for a cowardly sulk, and ostentatiously refused to drink the milk—though I later paid for it—rather than state plainly to the hostess, as I should have, why I had not drunk it, and would not pay for it.

So by the time the New Year ushered out the Old, riding in on my morning's indignation and stimulated by the gastric juices of resolution that flow so faithfully on New Year's Eve, I rendered my vow. Henceforward I would conquer my shyness, my despicable disposition to supineness. I would speak out like a man against the unnecessary annoyances of our time.

Forty-eight hours later, I was standing in line at the ski-repair store in Pico Peak, Vermont. All I needed, to get on with my skiing, was the loan, for one minute, of a small screw driver, to tighten a loose binding. Behind the counter in the workshop were two men. One was industriously engaged in servicing the complicated requirements of a young lady at the head of the line, and obviously he would be tied up for quite a while. The other—"Jiggs," his work-

---

1. After Caspar Milquetoast, a meek and timid character in a comic strip created by Harold Tucker Webster (1885–1952).

mate called him—was a middle-aged man, who sat in a chair puffing a pipe, exchanging small talk with his working partner. My pulse began its telltale acceleration. The minutes ticked on. I stared at the idle shopkeeper, hoping to shame him into action, but he was impervious to my telepathic reproof and continued his small talk with his friend, brazenly insensitive to the nervous demands of six good men who were raring to ski.

Suddenly my New Year's Eve resolution struck me. It was now or never. I broke from my place in line and marched to the counter. I was going to control myself. I dug my nails into my palms. My effort was only partially successful:

"If you are not too busy," I said icily, "would you mind handing me a screw driver?"

Work stopped and everyone turned his eyes on me, and I experienced that mortification I always feel when I am the center of centripetal shafts of curiosity, resentment, perplexity.

But the worst was yet to come. "I am sorry, sir," said Jiggs deferentially, moving the pipe from his mouth. "I am not supposed to move. I have just had a heart attack." That was the signal for a great whirring noise that descended from heaven. We looked, stricken, out the window, and it appeared as though a cyclone had suddenly focused on the snowy courtyard between the shop and the ski lift. Suddenly a gigantic Army helicopter materialized, and hovered down to a landing. Two men jumped out of the plane carrying a stretcher, tore into the ski shop, and lifted the shopkeeper onto the stretcher. Jiggs bade his companion good-by, was whisked out the door, into the plane, up to the heavens, down—we learned—to a near-by Army hospital. I looked up manfully—into a score of man-eating eyes. I put the experience down as a reversal.

As I write this, on an airplane, I have run out of paper and need to reach into my brief case under my legs for more. I cannot do this until my empty lunch tray is removed from my lap. I arrested the stewardess as she passed empty-handed down the aisle on the way to the kitchen to fetch the lunch trays for the passengers up forward who haven't been served yet. "Would you please take my tray?" "Just a *moment*, sir," she said, and marched on sternly. Shall I tell her that since she is headed for the kitchen *anyway*, it cannot delay the feeding of the other passengers by the two seconds necessary to stash away my empty tray? Or remind her that not fifteen minutes ago she spoke unctuously into the loud-speaker the words undoubtedly devised by the airline's highly paid public-relations counselor: "If there is anything I or Miss French can do for you to make your trip more enjoyable, *please* let us—" I have run out of paper.

I think the observable reluctance of the majority of Americans to assert themselves in minor matters is related to our increased sense of helplessness in an age of technology and centralized political and economic power. For generations, Americans who were too hot, or too cold, got up and did something about it. Now we call the plumber, or the electrician, or the furnace man. The habit of looking after our own needs obviously had something to do with the assertiveness that characterized the American family familiar to readers of American literature. With the technification of life goes our direct responsibility for our material environment, and we are conditioned to adopt a position of helplessness not only as regards the broken air conditioner, but as regards the overheated train. It takes an expert to fix the former, but not the latter: yet these distinctions, as we withdrew into helplessness, tend to fade away.

Our notorious political apathy is a related phenomenon. Every year, whether the Republican or the Democratic Party is in office, more and more power drains away from the individual to feed vast reservoirs in far-off places; and we have less and less say about the shape of events which shape our future. From this aberration of personal power comes the sense of resignation with which we accept the political dispensations of a powerful government whose hold upon us continues to increase.

An editor of a national weekly news magazine told me a few years ago that as few as a dozen letters of protest against an editorial stance of his magazine was enough to convene a plenipotentiary meeting of the board of editors to review policy. "So few people complain, or make their voices heard," he explained to me, "that we assume a dozen letters represent the inarticulated views of thousands of readers." In the past ten years, he said, the volume of mail has noticeably decreased, even though the circulation of his magazine has risen.

When our voices are finally mute, when we have finally suppressed the natural instinct to complain, whether the vexation is trivial or grave, we shall have become automatons, incapable of feeling. When Premier Khrushchev[2] first came to this country late in 1959 he was primed, we are informed, to experience the bitter resentment of the American people against his tyranny, against his persecutions, against the movement which is responsible for the then great number of American deaths in Korea,[3] for billions in taxes every year, and for life everlasting on the brink of disasters; but Khrushchev was pleasantly surprised, and reported back to the Russian people that he had been met with overwhelming cordiality (read: apathy), except, to be sure, for "a few fascists who followed me around with their wretched posters, and should be . . . horse-whipped."

I may be crazy, but I say there would have been lots more posters in a society where train temperatures in the dead of winter are not allowed to climb up to 85 degrees without complaint.

1961

Rachel Carson
1907–1964

Carson, a marine biologist, published her book Silent Spring *in 1962. She wanted to tell her readers that modern chemical pesticides, especially DDT, were destroying the environment. Ultimately, she hoped to change the way we think about our relationship to nature—to stop us from imagining humans as nature's conquerer and to prompt us to see ourselves as but one member in a delicate collaboration. It is notoriously difficult to measure the effect any single work has on a culture, but* Silent Spring *is generally credited with sparking the public debate about the environment that led to a sea change in the American consciousness. The immediate purpose of "A Fable for Tomorrow," the first chapter in* Silent Spring, *is to get people to read the following chapters, in*

2. Nikita Khrushchev (1894–1971), leader of the Soviet Union, 1953–64.

3. More than fifty thousand U.S. servicemen were killed during the Korean conflict, a war between communist North Korea (supported by the People's Republic of China) and South Korea (supported by the United Nations, with the United States the principal participant).

*which she presents and analyzes the dangers of pesticides. In and of
itself, then, this short excerpt does not offer an argument. The evidence that supports Carson's position comes later in the book. As
you read the description of what has befallen the small town described in this piece, you might think of this tale, not as a realistic
depiction of life in the United States in 1962, but rather as the fruit
of Carson's "fabulous" imagination. Carson expects that reaction. In
fact, the power of the final two paragraphs presumes it.*

A Fable for Tomorrow

There was once a town in the heart of America where all life
seemed to live in harmony with its surroundings. The town
lay in the midst of a checkerboard of prosperous farms, with
fields of grain and hillsides of orchards where, in spring, white
clouds of bloom drifted above the green fields. In autumn, oak and
maple and birch set up a blaze of color that flamed and flickered
across a backdrop of pines. Then foxes barked in the hills and deer
silently crossed the fields, half hidden in the mists of the fall mornings.

Along the roads, laurel, viburnum and alder, great ferns and
wildflowers delighted the traveler's eye through much of the year.
Even in winter the roadsides were places of beauty, where countless
birds came to feed on the berries and on the seed heads of the dried
weeds rising above the snow. The countryside was, in fact, famous
for the abundance and variety of its bird life, and when the flood of
migrants was pouring through in spring and fall people traveled
from great distances to observe them. Others came to fish the
streams, which flowed clear and cold out of the hills and contained
shady pools where trout lay. So it had been from the days many
years ago when the first settlers raised their houses, sank their wells,
and built their barns.

Then a strange blight crept over the area and everything began to
change. Some evil spell had settled on the community: mysterious
maladies swept the flocks of chickens; the cattle and sheep sickened
and died. Everywhere was a shadow of death. The farmers spoke of
much illness among their families. In the town the doctors had become more and more puzzled by new kinds of sickness appearing

among their patients. There had been several sudden and unexplained deaths, not only among adults but even among children, who would be stricken suddenly while at play and die within a few hours.

There was a strange stillness. The birds, for example—where had they gone? Many people spoke of them, puzzled and disturbed. The feeding stations in the backyards were deserted. The few birds seen anywhere were moribund; they trembled violently and could not fly. It was a spring without voices. On the mornings that had once throbbed with the dawn chorus of robins, catbirds, doves, jays, wrens, and scores of other bird voices there was now no sound; only silence lay over the fields and woods and marsh.

On the farms the hens brooded, but no chicks hatched. The farmers complained that they were unable to raise any pigs—the litters were small and the young survived only a few days. The apple trees were coming into bloom but no bees droned among the blossoms, so there was no pollination and there would be no fruit.

The roadsides, once so attractive, were now lined with browned and withered vegetation as though swept by fire. These, too, were silent, deserted by all living things. Even the streams were now lifeless. Anglers no longer visited them, for all the fish had died.

In the gutters under the eaves and between the shingles of the roofs, a white granular powder still showed a few patches; some weeks before it had fallen like snow upon the roofs and the lawns, the fields and streams.

No witchcraft, no enemy action had silenced the rebirth of new life in this stricken world. The people had done it themselves.

This town does not actually exist, but it might easily have a thousand counterparts in America or elsewhere in the world. I know of no community that has experienced all the misfortunes I describe. Yet every one of these disasters has actually happened somewhere, and many real communities have already suffered a substantial number of them. A grim specter has crept upon us almost unnoticed, and this imagined tragedy may easily become a stark reality we all shall know.

What has already silenced the voices of spring in countless towns in America? This book is an attempt to explain.

1962

Richard Dawkins
b. 1941
Jerry Coyne
b. 1949

Though the 1925 Scopes trial led many school districts to teach evolution, evolution only gradually became standard fare in most American high schools. The teaching of evolution accelerated in the 1960s, when the United States, fearful that Russia was winning the race in the sciences, seriously expanded support for the sciences in education. But in the 1980s, a reactionary movement gained ground, forcing some schools to teach creationism, or at least to treat evolution as an unproved theory. In Louisiana, for example, a new law required that creationism be taught alongside the theory of evolution. In 1987, the U.S. Supreme Court declared that such a requirement violated the Constitutional principle of the separation of church and state. Shortly afterward, "creation-science" was renamed "intelligent design" by opponents of evolutionary theory. In 1991, the Discovery Institute, a Seattle-based think tank, began promoting the position that some evolutionary change in species does take place, but certain complex features, such as the eye and the little whip-like flagella that propel bacteria, could not have been developed through natural evolutionary processes. Proponents of intelligent design believe that these and other "problems" that are as yet unsatisfactorily explained by evolutionists can only be explained by a supernatural intelligence, an invisible hand helping species leap from lesser to greater complexities when natural processes cannot do the trick. Through skillful publicity and lobbying campaigns, the Discovery Institute has influenced a number of school districts and President George W. Bush, who famously urged schools to teach intelligent design along with evolution. The school board of Dover, Pennsylvania, complied. However, in a landmark decision in 2004, the U.S. District Court for the Middle District of Pennsylvania concluded that "intelligent design" is "creationism" and cannot be required in public schools. Meanwhile, the Discovery Institute has been supporting an affiliated organization in England called Truth in Science. Disputing such groups, Dawkins and Coyne, evolutionary biologists at Oxford University and the Uni-

versity of Chicago, respectively, published this essay in The Guardian, *a liberal English newspaper, in September 2005.*

One Side Can Be Wrong

It sounds so reasonable, doesn't it? Such a modest proposal. Why not teach "both sides" and let the children decide for themselves? As President Bush said, "You're asking me whether or not people ought to be exposed to different ideas, the answer is yes." At first hearing, everything about the phrase "both sides" warms the hearts of educators like ourselves.

One of us spent years as an Oxford tutor and it was his habit to choose controversial topics for the students' weekly essays. They were required to go to the library, read about both sides of an argument, give a fair account of both, and then come to a balanced judgment in their essay. The call for balance, by the way, was always tempered by the maxim, "When two opposite points of view are expressed with equal intensity, the truth does not necessarily lie exactly halfway between. It is possible for one side simply to be wrong."

As teachers, both of us have found that asking our students to analyse controversies is of enormous value to their education. What is wrong, then, with teaching both sides of the alleged controversy between evolution and creationism or "intelligent design" (ID)? And, by the way, don't be fooled by the disingenuous euphemism. There is nothing new about ID. It is simply creationism camouflaged with a new name to slip (with some success, thanks to loads of tax-free money and slick public-relations professionals) under the radar of the U.S. Constitution's mandate for separation between church and state.

Why, then, would two lifelong educators and passionate advocates of the "both sides" style of teaching join with essentially all biologists in making an exception of the alleged controversy between creation and evolution? What is wrong with the apparently sweet reasonableness of "it is only fair to teach both sides"? The answer is simple. This is not a scientific controversy at all. And it is a time-wasting distraction because evolutionary science, perhaps more than any other major science, is bountifully endowed with genuine controversy.

Among the controversies that students of evolution commonly face, these are genuinely challenging and of great educational value: neutralism versus selectionism in molecular evolution; adaptationism; group selection; punctuated equilibrium; cladism; "evo-devo"; the "Cambrian Explosion"; mass extinctions; interspecies competition; sympatric speciation; sexual selection; the evolution of sex itself; evolutionary psychology; Darwinian medicine and so on. The point is that all these controversies, and many more, provide fodder for fascinating and lively argument, not just in essays but for student discussions late at night.

Intelligent design is not an argument of the same character as these controversies. It is not a scientific argument at all, but a religious one. It might be worth discussing in a class on the history of ideas, in a philosophy class on popular logical fallacies, or in a comparative religion class on origin myths from around the world. But it no more belongs in a biology class than alchemy belongs in a chemistry class, phlogiston in a physics class or the stork theory in a sex education class. In those cases, the demand for equal time for "both theories" would be ludicrous. Similarly, in a class on 20th-century European history, who would demand equal time for the theory that the Holocaust never happened?

So, why are we so sure that intelligent design is not a real scientific theory, worthy of "both sides" treatment? Isn't that just our personal opinion? It is an opinion shared by the vast majority of professional biologists, but of course science does not proceed by majority vote among scientists. Why isn't creationism (or its incarnation as intelligent design) just another scientific controversy, as worthy of scientific debate as the dozen essay topics we listed above? Here's why.

If ID really were a scientific theory, positive evidence for it, gathered through research, would fill peer-reviewed scientific journals. This doesn't happen. It isn't that editors refuse to publish ID research. There simply isn't any ID research to publish. Its advocates bypass normal scientific due process by appealing directly to the nonscientific public and—with great shrewdness—to the government officials they elect.

The argument the ID advocates put, such as it is, is always of the same character. Never do they offer positive evidence in favor of intelligent design. All we ever get is a list of alleged deficiencies in evolution. We are told of "gaps" in the fossil record. Or organs are stated, by flat and without supporting evidence, to be "irreducibly complex"; too complex to have evolved by natural selection.

In all cases there is a hidden (actually they scarcely even bother to hide it) "default" assumption that if Theory A has some difficulty in explaining Phenomenon X, we must automatically prefer Theory B without even asking whether Theory B (creationism in this case) is any better at explaining it. Note how unbalanced this is, and how it gives the lie to the apparent reasonableness of "let's teach both sides." One side is required to produce evidence, every step of the way. The other side is never required to produce one iota of evidence, but is deemed to have won automatically the moment the first side encounters a difficulty—the sort of difficulty that all sciences encounter every day, and go to work to solve, with relish.

What, after all, is a gap in the fossil record? It is simply the absence of a fossil which would otherwise have documented a particular evolutionary transition. The gap means that we lack a complete cinematic record of every step in the evolutionary process. But how incredibly presumptuous to demand a complete record, given that only a minuscule proportion of deaths result in a fossil anyway.

The equivalent evidential demand of creationism would be a complete cinematic record of God's behavior on the day that he went to work on, say, the mammalian ear bones or the bacterial flagellum—the small, hair-like organ that propels mobile bacteria. Not even the most ardent advocate of intelligent design claims that any such divine videotape will ever become available.

Biologists, on the other hand, can confidently claim the equivalent "cinematic" sequence of fossils for a very large number of evolutionary transitions. Not all, but very many, including our own descent from the bipedal ape *Australopithecus*. And—far more telling—not a single authentic fossil has ever been found in the "wrong" place in the evolutionary sequence. Such an anachronistic fossil, if one were ever unearthed, would blow evolution out of the water.

As the great biologist J. B. S. Haldane growled, when asked what might disprove evolution: "Fossil rabbits in the pre-Cambrian."

Evolution, like all good theories, makes itself vulnerable to disproof. Needless to say, it has always come through with flying colors.

Similarly, the claim that something—say the bacterial flagellum—[1] is too complex to have evolved by natural selection is alleged, by a lamentably common but false syllogism, to support the "rival" intelligent design theory by default. This kind of default reasoning leaves completely open the possibility that, if the bacterial flagellum is too complex to have evolved, it might also be too complex to have been created. And indeed, a moment's thought shows that any God capable of creating a bacterial flagellum (to say nothing of a universe) would have to be a far more complex, and therefore statistically improbable, entity than the bacterial flagellum (or universe) itself—even more in need of an explanation than the object he is alleged to have created.

If complex organisms demand an explanation, so does a complex designer. And it's no solution to raise the theologian's plea that God (or the Intelligent Designer) is simply immune to the normal demands of scientific explanation. To do so would be to shoot yourself in the foot. You cannot have it both ways. Either ID belongs in the science classroom, in which case it must submit to the discipline required of a scientific hypothesis. Or it does not, in which case get it out of the science classroom and send it back into the church, where it belongs.

In fact, the bacterial flagellum is certainly not too complex to have evolved, nor is any other living structure that has ever been carefully studied. Biologists have located plausible series of intermediates, using ingredients to be found elsewhere in living systems. But even if some particular case were found for which biologists could offer no ready explanation, the important point is that the "default" logic of the creationists remains thoroughly rotten.

---

1. The complex, tubelike projections that a single-cell organism uses to propel itself, in a manner similar to the screw on a boat's propeller. In his 1996 book *Darwin's Black Box*, Michael Behe suggested that bacterial flagellae, among other animal features, such as the clotting mechanism in blood, are "irreducibly complex." In other words, like machines, they depend on a concurrence of parts that have no individual functions; according to Behe, the random mechanisms of evolution could not have assembled such parts into a coherent, working "machine."

There is no evidence in favor of intelligent design: only alleged gaps in the completeness of the evolutionary account, coupled with the "default" fallacy we have identified. And, while it is inevitably true that there are incompletenesses in evolutionary science, the positive evidence for the fact of evolution is truly massive, made up of hundreds of thousands of mutually corroborating observations. These come from areas such as geology, paleontology, comparative anatomy, physiology, biochemistry, ethology, biogeography, embryology and—increasingly nowadays—molecular genetics.

The weight of the evidence has become so heavy that opposition to the fact of evolution is laughable to all who are acquainted with even a fraction of the published data. Evolution is a fact: as much a fact as plate tectonics or the heliocentric solar system.

Why, finally, does it matter whether these issues are discussed in science classes? There is a case for saying that it doesn't—that biologists shouldn't get so hot under the collar. Perhaps we should just accept the popular demand that we teach ID as well as evolution in science classes. It would, after all, take only about ten minutes to exhaust the case for ID, then we could get back to teaching real science and genuine controversy.

Tempting as this is, a serious worry remains. The seductive "let's teach the controversy" language still conveys the false, and highly pernicious, idea that there really are two sides. This would distract students from the genuinely important and interesting controversies that enliven evolutionary discourse. Worse, it would hand creationism the only victory it realistically aspires to. Without needing to make a single good point in any argument, it would have won the right for a form of supernaturalism to be recognized as an authentic part of science. And that would be the end of science education in America.

2005

Joan Didion
b. 1934

When she wrote "On Keeping a Notebook," Didion was a fairly obscure magazine contributor interpreting life on the West Coast in melancholy, fatalistic, liberal terms. She collected this and other essays in her 1968 book Slouching Towards Bethlehem, *which established her as one of America's best essayists. Most of her writing is at least tangentially political, but here Didion is not trying to persuade readers of anything. Rather, her purpose is to examine herself and expose what she finds. In the process, and in the tradition of the personal essay, she attempts to offer some ideas about the relationship between our present selves and our remembered past.*

On Keeping a Notebook

"That woman Estelle,'" the note reads, "'is partly the reason why George Sharp and I are separated today.' *Dirty crepe-de-Chine*[1] *wrapper, hotel bar, Wilmington RR, 9:45 a.m. August Monday morning.*"

Since the note is in my notebook, it presumably has some meaning to me. I study it for a long while. At first I have only the most general notion of what I was doing on an August Monday morning in the bar of the hotel across from the Pennsylvania Railroad station in Wilmington, Delaware (waiting for a train? missing one? 1960? 1961? why Wilmington?), but I do remember being there. The woman in the dirty crepe-de-Chine wrapper had come down from her room for a beer, and the bartender had heard before the reason why George Sharp and she were separated today. "Sure," he said, and went on mopping the floor. "You told me." At the other end of the bar is a girl. She is talking, pointedly, not to the man beside her but to a cat lying in the triangle of sunlight cast through the open door. She is wearing a plaid silk dress from Peck & Peck, and the hem is coming down.

---

1. A type of silk fabric.

Here is what it is: the girl has been on the Eastern Shore, and now she is going back to the city, leaving the man beside her, and all she can see ahead are the viscous summer sidewalks and the 3 a.m. long-distance calls that will make her lie awake and then sleep drugged through all the steaming mornings left in August (1960? 1961?). Because she must go directly from the train to lunch in New York, she wishes that she had a safety pin for the hem of the plaid silk dress, and she also wishes that she could forget about the hem and the lunch and stay in the cool bar that smells of disinfectant and malt and make friends with the woman in the crepe-de-Chine wrapper. She is afflicted by a little self-pity, and she wants to compare Estelles. That is what that was all about.

Why did I write it down? In order to remember, of course, but exactly what was it I wanted to remember? How much of it actually happened? Did any of it? Why do I keep a notebook at all? It is easy to deceive oneself on all those scores. The impulse to write things down is a peculiarly compulsive one, inexplicable to those who do not share it, useful only accidentally, only secondarily, in the way that any compulsion tries to justify itself. I suppose that it begins or does not begin in the cradle. Although I have felt compelled to write things down since I was five years old, I doubt that my daughter ever will, for she is a singularly blessed and accepting child, delighted with life exactly as life presents itself to her, unafraid to go to sleep and unafraid to wake up. Keepers of private notebooks are a different breed altogether, lonely and resistant rearrangers of things, anxious malcontents, children afflicted apparently at birth with some presentiment of loss.

My first notebook was a Big Five tablet, given to me by my mother with the sensible suggestion that I stop whining and learn to amuse myself by writing down my thoughts. She returned the tablet to me a few years ago; the first entry is an account of a woman who believed herself to be freezing to death in the Arctic night, only to find, when day broke, that she had stumbled onto the Sahara Desert, where she would die of the heat before lunch. I have no idea what turn of a five-year-old's mind could have prompted so insistently "ironic" and exotic a story, but it does reveal a certain predilection for the extreme which has dogged me into adult life; perhaps if I were analytically inclined I would find it a truer story than any I might have told about Donald Johnson's birthday party or the day my cousin Brenda put Kitty Litter in the aquarium.

So the point of my keeping a notebook has never been, nor is it now, to have an accurate factual record of what I have been doing or thinking. That would be a different impulse entirely, an instinct for reality which I sometimes envy but do not possess. At no point have I ever been able successfully to keep a diary; my approach to daily life ranges from the grossly negligent to the merely absent, and on those few occasions when I have tried dutifully to record a day's events, boredom has so overcome me that the results are mysterious at best. What is this business about "shopping, typing piece, dinner with E, depressed"? Shopping for what? Typing what piece? Who is E? Was this "E" depressed, or was I depressed? Who cares?

In fact I have abandoned altogether that kind of pointless entry; instead I tell what some would call lies. "That's simply not true," the members of my family frequently tell me when they come up against my memory of a shared event. "The party was *not* for you, the spider was *not* a black widow, *it wasn't that way at all.*" Very likely they are right, for not only have I always had trouble distinguishing between what happened and what merely might have happened, but I remain unconvinced that the distinction, for my purposes, matters. The cracked crab that I recall having for lunch the day my father came home from Detroit in 1945 must certainly be embroidery, worked into the day's pattern to lend verisimilitude; I was ten years old and would not now remember the cracked crab. The day's events did not turn on cracked crab. And yet it is precisely that fictitious crab that makes me see the afternoon all over again, a home movie run all too often, the father bearing gifts, the child weeping, an exercise in family love and guilt. Or that is what it was to me. Similarly, perhaps it never did snow that August in Vermont; perhaps there never were flurries in the night wind, and maybe no one else felt the ground hardening and summer already dead even as we pretended to bask in it, but that was how it felt to me, and it might as well have snowed, could have snowed, did snow.

How it felt to me: that is getting closer to the truth about a notebook. I sometimes delude myself about why I keep a notebook, imagine that some thrifty virtue derives from preserving everything observed. See enough and write it down, I tell myself, and then some morning when the world seems drained of wonder, some day when I am only going through the motions of doing what I am supposed to do, which is write—on that bankrupt morning I will simply open my notebook and there it will all be, a forgotten account with accumulated interest, paid passage back to the world out there: dialogue overheard in hotels and elevators and at the hat-check counter in Pavillon (one middle-aged man shows his hat check to another and says, "That's my old football number"); impressions of Bettina Aptheker and Benjamin Sonnenberg and Teddy ("Mr. Acapulco") Stauffer; careful *aperçus*[2] about tennis burns and failed fashion models and Greek shipping heiresses, one of whom taught me a significant lesson (a lesson I could have learned from F. Scott Fitzgerald, but perhaps we all must meet the very rich for ourselves) by asking, when I arrived to interview her in her orchid-filled sitting room on the second day of a paralyzing New York blizzard, whether it was snowing outside.

I imagine, in other words, that the notebook is about other people. But of course it is not. I have no real business with what one stranger said to another at the hat-check counter in Pavillon; in fact I suspect that the line "That's my old football number" touched not my own imagination at all, but merely some memory of something once read, probably "The Eighty-Yard Run." Nor is my concern with a woman in a dirty crepe-de-Chine wrapper in a Wilmington bar. My stake is always, of course, in the unmentioned girl in the plaid silk dress. *Remember what it was to be me:* that is always the point.

It is a difficult point to admit. We are brought up in the ethic that others, any others, all others, are by definition more interesting than ourselves; taught to be diffident, just this side of self-effacing. ("You're the least important person in the room and don't forget it," Jessica Mitford's[3] governess would hiss in her ear on the advent of any social occasion; I copied that into my notebook because it is only recently that I have been able to enter a room without hearing

---

2. Insights (French).
3. Jessica Mitford (1917–1996), aristocratic and eccentric English author.

some such phrase in my inner ear.) Only the very young and the very old may recount their dreams at breakfast, dwell upon self, interrupt with memories of beach picnics and favorite Liberty lawn dresses and the rainbow trout in a creek near Colorado Springs. The rest of us are expected, rightly, to affect absorption in other people's favorite dresses, other people's trout.

And so we do. But our notebooks give us away, for however dutifully we record what we see around us, the common denominator of all we see is always, transparently, shamelessly, the implacable "I." We are not talking here about the kind of notebook that is patently for public consumption, a structural conceit for binding together a series of graceful *pensées*;[4] we are talking about something private, about bits of the mind's string too short to use, an indiscriminate and erratic assemblage with meaning only for its maker.

And sometimes even the maker has difficulty with the meaning. There does not seem to be, for example, any point in my knowing for the rest of my life that, during 1964, 720 tons of soot fell on every square mile of New York City, yet there it is in my notebook, labeled "FACT." Nor do I really need to remember that Ambrose Bierce liked to spell Leland Stanford's[5] name "£eland $tanford" or that "smart women almost always wear black in Cuba," a fashion hint without much potential for practical application. And does not the relevance of these notes seem marginal at best?:

> In the basement museum of the Inyo County Courthouse in Independence, California, sign pinned to a mandarin coat: "This MANDARIN COAT was often worn by Mrs. Minnie S. Brooks when giving lectures on her TEAPOT COLLECTION."
> Redhead getting out of car in front of Beverly Wilshire Hotel, chinchilla stole, Vuitton bags with tags reading:
> > MRS LOU FOX
> > HOTEL SAHARA
> > VEGAS

Well, perhaps not entirely marginal. As a matter of fact, Mrs. Minnie S. Brooks and her MANDARIN COAT pull me back into my

4. Thoughts, reflections (French).
5. Bierce (1842–1914), American satirist, journalist, and short-story writer; Stanford: nineteenth-century American millionaire.

own childhood, for although I never knew Mrs. Brooks and did not visit Inyo County until I was thirty, I grew up in just such a world, in houses cluttered with Indian relics and bits of gold ore and ambergris and the souvenirs my Aunt Mercy Farnsworth brought back from the Orient. It is a long way from that world to Mrs. Lou Fox's world, where we all live now, and is it not just as well to remember that? Might not Mrs. Minnie S. Brooks help me to remember what I am? Might not Mrs. Lou Fox help me to remember what I am not?

But sometimes the point is harder to discern. What exactly did I have in mind when I noted down that it cost the father of someone I know $650 a month to light the place on the Hudson in which he lived before the Crash?[6] What use was I planning to make of this line by Jimmy Hoffa:[7] "I may have my faults, but being wrong ain't one of them"? And although I think it interesting to know where the girls who travel with the Syndicate have their hair done when they find themselves on the West Coast, will I ever make suitable use of it? Might I not be better off just passing it on to John O'Hara?[8] What is a recipe for sauerkraut doing in my notebook? What kind of magpie keeps this notebook? "*He was born the night the Titanic went down.*" That seems a nice enough line, and I even recall who said it, but is it not really a better line in life than it could ever be in fiction?

But of course that is exactly it: not that I should ever use the line, but that I should remember the woman who said it and the afternoon I heard it. We were on her terrace by the sea, and we were finishing the wine left from lunch, trying to get what sun there was, a California winter sun. The woman whose husband was born the night the *Titanic* went down wanted to rent her house, wanted to go back to her children in Paris. I remember wishing that I could afford the house, which cost $1,000 a month. "Someday you will," she said lazily. "Someday it all comes." There in the sun on her terrace it seemed easy to believe in someday, but later I had a low-grade afternoon hangover and ran over a black snake on the way to

---

6. The stock market crash of 1929.

7. American labor leader and president of the Teamsters Union with close ties to the Mafia; he disappeared in 1975 and is presumed dead.

8. Sardonic American novelist and short-story writer (1905–1970).

the supermarket and was flooded with inexplicable fear when I heard the checkout clerk explaining to the man ahead of me why she was finally divorcing her husband. "He left me no choice," she said over and over as she punched the register. "He has a little seven-month-old baby by her, he left me no choice." I would like to believe that my dread then was for the human condition, but of course it was for me, because I wanted a baby and did not then have one and because I wanted to own the house that cost $1,000 a month to rent and because I had a hangover.

It all comes back. Perhaps it is difficult to see the value in having one's self back in that kind of mood, but I do see it; I think we are well advised to keep on nodding terms with the people we used to be whether we find them attractive company or not. Otherwise they turn up unannounced and surprise us, come hammering on the mind's door at 4 a.m. of a bad night and demand to know who deserted them, who betrayed them, who is going to make amends. We forget all too soon the things we thought we could never forget. We forget the loves and the betrayals alike, forget what we whispered and what we screamed, forget who we were. I have already lost touch with a couple of people I used to be; one of them, a seventeen-year-old, presents little threat, although it would be of some interest to me to know again what it feels like to sit on a river levee drinking vodka-and-orange-juice and listening to Les Paul and Mary Ford and their echoes sing "How High the Moon" on the car radio. (You see I still have the scenes, but I no longer perceive myself among those present, no longer could even improvise the dialogue.) The other one, a twenty-three-year-old, bothers me more. She was always a good deal of trouble, and I suspect she will reappear when I least want to see her, skirts too long, shy to the point of aggravation, always the injured party, full of recriminations and little hurts and stories I do not want to hear again, at once saddening me and angering me with her vulnerability and ignorance, an apparition all the more insistent for being so long banished.

It is a good idea, then, to keep in touch, and I suppose that keeping in touch is what notebooks are all about. And we are all on our own when it comes to keeping those lines open to ourselves: your notebook will never help me, nor mine you. "*So what's new in the whiskey business?*" What could that possibly mean to you? To me it means a blonde in a Pucci[9] bathing suit sitting with a couple of fat men by the pool at the Beverly Hills Hotel. Another man approaches, and they all regard one another in silence for a while. "So what's new in the whiskey business?" one of the fat men finally says by way of welcome, and the blonde stands up, arches one foot and dips it in the pool, looking all the while at the cabaña where Baby Pignatari is talking on the telephone. That is all there is to that, except that several years later I saw the blonde coming out of Saks Fifth Avenue in New York with her California complexion and a voluminous mink coat. In the harsh wind that day she looked old and irrevocably tired to me, and even the skins in the mink coat were not worked the way they were doing them that year, not the way she would have wanted them done, and there is the point of the story. For a while after that I did not like to look in the mirror, and my eyes would skim the newspapers and pick out only the deaths, the cancer victims, the premature coronaries, the suicides, and I stopped riding the Lexington Avenue IRT[1] because I noticed for the first time that all the strangers I had seen for years—the man with the seeing-eye dog, the spinster who read the classified pages every day, the fat girl who always got off with me at Grand Central— looked older than they once had.

It all comes back. Even that recipe for sauerkraut: even that brings it back. I was on Fire Island when I first made that sauerkraut, and it was raining, and we drank a lot of bourbon and ate the sauerkraut and went to bed at ten, and I listened to the rain and the Atlantic and felt safe. I made the sauerkraut again last night and it did not make me feel any safer, but that is, as they say, another story.

1968

9. Italian fashion designer (1914–1992).   1. A subway line in New York City that stops at Grand Central Station.

Annie Dillard

b. 1945

Dillard might be described as a metaphysical essayist. She is a poet, but it was her Pulitzer Prize–winning, non-fiction observations of the natural world in her book Pilgrim at Tinker Creek *that demonstrated her real genius. In lyrical prose she tells us about seeing the unseen, about how the physical world indicates the metaphysical. Her technique is often metaphorical—the aggregate of comparisons ("We stuck to the plane's sides like flung paint")— building in readers a sense of those things that cannot be expressed directly. Her prose is like the writing of mystics, a pursuit of knowledge that logic cannot approach. This essay appears in Dillard's book* The Writing Life, *which takes art as its theme. A stunt pilot might seem an unusual subject of such a piece, at least as one begins to read the essay, not when one finishes. Dillard's view of art is similar to the nineteenth-century Romantics, who also compared artists to priests, special people able to "see into the life of things," as William Wordsworth put it, and mediators between regular people and the ineffable world we do not see.*

The Stunt Pilot*

D ave Rahm lived in Bellingham, Washington, north of Seattle. Bellingham, a harbor town, lies between the San Juan Islands in Haro Strait and the alpine North Cascade Mountains. I lived there between stints on the island. Dave Rahm was a stunt pilot, the air's own genius.

In 1975, with a newcomer's willingness to try anything once, I attended the Bellingham Air Show. The Bellingham airport was a wide clearing in a forest of tall Douglas firs; its runways suited small planes. It was June. People wearing blue or tan zipped jackets stood loosely on the concrete walkways and runways outside the coffee shop. At that latitude in June, you stayed outside because you

---

*This piece is an originally untitled excerpt from Dillard's book *The Writing Life* (chapter 7, pages 93–111).

could, even most of the night, if you could think up something to do. The sky did not darken until ten o'clock or so, and it never got very dark. Your life parted and opened in the sunlight. You tossed your dark winter routines, thought up mad projects, and improvised everything from hour to hour. Being a stunt pilot seemed the most reasonable thing in the world; you could wave your arms in the air all day and all night, and sleep next winter.

I saw from the ground a dozen stunt pilots; the air show scheduled them one after the other, for an hour of aerobatics. Each pilot took up his or her plane and performed a batch of tricks. They were precise and impressive. They flew upside down, and straightened out; they did barrel rolls, and straightened out; they drilled through dives and spins, and landed gently on a far runway.

For the end of the day, separated from all other performances of every sort, the air show director had scheduled a program titled "DAVE RAHM." The leaflet said that Rahm was a geologist who taught at Western Washington University. He had flown for King Hussein in Jordan. A tall man in the crowd told me Hussein had seen Rahm fly on a visit the king made to the United States; he had invited him to Jordan to perform at ceremonies. Hussein was a pilot, too. "Hussein thought he was the greatest thing in the world."

Idly, paying scant attention, I saw a medium-sized, rugged man dressed in brown leather, all begoggled, climb in a black biplane's open cockpit. The plane was a Bücker Jungman, built in the thirties. I saw a tall, dark-haired woman seize a propeller tip at the plane's nose and yank it down till the engine caught. He was off; he climbed high over the airport in his biplane, very high until he was barely visible as a mote, and then seemed to fall down the air, diving headlong, and streaming beauty in spirals behind him.

The black plane dropped spinning, and flattened out spinning the other way; it began to carve the air into forms that built wildly and musically on each other and never ended. Reluctantly, I started paying attention. Rahm drew high above the world an inexhaustibly glorious line; it piled over our heads in loops and arabesques. It was like a Saul Steinberg fantasy;[1] the plane was the pen. Like Steinberg's contracting and billowing pen line, the line Rahm spun moved to form new, punning shapes from the edges of the old. Like a Klee line, it smattered the sky with landscapes and systems.[2]

The air show announcer hushed. He had been squawking all day, and now he quit. The crowd stilled. Even the children watched dumbstruck as the slow, black biplane buzzed its way around the air. Rahm made beauty with his whole body; it was pure pattern, and you could watch it happen. The plane moved every way a line can move, and it controlled three dimensions, so the line carved massive and subtle slits in the air like sculptures. The plane looped the loop, seeming to arch its back like a gymnast; it stalled, dropped, and spun out of it climbing; it spiraled and knifed west on one side's wings and back east on another; it turned cartwheels, which must be physically impossible; it played with its own line like a cat with yarn. How did the pilot know where in the air he was? If he got lost, the ground would swat him.

Rahm did everything his plane could do: tailspins, four-point rolls, flat spins, figure 8's, snap rolls, and hammerheads. He did pirouettes on the plane's tail. The other pilots could do these stunts, too, skillfully, one at a time. But Rahm used the plane inexhaustibly, like a brush marking thin air.

His was pure energy and naked spirit. I have thought about it for years. Rahm's line unrolled in time. Like music, it split the bulging rim of the future along its seam. It pried out the present. We watchers waited for the split-second curve of beauty in the present to reveal itself. The human pilot, Dave Rahm, worked in the cockpit right at the plane's nose; his very body tore into the future for us and reeled it down upon us like a curling peel.

Like any fine artist, he controlled the tension of the audience's longing. You desired, unwittingly, a certain kind of roll or climb, or a return to a certain portion of the air, and he fulfilled your hope

1. Steinberg (1914–1999), artist known for line drawings done for *The New Yorker* and humorous covers for that magazine, including the much-copied *View of the World from 9th Avenue*.

2. Paul Klee (1879–1940), Swiss artist; Klee's paintings are dominated by lines and colors that express an almost abstract spirituality.

slantingly, like a poet, or evaded it until you thought you would burst, and then fulfilled it surprisingly, so you gasped and cried out.

The oddest, most exhilarating and exhausting thing was this: he never quit. The music had no periods, no rests or endings; the poetry's beautiful sentence never ended; the line had no finish; the sculptured forms piled overhead, one into another without surcease. Who could breathe, in a world where rhythm itself had no periods?

It had taken me several minutes to understand what an extraordinary thing I was seeing. Rahm kept all that embellished space in mind at once. For another twenty minutes I watched the beauty unroll and grow more fantastic and unlikely before my eyes. Now Rahm brought the plane down slidingly, and just in time, for I thought I would snap from the effort to compass and remember the line's long intelligence; I could not add another curve. He brought the plane down on a far runway. After a pause, I saw him step out, an ordinary man, and make his way back to the terminal.

The show was over. It was late. Just as I turned from the runway, something caught my eye and made me laugh. It was a swallow, a blue-green swallow, having its own air show, apparently inspired by Rahm. The swallow climbed high over the runway, held its wings oddly, tipped them, and rolled down the air in loops. The inspired swallow. I always want to paint, too, after I see the Rembrandts. The blue-green swallow tumbled precisely, and caught itself and flew up again as if excited, and looped down again, the way swallows do, but tensely, holding its body carefully still. It was a stunt swallow.

I went home and thought about Rahm's performance that night, and the next day, and the next.

I had thought I knew my way around beauty a little bit. I knew I had devoted a good part of my life to it, memorizing poetry and focusing my attention on complexity of rhythm in particular, on force, movement, repetition, and surprise, in both poetry and prose. Now I had stood among dandelions between two asphalt runways in Bellingham, Washington, and begun learning about beauty. Even the Boston Museum of Fine Arts was never more inspiriting than this small northwestern airport on this time-killing Sunday afternoon in June. Nothing on earth is more gladdening than knowing we must roll up our sleeves and move back the boundaries of the humanly possible once more.

Later I flew with Dave Rahm; he took me up. A generous geographer, Dick Smith, at Western Washington University, arranged it, and came along. Rahm and Dick Smith were colleagues at the university. In geology, Rahm had published two books and many articles. Rahm was handsome in a dull sort of way, blunt-featured, wide-jawed, wind-burned, keen-eyed, and taciturn. As anyone would expect. He was forty. He wanted to show me the Cascade Mountains; these enormous peaks, only fifty miles from the coast, rise over nine thousand feet; they are heavily glaciated. Whatcom County has more glaciers than the lower forty-eight states combined; the Cascades make the Rocky Mountains look like hills. Mount Baker is volcanic, like most Cascade peaks. That year, Mount Baker was acting up. Even from my house at the shore I could see, early in the morning on clear days, volcanic vapor rise near its peak. Often the vapor made a cloud which swelled all morning and hid the snows. Every day the newspapers reported on Baker's activity: would it blow? (A few years later, Mount St. Helens did blow.)

Rahm was not flying his trick biplane that day, but a faster, enclosed plane, a single-engine Cessna. We flew from a bumpy grass airstrip near my house, out over the coast and inland. There was coastal plain down there, but we could not see it for clouds. We were over the clouds at five hundred feet and inside them too, heading for an abrupt line of peaks we could not see. I gave up on everything, the way you do in airplanes; it was out of my hands. Every once in a while Rahm saw a peephole in the clouds and buzzed over for a look. "That's Larsen's pea farm," he said, or "That's Nooksack Road," and he changed our course with a heave.

When we got to the mountains, he slid us along Mount Baker's flanks sideways.

Our plane swiped at the mountain with a roar. I glimpsed a windshield view of dirty snow traveling fast. Our shaking, swooping belly seemed to graze the snow. The wings shuddered; we peeled away and the mountain fell back and the engines whined. We felt flung, because we were in fact flung; parts of our faces and internal organs trailed pressingly behind on the curves. We came back for another pass at the mountain, and another. We dove at the snow headlong like suicides; we jerked up, down, or away at the last second, so late we left our hearts, stomachs, and lungs behind. If I forced myself to hold my heavy head up against the g's, and to raise my eyelids, heavy as barbells, and to notice what I saw, I could see the wrinkled green crevasses cracking the glaciers' snow.

Pitching snow filled all the windows, and shapes of dark rock. I had no notion which way was up. Everything was black or gray or white except the fatal crevasses; everything made noise and shook. I felt my face smashed sideways and saw rushing abstractions of snow in the windshield. Patches of cloud obscured the snow fleetingly. We straightened out, turned, and dashed at the mountainside for another pass, which we made, apparently, on our ear, an inch or two away from the slope. Icefalls and cornices jumbled and fell away. If a commercial plane's black box, such as the FAA painstakingly recovers from crash sites, could store videotapes as well as pilots' last words, some videotapes would look like this: a mountainside coming up at the windows from all directions, ice and snow and rock filling the screen up close and screaming by.

Rahm was just being polite. His geographer colleague wanted to see the fissure on Mount Baker from which steam escaped. Everybody in Bellingham wanted to see that sooty fissure, as did every geologist in the country; no one on earth could fly so close to it as Rahm. He knew the mountain by familiar love and feel, like a face; he knew what the plane could do and what he dared to do.

When Mount Baker inexplicably let us go, he jammed us into cloud again and soon tilted. "The Sisters!" someone shouted, and I saw the windshield fill with red rock. This mountain looked infernal, a drear and sheer plane of lifeless rock. It was red and sharp; its gritty blades cut through the clouds at random. The mountain was quiet. It was in shade. Careening, we made sideways passes at these brittle peaks too steep for snow. Their rock was full of iron, somebody shouted at me then or later; the iron had rusted, so they were red. Later, when I was back on the ground, I recalled that, from a distance, the two jagged peaks called the Twin Sisters looked translucent against the sky; they were sharp, tapered, and fragile as arrowheads.

I talked to Rahm. He was flying us out to the islands now. The islands were fifty or sixty miles away. Like many other people, I had picked Bellingham, Washington, by looking at an atlas. It was clear from the atlas that you could row in the salt water and see snow-covered mountains; you could scale a glaciated mountainside with an ice ax in August, skirting green crevasses two hundred feet deep, and look out on the islands in the sea. Now, in the air, the clouds had risen over us; dark forms lay on the glinting water. There was almost no color to the day, just blackened green and some yellow. I knew the islands were forested in dark Douglas firs the size of sky-scrapers. Bald eagles scavenged on the beaches; robins the size of herring gulls sang in the clearings. We made our way out to the islands through the layer of air between the curving planet and its held, thick clouds.

"When I started trying to figure out what I was going to do with my life, I decided to become an expert on mountains. It wasn't much to be, it wasn't everything, but it was something. I was going to know everything about mountains from every point of view. So I started out in geography." Geography proved too pedestrian for Rahm, too concerned with "how many bushels of wheat an acre." So he ended up in geology. Smith had told me that geology departments throughout the country used Rahm's photographic slides—close-ups of geologic features from the air.

"I used to climb mountains. But you know, you can get a better feel for a mountain's power flying around it, flying all around it, than you can from climbing it tied to its side like a flea."

He talked about his flying performances. He thought of the air as a line, he said. "This end of the line, that end of the line—like a rope." He improvised. "I get a rhythm going and stick with it." While he was performing in a show, he paid attention, he said, to the lighting. He didn't play against the sun. That was all he said about what he did.

In aerobatic maneuvers, pilots pull about seven positive g's on some stunts and six negative g's on others. Some gyrations push; others pull. Pilots alternate the pressures carefully, so they do not gray out or black out.

Later I learned that some stunt pilots tune up by wearing gravity boots. These are boots made to hook over a doorway; wearing them, you hang in the doorway upside-down. It must startle a pilot's children, to run into their father or mother in the course of their home wanderings—the parent hanging wide-eyed upside-down in the doorway like a bat.

We were landing; here was the airstrip on Stuart Island—that island to which Ferrar Burn was dragged by the tide. We put down, climbed out of the plane, and walked. We wandered a dirt track through fields to a lee shore where yellow sandstone ledges slid into the sea. The salt chuck, people there called salt water. The sun came out. I caught a snake in the salt chuck; the snake, eighteen inches long, was swimming in the green shallows.

I had a survivor's elation. Rahm had found Mount Baker in the clouds before Mount Baker found the plane. He had wiped it with the fast plane like a cloth and we had lived. When we took off from Stuart Island and gained altitude, I asked if we could turn over— could we do a barrel roll? The plane was making a lot of noise, and Dick Smith did not hear any of this, I learned later. "Why not?" Rahm said, and added surprisingly, "It won't hurt the plane." Without ado he leaned on the wheel and the wing went down and we went somersaulting over it. We upended with a roar. We stuck to the plane's sides like flung paint. All the blood in my body bulged on my face; it piled between my skull and skin. Vaguely I could see the chrome sea twirling over Rahm's head like a baton, and the dark islands sliding down the skies like rain.

The g's slammed me into my seat like thugs and pinned me while my heart pounded and the plane turned over slowly and compacted each organ in turn. My eyeballs were newly spherical and full of heartbeats. I seemed to hear a crescendo; the wing rolled shuddering down the last ninety degrees and settled on the flat. There were the islands, admirably below us, and the clouds, admirably above. When I could breathe, I asked if we could do it again, and we did. He rolled the other way. The brilliant line of the sea slid up the side window bearing its heavy islands. Through the shriek of my blood and the plane's shakes I glimpsed the line of the sea over the windshield, thin as a spear. How in performance did Rahm keep track while his brain blurred and blood roared in his ears without ceasing? Every performance was a tour de force and a show of will, a *macht-*

spruch.[3] I had seen the other stunt pilots straighten out after a trick or two; their blood could drop back and the planet simmer down. An Olympic gymnast, at peak form, strings out a line of spins ten stunts long across a mat, and is hard put to keep his footing at the end. Rahm endured much greater pressure on his faster spins using the plane's power, and he could spin in three dimensions and keep twirling till he ran out of sky room or luck.

When we straightened out, and had flown straightforwardly for ten minutes toward home, Dick Smith, clearing his throat, brought himself to speak. "What was that we did out there?"

"The barrel rolls?" Rahm said. "They were barrel rolls." He said nothing else. I looked at the back of his head; I could see the serious line of his cheek and jaw. He was in shirtsleeves, tanned, strong-wristed. I could not imagine loving him under any circumstance; he was alien to me, unfazed. He looked like G.I. Joe. He flew with that matter-of-fact, bored gesture pilots use. They click overhead switches and turn dials as if only their magnificent strength makes such dullness endurable. The half circle of wheel in their big hands looks like a toy they plan to crush in a minute; the wiggly stick the wheel mounts seems barely attached.

A crop-duster pilot in Wyoming told me the life expectancy of a crop-duster pilot is five years. They fly too low. They hit buildings and power lines. They have no space to fly out of trouble, and no space to recover from a stall. We were in Cody, Wyoming, out on the North Fork of the Shoshone River. The crop duster had wakened me that morning flying over the ranch house and clearing my bedroom roof by half an inch. I saw the bolts on the wheel assembly a few feet from my face. He was spraying with pesticide the plain old grass. Over breakfast I asked him how long he had been dusting crops. "Four years," he said, and the figure stalled in the air between us for a moment. "You know you're going to die at it someday," he added. "We all know it. We accept that; it's part of it." I think now that, since the crop duster was in his twenties, he accepted only that he had to say such stuff; privately he counted on skewing the curve.

3. Powerful or willful decision (German).

I suppose Rahm knew the fact, too. I do not know how he felt about it. "It's worth it," said the early French aviator Mermoz. He was Antoine de Saint-Exupéry's[4] friend. "It's worth the final smashup."

Rahm smashed up in front of King Hussein, in Jordan, during a performance. The plane spun down and never came out of it; it nosedived into the ground and exploded. He bought the farm. I was living then with my husband out on that remote island in the San Juans, cut off from everything. Battery radios picked up the Canadian Broadcasting Company out of Toronto, half a continent away; island people would, in theory, learn if the United States blew up, but not much else. There were no newspapers. One friend got the Sunday *New York Times* by mailboat on the following Friday. He saved it until Sunday and had a party, every week; we all read the Sunday *Times* and no one mentioned that it was last week's.

One day, Paul Glenn's brother flew out from Bellingham to visit; he had a seaplane. He landed in the water in front of the cabin and tied up to our mooring. He came in for coffee, and he gave out news of this and that, and—Say, did we know that stunt pilot Dave Rahm had cracked up? In Jordan, during a performance: he never came out of a dive. He just dove right down into the ground, and his wife was there watching. "I saw it on CBS News last night." And then—with a sudden sharp look at my filling eyes—"What, did you know him?" But no, I did not know him. He took me up once. Several years ago. I admired his flying. I had thought that danger was the safest thing in the world, if you went about it right.

Later I found a newspaper. Rahm was living in Jordan that year; King Hussein invited him to train the aerobatics team, the Royal Jordanian Falcons. He was also visiting professor of geology at the University of Jordan. In Amman that day he had been flying a Pitt Special, a plane he knew well. Katy Rahm, his wife of six months, was sitting beside Hussein in the viewing stands, with her daughter. Rahm died performing a Lomcevak combined with a tail slide and hammerhead. In a Lomcevak, the pilot brings the plane up on a slant and pirouettes. I had seen Rahm do this: the falling plane

---

4. Saint-Exupéry (1900–1944) was a French writer and aviator. His most famous work is *The Little Prince*. He died, presumably in a plane crash, while on a reconnaissance mission over Nazi-occupied France.

twirled slowly like a leaf. Like a ballerina, the plane seemed to hold its head back stiff in concentration at the music's slow, painful beauty. It was one of Rahm's favorite routines. Next the pilot flies straight up, stalls the plane, and slides down the air on his tail. He brings the nose down—the hammerhead—kicks the engine, and finishes with a low loop.

It is a dangerous maneuver at any altitude, and Rahm was doing it low. He hit the ground on the loop; the tail slide had left him no height. When Rahm went down, King Hussein dashed to the burning plane to pull him out, but he was already dead.

A few months after the air show, and a month after I had flown with Rahm, I was working at my desk near Bellingham, where I lived, when I heard a sound so odd it finally penetrated my concentration. It was the buzz of an airplane, but it rose and fell musically, and it never quit; the plane never flew out of earshot. I walked out on the porch and looked up: it was Rahm in the black and gold biplane, looping all over the air. I had been wondering about his performance flight: could it really have been so beautiful? It was, for here it was again. The little plane twisted all over the air like a vine. It trailed a line like a very long mathematical proof you could follow only so far, and then it lost you in its complexity. I saw Rahm flying high over the Douglas firs, and out over the water, and back over farms. The air was a fluid, and Rahm was an eel.

It was as if Mozart could move his body through his notes, and you could walk out on the porch, look up, and see him in periwig and breeches, flying around in the sky. You could hear the music as he dove through it; it streamed after him like a contrail.

I lost myself; standing on the firm porch, I lost my direction and reeled. My neck and spine rose and turned, so I followed the plane's line kinesthetically. In his open-cockpit, black plane, Rahm demonstrated curved space. He slid down ramps of air, he vaulted and wheeled. He piled loops in heaps and praised height. He unrolled the scroll of the air, extended it, and bent it into Möbius strips; he furled line in a thousand new ways, as if he were inventing a script and writing it in one infinitely recurring utterance until I thought the bounds of beauty must break.

From inside, the looping plane had sounded tinny, like a kazoo.

Outside, the buzz rose and fell to the Doppler effect as the plane looped near or away. Rahm cleaved the sky like a prow and tossed out time left and right in his wake. He performed for forty minutes; then he headed the plane, as small as a wasp, back to the airport inland. Later I learned Rahm often practiced acrobatic flights over this shore. His idea was that if he lost control and was going to go down, he could ditch in the salt chuck, where no one else would get hurt.

If I had not turned two barrel rolls in an airplane, I might have fancied Rahm felt good up there, and playful. Maybe Jackson Pollock[5] felt a sort of playfulness, in addition to the artist's usual deliberate and intelligent care. In my limited experience, painting, unlike writing, pleases the senses while you do it, and more while you do it than after it is done. Drawing lines with an airplane, unfortunately, tortures the senses. Jet bomber pilots black out. I knew Rahm felt as if his brain were bursting his eardrums, felt that if he let his jaws close as tight as centrifugal force pressed them, he would bite through his lungs.

"All virtue is a form of acting," Yeats[6] said. Rahm deliberately turned himself into a figure. Sitting invisible at the controls of a distant airplane, he became the agent and the instrument of art and invention. He did not tell me how he felt, when we spoke of his performance flying; he told me instead that he paid attention to how his plane and its line looked to the audience against the lighted sky. If he had noticed how he felt, he could not have done the work. Robed in his airplane, he was as featureless as a priest. He was lost in his figural aspect like an actor or a king. Of his flying, he had said only, "I get a rhythm and stick with it." In its reticence, this statement reminded me of Veronese's[7] "Given a large canvas, I enhanced it as I saw fit." But Veronese was ironic, and Rahm was not; he was literal as an astronaut; the machine gave him tongue.

When Rahm flew, he sat down in the middle of art, and strapped

---

5. Pollock (1912–1956), an American painter, known for his abstract-expressionist canvasses covered in streaks and splashes of paint.

6. William Butler Yeats (1865–1939), Irish poet and playwright, well known for

presenting a masklike, self-fashioned persona to the public.

7. Paolo Veronese (1528–1588), Italian painter from the city of Verona. His reflections on painting were occasioned by his interrogation by the Inquisition.

himself in. He spun it all around him. He could not see it himself. If he never saw it on film, he never saw it at all—as if Beethoven could not hear his final symphonies not because he was deaf, but because he was inside the paper on which he wrote. Rahm must have felt it happen, that fusion of vision and metal, motion and idea. I think of this man as a figure, a college professor with a Ph.D. upside down in the loud band of beauty. What are we here for? *Propter chorum*, the monks say: for the sake of the choir.

"Purity does not lie in separation from but in deeper penetration into the universe," Teilhard de Chardin[8] wrote. It is hard to imagine a deeper penetration into the universe than Rahm's last dive in his plane, or than his inexpressible wordless selfless line's inscribing the air and dissolving. Any other art may be permanent. I cannot recall one Rahm sequence. He improvised. If Christo[9] wraps a building or dyes a harbor, we join his poignant and fierce awareness that the work will be gone in days. Rahm's plane shed a ribbon in space, a ribbon whose end unraveled in memory while its beginning unfurled as surprise. He may have acknowledged that what he did could be called art, but it would have been, I think, only in the common misusage, which holds art to be the last extreme of skill. Rahm rode the point of the line to the possible; he discovered it and wound it down to show. He made his dazzling probe on the run. "The world is filled, and filled with the Absolute," Teilhard de Chardin wrote. "To see this is to be made free."

1989

---

8. De Chardin (1881–1955), controversial Catholic theologian and paleontologist who was an early advocate of reading the book of Genesis metaphorically rather than literally. His works were condemned by the Vatican but his ideas, especially about the perfectability of humankind, inspired many twentieth-century spiritual thinkers.

9. Christo (b. 1935), Bulgarian-born artist whose installations include "wrapping" the German Reichstag (parliament building) in colored fabric and building "gates" of hung fabric in Central Park. Each of his projects is taken down after a relatively short period.

Frederick Douglass
c. 1817–1895

> *Douglass escaped from slavery in Maryland when he was about twenty-one. Three years later, at a meeting of abolitionists in Nantucket, Massachusetts, he rose from the audience to speak of his experiences. William Garrison, the most prominent abolitionist in America, was so moved that he hired Douglass to lecture for the Anti-Slavery Society, which he did very effectively for four years. When he was accused of being an imposter in 1845, he wrote the* Narrative of the Life of Frederick Douglass. *It was published by the Anti-Slavery Society and was an instant success. Within two years, 30,000 copies had been printed in America, Ireland, England, France, and Holland. Its reach extended even further: One reviewer in 1846 estimated that the book influenced more than a million people in Great Britain and Ireland alone. This essay is a short excerpt from the* Narrative, *which Douglass hoped would "do something toward throwing light on the American slave system, and hastening the glad day of deliverance to the millions of my brethren in bonds." Douglass wrote to affect broad public opinion, which, in a democracy, can influence public policy. He knew that state-sponsored censorship would prevent even sympathetic Southerners from seeing the book, so Douglass took aim at Northerners. Garrison declared in his preface that the* Narrative *would strike "a stunning blow . . . on northern prejudice against [blacks]." The* Narrative *did not expose just the material degradations of slavery—like the brutal punishments some masters inflicted on the bodies of their slaves—it also exposed the psychological and spiritual effects, what Garrison called "the outrage which is inflicted by [slavery] on the godlike nature of its victims."*

Learning to Read

I lived in Master Hugh's family about seven years. During this time, I succeeded in learning to read and write. In accomplishing this, I was compelled to resort to various stratagems. I had no regular teacher. My mistress, who had kindly commenced to instruct me, had, in compliance with the advice and direction of her husband, not only ceased to instruct, but had set her face against my being instructed by any one else. It is due, however, to my mistress to say of her, that she did not adopt this course of treatment immediately. She at first lacked the depravity indispensable to shutting me up in mental darkness. It was at least necessary for her to have some training in the exercise of irresponsible power, to make her equal to the task of treating me as though I were a brute.

My mistress was, as I have said, a kind and tender-hearted woman; and in the simplicity of her soul she commenced, when I first went to live with her, to treat me as she supposed one human being ought to treat another. In entering upon the duties of a slaveholder, she did not seem to perceive that I sustained to her the relation of a mere chattel, and that for her to treat me as a human being was not only wrong, but dangerously so. Slavery proved as injurious to her as it did to me. When I went there, she was a pious, warm, and tender-hearted woman. There was no sorrow or suffering for which she had not a tear. She had bread for the hungry, clothes for the naked, and comfort for every mourner that came within her reach. Slavery soon proved its ability to divest her of these heavenly qualities. Under its influence, the tender heart became stone, and the lamblike disposition gave way to one of tiger-like fierceness. The first step in her downward course was in her ceasing to instruct me. She now commenced to practise her husband's precepts. She finally became even more violent in her opposition than her husband himself. She was not satisfied with simply doing as well as he had commanded; she seemed anxious to do better. Nothing seemed to make her more angry than to see me with a newspaper. She seemed to think that here lay the danger. I have had her rush at me with a face made all up of fury, and snatch from me a newspaper, in a manner that fully revealed her apprehension. She was an apt woman; and a little experience soon demonstrated, to her satisfaction, that education and slavery were incompatible with each other.

From this time I was most narrowly watched. If I was in a separate room any considerable length of time, I was sure to be suspected of having a book, and was at once called to give an account of myself. All this, however, was too late. The first step had been taken. Mistress, in teaching me the alphabet, had given me the *inch*, and no precaution could prevent me from taking the *ell*.[1]

The plan which I adopted, and the one by which I was most successful, was that of making friends of all the little white boys whom I met in the street. As many of these as I could, I converted into teachers. With their kindly aid, obtained at different times and in different places, I finally succeeded in learning to read. When I was sent of errands, I always took my book with me, and by going one part of my errand quickly, I found time to get a lesson before my return. I used also to carry bread with me, enough of which was always in the house, and to which I was always welcome; for I was much better off in this regard than many of the poor white children in our neighborhood. This bread I used to bestow upon the hungry little urchins, who, in return, would give me that more valuable bread of knowledge. I am strongly tempted to give the names of two or three of those little boys, as a testimonial of the gratitude and affection I bear them; but prudence forbids;—not that it would injure me, but it might embarrass them; for it is almost an unpardonable offence to teach slaves to read in this Christian country. It is enough to say of the dear little fellows, that they lived on Philpot Street, very near Durgin and Bailey's ship-yard. I used to talk this matter of slavery over with them. I would sometimes say to them, I wished I could be as free as they would be when they got to be men. "You will be free as soon as you are twenty-one, *but I am a slave for life!* Have not I as good a right to be free as you have?" These words used to trouble them; they would express for me the liveliest sympathy, and console me with the hope that something would occur by which I might be free.

I was now about twelve years old, and the thought of being *a slave for life* began to bear heavily upon my heart. Just about this time, I got hold of a book entitled "The Columbian Orator."[2] Every opportunity I got, I used to read this book. Among much of other interesting matter, I found in it a dialogue between a master and his slave. The slave was represented as having run away from his master three times. The dialogue represented the conversation which took

1. A unit of measurement equal to 45 inches.

2. A collection of poems, dialogues, plays, and speeches popular in the period.

place between them, when the slave was retaken the third time. In this dialogue, the whole argument in behalf of slavery was brought forward by the master, all of which was disposed of by the slave. The slave was made to say some very smart as well as impressive things in reply to his master—things which had the desired though unexpected effect; for the conversation resulted in the voluntary emancipation of the slave on the part of the master.

In the same book, I met with one of Sheridan's mighty speeches on and in behalf of Catholic emancipation.[3] These were choice documents to me. I read them over and over again with unabated interest. They gave tongue to interesting thoughts of my own soul, which had frequently flashed through my mind, and died away for want of utterance. The moral which I gained from the dialogue was the power of truth over the conscience of even a slaveholder. What I got from Sheridan was a bold denunciation of slavery, and a powerful vindication of human rights. The reading of these documents enabled me to utter my thoughts, and to meet the arguments brought forward to sustain slavery; but while they relieved me of one difficulty, they brought on another even more painful than the one of which I was relieved. The more I read, the more I was led to abhor and detest my enslavers. I could regard them in no other light than a band of successful robbers, who had left their homes, and gone to Africa, and stolen us from our homes, and in a strange land reduced us to slavery. I loathed them as being the meanest as well as the most wicked of men. As I read and contemplated the subject, behold! that very discontentment which Master Hugh had predicted would follow my learning to read had already come, to torment and sting my soul to unutterable anguish. As I writhed under it, I would at times feel that learning to read had been a curse rather than a blessing. It had given me a view of my wretched condition, without the remedy. It opened my eyes to the horrible pit, but to no ladder upon which to get out. In moments of agony, I envied my fellow-slaves for their stupidity. I have often wished myself a beast. I preferred the condition of the meanest reptile to my own. Any

3. Richard Brinsley Sheridan (1751–1816) was an Irish-born playwright and politician favoring Catholic emancipation; however, the speech arguing for civil and political rights for Catholics in England and Ireland was actually made by Arthur O'Connor, an Irish patriot.

thing, no matter what, to get rid of thinking! It was this everlasting thinking of my condition that tormented me. There was no getting rid of it. It was pressed upon me by every object within sight or hearing, animate or inanimate. The silver trump of freedom had roused my soul to eternal wakefulness. Freedom now appeared, to disappear no more forever. It was heard in every sound, and seen in every thing. It was ever present to torment me with a sense of my wretched condition. I saw nothing without seeing it, I heard nothing without hearing it, and felt nothing without feeling it. It looked from every star, it smiled in every calm, breathed in every wind, and moved in every storm.

I often found myself regretting my own existence, and wishing myself dead; and but for the hope of being free, I have no doubt but that I should have killed myself, or done something for which I should have been killed. While in this state of mind, I was eager to hear any one speak of slavery. I was a ready listener. Every little while, I could hear something about the abolitionists. It was some time before I found what the word meant. It was always used in such connections as to make it an interesting word to me. If a slave ran away and succeeded in getting clear, or if a slave killed his master, set fire to a barn, or did any thing very wrong in the mind of a slave-holder, it was spoken of as the fruit of *abolition*. Hearing the word in this connection very often, I set about learning what it meant. The dictionary afforded me little or no help. I found it was "the act of abolishing"; but then I did not know what was to be abolished. Here I was perplexed. I did not dare to ask any one about its meaning, for I was satisfied that it was something they wanted me to know very little about. After a patient waiting, I got one of our city papers, containing an account of the number of petitions from the north, praying for the abolition of slavery in the District of Columbia, and of the slave trade between the States. From this time I understood the words *abolition* and *abolitionist*, and always drew near when that word was spoken, expecting to hear something of importance to myself and fellow-slaves. The light broke in upon me by degrees. I went one day down on the wharf of Mr. Waters; and seeing two Irishmen unloading a scow of stone, I went, unasked, and helped them. When we had finished, one of them came to me and asked me if I were a slave. I told him I was. He asked, "Are ye a slave for life?" I told him that I was. The good Irishman seemed to be deeply affected by the statement. He said to the other that it was a pity so fine a little fellow as myself should be a slave for life. He said it was a shame to hold me. They both advised me to run away to the north; that I should find friends there, and that I should be free. I pretended not to be interested in what they said, and treated them as if I did not understand them; for I feared they might be treacherous. White men have been known to encourage slaves to escape, and then, to get the reward, catch them and return them to their masters. I was afraid that these seemingly good men might use me so; but I nevertheless remembered their advice, and from that time I resolved to run away. I looked forward to a time at which it would be safe for me to escape. I was too young to think of doing so immediately; besides, I wished to learn how to write, as I might have occasion to write my own pass. I consoled myself with the hope that I should one day find a good chance. Meanwhile, I would learn to write.

The idea as to how I might learn to write was suggested to me by being in Durgin and Bailey's ship-yard, and frequently seeing the ship carpenters, after hewing, and getting a piece of timber ready for use, write on the timber the name of that part of the ship for which it was intended. When a piece of timber was intended for the larboard side, it would be marked thus—"L." When a piece was for the starboard side, it would be marked thus—"S." A piece for the larboard side forward, would be marked thus—"L. F." When a piece was for starboard side forward, it would be marked thus—"S. F." For larboard aft, it would be marked thus—"L. A." For starboard aft, it would be marked thus—"S. A." I soon learned the names of these letters, and for what they were intended when placed upon a piece of timber in the ship-yard. I immediately commenced copying them, and in a short time was able to make the four letters named. After that, when I met with any boy who I knew could write, I would tell him I could write as well as he. The next word would be, "I don't believe you. Let me see you try it." I would then make the letters which I had been so fortunate as to learn, and ask him to beat that. In this way I got a good many lessons in writing, which it is quite possible I should never have gotten in any other way. During this time, my copy-book was the board fence, brick wall, and pavement; my pen and ink was a lump of chalk. With

these, I learned mainly how to write. I then commenced and continued copying the Italics in Webster's Spelling Book,[4] until I could
make them all without looking on the book. By this time, my little
Master Thomas had gone to school, and learned how to write, and
had written over a number of copy-books. These had been brought
home, and shown to some of our near neighbors, and then laid
aside. My mistress used to go to class meeting at the Wilk Street
meetinghouse every Monday afternoon, and leave me to take care of
the house. When left thus, I used to spend the time in writing in
the spaces left in Master Thomas's copy-book, copying what he had
written. I continued to do this until I could write a hand very similar to that of Master Thomas. Thus, after a long, tedious effort for
years, I finally succeeded in learning how to write.

1845

---

4. Italics were used to make type resemble handwriting in *The American Spelling Book*
(1783), by the American lexicographer Noah Webster (1758–1843).

Barbara Ehrenreich

b. 1941

Barbara Ehrenreich is one of our age's most provocative social com-
mentators. She has a Ph.D. in biology, and much of her early work
exposed the ideological biases of the American health-care system.
But more recently she has widened her scope to include an exami-
nation of class consciousness in America. Her analyses of the ascen-
dant American middle class have confirmed her commitments to
feminism and socialism (she is honorary chair of the Democratic
Socialists of America's National Political Committee). She often
adopts the traditional role of essayist—the surveyor and disputant
of accepted social judgments—as she does in this essay. William
Bennett, secretary of education under Ronald Reagan and "drug
czar" under George H. W. Bush, exemplifies much of what Ehren-
reich considers wrong with America: the powerful, smug, middle-
class moralist blind to the injustices underlying his judgments.

In Defense of Talk Shows

U p until now, the targets of Bill (*The Book of Virtues*) Bennett's crusades have at least been plausible sources of evil.
But the latest victim of his wrath—TV talk shows of the
Sally Jessy Raphael variety—are in a whole different category from
drugs and gangsta rap. As anyone who actually watches them
knows, the talk shows are one of the most excruciatingly moralistic
forums the culture has to offer. Disturbing and sometimes disgusting, yes, but their very business is to preach the middle-class virtues
of responsibility, reason and self-control.

Take the case of Susan, recently featured on *Montel Williams* as
an example of a woman being stalked by her ex-boyfriend. Turns
out Susan is also stalking the boyfriend and—here's the sexual
frisson—has slept with him only days ago. In fact Susan is neck
deep in trouble without any help from the boyfriend: she's serving a
yearlong stretch of home incarceration for assaulting another
woman, and home is the tiny trailer she shares with her nine-year-
old daughter.

But no one is applauding this life spun out of control. Montel scolds Susan roundly for neglecting her daughter and failing to confront her role in the mutual stalking. A therapist lectures her about this unhealthy "obsessive kind of love." The studio audience jeers at her every evasion. By the end Susan has lost her cocky charm and dissolved into tears of shame.

The plot is always the same. People with problems—"husband says she looks like a cow," "pressured to lose her virginity or else," "mate wants more sex than I do"—are introduced to rational methods of problem solving. People with moral failings—"boy crazy," "dresses like a tramp," "a hundred sex partners"—are introduced to external standards of morality. The preaching—delivered alternately by the studio audience, the host and the ever present guest therapist—is relentless. "This is wrong to do this," Sally Jessy tells a cheating husband. "Feel bad?" Geraldo asks the girl who stole her best friend's boyfriend, "Any sense of remorse?" The expectation is that the sinner, so hectored, will see her way to reform. And indeed, a *Sally Jessy* update found "boy crazy," who'd been a guest only weeks ago, now dressed in schoolgirlish plaid and claiming her "attitude [had] changed"—thanks to the rough-and-ready therapy dispensed on the show.

All right, the subjects are often lurid and even bizarre. But there's no part of the entertainment spectacle, from *Hard Copy* to *Jade,*[1] that doesn't trade in the lurid and bizarre. At least in the talk shows, the moral is always loud and clear: Respect yourself, listen to others, stop beating on your wife. In fact it's hard to see how *The Bill Bennett Show,* if there were to be such a thing, could deliver a more pointed sermon. Or would he prefer to see the feckless Susan, for example, tarred and feathered by the studio audience instead of being merely booed and shamed?

There *is* something morally repulsive about the talks, but it's not anything Bennett or his co-crusader Senator Joseph Lieberman has seen fit to mention. Watch for a few hours, and you get the claustrophobic sense of lives that have never seen the light of some external judgment, of people who have never before been listened to,

---

1. *Hard Copy:* a current affairs television program; *Jade:* a controversial 1995 film, rated R for its sexual and violent content.

and certainly never been taken seriously if they were. "What kind of people would let themselves be humiliated like this?" is often asked, sniffily, by the shows' detractors. And the answer, for the most part, is people who are so needy—of social support, of education, of material resources and self-esteem—that they mistake being the center of attention for being actually loved and respected.

What the talks are about, in large part, is poverty and the distortions it visits on the human spirit. You'll never find investment bankers bickering on *Rolonda*, or the host of *Gabrielle* recommending therapy to sobbing professors. With few exceptions the guests are drawn from trailer parks and tenements, from bleak streets and narrow, crowded rooms. Listen long enough, and you hear references to unpaid bills, to welfare, to 12-hour workdays and double shifts. And this is the real shame of the talks: that they take lives bent out of shape by poverty and hold them up as entertaining exhibits. An announcement appearing between segments of *Montel* says it all; the show is looking for "pregnant women who sell their bodies to make ends meet."

This is class exploitation, pure and simple. What next—"homeless people so hungry they eat their own scabs"? Or would the next step be to pay people outright to submit to public humiliation? For $50 would you confess to adultery in your wife's presence? For $500 would you reveal your 13-year-old's girlish secrets on *Ricki Lake*? If you were poor enough, you might.

It is easy enough for those who can afford spacious homes and private therapy to sneer at their financial inferiors and label their pathetic moments of stardom vulgar. But if I had a talk show, it would feature a whole different cast of characters and category of crimes than you'll ever find on the talks: "CEOs who take in millions while their employees get downsized" would be an obvious theme, along with "Senators who voted for welfare and Medicaid cuts"—and, if he'll agree to appear, "Well-fed Republicans who dithered about talk shows while trailer-park residents slipped into madness and despair."

1995

Louise Erdrich
b. 1954

> Z, a 1969 French film, was a thinly veiled telling of the assassina-
> tion of Gregoris Lambrakis in Greece in 1963. A pacifist and left-
> leaning social activist, Lambrakis led protests against the repressive
> Greek government. After World War II, Greece was convulsed by a
> civil war that reflected the larger world struggle between commu-
> nists and capitalists. With American aid, the communists were de-
> feated, and Greece enjoyed a period of growing prosperity and
> diminishing political freedom under rightist regimes. By the early
> 1960s, a number of leftist politicians had begun grass roots cam-
> paigns for reform. Lambrakis, the most popular of these, was delib-
> erately run down by a delivery truck driven by right-wing
> extremists. The subsequent investigation revealed connections be-
> tween these extremists and the police and army. Half a million peo-
> ple attended Lambrakis's funeral, and massive political rallies
> marked the anniversary of his death for years. The letter "Z" be-
> came a political symbol connoting solidarity with Lambrakis's left-
> ist ideals, appearing in graffiti all over Greece, especially after 1967,
> when certain army officers staged a coup d'état, wresting power
> from the elected government.

Z: The Movie That Changed My Life

Next to writing full time, the best job I ever had combined two passions—popcorn and narrative. At fourteen, I was hired as a concessioner at the Gilles Theater in Wahpeton, North Dakota. Behind a counter of black marbleized glass, I sold Dots, Red Hot Tamales, Jujubes, Orange Crush, and, of course, hot buttered popcorn. My little stand was surrounded by art deco mirrors, and my post, next to the machine itself, was bathed in an aura of salt and butter. All of my sophomore year, I exuded a light nutty fragrance that turned, on my coats and dresses, to the stale odor of mouse nests. The best thing about that job was that, once I had wiped the counters, dismantled the machines, washed the stainless steel parts, totaled up the take, and refilled the syrup cannisters and wiped off the soft drink machine, I could watch the show, free.

I saw everything that came to Wahpeton in 1969—watched every movie seven times, in fact, since each one played a full week. I saw Zeffirelli's *Romeo and Juliet*, and did not weep. I sighed over Charlton Heston in *Planet of the Apes*, and ground my teeth at the irony of the ending shot. But the one that really got to me was Costa-Gavras's *Z*.

Nobody in Wahpeton walked into the Gilles knowing that the film was about the assassination in Greece of a leftist peace leader by a secret right-wing organization and the subsequent investigation that ended in a bloody coup. The ad in the paper said only "Love Thriller" and listed Yves Montand and Irene Papas as the stars.

"Dear Diary," I wrote the morning after I'd seen *Z* for the first time. "The hypocrites are exposed. He is alive! Just saw the best movie of my life. Must remember to dye my bra and underwear to match my cheerleading outfit."

I forgot to rinse out the extra color, so during the week that *Z* was playing, I had purple breasts. The school color of my schizophrenic adolescence. My parents strictly opposed my career as a wrestling cheerleader, on the grounds that it would change me into someone they wouldn't recognize. Now, they were right, though of course I never let anyone know my secret.

I had changed in other ways, too. Until I was fourteen, my dad and I would go hunting on weekends or skating in the winter. Now I practiced screaming S-U-C-C-E-S-S and K-I-L-L for hours, and then, of course, had to run to work during the matinee. Not that I was utterly socialized. Over my cheerleading outfit I wore Dad's army jacket, and on my ankle, a bracelet made of twisted blasting-wire given to me by a guitar-playing Teen Corps volunteer, Kurt, who hailed from The Valley of the Jolly Green Giant, a real town in eastern Minnesota.

No, I was not yet completely subsumed into small-town female-hood. I knew there was more to life than the stag leap, or the flying T, but it wasn't until I saw *Z* that I learned language for what that "more" was.

After the third viewing, phrases began to whirl in my head. "The forces of greed and hatred cannot tolerate us"; "There are not enough hospitals, not enough doctors, yet one half of the budget goes to the military"; "Peace at all costs"; and, of course, the final words, "He is alive!" But there was more to it than the language. It was the first *real* movie I had ever seen—one with a cynical, unromantic, deflating ending.

At the fourth viewing of the movie, I had a terrible argument with Vincent, the Gilles's pale, sad ticket taker, who was also responsible for changing the wooden letters on the marquee. At the beginning of the week, he had been pleased. He had looked forward to this title for a month. Just one letter. It was he who thought of the ad copy, "Love Thriller." By the middle of the run, he was unhappy, for he sided with the generals, just as he sided with our boss.

Vincent always wore a suit and stood erect. He was officious, a tiger with gatecrashers and tough with those who had misplaced their stubs while going to the bathroom. I, on the other hand, waved people in free when I was left in charge, and regarded our boss with absolute and burning hatred, for he was a piddling authority, a man who enjoyed setting meaningless tasks. I hated being made to rewash the butter dispenser. Vincent liked being scolded for not tearing the tickets exactly in half. Ours was an argument of more than foreign ideologies.

Vincent insisted that the boss was a fair man who made lots of money. I maintained that we were exploited. Vincent said the film was lies, while I insisted it was based on fact. Neither of us checked for the truth in the library. Neither of us knew the first thing about modern Greece, yet I began comparing the generals to our boss. Their pompous egotism, the way they bumbled and puffed when they were accused of duplicity, their self-righteous hatred of "long-haired hippies and dope addicts of indefinite sex."

When I talked behind the boss's back, Vincent was worse than horrified; he was incensed.

"Put what's-his-name in a uniform and he'd be the head of the security police," I told Vincent, who looked like he wanted to pound my head.

But I knew what I knew. I had my reasons. Afraid that I might eat him out of Junior Mints, the boss kept a running tab of how many boxes of each type of candy reposed in the bright glass case.

Every day, I had to count the boxes and officially request more to fill the spaces. I couldn't be off by so much as a nickel at closing.

One night, made bold by Z, I opened each candy box and ate one Jujube, one Jordan Almond, one Black Crow, and so on, out of each box, just to accomplish something subversive. When I bragged, Vincent cruelly pointed out that I had just cheated all my proletarian customers. I allowed that he was right, and stuck to popcorn after that, eating handfuls directly out of the machine. I had to count the boxes, and the buckets, too, and empty out the ones unsold and fold them flat again and mark them. There was an awful lot of paperwork involved in being a concessioner.

As I watched Z again and again, the generals took on aspects of other authorities. I memorized the beginning, where the military officers, in a secret meeting, speak of the left as "political mildew" and deplored "the dry rot of subversive ideologies." It sounded just like the morning farm report on our local radio, with all the dire warnings of cow brucellosis and exhortations to mobilize against the invasion of wild oats. I knew nothing about metaphor, nothing, in fact, of communism or what a dictatorship was, but the language grabbed me and would not let go. Without consciously intending it, I had taken sides.

Then, halfway into Christmas vacation, Vincent told on me. The boss took me down into his neat little office in the basement and confronted me with the denouncement that I had eaten one piece of candy from every box in the glass case. I denied it.

"Vincent does it all the time," I lied with a clear conscience.

So there we were, a nest of informers and counterinformers, each waiting to betray the other over a Red Hot Tamale. It was sad. I accused Vincent of snitching; he accused me of the same. We no longer had any pretense of solidarity. He didn't help me when I had a line of customers, and I didn't give him free pop.

Before watching Z again the other night, I took a straw poll of people I knew to have been conscientious in 1969, asking them what they remembered about the movie. It was almost unanimous. People running, darkness, a little blue truck, and Irene Papas. Michael[1]

---

1. Michael Dorris, Erdrich's husband when she wrote this essay.

and I sat down and put the rented tape of *Z* into the video recorder. Between us we shared a bowl of air-popped corn. No salt. No butter anymore. Back in 1969, Michael had purchased the soundtrack to the movie and reviewed it for his school newspaper. It had obviously had an effect on both of us, and yet we recalled no more about it than the viewers in our poll. My memories were more intense because of the argument that almost got me fired from my first indoor job, but all was very blurred except for Irene Papas. As the credits rolled I looked forward to seeing the star. Moment after moment went by, and she did not appear. The leftist organizer went to the airport to pick up the peace leader, and somehow I expected Irene to get off the plane and stun everyone with her tragic, moral gaze.

Of course, Yves was the big star, the peace leader. We watched. I waited for Irene, and then, when it became clear she was only a prop for Yves, I began to watch for *any* woman with a speaking role.

The first one who appeared spoke into a phone. The second woman was a maid, the third a secretary, then a stewardess, then, finally, briefly, Irene, looking grim, and then a woman in a pink suit handing out leaflets. Finally, a woman appeared in a demonstration, only to get kicked in the rear end.

Not only that, the man who kicked her was gay, and much was made of his seduction of a pinball-playing boy, his evil fey grin, his monstrosity. To the Costa-Gavras of 1969, at least, the lone gay man was a vicious goon, immoral and perverted.

Once Yves was killed, Irene was called in to mourn, on cue. Her main contribution to the rest of the movie was to stare inscrutably, to weep uncontrollably, and to smell her deceased husband's aftershave. How had I gotten the movie so wrong?

By the end, I knew I hadn't gotten it so wrong after all. In spite of all that is lacking from the perspective of twenty years, *Z* is still a good political film. It still holds evil to the light and makes hypocrisy transparent. The witnesses who come forward to expose the assassination are bravely credible, and their loss at the end is terrible and stunning. *Z* remains a moral tale, a story of justice done and vengeance sought. It deals with stupidity and avarice, with hidden motives and the impact that one human being can have on others' lives. I still got a thrill when the last line was spoken, telling us that *Z*, in the language of the ancient Greeks, means "He is alive." I

remember feeling that the first time I saw the movie, and now I recalled one other thing. The second evening the movie showed, I
watched Vincent, who hadn't even waited for the end, unhook the
red velvet rope from its silver post.

Our argument was just starting in earnest. Normally, after everyone was gone and the outside lights were doused, he spent an hour,
maybe two if a Disney had played, cleaning up after the crowd. He
took his time. After eleven o'clock, the place was his. He had the
keys and the boss was gone. Those nights, Vincent walked down
each aisle with a bag, a mop, and a bucket filled with the same pink
soapy solution I used on the butter machine. He went after the
spilled Coke, the mashed chocolate, the Jujubes pressed flat. He
scraped the gum off the chairs before it hardened. And there were
things people left, things so inconsequential that the movie goers
rarely bothered to claim them—handkerchiefs, lipsticks, buttons,
pens, and small change. One of the things I knew Vincent liked
best about his job was that he always got to keep what he found.

There was nothing to find that night, however, not a chewed
pencil or hair pin. No one had come. We'd have only a few strag-
glers the next few nights, then the boss canceled the film. Vincent
and I locked the theater and stood for a moment beneath the dark
marquee, arguing. Dumb as it was, it was the first time I'd disagreed
with anyone over anything but hurt feelings and boyfriends. It was
intoxicating. It seemed like we were the only people in the town.

There have been many revolutions, but never one that so thoroughly changed the way women are perceived and depicted as the
movement of the last twenty years. In Costa-Gravras's *Missing*, *Betrayed*, and *Music Box*, strong women are the protagonists, the jug-
glers of complicated moral dilemmas. These are not women who
dye their underwear to lead cheers, and neither am I anymore,
metaphorically I mean, but it is hard to escape from expectations.
The impulse never stops. Watching *Z* in an empty North Dakota
theater was one of those small, incremental experiences that fed into
personal doubt, the necessary seed of any change or growth. The
country in *Z* seemed terribly foreign, exotic, a large and threatened
place—deceptive, dangerous, passionate. As it turned out, it was my
first view of the world.

1993

Stephen Jay Gould
1941–2002

> *When Gould wrote this essay, he was already a well-known scientist, popularizing technical debates in laymen's language in his monthly column for* Natural History *magazine. Periodically, those essays were republished in best-selling books. He devoted himself to explaining the marvelous and messy mechanisms of natural evolution, a role that was, by the early 1980s, bringing him into conflict with creationists. So the announcement that he had been diagnosed with fatal cancer and was given, essentially, a death sentence that was to be carried out shortly, struck readers with a special urgency. How would one of science's greatest champions face death? At least in part, his is a cautionary tale about the scientific view of life. But there is another part also. In the second-to-last paragraph, Gould paraphrases Dylan Thomas's famous villanelle, advising his aged and failing father, "Do not go gentle into that good night." Dylan's poem presumes that life is rounded out only by darkness, nothing else, no afterlife. Ironically, Gould was cured of the abdominal cancer that sickened him the 1980s, but died of a different cancer nearly two decades later.*

The Median Isn't the Message

My life has recently intersected, in a most personal way, two of Mark Twain's famous quips. One I shall defer to the end of this essay. The other (sometimes attributed to Disraeli)[1] identifies three species of mendacity, each worse than the one before—lies, damned lies, and statistics.

Consider the standard example of stretching truth with numbers—a case quite relevant to my story. Statistics recognizes different measures of an "average," or central tendency. The *mean* represents our usual concept of an overall average—add up the items and divide them by the number of sharers (100 candy bars collected for five kids next Halloween will yield twenty for each in a

---

1. Benjamin Disraeli (1804–1881), British novelist and prime minister (1868, 1874–80).

fair world). The *median*, a different measure of central tendency, is the halfway point. If I line up five kids by height, the median child is shorter than two and taller than the other two (who might have trouble getting their mean share of the candy). A politician in power might say with pride, "The mean income of our citizens is $15,000 per year." The leader of the opposition might retort, "But half our citizens make less than $10,000 per year." Both are right, but neither cites a statistic with impassive objectivity. The first invokes a mean, the second a median. (Means are higher than medians in such cases because one millionaire may outweigh hundreds of poor people in setting a mean, but can balance only one mendicant in calculating a median.)

The larger issue that creates a common distrust or contempt for statistics is more troubling. Many people make an unfortunate and invalid separation between heart and mind, or feeling and intellect. In some contemporary traditions, abetted by attitudes stereotypically centered upon Southern California, feelings are exalted as more "real" and the only proper basis for action, while intellect gets short shrift as a hang-up of outmoded elitism. Statistics, in this absurd dichotomy, often becomes the symbol of the enemy. As Hilaire Belloc[2] wrote, "Statistics are the triumph of the quantitative method, and the quantitative method is the victory of sterility and death."

This is a personal story of statistics, properly interpreted, as profoundly nurturant and life-giving. It declares holy war on the downgrading of intellect by telling a small story to illustrate the utility of dry, academic knowledge about science. Heart and head are focal points of one body, one personality.

In July 1982, I learned that I was suffering from abdominal mesothelioma, a rare and serious cancer usually associated with exposure to asbestos. When I revived after surgery, I asked my first question of my doctor and chemotherapist: "What is the best technical literature about mesothelioma?" She replied, with a touch of diplomacy (the only departure she has ever made from direct frankness), that the medical literature contained nothing really worth reading.

2. Belloc (1870–1953), British essayist, poet, and travel writer, noted for his devotion to Catholicism.

Of course, trying to keep an intellectual away from literature works about as well as recommending chastity to *Homo sapiens*, the sexiest primate of all. As soon as I could walk, I made a beeline for Harvard's Countway medical library and punched mesothelioma into the computer's bibliographic search program. An hour later, surrounded by the latest literature on abdominal mesothelioma, I realized with a gulp why my doctor had offered that humane advice. The literature couldn't have been more brutally clear: Mesothelioma is incurable, with a median mortality of only eight months after discovery. I sat stunned for about fifteen minutes, then smiled and said to myself: So that's why they didn't give me anything to read. Then my mind started to work again, thank goodness.

If a little learning could ever be a dangerous thing, I had encountered a classic example. Attitude clearly matters in fighting cancer. We don't know why (from my old-style materialistic perspective, I suspect that mental states feed back upon the immune system). But match people with the same cancer for age, class, health, and socioeconomic status, and, in general, those with positive attitudes, with a strong will and purpose for living, with commitment to struggle, and with an active response to aiding their own treatment and not just a passive acceptance of anything doctors say, tend to live longer. A few months later I asked Sir Peter Medawar, my personal scientific guru and a Nobelist in immunology, what the best prescription for success against cancer might be. "A sanguine personality," he replied. Fortunately (since one can't reconstruct oneself at short notice and for a definite purpose), I am, if anything, even-tempered and confident in just this manner.

Hence the dilemma for humane doctors: Since attitude matters so critically, should such a somber conclusion be advertised, especially since few people have sufficient understanding of statistics to evaluate what the statements really mean? From years of experience with the small-scale evolution of Bahamian land snails treated quantitatively, I have developed this technical knowledge—and I am convinced that it played a major role in saving my life. Knowledge is indeed power, as Francis Bacon[3] proclaimed.

---

3. English scientist and diplomat, (1561–1626) credited with helping to establish the scientific method of inquiry.

The problem may be briefly stated: What does "median mortality of eight months" signify in our vernacular? I suspect that most people, without training in statistics, would read such a statement as "I will probably be dead in eight months"—the very conclusion that must be avoided, both because this formulation is false, and because attitude matters so much.

I was not, of course, overjoyed, but I didn't read the statement in this vernacular way either. My technical training enjoined a different perspective on "eight months median mortality." The point may seem subtle, but the consequences can be profound. Moreover, this perspective embodies the distinctive way of thinking in my own field of evolutionary biology and natural history.

We still carry the historical baggage of a Platonic heritage that seeks sharp essences and definite boundaries. (Thus we hope to find an unambiguous "beginning of life" or "definition of death," although nature often comes to us as irreducible continua.) This Platonic heritage, with its emphasis on clear distinctions and separated immutable entities, leads us to view statistical measures of central tendency wrongly, indeed opposite to the appropriate interpretation in our actual world of variation, shadings, and continua. In short, we view means and medians as hard "realities," and the variation that permits their calculation as a set of transient and imperfect measurements of this hidden essence. If the median is the reality and variation around the median just a device for calculation, then "I will probably be dead in eight months" may pass as a reasonable interpretation.

But all evolutionary biologists know that variation itself is nature's only irreducible essence. Variation is the hard reality, not a set of imperfect measures for a central tendency. Means and medians are the abstractions. Therefore, I looked at the mesothelioma statistics quite differently—and not only because I am an optimist who tends to see the doughnut instead of the hole, but primarily because I know that variation itself is the reality. I had to place myself amidst the variation.

When I learned about the eight-month median, my first intellectual reaction was: Fine, half the people will live longer; now what are my chances of being in that half? I read for a furious and nervous hour and concluded, with relief: damned good. I possessed every one of the characteristics conferring a probability of longer life: I was young; my disease had been recognized in a relatively early stage; I would receive the nation's best medical treatment; I had the world to live for; I knew how to read the data properly and not despair.

Another technical point then added even more solace. I immediately recognized that the distribution of variation about the eight-month median would almost surely be what statisticians call "right skewed." (In a symmetrical distribution, the profile of variation to the left of the central tendency is a mirror image of variation to the right. Skewed distributions are asymmetrical, with variation stretching out more in one direction than the other—left skewed if extended to the left, right skewed if stretched out to the right.) The distribution of variation had to be right skewed, I reasoned. After all, the left of the distribution contains an irrevocable lower boundary of zero (since mesothelioma can only be identified at death or before). Thus, little space exists for the distribution's lower (or left) half—it must be scrunched up between zero and eight months. But the upper (or right) half can extend out for years and years, even if nobody ultimately survives. The distribution must be right skewed, and I needed to know how long the extended tail ran—for I had already concluded that my favorable profile made me a good candidate for the right half of the curve.

The distribution was, indeed, strongly right skewed, with a long tail (however small) that extended for several years above the eight-month median. I saw no reason why I shouldn't be in that small tail, and I breathed a very long sigh of relief. My technical knowledge had helped. I had read the graph correctly. I had asked the right question and found the answers. I had obtained, in all probability, that most precious of all possible gifts in the circumstances—substantial time. I didn't have to stop and immediately follow Isaiah's injunction to Hezekiah[4]—set thine house in order: for thou shalt die, and not live. I would have time to think, to plan, and to fight.

One final point about statistical distributions. They apply only to a prescribed set of circumstances—in this case to survival with

4. In Isaiah 38.1, the prophet Isaiah tells Hezekiah, the King of Judah between 715 and 687 B.C.E., to prepare himself for death

mesothelioma under conventional modes of treatment. If circumstances change, the distribution may alter. I was placed on an experimental protocol of treatment and, if fortune holds, will be in the first cohort of a new distribution with high median and a right tail extending to death by natural causes at advanced old age.

It has become, in my view, a bit too trendy to regard the acceptance of death as something tantamount to intrinsic dignity. Of course I agree with the preacher of Ecclesiastes[5] that there is a time to love and a time to die—and when my skein runs out I hope to face the end calmly and in my own way. For most situations, however, I prefer the more martial view that death is the ultimate enemy—and I find nothing reproachable in those who rage mightily against the dying of the light.

The swords of battle are numerous, and none more effective than humor. My death was announced at a meeting of my colleagues in Scotland, and I almost experienced the delicious pleasure of reading my obituary penned by one of my best friends (the so-and-so got suspicious and checked; he too is a statistician, and didn't expect to find me so far out on the left tail). Still, the incident provided my first good laugh after the diagnosis. Just think, I almost got to repeat Mark Twain's most famous line of all: The reports of my death are greatly exaggerated.

1985

Angelina Grimké
1805–1879

> *Grimké, the daughter of a judge in Charleston, South Carolina, wrote a letter of support to the abolitionist paper* The Liberator *in 1835. Without her permission the editor, William Garrison, published it, and Grimké found herself instantly notorious in both the South and the North for being an inflammatory radical. She was vilified and insulted; her own Quaker brethren ostracized her. In her hometown, her writings were publicly burned, and she was warned that if she returned to Charleston she would be jailed. But*

---

5. See Ecclesiastes 3.8.

she relished the fight against slavery, dangerous as it was for a woman to write and speak publicly on this topic in the mid-nineteenth century. She delivered the speech that follows to members of the Anti-Slavery Convention of American Women and the Pennsylvania State Anti-Slavery Society, which met on May 16, 1837, in the brand-new Pennsylvania Hall for Free Discussion. The next day a mob burnt the auditorium to the ground.

Speech in Pennsylvania Hall

Men, brethren and fathers—mothers, daughters and sisters, what came ye out for to see? A reed shaken with the wind? Is it curiosity merely, or a deep sympathy with the perishing slave, that has brought this large audience together? Those voices without[1] ought to awaken and call out our warmest sympathies. Deluded beings! "they know not what they do."[2] They know not that they are undermining their own rights and their own happiness, temporal and eternal. Do you ask, "what has the North to do with slavery?" Hear it—hear it. Those voices without tell us that the spirit of slavery is *here*, and has been roused to wrath by our abolition speeches and conventions: for surely liberty would not foam and tear herself with rage, because her friends are multiplied daily, and meetings are held in quick succession to set forth her virtues and extend her peaceful kingdom. This opposition shows that slavery has done its deadliest work in the hearts of our citizens. Do you ask, then, "what has the North to do?" I answer, cast out first the spirit of slavery from your own hearts, and then lend your aid to convert the South. Each one present has a work to do, be his or her situation what it may, however limited their means, or insignificant their supposed influence. The great men of this country will not do this work; the church will never do it. A desire to please the world, to keep the favor of all parties and of all conditions, makes them dumb on this and every other unpopular subject. They have become worldly-wise, and therefore God, in his wisdom, em-

1. A mob outside the auditorium was shouting.
2. Luke 23.34.

ploys them not to carry on his plans of reformation and salvation. He hath chosen the foolish things of the world to confound the wise, and the weak to overcome the mighty.

As a Southerner I feel that it is my duty to stand up here tonight and bear testimony against slavery. I have seen it—I have seen it. I know it has horrors that can never be described. I was brought up under its wing: I witnessed for many years its demoralizing influences, and its destructiveness to human happiness. It is admitted by some that the slave is not happy under the *worst* forms of slavery. But I have *never* seen a happy slave. I have seen him dance in his chains, it is true; but he was not happy. There is a wide difference between happiness and mirth. Man cannot enjoy the former while his manhood is destroyed, and that part of the being which is necessary to the making, and to the enjoyment of happiness, is completely blotted out. The slaves, however, may be, and sometimes are, mirthful. When hope is extinguished, they say, "let us eat and drink, for tomorrow we die."[3] What is a mob? What would the breaking of every window be?[4] What would the levelling of this Hall be? Any evidence that we are wrong, or that slavery is a good and wholesome institution? What if the mob should now burst in upon us, break up our meeting and commit violence upon our persons—would this be anything compared with what the slaves endure? No, no: and we do not remember them "as bound with them,"[5] if we shrink in the time of peril, or feel unwilling to sacrifice ourselves, if need be, for their sake. I thank the Lord that there is yet left life enough to feel the truth, even though it rages at it—that conscience is not so completely seared as to be unmoved by the truth of the living God.

Many persons go to the South for a season, and are hospitably entertained in the parlor and at the table of the slaveholder. They never enter the huts of the slaves; they know nothing of the dark side of the picture, and they return home with praises on their lips of the generous character of those with whom they had tarried. Or if they have witnessed the cruelties of slavery, by remaining silent spectators they have naturally become callous—an insensibility has ensued which prepares them to apologize even for barbarity. Noth-

3. Isaiah 22.13.
4. The mob had begun throwing stones at the windows of the hall.
5. Hebrews 13.3.

ing but the corrupting influence of slavery on the hearts of the Northern people can induce them to apologize for it; and much will have been done for the destruction of Southern slavery when we have so reformed the North that no one here will be willing to risk his reputation by advocating or even excusing the holding of men as property. The South know it, and acknowledge that as fast as our principles prevail, the hold of the master must be relaxed.

How wonderfully constituted is the human mind! How it resists, as long as it can, all efforts made to reclaim from error! I feel that all this disturbance[6] is but an evidence that our efforts are the best that could have been adopted, or else the friends of slavery, would not care for what we say and do. The South know what we do. I am thankful that they are reached by our efforts. Many times have I wept in the land of my birth over the system of slavery. I knew of none who sympathized in my feelings—I was unaware that any efforts were made to deliver the oppressed—no voice in the wilderness was heard calling on the people to repent and do works meet for repentance—and my heart sickened within me. Oh, how should I have rejoiced to know that such efforts as these were being made. I only wonder that I had such feelings. I wonder when I reflect under what influence I was brought up, that my heart is not harder than the nether millstone. But in the midst of temptation I was preserved, and my sympathy grew warmer, and my hatred of slavery more inveterate, until at last I have exiled myself from my native land because I could no longer endure to hear the wailing of the slave. I fled to the land of Penn;[7] for here, thought I, sympathy for the slave will surely be found. But I found it not. The people were kind and hospitable, but the slave had no place in their thoughts. Whenever questions were put to me as to his condition, I felt that they were dictated by an idle curiosity, rather than by that deep feeling which would lead to effort for his rescue. I therefore shut up my grief in my own heart. I remembered that I was a Carolinian, from a state which framed this iniquity by law. I knew that throughout her territory was continued suffering, on the one part, and continual brutality and sin on the other. Every Southern breeze wafted to

6. A reference to the continuing uproar of the mob outside the hall.
7. William Penn (1644–1718), founder of the state of Pennsylvania.

me the discordant tones of weeping and wailing, shrieks and groans, mingled with prayers and blasphemous curses. I thought there was no hope; that the wicked would go on in his wickedness, until he had destroyed both himself and his country. My heart sunk within me at the abominations in the midst of which I had been born and educated. What will it avail, cried I in bitterness of spirit, to expose to the gaze of strangers the horrors and pollutions of slavery, when there is no ear to hear nor heart to feel and pray for the slave. The language of my soul was, "Oh tell it not in Gath, publish it not in the streets of Askelon."[8] But how different do I feel now! Animated with hope, nay, with an assurance of the triumph of liberty and good will to man, I will lift up my voice like a trumpet, and show this people their transgression, their sins of omission towards the slave, and what they can do towards affecting Southern mind, and overthrowing Southern oppression.

We may talk of occupying neutral ground, but on this subject, in its present attitude, there is no such thing as neutral ground. He that is not for us is against us, and he that gathereth not with us, scattereth abroad. If you are on what you suppose to be neutral ground, the South look upon you as on the side of the oppressor. And is there one who loves his country willing to give his influence, even indirectly, in favor of slavery—that curse of nations? God swept Egypt with the besom of destruction, and punished Judea also with a sore punishment, because of slavery.[9] And have we any reason to believe that he is less just now?—or that he will be more favorable to us than to his own "peculiar people?"

There is nothing to be feared from those who would stop our mouths, but they themselves should fear and tremble. The current is even now setting fast against them. If the arm of the North had not caused the Bastille[1] of slavery to totter to its foundation, you would not hear those cries. A few years ago, and the South felt secure, and with a contemptuous sneer asked, "Who are the abolitionists? The abolitionists are nothing?"—Ay, in one sense they were nothing, and they are nothing still. But in this we rejoice, that

---

8. 2 Samuel 1.20, meaning keep our adversaries from knowing of our plight.
9. See Exodus.

1. A Parisian prison, the storming of which marked the beginning of the French Revolution.

"God has chosen things that are not to bring to nought things that are."[2]

We often hear the question asked, "What shall we do?" Here is an opportunity for doing something now. Every man and every woman present may do something by showing that we fear not a mob, and, in the midst of threatenings and revilings, by opening our mouths for the dumb and pleading the cause of those who are ready to perish.

To work as we should in this cause, we must know what Slavery is. Let me urge you then to buy the books which have been written on this subject and read them, and then lend them to your neighbors. Give your money no longer for things which pander to pride and lust, but aid in scattering "the living coals of truth"[3] upon the naked heart of this nation,—in circulating appeals to the sympathies of Christians in behalf of the outraged and suffering slave. But, it is said by some, our "books and papers do not speak the truth." Why, then, do they not contradict what we say? They cannot. Moreover the South has entreated, nay commanded us to be silent; and what greater evidence of the truth of our publications could be desired?

Women of Philadelphia! allow me as a Southern woman with much attachment to the land of my birth, to entreat you to come up to this work. Especially let me urge you to petition. *Men* may settle this and other questions at the ballot box, but you have no such right; it is only through petition that you can reach the Legislature. It is therefore peculiarly *your* duty to petition. Do you say, "It does no good?" The South already turns pale at the number sent. They have read the reports of the proceedings of Congress, and there have seen that among other petitions were very many from the women of the North on the subject of slavery. This fact has called the attention of the South to the subject. How could we expect to have done more as yet? Men who hold the rod over slaves, rule in the councils of the nation: and they deny our right to petition and to remonstrate against abuses of our sex and of our kind. We have

2. 1 Corinthians 26.31, meaning that everything is a part of God's plan.

3. From the poem "Our Countrymen in Chains" (1837) by abolitionist poet John Greenleaf Whittier (1807–1892).

these rights, however, from our God. Only let us exercise them: and though often turned away unanswered, let us remember the influence of importunity upon the unjust judge, and act accordingly. The fact that the South look with jealousy upon our measures shows that they are effectual. There is, therefore, no cause for doubting or despair, but rather for rejoicing.

It was remarked in England that women did much to abolish Slavery in her colonies. Nor are they now idle. Numerous petitions from them have recently been presented to the Queen,[4] to abolish the apprenticeship with its cruelties nearly equal to those of the system whose place it supplies. One petition two miles and a quarter long has been presented. And do you think these labors will be in vain? Let the history of the past answer. When the women of these States send up to Congress such a petition, our legislators will arise as did those of England, and say, "When all the maids and matrons of the land are knocking at our doors we must legislate." Let the zeal and love, the faith and works of our English sisters quicken ours—that while the slaves continue to suffer, and when they shout deliverance, we may feel the satisfaction of *having done what we could.*

1837

Sam Harris
b. 1967

Since Galileo first confirmed that, contrary to scripture, the Earth revolved around the sun, intellectuals have used reason to challenge revealed religions, such as Christianity. The debate became very timely when the American republic proposed to separate the state from its association with any particular religion. For example, Thomas Paine's 1794 The Age of Reason *argued against the truth of revelation. With many scientific advancements, the debate grew hotter, as it did, for example, when nineteenth-century geologists suggested that the Earth is millions of years old, and when Charles*

---

4. Queen Victoria (1819–1901), who ascended to the throne in 1837; slavery was abolished throughout the British Empire in 1833.

Darwin, borrowing from these geologists, suggested that long, slow processes of natural selection accounted for the remarkable variety and complexity of species. So Harris's position is not a new one; but his argument was spurred by recent history, especially by religions' regaining influence in politics. The Iranian revolution in the 1970s, for example, established a theocracy in that country, and the goal of groups like Al-Qaeda are obviously theocratic as well. But Harris is also responding to what he calls "intrusions of religion into [American] public policy." This particular essay is part of Harris's larger argument in his book The End of Faith, *which links religious moderation, not just fundamentalism, to the perpetuation of injustice and violence.*

The Myth of "Moderation" in Religion

The idea that any one of our religions represents the infallible word of the One True God requires an encyclopedic ignorance of history, mythology, and art even to be entertained—as the beliefs, rituals, and iconography of each of our religions attest to centuries of cross-pollination among them. Whatever their imagined source, the doctrines of modern religions are no more tenable than those which, for lack of adherents, were cast upon the scrap heap of mythology millennia ago; for there is no more evidence to justify a belief in the literal existence of Yahweh and Satan than there was to keep Zeus perched upon his mountain throne or Poseidon churning the seas.

According to Gallup,[1] 35 percent of Americans believe that the Bible is the literal and inerrant word of the Creator of the universe. Another 48 percent believe that it is the "inspired" word of the same—still inerrant, though certain of its passages must be interpreted symbolically before their truth can be brought to light. Only 17 percent of us remain to doubt that a personal God, in his infinite wisdom, is likely to have authored this text—or, for that matter, to have created the earth with its 250,000 species of beetles. Some

---

1. The Gallup Organization, founded in 1935, uses statistical analyses of surveys to determine public opinion on a wide range of issues.

46 percent of Americans take a literalist view of creation (40 percent believe that God has guided creation over the course of millions of years). This means that 120 million of us place the big bang 2,500 years *after* the Babylonians and Sumerians learned to brew beer. If our polls are to be trusted, nearly 230 million Americans believe that a book showing neither unity of style nor internal consistency was authored by an omniscient, omnipotent, and omnipresent deity. A survey of Hindus, Muslims, and Jews around the world would surely yield similar results, revealing that we, as a species, have grown almost perfectly intoxicated by our myths. How is it that, in this one area of our lives, we have convinced ourselves that our beliefs about the world can float entirely free of reason and evidence?

It is with respect to this rather surprising cognitive scenery that we must decide what it means to be a religious "moderate" in the twenty-first century. Moderates in every faith are obliged to loosely interpret (or simply ignore) much of their canons in the interests of living in the modern world. No doubt an obscure truth of economics is at work here: societies appear to become considerably less productive whenever large numbers of people stop making widgets and begin killing their customers and creditors for heresy. The first thing to observe about the moderate's retreat from scriptural literalism is that it draws its inspiration not from scripture but from cultural developments that have rendered many of God's utterances difficult to accept as written. In America, religious moderation is further enforced by the fact that most Christians and Jews do not read the Bible in its entirety and consequently have no idea just how vigorously the God of Abraham wants heresy expunged. One look at the book of Deuteronomy[2] reveals that he has something very specific in mind should your son or daughter return from yoga class advocating the worship of Krishna.[3]

If your brother, the son of your father or of your mother, or your son or daughter, or the spouse whom you embrace, or your most

2. The fifth book in the Bible, Deuteronomy presents discourses by Moses, including long lists of proscriptive laws.

3. Hindu god often considered an avatar of Vishnu.

intimate friend, tries to secretly seduce you, saying, "Let us go and serve other gods," unknown to you or your ancestors before you, gods of the peoples surrounding you, whether near you or far away, anywhere throughout the world, you must not consent, you must not listen to him; you must show him no pity, you must not spare him or conceal his guilt. No, you must kill him, your hand must strike the first blow in putting him to death and the hands of the rest of the people following. You must stone him to death, since he has tried to divert you from Yahweh your God . . . (Deuteronomy 13:7–11)

While the stoning of children for heresy has fallen out of fashion in our country, you will not hear a moderate Christian or Jew arguing for a "symbolic" reading of passages of this sort. (In fact, one seems to be explicitly blocked by God himself in Deuteronomy 13:1— "Whatever I am now commanding you, you must keep and observe, adding nothing to it, taking nothing away.") The above passage is as canonical as any in the Bible, and it is only by ignoring such barbarisms that the Good Book can be reconciled with life in the modern world. This is a problem for "moderation" in religion: it has nothing underwriting it other than the unacknowledged neglect of the letter of the divine law.

The only reason anyone is "moderate" in matters of faith these days is that he has assimilated some of the fruits of the last two thousand years of human thought (democratic politics, scientific advancement on every front, concern for human rights, an end to cultural and geographic isolation, etc.). The doors leading out of scriptural literalism do not open from the *inside*. The moderation we see among nonfundamentalists is not some sign that faith itself has evolved; it is, rather, the product of the many hammer blows of modernity that have exposed certain tenets of faith to doubt. Not the least among these developments has been the emergence of our tendency to value evidence and to be convinced by a proposition to the degree that there is evidence for it. Even most fundamentalists live by the lights of reason in this regard; it is just that their minds seem to have been partitioned to accommodate the profligate truth claims of their faith. Tell a devout Christian that his wife is cheating on him, or that frozen yogurt can make a man invisible, and he is

likely to require as much evidence as anyone else, and to be persuaded only to the extent that you give it. Tell him that the book he
keeps by his bed was written by an invisible deity who will punish
him with fire for eternity if he fails to accept its every incredible
claim about the universe, and he seems to require no evidence whatsoever.

Religious moderation springs from the fact that even the least educated person among us simply *knows* more about certain matters
than anyone did two thousand years ago—and much of this knowledge is incompatible with scripture. Having heard something about
the medical discoveries of the last hundred years, most of us no
longer equate disease processes with sin or demonic possession.
Having learned about the known distances between objects in our
universe, most of us (about half of us, actually) find the idea that
the whole works was created six thousand years ago (with light from
distant stars already in transit toward the earth) impossible to take
seriously. Such concessions to modernity do not in the least suggest
that faith is compatible with reason, or that our religious traditions
are in principle open to new learning: it is just that the utility of ignoring (or "reinterpreting") certain articles of faith is now overwhelming. Anyone being flown to a distant city for heart-bypass
surgery has conceded, tacitly at least, that we have learned a few
things about physics, geography, engineering, and medicine since
the time of Moses.

So it is not that these texts have maintained their integrity over
time (they haven't); it is just that they have been effectively edited
by our neglect of certain of their passages. Most of what remains—
the "good parts"—has been spared the same winnowing because we
do not yet have a truly modern understanding of our ethical intu-
itions and our capacity for spiritual experience. If we better understood the workings of the human brain, we would undoubtedly
discover lawful connections between our states of consciousness,
our modes of conduct, and the various ways we use our attention.
What makes one person happier than another? Why is love more
conducive to happiness than hate? Why do we generally prefer
beauty to ugliness and order to chaos? Why does it feel so good to
smile and laugh, and why do these shared experiences generally
bring people closer together? Is the ego an illusion, and, if so, what

implications does this have for human life? Is there life after death? These are ultimately questions for a mature science of the mind. If we ever develop such a science, most of our religious texts will be no more useful to mystics than they now are to astronomers.

While moderation in religion may seem a reasonable position to stake out, in light of all that we have (and have not) learned about the universe, it offers no bulwark against religious extremism and religious violence. From the perspective of those seeking to live by the letter of the texts, the religious moderate is nothing more than a failed fundamentalist. He is, in all likelihood, going to wind up in hell with the rest of the unbelievers. The problem that religious moderation poses for all of us is that it does not permit anything very critical to be said about religious literalism. We cannot say that fundamentalists are crazy, because they are merely practicing their freedom of belief; we cannot even say that they are mistaken in *religious* terms, because their knowledge of scripture is generally unrivaled. All we can say, as religious moderates, is that we don't like the personal and social costs that a full embrace of scripture imposes on us. This is not a new form of faith, or even a new species of scriptural exegesis; it is simply a capitulation to a variety of all-too-human interests that have nothing, in principle, to do with God. Religious moderation is the product of *secular* knowledge and scriptural *ignorance*—and it has no bona fides, in religious terms, to put it on a par with fundamentalism. The texts themselves are unequivocal: they are perfect in all their parts. By their light, religious moderation appears to be nothing more than an unwillingness to fully submit to God's law. By failing to live by the letter of the texts, while tolerating the irrationality of those who do, religious moderates betray faith and reason equally. Unless the core dogmas of faith are called into question—i.e., that we know there is a God, and that we know what he wants from us—religious moderation will do nothing to lead us out of the wilderness.

2004

S. I. Hayakawa
1906–1992

Hayakawa was trained as a literary scholar, but in the 1930s he began pursuing general semantics, the study of what words mean. He published a popular college textbook on the subject, Language in Thought and Action, *in 1939. Hayakawa thought contemporary language was degenerate. He believed that he and his contemporaries breathed "a poisoned air without knowing it": Their language was contaminated by the commercialism of newspapers and radio, and by "the propaganda technique of nationalistic madmen," by whom he meant the fascists, Hitler, Mussolini, and Franco.* Language in Thought and Action *was intended to innoculate American students against these abuses of language, and "How Dictionaries Are Made," an excerpt from this book, was part of his program.*

How Dictionaries Are Made

It is widely believed that every word has a correct meaning, that we learn these meanings principally from teachers and grammarians (except that most of the time we don't bother to, so that we ordinarily speak "sloppy English"), and that dictionaries and grammars are the supreme authority in matters of meaning and usage. Few people ask by what authority the writers of dictionaries and grammars say what they say. I once got into a dispute with an Englishwoman over the pronunciation of a word and offered to look it up in the dictionary. The Englishwoman said firmly "What for? I am English. I was born and brought up in England. The way I speak *is* English." Such self-assurance about one's own language is not uncommon among the English. In the United States, however, anyone who is willing to quarrel with the dictionary is regarded as either eccentric or mad.

Let us see how dictionaries are made and how the editors arrive at definitions. What follows applies, incidentally, only to those dictionary offices where first-hand, original research goes on—not those in which editors simply copy existing dictionaries. The task of writing a dictionary begins with reading vast amounts of the literature of the period or subject that the dictionary is to cover. As the editors read, they copy on cards every interesting or rare word, every unusual or peculiar occurrence of a common word, a large number of common words in their ordinary uses, and also the sentences in which each of these words appears, thus

> **pail**
> The dairy *pails* bring home increase of milk
> KEATS, *Endymion*
> I, 44–45

That is to say, the context of each word is collected, along with the word itself. For a really big job of dictionary-writing, such as the *Oxford English Dictionary* (usually bound in about twenty-five volumes), millions of such cards are collected, and the task of editing occupies decades. As the cards are collected, they are alphabetized and sorted. When the sorting is completed, there will be for each word anywhere from two or three to several hundred illustrative quotations, each on its card.

To define a word, then, the dictionary-editor places before him the stack of cards illustrating that word; each of the cards represents an actual use of the word by a writer of some literary or historical importance. He reads the cards carefully, discards some, rereads the rest, and divides up the stack according to what he thinks are the several senses of the word. Finally, he writes his definitions, following the hard-and-fast rule that each definition *must* be based on what the quotations in front of him reveal about the meaning of the word. The editor cannot be influenced by what *he* thinks a given word *ought* to mean. He must work according to the cards or not at all.

The writing of a dictionary, therefore, is not a task of setting up authoritative statements about the "true meanings" of words, but a task of *recording*, to the best of one's ability, what various words have *meant* to authors in the distant or immediate past. *The writer of a dictionary is a historian, not a lawgiver.* If, for example, we had been writing a dictionary in 1890, or even as late as 1919, we could have said that the word "broadcast" means "to scatter" (seed, for example), but we could not have decreed that from 1921 on, the most common meaning of the word should become "to disseminate audible messages, etc., by radio transmission." To regard the dictionary as an "authority," therefore, is to credit the dictionary-writer with gifts of prophecy which neither he nor anyone else possesses. In choosing our words when we speak or write, we can be *guided* by the historical record afforded us by the dictionary, but we cannot be *bound* by it, because new situations, new experiences, new inventions, new feelings are always compelling us to give new uses to old words. Looking under a "hood," we should ordinarily have found, five hundred years ago, a monk; today, we find a motorcar engine.

1939

Jim Hightower
b. 1943

Hightower is one of the best examples of a populist in American politics today. Broadly speaking, any political movement that champions the common people against the elites who dominate government is "populist." In Hightower's case, that has generally meant attacking the influence of corporations in American politics, whether that influence has been channeled through the Republican or the Democratic party. Hightower himself has a well-defined and nuanced political perspective, which leads him to unequivocal positions on just about every public policy and puts him on the fringe of mainstream American politics. But in this essay he discusses the centrality of populism, suggesting that it transcends the political affiliations of ordinary Republicans and Democrats. He wrote this essay in 1997, but on Christmas 2006 Hightower delivered a shorter version of it on his two-minute radio program, Common Sense Commentary, *which is aired on nearly a hundred stations across the United States.*

Daddy's Philosophy

My daddy is buried in the rolling Texas prairie at Denison, with a modest marble headstone to mark his grave. But there is another monument in town with his name on it, too, a couple of miles from the cemetery, where West Woodard Street dead-ends at Maurice. Right there is a Little League baseball field, the first that Denison had, and at the edge of the field is a small sandstone monument with a brass plaque acknowledging the half-dozen men who started Little League ball in our town, including W. F. "High" Hightower.

The marble stone marks his grave, but this stone marks the way he lived and what he valued. Daddy and his Lions Club[1] buddies got the city to donate the vacant lots that now form the ballfield;

---

1. The Lions Club, founded in 1917, is an international service organization whose members volunteer in projects that help their communities.

they organized the teams and came up with a few dollars to buy equipment, uniforms, and such; then they "volunteered" us boys to clear the lots of rocks (approximately 117 billion of them, as I recall) and to do the shoveling, hauling, leveling, planting, and other chores necessary to turn this raw space into a ballpark. Once we made a place to play, Daddy and other folks in town coached the teams, did the official scoring, ran the snowcone stand, and announced the games on the squawking P.A. system.

I played five summers on that field—once batting .517 (a far better year than I have averaged since; little did I know I had peaked at age twelve). Even after I moved on, though, Daddy stayed involved in the Little League program, because it was what the community needed. He was not doing it only for his boys, but for the community.

He believed in that concept. He believed that everyone should pool efforts when the common good calls for it, whether pitching in locally to start a Little League or being taxed nationally to assure everyone's social security. "You're no better than anyone else," he would tell me as a maturing boy, "and they're no better than you. We're all just people and we need each other." Not that he was any kind of philosopher, for God's sake, or any do-gooder, either—just an ordinary American of common sense and goodwill who grew up on a hardscrabble, Depression-era tenant farm[2] and had learned from life that *everyone does better when everyone does better.* That is what passes for political philosophy in Denison, and it remains the best I have found in all my years wandering and studying.

Also I found that his outlook is shared by a majority of folks everywhere, today just as surely as it was in Daddy's time. Yet it is this very concept of the common good that the powerful in our society are rending as fast as their fat little hands can rip.

In the class war of the past couple decades, the corporate and investor elites have made out like bandits by shortchanging the middle class on economic gains that the whole society has produced.

2. A tenant farm is worked by farmers who rent their land; during the Great Depression (roughly 1929–41), many tenant farmers, especially in the Oklahoma/north Texas region, suffered through the drought known as the Dust Bowl. Franklin Delano Roosevelt's New Deal, which helped ease the economic crisis, was based on a philosophy of mutual help rather than independence.

They have forcibly held down wages (interestingly, "wages" is a term derived from the same Latin root as the term for "waging war"), just as they have depressed the paychecks of nearly every salaried employee not working on the top floor. The result is that the prosperity generated by the many has been stolen by the few, especially by the million or so richest Americans, and there is a widening chasm between the wealth of these elites and the well-being of the great majority. Writing about the last time such a separation was made in our country, in the 1920s and 1930s, Woody Guthrie[3] penned these lyrics: "As through this world I've traveled/I've seen lots of funny men/Some'll rob you with a six gun/Some with a fountain pen."

Today's fountain-pen bandits do their finagling in the name of "global competitiveness," but they are merely feeding us globaloney when they say that. These privileged and powerful ones have severed themselves from the common good (1) because they can, and (2) because there is a "screw you" imperative built into the corporate system that commands top managers to produce as much money as possible for the big shareholders (including the top managers) as quickly as possible, no matter who or what has to be run over.

While the bandits are loose in the private sector, plundering the middle class by day and stealing back at night to their gated-and-guarded compounds of wealth, those running our public sector have adopted the same pernicious philosophy of "I got mine, you get yours." Health care for all? Hey, Newt[4] and his gang of money-corrupted cutthroats shout, buy yourself a medical savings account. Universal education, the notion that our communities and our nation will be enriched if we are smart enough to provide a system of quality public schools for all? Hey, the ideologues of separation shout, we want to take our tax dollars out of the common pool and fund exclusive academies for our kids, the hell with your ragamuffins. Old-age protection through a shared retirement fund? Hey, shout Wall Street's minions in Congress and the White House, sever

3. Oklahoma folk singer and song writer (1912–1967), most famous for his 1940 song "This Land Is Your Land."

4. Newt Gingrich (b. 1943), Speaker of the House of Representatives from 1995 to 1999 and chief architect of the 1994 "Con-tract with America" that helped Republicans win a majority in the House for the first time in fifty years. The Contract promised, among other things, to reduce federal spending on welfare.

the bonds of common responsibility and let everyone bet the farm by putting their social security money in a dazzling array of Wall Street schemes and scams.

The disuniting of our society is the result of a historic failure of our political system. The workaday majority, the folks who believe in America's concept of the common good, have no home in the two major parties, both of which have been molded into branches of one Corporate Party that is pushing hard for disunification. There is no political redress in Washington (or in state capitals) for working people, inner city and rural residents, old folks and children, small farmers, the poor (working and otherwise)—no redress for the middle class and less fortunate.

Bill Clinton himself is a quisling in the class war. Ironically, Clinton's inauguration this year was held on the national holiday established to honor Martin Luther King Jr., and of course Clinton invoked the King name to demonstrate his concern for racial tolerance. But Dr. King was not only a martyr for minorities and the racial cause—his agenda was one of economic power for the working class. He was assassinated in Memphis, where he had gone in 1968 not to register African-Americans to vote, but to support striking garbage workers and to organize white and black folks alike to join him in the massive "Poor People's March" he had scheduled for Washington—a trip he never got to take. In the eyes of the country's power brokers, King had moved from being an acceptable missionary of civil rights to being an unacceptable meddler in economic rights. Clinton did not mention this richly heroic side of Dr. King, much less invoke any of the great crusader's populist message. No surprise, given Clinton's essential Republicanism. Indeed, had King been alive on January 20, 1997, he most certainly would have shunned the inauguration of this pusillanimous President, probably instead organizing a march of the "Other Americans" for a show of strength against a "Democratic" administration that is owned and managed by the comfortable and the corporate.

Clinton-the-Democrat campaigned in '92 as the candidate of economic justice, but he has governed as the President of economic privilege. Again in the '96 campaign he sounded populist themes, jumping the Republicans for their assault on Medicare, but now he has met in back rooms with the GOP to plot a bipartisan raid not only on Medicare, but also on Medicaid and social security. Ironically, he agreed to this Republican assault on the elderly and the poor the same week he participated in the dedication of the Franklin and Eleanor Roosevelt[5] memorial in Washington, thus setting a new Olympic record in political hypocrisy.

Having Clinton as a Democratic President is like getting bitten by your pet dog—the bite will heal, but you never feel the same about that dog again.

Have heart, though, for a change is coming. It's coming because it must, just as it has had to come periodically in our history when economic elites have set themselves too far above the rest of us. "The fruits of the toil of millions are boldly stolen to build up colossal fortunes for a few, unprecedented in the history of mankind," proclaimed the preamble to the 1892 platform of the People's Party, rallying the Populist movement to a historic reshaping of America's political landscape. "We have witnessed for more than a quarter of a century the struggles of the two great political parties for power and plunder," the platform raged, "while grievous wrongs have been inflicted upon the suffering people. We charge that the controlling influences dominating both these parties have permitted the existing dreadful conditions to develop without serious effort to prevent or restrain them. Neither do they now promise us any substantial reform. . . . They propose to sacrifice our homes, lives and children on the altar of mammon; to destroy the multitude in order to secure corruption funds from the millionaires."

No need to appoint a drafting committee to put forward the particulars of today's populist manifesto—just fax this one across the country.

A change is coming because there is no party representing the worker majority of our country, creating a political vacuum that a civil society cannot survive. The vacuum exists because today's national Democratic Party is immobilized by its corporate sponsors and its craven leadership, no longer having either the inclination or the political freedom to nod to that majority, much less represent it.

5. During the Great Depression, President Franklin Delano Roosevelt (1882–1945) established many government-funded programs, such as Social Security, which he and his wife, Eleanor (1884–1962) advocated. Medicaid, the largest provider of health care to low-income families, was established by the Social Security Act of 1965.

The good news is that a change is coming because it *is* coming, already organizing and gaining strength at the country's grassroots. One vital development is that organized labor has shaken itself awake and is on the move again, with savvy and aggressive new leadership at all levels, adding energy, focus, and resources to the long-term process of building a new political path. There are groups like ACORN, Citizen Action, the PIRGs (Public Interest Research Groups), and Clean Water Action working door-to-door in thousands of neighborhoods all across the country, organizing and training "just folks" to fight back. There are now serious-minded third parties that are beginning to crack the lock that the Democrat and Republican parties have had on the system—a smart and well-organized group called the New Party, for example, already has more dues-paying members than the national Democratic Party; it is running candidates for school boards, city councils, state legislatures, and other local offices in dozens of cities and towns (of 185 campaigns it has run so far, it has won 126); it has teamed with ACORN and others to win "living-wage" campaigns in cities across the country, effectively raising the local minimum wage to as high as $7.50 an hour; and it has had the brains and chutzpah to challenge the election laws that presently rig the political system for the perpetuation of the two major parties. In addition there are groups like the Labor Party and the Alliance for Democracy that are not yet running candidates, but are working throughout the country to inform, educate, and activate citizens to take charge. Also, an essential network of communications already is in place for this burgeoning progressive political movement, including magazines and papers, hundreds of important Internet sites, radio talk shows, newsletters, cable television broadcasts, videos, cartoonists, and musicians.

Most significantly, though, people themselves are ready to fight back and are actively in search of a new politics that enlists them, that stands unequivocally for working families against the bandits, that rejects trickle-down policies in favor of percolate-up economics, and that is centered on that philosophical notion I first learned from my ol' daddy, which bears repeating here: *Everyone does better when everyone does better.*

There is no need to "create" a progressive movement, because it already exists in the hearts and minds of America's ordinary folks.

Instead the chore of progressive strategists and organizers is to connect these folks nationally and help them build an independent political mechanism that frees them from reliance on either branch of today's corporate, one-party structure.

There was a moving company here in Austin that had an advertising slogan I liked: "If we can get it loose, we can move it." That's the spirit! If we give people a means to get loose from the old politics, they'll get moving—and they'll take America back.

1997

Zora Neale Hurston
1903–1960

Hurston was a young member of the Harlem Renaissance, a movement of black writers, musicians, artists, dancers, and scholars, when she published "How It Feels to Be Colored Me" in 1928. Her mentor, Alain Locke, who edited the influential journal The New Negro, *wanted his writers to win equal citizenship not by arguing for it but by producing art of equal greatness with any produced by whites. This was a departure from Frederick Douglass's writing, for example, which was overtly persuasive. Although Hurston later broke with Locke, she wrote this essay in the spirit Locke advocated. It was published in the journal* World Tomorrow, *which was read largely by whites who were already sympathetic to civil rights for African Americans. In this essay, Hurston is trying to explain the "New Negro" to this audience. Her patriotism would have reassured her readers, who would have been aware of the angrier speeches of black nationalists like Marcus Garvey. But while Locke liked her essay, he believed it pandered to her audience. Hurston presumes that there are essential differences between blacks and whites, a presumption that few intellectuals—white or black— would accept today. In fact, in her 1979 edition of Hurston's work* I Love Myself When I'm Laughing, *the black writer Alice Walker went so far as to say that this essay "makes one's flesh crawl" because it confirms white stereotypes of blacks, including the belief that "the educated black person . . . is, underneath the thin veneer of civilization, still a 'heathen.' "*

How It Feels to Be Colored Me

I am colored but I offer nothing in the way of extenuating circumstances except the fact that I am the only Negro in the United States whose grandfather on the mother's side was *not* an Indian chief.

I remember the very day that I became colored. Up to my thirteenth year I lived in the little Negro town of Eatonville, Florida. It is exclusively a colored town. The only white people I knew passed through the town going to or coming from Orlando. The native whites rode dusty horses, the Northern tourists chugged down the sandy village road in automobiles. The town knew the Southerners and never stopped cane[1] chewing when they passed. But the Northerners were something else again. They were peered at cautiously from behind curtains by the timid. The more venturesome would come out on the porch to watch them go past and got just as much pleasure out of the tourists as the tourists got out of the village.

The front porch might seem a daring place for the rest of the town, but it was a gallery seat for me. My favorite place was atop the gate-post. Proscenium box for a born first-nighter. Not only did I enjoy the show, but I didn't mind the actors knowing that I liked it. I usually spoke to them in passing. I'd wave at them and when they returned my salute, I would say something like this: "Howdy-do-well-I-thank-you-where-you-goin'?" Usually automobile or the horse paused at this, and after a queer exchange of compliments, I would probably "go a piece of the way" with them, as we say in farthest Florida. If one of my family happened to come to the front in time to see me, of course negotiations would be rudely broken off. But even so, it is clear that I was the first "welcome-to-our-state" Floridian, and I hope the Miami Chamber of Commerce will please take notice.

During this period, white people differed from colored to me only in that they rode through town and never lived there. They liked to hear me "speak pieces" and sing and wanted to see me dance the parse-me-la, and gave me generously of their small silver

---

1. Sugarcane.

for doing these things, which seemed strange to me for I wanted to do them so much that I needed bribing to stop. Only they didn't know it. The colored people gave no dimes. They deplored any joyful tendencies in me, but I was their Zora nevertheless. I belonged to them, to the nearby hotels, to the county—everybody's Zora.

But changes came in the family when I was thirteen, and I was sent to school in Jacksonville. I left Eatonville, the town of the oleanders,[2] as Zora. When I disembarked from the river-boat at Jacksonville, she was no more. It seemed that I had suffered a sea change. I was not Zora of Orange County any more, I was now a little colored girl. I found it out in certain ways. In my heart as well as in the mirror, I became a fast[3] brown—warranted not to rub nor run.

But I am not tragically colored. There is no great sorrow dammed up in my soul, nor lurking behind my eyes. I do not mind at all. I do not belong to the sobbing school of Negrohood who hold that nature somehow has given them a lowdown dirty deal and whose feelings are all hurt about it. Even in the helter-skelter skirmish that is my life, I have seen that the world is to the strong regardless of a little pigmentation more or less. No, I do not weep at the world—I am too busy sharpening my oyster knife.[4]

Someone is always at my elbow reminding me that I am the granddaughter of slaves. It fails to register depression with me. Slavery is sixty years in the past. The operation was successful and the patient is doing well, thank you. The terrible struggle[5] that made me an American out of a potential slave said "On the line!" The Reconstruction said "Get set!"; and the generation before said "Go!" I am off to a flying start and I must not halt in the stretch to look behind and weep. Slavery is the price I paid for civilization, and the choice was not with me. It is a bully adventure and worth all that I have paid through my ancestors for it. No one on earth ever had a greater chance for glory. The world to be won and nothing to be lost. It is thrilling to think—to know that for any act of mine, I

2. A flowering tropical shrub.
3. Colorfast.
4. A reference to the expression "The world is my oyster."

5. The Civil War; the Reconstruction was the period immediately following the war.

shall get twice as much praise or twice as much blame. It is quite exciting to hold the center of the national stage, with the spectators not knowing whether to laugh or to weep.

The position of my white neighbor is much more difficult. No brown specter pulls up a chair beside me when I sit down to eat. No dark ghost thrusts its leg against mine in bed. The game of keeping what one has is never so exciting as the game of getting.

I do not always feel colored. Even now I often achieve the unconscious Zora of Eatonville before the Hegira.[6] I feel most colored when I am thrown against a sharp white background.

For instance at Barnard.[7] "Beside the waters of the Hudson" I feel my race. Among the thousand white persons, I am a dark rock surged upon, and overswept, but through it all, I remain myself. When covered by the waters, I am; and the ebb but reveals me again.

Sometimes it is the other way around. A white person is set down in our midst, but the contrast is just as sharp for me. For instance, when I sit in the drafty basement that is The New World Cabaret with a white person, my color comes. We enter chatting about any little nothing that we have in common and are seated by the jazz waiters. In the abrupt way that jazz orchestras have, this one plunges into a number. It loses no time in circumlocutions, but gets right down to business. It constricts the thorax and splits the heart with its tempo and narcotic harmonies. This orchestra grows rambunctious, rears on its hind legs and attacks the tonal veil with primitive fury, rending it, clawing it until it breaks through to the jungle beyond. I follow those heathen—follow them exultingly. I dance wildly inside myself; I yell within, I whoop; I shake my assegai[8] above my head, I hurl it true to the mark *yeeeeooww!* I am in the jungle and living in the jungle way. My face is painted red and yellow and my body is painted blue. My pulse is throbbing like a war drum. I want to slaughter something—give paid, give death to what, I do not know. But the piece ends. The men of the orchestra wipe their lips and rest their fingers. I creep back slowly to the ve-

6. Flight from a dangerous situation to a more desirable one; an exodus.

7. A women's college in New York City

at which Hurston studied anthropology, 1925–28.

8. African spear.

neer we call civilization with the last tone and find the white friend sitting motionless in his seat, smoking calmly.

"Good music they have here," he remarks, drumming the table with his fingertips.

Music. The great blobs of purple and red emotion have not touched him. He has only heard what I felt. He is far away and I see him but dimly across the ocean and the continent that have fallen between us. He is so pale with his whiteness then and I am *so* colored.

At certain times I have no race, I am *me*. When I set my hat at a certain angle and saunter down Seventh Avenue, Harlem City, feeling as snooty as the lions in front of the Forty-Second Street Library, for instance. So far as my feelings are concerned, Peggy Hopkins Joyce on the Boule Mich[9] with her gorgeous raiment, stately carriage, knees knocking together in a most aristocratic manner, has nothing on me. The cosmic Zora emerges. I belong to no race nor time. I am the eternal feminine with its string of beads.

I have no separate feeling about being an American citizen and colored. I am merely a fragment of the Great Soul that surges within the boundaries. My country, right or wrong.

Sometimes, I feel discriminated against, but it does not make me angry. It merely astonishes me. How *can* any deny themselves the pleasure of my company? It's beyond me.

But in the main, I feel like a brown bag of miscellany propped against a wall. Against a wall in company with other bags, white, red and yellow. Pour out the contents, and there is discovered a jumble of small things priceless and worthless. A first-water diamond, an empty spool, bits of broken glass, lengths of string, a key to a door long since crumbled away, a rusty knife-blade, old shoes saved for a road that never was and never will be, a nail bent under the weight of things too heavy for any nail, a dried flower or two still a little fragrant. In your hand is the brown bag. On the ground before you is the jumble it held—so much like the jumble in the bags, could they be emptied, that all might be dumped in a single heap and the bags refilled without altering the content of any

9. Peggy Hopkins Joyce: a beautiful and fashionable white American in the 1920s; Boule Mich: Boulevard Saint-Michel, a fashionable street in Paris

greatly. A bit of colored glass more or less would not matter. Perhaps that is how the Great Stuffer of Bags filled them in the first place— who knows?

1928

Molly Ivins
1944–2007

The Republicans were quite vulnerable in the voting booths in 1976. Vice President Spiro Agnew, charged with tax evasion, had resigned in 1973; Richard Nixon picked Gerald Ford to replace him. Then, in 1974, in the midst of the Watergate scandal, Nixon himself resigned the presidency, elevating Ford to that office, and Ford became the first man to serve without being elected as either president or vice president. The Democrats were in a good position to win the White House, though early in the year none of the possible candidates was an obvious choice; none had a strong national reputation. The field was wide open, and early media reports, like the one Ivins recounts here, were unusually influential. The eventual winner, Jimmy Carter, was more obscure than most. Carter benefited from the general anti-Washington sentiment in the mid-1970s, but he also benefited from the news agencies. Morris Udall ran a close second in the primaries, winning 36 percent to Carter's 37 percent of the crucial Michigan delegation in an early vote. Many attribute that result to inaccurate suggestions that Udall was a racist, which circulated in the media on the eve of the election. Ivins probably was not responsible for Udall's demise, but she contributed to it. She wrote this confession years later, after establishing herself as the most acerbic and funny liberal columnist in America.

What I Did to Morris Udall

Tucson, Arizona—Life's a funny ol' female-dog, idn't she? Here I am back in Tucson, one of my favorite places in the U.S. of A., and also the place of one of my most bitter professional regrets.

I did a man wrong here one time. I didn't mean to, and it didn't make much difference, but there it is. The man's name is Morris Udall, congressman from Tucson, and the year was 1976.

Six, I think it was, Democrats were scrapping for the presidential nomination that year. Ol' Gerry Ford looked beatable. Among the less likely contenders were Jimmy Carter, a former governor of Georgia with the charisma of a day-old pizza, and Mo Udall, an ace guy with the misfortune to be from Arizona (three electoral votes).

The New York Times Magazine was fixing to run profiles on each of these six candidates, and they called me to profile Udall—I think because I was the farthest-West journalist they'd ever heard of; Texas, Arizona—they all look the same from New York.

In those days I was what is known in our trade as "hungry," which is supposed to mean "feisty, ambitious, willin' to go after a story like a starvin' dog." Actually, I was plain hungry: Six years at the *Texas Observer* left me below the poverty line, and I jumped at that assignment.

So I came over to Arizona and investigated Mo Udall's life, times, finances, family life, psychological health, and public record back to Year Aught. I'll tell you now what I should have told you then: Udall is a man of exceptional decency, integrity, courage, honesty, and intelligence. On top of which, he's funny. If you could have forced Congress to take a vote back then just on the question of who was the finest human being then serving—secret ballot, no consequences, just vote your conscience—I swear to you that Udall would have won hands down.

And did I report this? No. I was looking for warts; I wanted dirt. Besides, I was afraid of being conned, of looking like a naïve hick. I dug through his campaign contributions. (I found union money! Do you know how brave you have to be to support unions in Arizona?) I dug through his psycho history (The Udalls are a famous Mormon family. Mo split from the church and became a Jack Mormon[1] after commanding an all-black troop in the Army). I wrote about his being one-eyed. (At one point, he was a one-eyed professional basketball player—some handicap.)

---

1. Someone who has left the Mormon Church but retains friendly relations with the organization, its members, and its beliefs.

Faced with the disgusting reality of a truly decent politician, I did my dead-level best to be tougher than a fifty-cent steak. I didn't cut him an inch of slack; I thought that was my job, the way they did it in the big leagues.

My grudging report that I hadn't been able to find anything actually wrong with Udall duly appeared in print. Imagine my surprise when *The New York Times's* famed political correspondent R. W. Apple followed my reserved appraisal of Udall with a puff piece about Jimmy Carter. (Johnny Apple, you know perfectly well that was a puff piece.) Every venial sin of Udall's that I had held up to the merciless light of day, Apple glossed over gaily in the case of Carter. The profiles appeared from one Sunday to the next, but the politicians described in them were not judged by a single standard. To put it mildly.

Well, Jimmy Carter turned out to be a man of character and decency, too—he just wasn't much of a politician, and Mo Udall was a good one.

My continuing regret is that what I wrote was accurate, but it wasn't *true*. I was trying so hard to prove I could be a major-league, hard-hitting journalist that I let the real story go hang itself.

The real story is the sheer decency of Morris Udall. When I am asked if there are any heroes left in politics, I always think of Udall. He's retired now, victim of a sad, slow, wasting disease. I suppose you could say that Udall is to Arizona liberals what Barry Goldwater[2] is to Arizona conservatives: an incurably honest man of principle. Or you could say that Morris Udall is to Arizona liberals what Ev Meacham[3] is to Arizona kooks. I think he'd like to have it end with a joke.

1994

2. Goldwater (1909–1998) was a U.S. Senator from Arizona for five terms. The Republican nominee for president in 1964, he opposed the New Deal policies established by Franklin Delano Roosevelt and Lyndon Johnson's proposed expansion of those programs. He was defeated in a landslide election, but most conservatives credit him with starting the modern conservative movement in American politics.

3. Evan Meacham (b. 1924), governor of Arizona from 1987 to 1988, was impeached in 1988 and convicted of obstructing justice. Enjoying only tepid support from his own Republican Party, he is best known for canceling Martin Luther King Jr. Day in the state shortly after his election.

Thomas Jefferson
1743–1826

> In June 1776, the American colonies had been at war with England
> for a year. Congress had raised an army, put it in the field, and even
> published a declaration (also drafted by Jefferson) explaining the
> reasons for these drastic steps. The escalating conflict persuaded Con-
> gress to instruct Jefferson, John Adams, Benjamin Franklin, and two
> others to draft a second declaration, the Declaration of Indepen-
> dence, explaining why Americans felt compelled to separate them-
> selves permanently from the King's jurisdiction. Harried by the more
> pressing business of running the new government and supplying the
> army, the other committee members left the job to Jefferson, who
> drafted this document. Adams and Franklin revised it slightly, and
> it was submitted to Congress, where it was again revised before be-
> ing adopted on July 4, 1776. Loyalists attacked the argument by dis-
> puting the truth or importance of many of the grievances, but
> Congress didn't expect to persuade hostile readers to the cause of in-
> dependence. The target audience was sympathetic Americans: Con-
> gress instructed that the document be published domestically,
> distributed to each state's legislature, and (perhaps most signifi-
> cantly) read publicly to the army. The opening paragraph must have
> been especially calculated to hearten dispirited soldiers by persuad-
> ing them that they fought for a just cause and a place in history. An-
> other important audience was Europe—the English, French, and
> Dutch, who might aid the cause, especially King Louis of France.
> Congress sent a copy to its ambassador in France and instructed him
> to present it to the French court and distribute it to other European
> governments. The Declaration of Independence has inspired many
> similar documents by peoples around the world struggling to win
> their right of self-rule from foreign, imperial governments.

The Declaration of Independence

In Congress, July 4, 1776
The unanimous Declaration of the
thirteen United States of America

When in the Course of human events it becomes necessary for one people to dissolve the political bands which have connected them with another, and to assume among the powers of the earth, the separate and equal station to which the Laws of Nature and of Nature's God entitle them, a decent respect to the opinions of mankind requires that they should declare the causes which impel them to the separation.

We hold these truths to be self-evident, that all men are created equal, that they are endowed by their Creator with certain unalienable Rights, that among these are Life, Liberty and the pursuit of Happiness. That to secure these rights, Governments are instituted among Men, deriving their just powers from the consent of the governed. That whenever any Form of Government becomes destructive of these ends, it is the Right of the People to alter or to abolish it, and to institute new Government, laying its foundation on such principles and organizing its powers in such form, as to them shall seem most likely to effect their Safety and Happiness. Prudence, indeed, will dictate that Governments long established should not be changed for light and transient causes; and accordingly all experience hath shewn that mankind are more disposed to suffer, while evils are sufferable, than to right themselves by abolishing the forms to which they are accustomed. But when a long train of abuses and usurpations, pursuing invariably the same Object evinces a design to reduce them under absolute Despotism, it is their right, it is their duty, to throw off such Government, and to provide new Guards for their future security. Such has been the patient sufferance of these Colonies; and such is now the necessity which constrains them to alter their former Systems of Government. The history of the present King of Great Britain is a history of repeated injuries and usurpations, all having in direct object the establishment of an absolute Tyranny over these States. To prove this, let Facts be submitted to a candid world.

He has refused his Assent to Laws, the most wholesome and necessary for the public good.

He has forbidden his Government to pass laws of immediate and pressing importance, unless suspended in their operation till his Assent should be obtained; and when so suspended, he has utterly neglected to attend to them.

He has refused to pass other Laws for the accommodation of large districts of people, unless those people would relinquish the right of Representation in the Legislature, a right inestimable to them and formidable to tyrants only.

He has called together legislative bodies at places unusual, uncomfortable, and distant from the depository of their Public Records, for the sole purpose of fatiguing them into compliance with his measures.

He has dissolved Representative Houses repeatedly, for opposing with manly firmness his invasions on the rights of the people.

He has refused for a long time, after such dissolutions, to cause others to be elected; whereby the Legislative Powers, incapable of Annihilation, have returned to the People at large for their exercise; the State remaining in the mean time exposed to all the dangers of invasion from without, and convulsions within.

He has endeavored to prevent the population of these States; for that purpose obstructing the Laws for Naturalization of Foreigners; refusing to pass others to encourage their migration hither, and raising the conditions of new Appropriations of Lands.

He has obstructed the Administration of Justice, by refusing his Assent to Laws for establishing Judiciary Powers.

He has made Judges dependent on his Will alone, for the tenure of their offices, and the amount and payment of their salaries.

He has erected a multitude of New Offices, and sent hither swarms of Officers to harass our people, and eat out their substance.

He has kept among us, in times of peace, Standing Armies without the Consent of our legislatures.

He has affected to render the Military independent of and superior to the Civil Power.

He has combined with others to subject us to a jurisdiction foreign to our constitution, and unacknowledged by our laws; giving his Assent to their Acts of pretended Legislation: For quartering large bodies of armed troops among us: For protecting them, by a mock Trial, from punishment for any Murders which they should commit on the Inhabitants of these States: For cutting off our Trade with all parts of the world: For imposing Taxes on us without our Consent: For depriving us in many cases, of the benefits of Trial by Jury; For transporting us beyond Seas to be tried for pretended offenses: for abolishing the free System of English Laws in a neighboring Province, establishing therein an Arbitrary government, and enlarging its Boundaries so as to render it at once an example and fit instrument for introducing the same absolute rule into these Colonies: For taking away our Charters, abolishing our most valuable Laws and altering fundamentally the Forms of our Governments: For suspending our own Legislatures, and declaring themselves invested with power to legislate for us in all cases whatsoever.

He has abdicated Government here, by declaring us out of his Protection and waging War against us.

He has plundered our seas, ravaged our Coasts, burnt our towns, and destroyed the lives of our people.

He is at this time transporting large Armies of foreign Mercenaries to complete the works of death, desolation and tyranny, already begun with circumstances of Cruelty & Perfidy scarcely paralleled in the most barbarous ages, and totally unworthy of the Head of a civilized nation.

He has constrained our fellow Citizens taken Captive on the high Seas to bear Arms against their Country, to become the executioners of their friends and Brethren, or to fall themselves by their Hands.

He has excited domestic insurrections amongst us, and has endeavored to bring on the inhabitants of our frontiers, the merciless Indian Savages, whose known rule of warfare, is an undistinguished destruction of all ages, sexes, and conditions.

In every stage of these Oppressions We have Petitioned for Redress in the most humble terms: Our repeated Petitions have been answered only by repeated injury. A Prince, whose character is thus marked by every act which may define a Tyrant, is unfit to be the ruler of a free people.

Nor have We been wanting in attention to our British brethren. We have warned them from time to time of attempts by their legislature to extend an unwarrantable jurisdiction over us. We have reminded them of the circumstances of our emigration and settlement here. We have appealed to their native justice and magnanimity, and we have conjured them by the ties of our common kindred to disavow these usurpations, which would inevitably interrupt our connections and correspondence. They too have been deaf to the voice of justice and of consaguinity. We must, therefore, acquiesce in the necessity, which denounces our Separation, and hold them, as we hold the rest of mankind, Enemies in War, in Peace Friends.

We, THEREFORE the Representatives of the UNITED STATES OF AMERICA, in General Congress, Assembled, appealing to the Supreme Judge of the world for the rectitude of our intentions, do, in the Name, and by Authority of the good People of these Colonies, solemnly publish and declare, That these United Colonies are, and of Right ought to be FREE AND INDEPENDENT STATES; that they are Absolved from all Allegiance to the British Crown, and that all political connection between them and the State of Great Britain, is and ought to be totally dissolved; and that as Free and Independent States, they have full Power to levy War, conclude Peace, contract Alliances, establish Commerce, and to do all other Acts and Things which Independent States may of right do. And for the support of this Declaration, with a firm reliance on the protection of Divine Providence, we mutually pledge to each other our Lives, our Fortunes, and our sacred Honor.

1776

Robert F. Kennedy
1925–1968

Robert F. Kennedy was running for president when he gave this speech in 1968. All campaigns are contentious, but in 1968 the United States was in extraordinary turmoil. President Lyndon Johnson, who ascended to that office when Robert's brother, John Kennedy, was assassinated, withdrew from the race because Eugene McCarthy, who vowed to remove American troops from Vietnam, nearly defeated him in the New Hampshire Democratic primary. Johnson was further discouraged when Robert Kennedy announced that he would seek the Democratic nomination. Also joining the race was George Wallace, governor of Mississippi, who, running on a platform that advocated white supremacy, was popular in the South. Whoever was elected would have much to deal with. Civil rights for African Americans, made law by key victories in Congress, were being imposed upon reluctant, sometimes militant Southern whites. Vietnam War protesters more and more defiantly opposed American foreign policy. College campuses were torn apart. Then, early in the primary season, Martin Luther King Jr. was assassinated in Memphis, threatening to provoke yet further conflict. Kennedy was scheduled to give a speech in a poor, African American section of Indianapolis when he learned that King was murdered. Rather than cancel the event, he gave this impromptu speech to a crowd of people who had not yet heard about the assassination. This speech is generally praised for the ethos Kennedy displays, and that ethos surely contributed to his victory, two months later, in the California primary. It looked like he was well on the way to being nominated by the Democratic party, but within hours of his California victory, Kennedy himself was assassinated. That summer, at one of the most violent political conventions in American history, the Democrats nominated Hubert Humphrey, who lost the presidential election to Richard Nixon.

On the Death of the Reverend Dr. Martin Luther King, Jr.

I have bad news for you, for all of our fellow citizens, and people who love peace all over the world, and that is that Martin Luther King was shot and killed tonight.

Martin Luther King dedicated his life to love and to justice for his fellow human beings, and he died because of that effort.

In this difficult day, in this difficult time for the United States, it is perhaps well to ask what kind of a nation we are and what direction we want to move in. For those of you who are black—considering the evidence there evidently is that there were white people who were responsible—you can be filled with bitterness, with hatred, and a desire for revenge. We can move in that direction as a country, in great polarization—black people amongst black, white people amongst white, filled with hatred toward one another.

Or we can make an effort, as Martin Luther King did, to understand and to comprehend, and to replace that violence, that stain of bloodshed that has spread across our land, with an effort to understand with compassion and love.

For those of you who are black and are tempted to be filled with hatred and distrust at the injustice of such an act, against all white people, I can only say that I feel in my own heart the same kind of feeling. I had a member of my family killed, but he was killed by a white man. But we have to make an effort in the United States, we have to make an effort to understand, to go beyond these rather difficult times.

My favorite poet was Aeschylus. He wrote: "In our sleep, pain which cannot forget falls drop by drop upon the heart until, in our own despair, against our will, comes wisdom through the awful grace of God."

What we need in the United States is not division; what we need in the United States is not hatred; what we need in the United States is not violence or lawlessness; but love and wisdom, and compassion toward one another, and a feeling of justice toward those who still suffer within our country, whether they be white or they be black.

So I shall ask you tonight to return home, to say a prayer for the family of Martin Luther King, that's true, but more importantly to say a prayer for our own country, which all of us love—a prayer for understanding and that compassion of which I spoke.

We can do well in this country. We will have difficult times; we've had difficult times in the past; we will have difficult times in the future. It is not the end of violence; it is not the end of lawlessness; it is not the end of disorder.

But the vast majority of white people and the vast majority of black people in this country want to live together, want to improve the quality of our life, and want justice for all human beings who abide in our land.

Let us dedicate ourselves to what the Greeks wrote so many years ago: to tame the savageness of man and make gentle the life of this world.

Let us dedicate ourselves to that, and say a prayer for our country and for our people.

1968

Martin Luther King Jr.
1929–1968

> *In the early days of 1963, new orders from the federal courts were about to outlaw racial segregation in Alabama's schools and colleges. Local officials, including Commissioner of Public Safety Eugene "Bull" Connor and Governor George Wallace, publicly threatened to break these laws. On January 17, 1963, eleven white clergymen criticized Connor and Wallace in a letter to the* Birmingham News. *Connor's subsequent defeat in the mayoral election seemed to promise some lessening of the city's systematic oppression of blacks, at least to moderate whites like these ministers. Nevertheless, on April 3, 1963, black men and women, impatient for equality, opened a campaign to desegregate businesses in downtown Birmingham. For a week protestors openly defied segregation laws and, as a consequence, filled Bull Connor's jail cells beyond capacity. When the state courts of Alabama issued an injunction against such protests, King decided to defy the law and suffer the consequences.*

On Good Friday, he and about fifty other blacks marched in the streets and were summarily arrested. Connor put King in solitary confinement and near-total darkness for three days, and only pressure from the U.S. attorney general, Robert Kennedy, softened the conditions of his imprisonment. (It would be eight days before bail money, raised by the singer Harry Belafonte, secured his release.) On the day King was arrested, eight of the eleven white clergymen— Catholic, Episcopal, Presbyterian, Baptist, Methodist, and Jewish— published a second letter in the Birmingham News, *this one criticizing Dr. King. While ostensibly addressed to this group, King's response to their letter, composed on slips of paper sneaked into his cell by black jailers, was really designed to address a national audience. A million copies of his "Letter from Birmingham Jail" were distributed in churches throughout the country, and published in various newspapers and magazines, including the* New York Post *and* Atlantic Monthly. *By inspiring weary, long-suffering blacks and motivating sympathetic yet sluggish whites, this essay became, perhaps, the most influential document of the civil rights era.*

Letter from Birmingham Jail

My Dear Fellow Clergymen:

While confined here in the Birmingham city jail, I came across your recent statement calling my present activities "unwise and untimely." Seldom do I pause to answer criticism of my work and ideas. If I sought to answer all the criticisms that cross my desk, my secretaries would have little time for anything other than such correspondence in the course of the day, and I would have no time for constructive work. But since I feel that you are men of genuine good will and that your criticisms are sincerely set forth, I want to try to answer your statement in what I hope will be patient and reasonable terms.

I think I should indicate why I am here in Birmingham, since you have been influenced by the view which argues against "outsiders coming in." I have the honor of serving as president of the Southern Christian Leadership Conference, an organization operating in every southern state, with headquarters in Atlanta, Georgia.

We have some eighty-five affiliated organizations across the South, and one of them is the Alabama Christian Movement for Human Rights. Frequently we share staff, educational, and financial resources with our affiliates. Several months ago the affiliate here in Birmingham asked us to be on call to engage in a nonviolent direct-action program if such were deemed necessary. We readily consented, and when the hour came we lived up to our promise. So I, along with several members of my staff, am here because I was invited here. I am here because I have organizational ties here.

But more basically, I am in Birmingham because injustice is here. Just as the prophets of the eighth century B.C. left their villages and carried their "thus saith the Lord" far beyond the boundaries of their home towns, and just as the Apostle Paul left his village of Tarsus and carried the gospel of Jesus Christ to the far corners of the Greco-Roman world, so am I compelled to carry the gospel of freedom beyond my own home town. Like Paul, I must constantly respond to the Macedonian call for aid.

Moreover, I am cognizant of the interrelatedness of all communities and states. I cannot sit idly by in Atlanta and not be concerned about what happens in Birmingham. Injustice anywhere is a threat to justice everywhere. We are caught in an inescapable network of mutuality, tied in a single garment of destiny. Whatever affects one directly, affects all indirectly. Never again can we afford to live with the narrow, provincial "outside agitator" idea. Anyone who lives inside the United States can never be considered an outsider anywhere within its bounds.

You deplore the demonstrations taking place in Birmingham. But your statement, I am sorry to say, fails to express a similar concern for the conditions that brought about the demonstrations. I am sure that none of you would want to rest content with the superficial kind of social analysis that deals merely with effects and does not grapple with underlying causes. It is unfortunate that demonstrations are taking place in Birmingham, but it is even more unfortunate that the city's white power structure left the Negro community with no alternative.

In any nonviolent campaign there are four basic steps: collection of the facts to determine whether injustices exist; negotiation; self-purification; and direct action. We have gone through all these steps in Birmingham. There can be no gainsaying the fact that racial injustice engulfs this community. Birmingham is probably the most thoroughly segregated city in the United States. Its ugly record of brutality is widely known. Negroes have experienced grossly unjust treatment in the courts. There have been more unsolved bombings of Negro homes and churches in Birmingham than in any other city in the nation. These are the hard, brutal facts of the case. On the basis of these conditions, Negro leaders sought to negotiate with the city fathers. But the latter consistently refused to engage in good-faith negotiation.

Then, last September, came the opportunity to talk with leaders of Birmingham's economic community. In the course of the negotiations, certain promises were made by the merchants—for example, to remove the stores' humiliating racial signs. On the basis of these promises, the Reverend Fred Shuttlesworth and the leaders of the Alabama Christian Movement for Human Rights agreed to a moratorium on all demonstrations. As the weeks and months went by, we realized that we were the victims of a broken promise. A few signs, briefly removed, returned; the others remained.

As in so many past experiences, our hopes had been blasted, and the shadow of deep disappointment settled upon us. We had no alternative except to prepare for direct action, whereby we would present our very bodies as a means of laying our case before the conscience of the local and the national community. Mindful of the difficulties involved, we decided to undertake a process of self-purification. We began a series of workshops on nonviolence, and we repeatedly asked ourselves: "Are you able to accept blows without retaliating?" "Are you able to endure the ordeal of jail?" We decided to schedule our direct-action program for the Easter season, realizing that except for Christmas, this is the main shopping period of the year. Knowing that a strong economic-withdrawal program would be the by-product of direct action, we felt that this would be the best time to bring pressure to bear on the merchants for the needed change.

Then it occurred to us that Birmingham's mayoral election was coming up in March, and we speedily decided to postpone action until after election day. When we discovered that the Commissioner of Public Safety, Eugene "Bull" Connor, had piled up enough votes to be in the run-off, we decided again to postpone action until the day after the run-off so that the demonstrations could not be used to cloud the issues. Like many others, we wanted to see Mr. Connor defeated, and to this end we endured postponement after postponement. Having aided in this community need, we felt that our direct-action program could be delayed no longer.

You may well ask, "Why direct action? Why sit-ins, marches, and so forth? Isn't negotiation a better path?" You are quite right in calling for negotiation. Indeed, this is the very purpose of direct action. Nonviolent direct action seeks to create such a crisis and foster such a tension that a community which has constantly refused to negotiate is forced to confront the issue. It seeks so to dramatize the issue that it can no longer be ignored. My citing the creation of tension as part of the work of the nonviolent-resister may sound rather shocking. But I must confess that I am not afraid of the word "tension." I have earnestly opposed violent tension, but there is a type of constructive, nonviolent tension which is necessary for growth. Just as Socrates felt that it was necessary to create a tension in the mind so that individuals could rise from the bondage of myths and half-truths to the unfettered realm of creative analysis and objective appraisal, so must we see the need for nonviolent gadflies to create the kind of tension in society that will help men rise from the dark depths of prejudice and racism to the majestic heights of understanding and brotherhood.

The purpose of our direct-action program is to create a situation so crisis-packed that it will inevitably open the door to negotiation. I therefore concur with you in your call for negotiation. Too long has our beloved Southland been bogged down in a tragic effort to live in monologue rather than dialogue.

One of the basic points in your statement is that the action that I and my associates have taken in Birmingham is untimely. Some have asked: "Why didn't you give the new city administration time to act?" The only answer that I can give to this query is that the new Birmingham administration must be prodded about as much as the outgoing one, before it will act. We are sadly mistaken if we feel that the election of Albert Boutwell as mayor will bring the millennium to Birmingham. While Mr. Boutwell is a much more gentle person than Mr. Connor, they are both segregationists, dedicated to maintenance of the status quo. I have hoped that Mr. Boutwell will be reasonable enough to see the futility of massive resistance to deseg-regation. But he will not see this without pressure from devotees of civil rights. My friends, I must say to you that we have not made a single gain in civil rights without determined legal and nonviolent pressure. Lamentably, it is an historical fact that privileged groups seldom give up their privileges voluntarily. Individuals may see the moral light and voluntarily give up their unjust posture; but, as Reinhold Niebuhr[1] has reminded us, groups tend to be more immoral than individuals.

We know through painful experience that freedom is never vol-untarily given by the oppressor; it must be demanded by the op-pressed. Frankly, I have yet to engage in a direct-action campaign that was "well timed" in the view of those who have not suffered unduly from the disease of segregation. For years now I have heard the word "Wait!" It rings in the ear of every Negro with piercing fa-miliarity. This "Wait" has almost always meant "Never." We must come to see, with one of our distinguished jurists, that "justice too long delayed is justice denied."

We have waited for more than 340 years for our constitutional and God-given rights. The nations of Asia and Africa are moving with jetlike speed toward gaining political independence, but we still creep at horse-and-buggy pace toward gaining a cup of coffee at a lunch counter. Perhaps it is easy for those who have never felt the stinging darts of segregation to say, "Wait." But when you have seen vicious mobs lynch your mothers and fathers at will and drown your sisters and brothers at whim; when you have seen hate-filled policemen curse, kick, and even kill your black brothers and sisters; when you see the vast majority of your twenty million Negro broth-ers smothering in an airtight cage of poverty in the midst of an af-fluent society; when you suddenly find your tongue twisted and your speech stammering as you seek to explain to your six-year-old daughter why she can't go to the public amusement park that has just been advertised on television, and see tears welling up in her eyes when she is told that Funtown is closed to colored children, and see ominous clouds of inferiority beginning to form in her little mental sky, and see her beginning to distort her personality by de-

1. American Protestant theologian (1892–1971).

veloping an unconscious bitterness toward white people; when you have to concoct an answer for a five-year-old son who is asking, "Daddy, why do white people treat colored people so mean?"; when you take a cross-country drive and find it necessary to sleep night after night in the uncomfortable corners of your automobile because no motel will accept you; when you are humiliated day in and day out by nagging signs reading "white" and "colored"; when your first name becomes "nigger," your middle name becomes "boy" (however old you are) and your last name becomes "John," and your wife and mother are never given the respected title "Mrs."; when you are harried by day and haunted by night by the fact that you are a Negro, living constantly at tiptoe stance, never quite knowing what to expect next, and are plagued with inner fears and outer resentments; when you are forever fighting a degenerating sense of "nobodiness"—then you will understand why we find it difficult to wait. There comes a time when the cup of endurance runs over, and men are no longer willing to be plunged into the abyss of despair. I hope, sirs, you can understand our legitimate and unavoidable impatience.

You express a great deal of anxiety over our willingness to break laws. This is certainly a legitimate concern. Since we so diligently urge people to obey the Supreme Court's decision of 1954 outlawing segregation in the public schools, at first glance it may seem rather paradoxical for us consciously to break laws. One may well ask: "How can you advocate breaking some laws and obeying others?" The answer lies in the fact that there are two types of laws: just and unjust. I would be the first to advocate obeying just laws. One has not only a legal but a moral responsibility to obey just laws. Conversely, one has a moral responsibility to disobey unjust laws. I would agree with St. Augustine that "an unjust law is no law at all."[2]

Now, what is the difference between the two? How does one determine whether a law is just or unjust? A just law is a man-made code that squares with the moral law or the law of God. An unjust law is a code that is out of harmony with the moral law. To put it in the terms of St. Thomas Aquinas:[3] An unjust law is a human law

---

2. Early Christian theologian (354–430); the quotation comes from his *City of God.*

3. Medieval Christian philosopher and theologian (1224–1274).

that is not rooted in eternal law and natural law. Any law that uplifts human personality is just. Any law that degrades human personality is unjust. All segregation statutes are unjust because segregation distorts the soul and damages the personality. It gives the segregator a false sense of superiority and the segregated a false sense of inferiority. Segregation, to use the terminology of the Jewish philosopher Martin Buber,[4] substitutes an "I-it" relationship for an "I-thou" relationship and ends up relegating persons to the status of things. Hence segregation is not only politically, economically, and sociologically unsound, it is morally wrong and sinful. Paul Tillich[5] has said that sin is separation. Is not segregation an existential expression of man's tragic separation, his awful estrangement, his terrible sinfulness? Thus it is that I can urge men to obey the 1954 decision of the Supreme Court, for it is morally right; and I can urge them to disobey segregation ordinances, for they are morally wrong.

Let us consider a more concrete example of just and unjust laws. An unjust law is a code that a numerical or power majority group compels a minority group to obey but does not make binding on itself. This is *difference* made legal. By the same token, a just law is a code that a majority compels a minority to follow and that it is willing to follow itself. This is *sameness* made legal.

Let me give another explanation. A law is unjust if it is inflicted on a minority that, as a result of being denied the right to vote, had no part in enacting or devising the law. Who can say that the legislature of Alabama which set up that state's segregation laws was democratically elected? Throughout Alabama all sorts of devious methods are used to prevent Negroes from becoming registered voters, and there are some counties in which, even though Negroes constitute a majority of the population, not a single Negro is registered. Can any law enacted under such circumstances be considered democratically structured?

Sometimes a law is just on its face and unjust in its application. For instance, I have been arrested on a charge of parading without a permit. Now, there is nothing wrong in having an ordinance which

---

4. Austrian-born Israeli philosopher (1878–1965).

5. German-born American Protestant theologian (1886–1965); see his *History of Christian Thought* (1968).

requires a permit for a parade. But such an ordinance becomes unjust when it is used to maintain segregation and to deny citizens the First-Amendment privilege of peaceful assembly and protest.

I hope you are able to see the distinction I am trying to point out. In no sense do I advocate evading or defying the law, as would the rabid segregationist. That would lead to anarchy. One who breaks an unjust law must do so openly, lovingly, and with a willingness to accept the penalty. I submit that an individual who breaks a law that conscience tells him is unjust, and who willingly accepts the penalty of imprisonment in order to arouse the conscience of the community over its injustice, is in reality expressing the highest respect for law.

Of course, there is nothing new about this kind of civil disobedience. It was evidenced sublimely in the refusal of Shadrach, Meshach, and Abednego to obey the laws of Nebuchadnezzar,[6] on the ground that a higher moral law was at stake. It was practiced superbly by the early Christians, who were willing to face hungry lions and the excruciating pain of chopping blocks rather than submit to certain unjust laws of the Roman Empire. To a degree, academic freedom is a reality today because Socrates[7] practiced civil disobedience. In our own nation, the Boston Tea Party represented a massive act of civil disobedience.

We should never forget that everything Adolf Hitler did in Germany was "legal" and everything the Hungarian freedom fighters[8] did in Hungary was "illegal." It was "illegal" to aid and comfort a Jew in Hitler's Germany. Even so, I am sure that, had I lived in Germany at the time, I would have aided and comforted my Jewish brothers. If today I lived in a Communist country where certain principles dear to the Christian faith are suppressed, I would openly advocate disobeying that country's anti-religious laws.

---

6. See Daniel 3. Nebuchadnezzar, the king of Babylonia (c. 605–562 B.C.E.), commanded his people to worship a golden idol. When Shadrach, Meshach, and Abednego refused, they were thrown into a furnace but escaped unscathed. So Nebuchadnezzar forbade blasphemy against their god—Yahweh, the god of the Jews.

7. Ancient Greek philosopher who was tried for impiety and for corrupting Athenian youth through his skeptical, questioning teaching method; having refused to denounce his teachings, he was condemned to death and executed. See Plato's "Crito."

8. Anti-Communists whose 1956 revolution was quickly put down by the Soviet army.

I must make two honest confessions to you, my Christian and Jewish brothers. First, I must confess that over the past few years I have been gravely disappointed with the white moderate. I have almost reached the regrettable conclusion that the Negro's great stumbling block in his stride toward freedom is not the White Citizen's Counciler[9] or the Ku Klux Klanner, but the white moderate, who is more devoted to "order" than to justice; who prefers a negative peace which is the absence of tension to a positive peace which is the presence of justice; who constantly says, "I agree with you in the goal you seek, but I cannot agree with your methods of direct action"; who paternalistically believes he can set the timetable for another man's freedom; who lives by a mythical concept of time and who constantly advises the Negro to wait for a "more convenient season."[1] Shallow understanding from people of good will is more frustrating than absolute misunderstanding from people of ill will. Lukewarm acceptance is much more bewildering than outright rejection.

I had hoped that the white moderate would understand that law and order exist for the purpose of establishing justice and that when they fail in this purpose they become the dangerously structured dams that block the flow of social progress. I had hoped that the white moderate would understand that the present tension in the South is a necessary phase of the transition from an obnoxious negative peace, in which the Negro passively accepted his unjust plight, to a substantive and positive peace, in which all men will respect the dignity and worth of human personality. Actually, we who engage in nonviolent direct action are not the creators of tension. We merely bring to the surface the hidden tension that is already alive. We bring it out in the open, where it can be seen and dealt with. Like a boil that can never be cured so long as it is covered up but must be opened with all its ugliness to the natural medicines of air and light, injustice must be exposed, with all the tension its exposure creates, to the light of human conscience and the air of national opinion, before it can be cured.

9. A group formed in Mississippi to maintain segregation following the Supreme Court's decision in *Brown v. Board of Education of Topeka, Kansas* (1954/55).
1. Acts 24.25.

In your statement you assert that our actions, even though peaceful, must be condemned because they precipitate violence. But is this a logical assertion? Isn't this like condemning a robbed man because his possession of money precipitated the evil act of robbery? Isn't this like condemning Socrates because his unswerving commitment to truth and his philosophical inquiries precipitated the act by the misguided populace in which they made him drink hemlock? Isn't this like condemning Jesus because his unique God-consciousness and never-ceasing devotion to God's will precipitated the evil act of crucifixion? We must come to see that, as the federal courts have consistently affirmed, it is wrong to urge an individual to cease his efforts to gain his basic constitutional rights because the quest may precipitate violence. Society must protect the robbed and punish the robber.

I had also hoped that the white moderate would reject the myth concerning time in relation to the struggle for freedom. I have just received a letter from a white brother in Texas. He writes: "All Christians know that the colored people will receive equal rights eventually, but it is possible that you are in too great a religious hurry. It has taken Christianity almost two thousand years to accomplish what it has. The teachings of Christ take time to come to earth." Such an attitude stems from a tragic misconception of time, from the strangely irrational notion that there is something in the very flow of time that will inevitably cure all ills. Actually, time itself is neutral; it can be used either destructively or constructively. More and more I feel that the people of ill will have used time much more effectively than have the people of good will. We will have to repent in this generation not merely for the hateful words and actions of the bad people, but for the appalling silence of the good people. Human progress never rolls in on wheels of inevitability; it comes through the tireless efforts of men willing to be co-workers with God, and without this hard work, time itself becomes an ally of the forces of social stagnation. We must use time creatively, in the knowledge that the time is always ripe to do right. Now is the time to make real the promise of democracy and transform our pending national elegy into a creative psalm of brotherhood. Now is the time to lift our national policy from the quicksand of racial injustice to the solid rock of human dignity.

You speak of our activity in Birmingham as extreme. At first I was rather disappointed that fellow clergymen would see my nonviolent efforts as those of an extremist. I began thinking about the fact that I stand in the middle of two opposing forces in the Negro community. One is a force of complacency, made up in part of Negroes who, as a result of long years of oppression, are so drained of self-respect and a sense of "somebodiness" that they have adjusted to segregation; and in part of a few middle-class Negroes who, because of a degree of academic and economic security and because in some ways they profit by segregation, have become insensitive to the problems of the masses. The other force is one of bitterness and hatred, and it comes perilously close to advocating violence. It is expressed in the various black nationalist groups that are springing up across the nation, the largest and best-known being Elijah Muhammad's Muslim movement.[2] Nourished by the Negro's frustration over the continued existence of racial discrimination, this movement is made up of people who have lost faith in America, who have absolutely repudiated Christianity, and who have concluded that the white man is an incorrigible "devil."

I have tried to stand between these two forces, saying that we need emulate neither the "do-nothingism" of the complacent nor the hatred and despair of the black nationalist. For there is the more excellent way of love and nonviolent protest. I am grateful to God that, through the influence of the Negro church, the way of nonviolence became an integral part of our struggle.

If this philosophy had not emerged, by now many streets of the South would, I am convinced, be flowing with blood. And I am further convinced that if our white brothers dismiss as "rabblerousers" and "outside agitators" those of us who employ nonviolent direct action, and if they refuse to support our nonviolent efforts, millions of Negroes will, out of frustration and despair, seek solace and security in black-nationalist ideologies—a development that would inevitably lead to a frightening racial nightmare.

Oppressed people cannot remain oppressed forever. The yearning for freedom eventually manifests itself, and that is what has happened to the American Negro. Something within has reminded him

---

2. Elijah Muhammad (1897–1975), leader of the Nation of Islam.

of his birthright of freedom, and something without has reminded him that it can be gained. Consciously or unconsciously, he has been caught up by the *Zeitgeist*,[3] and with his black brothers of Africa and his brown and yellow brothers of Asia, South America, and the Caribbean, the United States Negro is moving with a sense of great urgency toward the promised land of racial justice. If one recognizes this vital urge that has engulfed the Negro community, one should readily understand why public demonstrations are taking place. The Negro has many pent-up resentments and latent frustrations, and he must release them. So let him march; let him make prayer pilgrimages to the city hall; let him go on freedom rides—and try to understand why he must do so. If his repressed emotions are not released in nonviolent ways, they will seek expression through violence; this is not a threat but a fact of history. So I have not said to my people, "Get rid of your discontent." Rather, I have tried to say that this normal and healthy discontent can be channeled into the creative outlet of nonviolent direct action. And now this approach is being termed extremist.

But though I was initially disappointed at being categorized as an extremist, as I continued to think about the matter I gradually gained a measure of satisfaction from the label. Was not Jesus an extremist for love: "Love your enemies, bless them that curse you, do good to them that hate you, and pray for them which despitefully use you, and persecute you."[4] Was not Amos an extremist for justice: "Let justice roll down like waters and righteousness like an ever-flowing stream."[5] Was not Paul an extremist for the Christian gospel: "I bear in my body the marks of the Lord Jesus."[6] Was not Martin Luther an extremist: "Here I stand; I cannot do otherwise, so help me God."[7] And John Bunyan: "I will stay in jail to the end of my days before I make a butchery of my conscience."[8] And Abraham Lincoln: "This nation cannot survive half slave and half

3. The spirit of the times (German).

4. Matthew 5.44.

5. Amos 5.24; Amos was an Old Testament prophet.

6. Galatians 6.17; Paul, a great missionary of the early Christian church, often suffered for his teaching. He wrote some of his own biblical letters from prison.

7. German theologian and leader of the Reformation (1483–1546); the quote is from Luther's defense of his teaching at the Trial of Worms, 1521.

8. English preacher (1628–1688) and author of *Pilgrim's Progress* (1678); this is a paraphrase of a passage in his *Confession of My Faith, and a Reason of My Practice.*

free."[9] And Thomas Jefferson: "We hold these truths to be self-evident, that all men are created equal. . . ." So the question is not whether we will be extremists, but what kind of extremists we will be. Will we be extremists for hate or for love? Will we be extremists for the preservation of injustice or for the extension of justice? In that dramatic scene on Calvary's hill three men were crucified. We must never forget that all three were crucified for the same crime—the crime of extremism. Two were extremists for immorality, and thus fell below their environment. The other, Jesus Christ, was an extremist for love, truth, and goodness, and thereby rose above his environment. Perhaps the South, the nation, and the world are in dire need of creative extremists.

I had hoped that the white moderate would see this need. Perhaps I was too optimistic; perhaps I expected too much. I suppose I should have realized that few members of the oppressor race can understand the deep groans and passionate yearnings of the oppressed race, and still fewer have the vision to see that injustice must be rooted out by strong, persistent, and determined action. I am thankful, however, that some of our white brothers in the South have grasped the meaning of this social revolution and committed themselves to it. They are still all too few in quantity, but they are big in quality. Some—such as Ralph McGill, Lillian Smith, Harry Golden, James McBridge Dabbs, Ann Braden, and Sarah Patton Boyle—have written about our struggle in eloquent and prophetic terms. Others have marched with us down nameless streets of the South. They have languished in filthy, roach-infested jails, suffering the abuse and brutality of policemen who view them as "dirty - nigger-lovers." Unlike so many of their moderate brothers and sisters, they have recognized the urgency of the moment and sensed the need for powerful "action" antidotes to combat the disease of segregation.

Let me take note of my other major disappointment. I have been so greatly disappointed with the white church and its leadership. Of course, there are some notable exceptions. I am not unmindful of the fact that each of you has taken some significant stands on this is-

9. From a speech given June 16, 1858; again, the quotation is slightly inaccurate.

sue. I commend you, Reverend Stallings,[1] for your Christian stand on this past Sunday, in welcoming Negroes to your worship service on a nonsegregated basis. I commend the Catholic leaders of this state for integrating Spring Hill College several years ago.

But despite these notable exceptions, I must honestly reiterate that I have been disappointed with the church. I do not say this as one of those negative critics who can always find something wrong with the church. I say this as a minister of the gospel, who loves the church; who was nurtured in its bosom; who has been sustained by its spiritual blessings and who will remain true to it as long as the cord of life shall lengthen.

When I was suddenly catapulted into the leadership of the bus protest in Montgomery, Alabama, a few years ago,[2] I felt we would be supported by the white church. I felt that the white ministers, priests, and rabbis of the South would be among our strongest allies. Instead, some have been outright opponents, refusing to understand the freedom movement and misrepresenting its leaders; all too many others have been more cautious than courageous and have remained silent behind the anesthetizing security of stained-glass windows.

In spite of my shattered dreams, I came to Birmingham with the hope that the white religious leadership of this community would see the justice of our cause and, with deep moral concern, would serve as the channel through which our just grievances could reach the power structure. I had hoped that each of you would understand. But again I have been disappointed.

I have heard numerous southern religious leaders admonish their worshipers to comply with a desegregation decision because it is the law, but I have longed to hear white ministers declare: "Follow this decree because integration is morally right and because the Negro is your brother." In the midst of blatant injustices inflicted upon the Negro, I have watched white churchmen stand on the sideline and mouth pious irrelevancies and sanctimonious trivialities. In the midst of a mighty struggle to rid our nation of racial and economic

---

1. One of the eight clergymen who criticized King's actions in their letter to the *Birmingham News.*

2. Inspired by the refusal of Rosa Parks (1913–2005) to move to the back of a bus in December 1955.

injustice, I have heard many ministers say: "Those are social issues, with which the gospel has no real concern." And I have watched many churches commit themselves to a completely otherworldly religion which makes a strange, un-Biblical distinction between body and soul, between the sacred and the secular.

I have traveled the length and breadth of Alabama, Mississippi, and all the other southern states. On sweltering summer days and crisp autumn mornings I have looked at the South's beautiful churches with their lofty spires pointing heavenward. I have beheld the impressive outlines of her massive religious-education buildings. Over and over I have found myself asking: "What kind of people worship here? Who is their God? Where were their voices when the lips of Governor Barnett[3] dripped with words of interposition and nullification? Where were they when Governor Wallace gave a clarion call for defiance and hatred? Where were their voices of support when bruised and weary Negro men and women decided to rise from the dark dungeons of complacency to the bright hills of creative protest?"

Yes, these questions are still in my mind. In deep disappointment I have wept over the laxity of the church. But be assured that my tears have been tears of love. There can be no deep disappointment where there is not deep love. Yes, I love the church. How could I do otherwise? I am in the rather unique position of being the son, the grandson, and the great-grandson of preachers. Yes, I see the church as the body of Christ. But, oh! How we have blemished and scarred that body through social neglect and through fear of being nonconformists.

There was a time when the church was very powerful—in the time when the early Christians rejoiced at being deemed worthy to suffer for what they believed. In those days the church was not merely a thermometer that recorded the ideas and principles of popular opinion; it was a thermostat that transformed the mores of society. Whenever the early Christians entered a town, the people in power became disturbed and immediately sought to convict the Christians for being "disturbers of the peace" and "outside agitators." But the Christians pressed on, in the conviction that they

---

3. Ross Barnett (1898–1988), governor of Mississippi who opposed the integration of the University of Mississippi.

were a colony of heaven,"[4] called to obey God rather than man. Small in number, they were big in commitment. They were too God-intoxicated to be "astronomically intimidated." By their effort and example they brought an end to such ancient evils as infanticide and gladiatorial contests.

Things are different now. So often the contemporary church is a weak, ineffectual voice with an uncertain sound. So often it is an archdefender of the status quo. Far from being disturbed by the presence of the church, the power structure of the average community is consoled by the church's silent—and often even vocal— sanction of things as they are.

But the judgment of God is upon the church as never before. If today's church does not recapture the sacrificial spirit of the early church, it will lose its authenticity, forfeit the loyalty of millions, and be dismissed as an irrelevant social club with no meaning for the twentieth century. Every day I meet young people whose disappointment with the church has turned into outright disgust.

Perhaps I have once again been too optimistic. Is organized religion too inextricably bound to the status quo to save our nation and the world? Perhaps I must turn my faith to the inner spiritual church, the church within the church, as the true *ekklesia*[5] and the hope of the world. But again I am thankful to God that some noble souls from the ranks of organized religion have broken loose from the paralyzing chains of conformity and joined us as active partners in the struggle for freedom. They have left their secure congregations and walked the streets of Albany, Georgia, with us. They have gone down the highways of the South on tortuous rides for freedom. Yes, they have gone to jail with us. Some have been dismissed from their churches, have lost the support of their bishops and fellow ministers. But they have acted in the faith that right defeated is stronger than evil triumphant. Their witness has been the spiritual salt that has preserved the true meaning of the gospel in these troubled times. They have carved a tunnel of hope through the dark mountain of disappointment.

I hope the church as a whole will meet the challenge of this deci-

4. Philippians 3.20.
5. Greek word for the early Christian church.

sive hour. But even if the church does not come to the aid of justice, I have no despair about the future. I have no fear about the outcome of our struggle in Birmingham, even if our motives are at present misunderstood. We will reach the goal of freedom in Birmingham and all over the nation, because the goal of America is freedom. Abused and scorned though we may be, our destiny is tied up with America's destiny. Before the pilgrims landed at Plymouth, we were here. Before the pen of Jefferson etched the majestic words of the Declaration of Independence across the pages of history, we were here. For more than two centuries our forebears labored in this country without wages; they made cotton king; they built the homes of their masters while suffering gross injustice and shameful humiliation—and yet out of a bottomless vitality they continued to thrive and develop. If the inexpressible cruelties of slavery could not stop us, the opposition we now face will surely fail. We will win our freedom because the sacred heritage of our nation and the eternal will of God are embodied in our echoing demands.

Before closing I feel impelled to mention one other point in your statement that has troubled me profoundly. You warmly commended the Birmingham police force for keeping "order" and "preventing violence." I doubt that you would have so warmly commended the police force if you had seen its dogs sinking their teeth into unarmed, nonviolent Negroes. I doubt that you would so quickly commend the policemen if you were to observe their ugly and inhumane treatment of Negroes here in the city jail; if you were to watch them push and curse old Negro women and young Negro girls; if you were to see them slap and kick old Negro men and young boys; if you were to observe them, as they did on two occasions, refuse to give us food because we wanted to sing our grace together. I cannot join you in your praise of the Birmingham police department.

It is true that the police have exercised a degree of discipline in handling the demonstrators. In this sense they have conducted themselves rather "non-violently" in public. But for what purpose? To preserve the evil system of segregation. Over the past few years I have consistently preached that nonviolence demands that the means we use must be as pure as the ends we seek. I have tried to make clear that it is wrong to use immoral means to attain moral ends. But now I must affirm that it is just as wrong, or perhaps even more so, to use moral means to preserve immoral ends. Perhaps Mr. Connor and his policemen have been rather nonviolent in public, as was Chief Pritchett[6] in Albany, Georgia, but they have used the moral means of nonviolence to maintain the immoral end of racial injustice. As T. S. Eliot has said, "The last temptation is the greatest treason: To do the right deed for the wrong reason."[7]

I wish you had commended the Negro sit-inners and demonstrators of Birmingham for their sublime courage, their willingness to suffer, and their amazing discipline in the midst of great provocation. One day the South will recognize its real heroes. They will be the James Merediths,[8] with the noble sense of purpose that enables them to face jeering and hostile mobs, and with the agonizing loneliness that characterizes the life of the pioneer. They will be old, oppressed, battered Negro women, symbolized in a seventy-two-year-old woman in Montgomery, Alabama, who rose up with a sense of dignity and with her people decided not to ride segregated buses, and who responded with ungrammatical profundity to one who inquired about her weariness: "My feets is tired, but my soul is at rest."[9] They will be the young high school and college students, the young ministers of the gospel and a host of their elders, courageously and nonviolently sitting in at lunch counters and willingly going to jail for conscience' sake. One day the South will know that when these disinherited children of God sat down at lunch counters, they were in reality standing up for what is best in the American dream and for the most sacred values in our Judaeo-Christian heritage, thereby bringing our nation back to those great wells of democracy which were dug deep by the founding fathers in their formulation of the Constitution and the Declaration of Independence.

Never before have I written so long a letter. I'm afraid it is much too long to take your precious time. I can assure you that it would have been much shorter if I had been writing from a comfortable

---

6. Chief of police who, in an effort to prevent violence, prosecuted anyone who violated segregation laws; he was a hero to those who valued peace over social justice.

7. American-born Modernist poet (1888–

1965); the quotation is from *Murder in the Cathedral* (1935).

8. Meredith was the first black to enroll at the University of Mississippi.

9. Mother Pollard, an elderly supporter of King.

desk, but what else can one do when he is alone in a narrow jail cell, other than write long letters, think long thoughts, and pray long prayers?

If I have said anything in this letter that overstates the truth and indicates an unreasonable impatience, I beg you to forgive me. If I have said anything that understates the truth and indicates my having a patience that allows me to settle for anything less than brotherhood, I beg God to forgive me.

I hope this letter finds you strong in the faith. I also hope that circumstances will soon make it possible for me to meet each of you, not as an integrationist or a civil-rights leader but as a fellow clergyman and a Christian brother. Let us all hope that the dark clouds of racial prejudice will soon pass away and the deep fog of misunderstanding will be lifted from our fear-drenched communities, and in some not too distant tomorrow the radiant stars of love and brotherhood will shine over our great nation with all their scintillating beauty.

> Yours for the cause of Peace and Brotherhood,
> Martin Luther King, Jr.

1963

Maxine Hong Kingston

b. 1940

> *"No Name Woman" is the first chapter in Kingston's award-winning book* The Woman Warrior *(1976), which deals with a girl's experience growing up in a Chinese American family. Because it is a mixture of autobiography, imaginative fiction, and even Chinese myth and folklore, critics have a hard time classifying Kingston's memoir. It is, perhaps, the least rhetorical piece in this collection: Certainly there is no overt persuasive agenda here. But Kingston does explore the problems of identity that confront all immigrants and, perhaps, everyone living in our multicultural society. It might be best to read "No Name Woman" as you would a short story. For example, examine the conflicting themes of individualism and community. Also consider point of view. Who can we trust? How much of the story is the narrator making up? Can we believe even the little bit of information that her mother gives her? Does the narrator honor or dishonor her aunt by publishing her story?*

No Name Woman

"You must not tell anyone," my mother said, "what I am about to tell you. In China your father had a sister who killed herself. She jumped into the family well. We say that your father has all brothers because it is as if she had never been born.

"In 1924 just a few days after our village celebrated seventeen hurry-up weddings—to make sure that every young man who went 'out on the road' would responsibly come home—your father and his brothers and your grandfather and his brothers and your aunt's new husband sailed for America, the Gold Mountain. It was your grandfather's last trip. Those lucky enough to get contracts waved goodbye from the decks. They fed and guarded the stowaways and helped them off in Cuba, New York, Bali, Hawaii. 'We'll meet in California next year,' they said. All of them sent money home.

"I remember looking at your aunt one day when she and I were dressing; I had not noticed before that she had such a protruding melon of a stomach. But I did not think, 'She's pregnant,' until she began to look like other pregnant women, her shirt pulling and the white tops of her black pants showing. She could not have been pregnant, you see, because her husband had been gone for years. No one said anything. We did not discuss it. In early summer she was ready to have the child, long after the time when it could have been possible.

"The village had also been counting. On the night the baby was to be born the villagers raided our house. Some were crying. Like a great saw, teeth strung with lights, files of people walked zigzag across our land, tearing the rice. Their lanterns doubled in the disturbed black water, which drained away through the broken bunds. As the villagers closed in, we could see that some of them, probably men and women we knew well, wore white masks. The people with long hair hung it over their faces. Women with short hair made it stand up on end. Some had tied white bands around their foreheads, arms, and legs.

"At first they threw mud and rocks at the house. Then they threw eggs and began slaughtering our stock. We could hear the animals scream their deaths—the roosters, the pigs, a last great roar from the ox. Familiar wild heads flared in our night windows; the villagers encircled us. Some of the faces stopped to peer at us, their eyes rushing like searchlights. The hands flattened against the panes, framed heads, and left red prints.

"The villagers broke in the front and the back doors at the same time, even though we had not locked the doors against them. Their knives dripped with the blood of our animals. They smeared blood on the doors and walls. One woman swung a chicken, whose throat she had slit, splattering blood in red arcs about her. We stood together in the middle of our house, in the family hall with the pictures and tables of the ancestors around us, and looked straight ahead.

"At that time the house had only two wings. When the men came back, we would build two more to enclose our courtyard and a third one to begin a second courtyard. The villagers pushed through both wings, even your grandparents' rooms, to find your aunt's, which was also mine until the men returned. From this room a new wing for one of the younger families would grow. They ripped up her clothes and shoes and broke her combs, grinding them underfoot. They tore her work from the loom. They scattered the cooking fire and rolled the new weaving in it. We could hear them in the kitchen breaking our bowls and banging the pots. They overturned the great waist-high earthenware jugs; duck eggs, pickled fruits, vegetables burst out and mixed in acrid torrents. The old woman from the next field swept a broom through the air and loosed the spirits-of-the-broom over our heads. 'Pig.' 'Ghost.' 'Pig,' they sobbed and scolded while they ruined our house.

"When they left, they took sugar and oranges to bless themselves. They cut pieces from the dead animals. Some of them took bowls that were not broken and clothes that were not torn. Afterward we swept up the rice and sewed it back up into sacks. But the smells from the spilled preserves lasted. Your aunt gave birth in the pigsty that night. The next morning when I went for the water, I found her and the baby plugging up the family well.

"Don't let your father know that I told you. He denies her. Now that you have started to menstruate, what happened to her could happen to you. Don't humiliate us. You wouldn't like to be forgotten as if you had never been born. The villagers are watchful."

Whenever she had to warn us about life, my mother told stories that ran like this one, a story to grow up on. She tested our strength to establish realities. Those in the emigrant generations who could not reassert brute survival died young and far from home. Those of us in the first American generations have had to figure out how the invisible world the emigrants built around our childhoods fits in solid America.

The emigrants confused the gods by diverting their curses, misleading them with crooked streets and false names. They must try to confuse their offspring as well, who, I suppose, threaten them in similar ways—always trying to get things straight, always trying to name the unspeakable. The Chinese I know hide their names; sojourners take new names when their lives change and guard their real names with silence.

Chinese-Americans, when you try to understand what things in you are Chinese, how do you separate what is peculiar to childhood, to poverty, insanities, one family, your mother who marked your growing with stories, from what is Chinese? What is Chinese tradition and what is the movies?

If I want to learn what clothes my aunt wore, whether flashy or ordinary, I would have to begin, "Remember Father's drowned-in-the-well sister?" I cannot ask that. My mother has told me once and for all the useful parts. She will add nothing unless powered by Necessity, a riverbank that guides her life. She plants vegetable gardens rather than lawns; she carries the odd-shaped tomatoes home from the fields and eats food left for the gods.

Whenever we did frivolous things, we used up energy; we flew high kites. We children came up off the ground over the melting cones our parents brought home from work and the American movie on New Year's Day—*Oh, You Beautiful Doll* with Betty Grable one year, and *She Wore a Yellow Ribbon* with John Wayne another year. After the one carnival ride each, we paid in guilt; our tired father counted his change on the dark walk home.

Adultery is extravagance. Could people who hatch their own chicks and eat the embryos and the heads for delicacies and boil the feet in vinegar for party food, leaving only the gravel, eating even the gizzard lining—could such people engender a prodigal aunt? To be a woman, to have a daughter in starvation time was a waste enough. My aunt could not have been the lone romantic who gave up everything for sex. Women in the old China did not choose. Some man had commanded her to lie with him and be his secret evil. I wonder whether he masked himself when he joined the raid on her family.

Perhaps she had encountered him in the fields or on the mountain where the daughters-in-law collected fuel. Or perhaps he first noticed her in the marketplace. He was not a stranger because the village housed no strangers. She had to have dealings with him other than sex. Perhaps he worked an adjoining field, or he sold her the cloth for the dress she sewed and wore. His demand must have surprised, then terrified her. She obeyed him; she always did as she was told.

When the family found a young man in the next village to be her husband, she had stood tractably beside the best rooster, his proxy, and promised before they met that she would be his forever. She was lucky that he was her age and she would be the first wife, an advantage secure now. The night she first saw him, he had sex with her. Then he left for America. She had almost forgotten what he looked like. When she tried to envision him, she only saw the black and white face in the group photograph the men had had taken before leaving.

The other man was not, after all, much different from her husband. They both gave orders: she followed. "If you tell your family, I'll beat you. I'll kill you. Be here again next week." No one talked sex, ever. And she might have separated the rapes from the rest of living if only she did not have to buy her oil from him or gather wood in the same forest. I want her fear to have lasted just as long as rape lasted so that the fear could have been contained. No drawn-out fear. But women at sex hazarded birth and hence lifetimes. The fear did not stop but permeated everywhere. She told the man, "I think I'm pregnant." He organized the raid against her.

On nights when my mother and father talked about their life back home, sometimes they mentioned an "outcast table" whose business they still seemed to be settling, their voices tight. In a commensal tradition, where food is precious, the powerful older people made wrongdoers eat alone. Instead of letting them start separate new lives like the Japanese, who could become samurais and geishas, the Chinese family, faces averted but eyes glowering sideways, hung on to the offenders and fed them leftovers. My aunt must have lived in the same house as my parents and eaten at an outcast table. My mother spoke about the raid as if she had seen it, when she and my aunt, a daughter-in-law to a different household, should not have been living together at all. Daughters-in-law lived with their husbands' parents, not their own; a synonym for marriage in Chinese is "taking a daughter-in-law." Her husband's parents could have sold her, mortgaged her, stoned her. But they had sent her back to her own mother and father, a mysterious act hinting at disgraces not told me. Perhaps they had thrown her out to deflect the avengers.

She was the only daughter; her four brothers went with her father, husband, and uncles "out on the road" and for some years became western men. When the goods were divided among the family, three of the brothers took land, and the youngest, my father, chose an education. After my grandparents gave their daughter away to her husband's family, they had dispensed all the adventure and all the property. They expected her alone to keep the traditional ways, which her brothers, now among the barbarians, could fumble without detection. The heavy, deep-rooted women were to maintain the past against the flood, safe for returning. But the rare urge west had fixed upon our family, and so my aunt crossed boundaries not delineated in space.

The work of preservation demands that the feelings playing about in one's guts not be turned into action. Just watch their passing like cherry blossoms. But perhaps my aunt, my forerunner, caught in a slow life, let dreams grow and fade and after some months or years went toward what persisted. Fear at the enormities of the forbidden kept her desires delicate, wire and bone. She looked at a man because she liked the way the hair was tucked behind his ears, or she liked the question-mark line of a long torso curving at the shoulder and straight at the hip. For warm eyes or a soft voice or a slow walk—that's all—a few hairs, a line, a brightness, a sound, a pace, she gave up family. She offered us up for a charm that vanished with tiredness, a pigtail that didn't toss when the wind died. Why, the wrong lighting could erase the dearest thing about him.

It could very well have been, however, that my aunt did not take subtle enjoyment of her friend, but, a wild woman, kept rollicking company. Imagining her free with sex doesn't fit, though. I don't know any women like that, or men either. Unless I see her life branching into mine, she gives me no ancestral help.

To sustain her being in love, she often worked at herself in the mirror, guessing at the colors and shapes that would interest him, changing them frequently in order to hit on the right combination. She wanted him to look back.

On a farm near the sea, a woman who tended her appearance reaped a reputation for eccentricity. All the married women bluntcut their hair in flaps about their ears or pulled it back in tight buns. No nonsense. Neither style blew easily into heart-catching tangles. And at their weddings they displayed themselves in their long hair for the last time. "It brushed the backs of my knees," my mother tells me. "It was braided, and even so, it brushed the backs of my knees."

At the mirror my aunt combed individuality into her bob. A bun could have been contrived to escape into black streamers blowing in the wind or in quiet wisps about her face, but only the older women in our picture album wear buns. She brushed her hair back from her forehead, tucking the flaps behind her ears. She looped a piece of thread, knotted into a circle between her index fingers and thumbs, and ran the double strand across her forehead. When she closed her fingers as if she were making a pair of shadow geese bite, the string twisted together catching the little hairs. Then she pulled the thread away from her skin, ripping the hairs out neatly, her eyes watering from the needles of pain. Opening her fingers, she cleaned the thread, then rolled it along her hairline and the tops of her eyebrows. My mother did the same to me and my sisters and herself. I used to believe that the expression "caught by the short hairs" meant a captive held with a depilatory string. It especially hurt at the temples, but my mother said we were lucky we didn't have to have our feet bound when we were seven. Sisters used to sit on their beds and cry together, she said, as their mothers or their slaves removed the bandages for a few minutes each night and let the blood gush back into their veins. I hope that the man my aunt loved appreciated a smooth brow, that he wasn't just a tits-and-ass man.

Once my aunt found a freckle on her chin, at a spot that the almanac said predestined her for unhappiness. She dug it out with a hot needle and washed the wound with peroxide.

More attention to her looks than these pullings of hairs and pickings at spots would have caused gossip among the villagers. They owned work clothes and good clothes, and they wore good clothes for feasting the new seasons. But since a woman combing her hair hexes beginnings, my aunt rarely found an occasion to look her best. Women looked like great sea snails—the corded wood, babies, and laundry they carried were the whorls on their backs. The Chinese did not admire a bent back; goddesses and warriors stood straight. Still there must have been a marvelous freeing of beauty when a worker laid down her burden and stretched and arched.

Such commonplace loveliness, however, was not enough for my aunt. She dreamed of a lover for the fifteen days of New Year's, the time for families to exchange visits, money, and food. She plied her secret comb. And sure enough she cursed the year, the family, the village, and herself.

Even as her hair lured her imminent lover, many other men

looked at her. Uncles, cousins, nephews, brothers would have looked, too, had they been home between journeys. Perhaps they had already been restraining their curiosity, and they left, fearful that their glances, like a field of nesting birds, might be startled and caught. Poverty hurt, and that was their first reason for leaving. But another, final reason for leaving the crowded house was the never-said.

She may have been unusually beloved, the precious only daughter, spoiled and mirror gazing because of the affection the family lavished on her. When her husband left, they welcomed the chance to take her back from the in-laws; she could live like the little daughter for just a while longer. There are stories that my grandfather was different from other people, "crazy ever since the little Jap bayoneted him in the head." He used to put his naked penis on the dinner table, laughing. And one day he brought home a baby girl, wrapped up inside his brown western-style greatcoat. He had traded one of his sons, probably my father, the youngest, for her. My grandmother made him trade back. When he finally got a daughter of his own, he doted on her. They must have all loved her, except perhaps my father, the only brother who never went back to China, having once been traded for a girl.

Brothers and sisters, newly men and women, had to efface their sexual color and present plain miens. Disturbing hair and eyes, a smile like no other, threatened the ideal of five generations living under one roof. To focus blurs, people shouted face to face and yelled from room to room. The immigrants I know have loud voices, unmodulated to American tones even after years away from the village where they called their friendships out across the fields. I have not been able to stop my mother's screams in public libraries or over telephones. Walking erect (knees straight, toes pointed forward, not pigeon-toed, which is Chinese-feminine) and speaking in an inaudible voice, I have tried to turn myself American-feminine. Chinese communication was loud, public. Only sick people had to whisper. But at the dinner table, where the family members came nearest one another, no one could talk, not the outcasts nor any eaters. Every word that falls from the mouth is a coin lost. Silently they gave and accepted food with both hands. A preoccupied child who took his bowl with one hand got a sideways glare. A complete moment of total attention is due everyone alike. Children and lovers have no singularity here, but my aunt used a secret voice, a separate attentiveness.

She kept the man's name to herself throughout her labor and dying; she did not accuse him that he be punished with her. To save her inseminator's name she gave silent birth.

He may have been somebody in her own household, but intercourse with a man outside the family would have been no less abhorrent. All the village were kinsmen, and the titles shouted in loud country voices never let kinship be forgotten. Any man within visiting distance would have been neutralized as a lover—"brother," "younger brother," "older brother"—one hundred and fifteen relationship titles. Parents researched birth charts probably not so much to assure good fortune as to circumvent incest in a population that has but one hundred surnames. Everybody has eight million relatives. How useless then sexual mannerisms, how dangerous.

As if it came from an atavism deeper than fear, I used to add "brother" silently to boys' names. It hexed the boys, who would or would not ask me to dance, and made them less scary and as familiar and deserving of benevolence as girls.

But, of course, I hexed myself also—no dates. I should have stood up, both arms waving, and shouted out across libraries, "Hey, you! Love me back." I had no idea, though, how to make attraction selective, how to control its direction and magnitude. If I made myself American-pretty so that the five or six Chinese boys in the class fell in love with me, everyone else—the Caucasian, Negro, and Japanese boys—would too. Sisterliness, dignified and honorable, made much more sense.

Attraction eludes control so stubbornly that whole societies designed to organize relationships among people cannot keep order, not even when they bind people to one another from childhood and raise them together. Among the very poor and the wealthy, brothers married their adopted sisters, like doves. Our family allowed some romance, paying adult brides' prices and providing dowries so that their sons and daughters could marry strangers. Marriage promises to turn strangers into friendly relatives—a nation of siblings.

In the village structure, spirits shimmered among the live creatures, balanced and held in equilibrium by time and land. But one human

being flaring up into violence could open up a black hole, a mael-
strom that pulled in the sky. The frightened villagers, who depended
on one another to maintain the real, went to my aunt to show her a
personal, physical representation of the break she had made in the
"roundness." Misallying couples snapped off the future, which was to
be embodied in true offspring. The villagers punished her for acting
as if she could have a private life, secret and apart from them.

If my aunt had betrayed the family at a time of large grain yields
and peace, when many boys were born, and wings were being built
on many houses, perhaps she might have escaped such severe punishment. But the men—hungry, greedy, tired of planting in dry
soil—had been forced to leave the village in order to send food-
money home. There were ghost plagues, bandit plagues, wars with
the Japanese, floods. My Chinese brother and sister had died of an
unknown sickness. Adultery, perhaps only a mistake during good
times, became a crime when the village needed food.

The round moon cakes and round doorways, the round tables of
graduated sizes that fit one roundness inside another, round windows and rice bowls—these talismans had lost their power to warn
this family of the law: a family must be whole, faithfully keeping the
descent line by having sons to feed the old and the dead, who in
turn look after the family. The villagers came to show my aunt and
her lover-in-hiding a broken house. The villagers were speeding up
the circling of events because she was too shortsighted to see that
her infidelity had already harmed the village, that waves of consequences would return unpredictably, sometimes in disguise, as now,
to hurt her. This roundness had to be made coin-sized so that she
would see its circumference: punish her at the birth of her baby.
Awaken her to the inexorable. People who refused fatalism because
they could invent small resources insisted on culpability. Deny accidents and wrest fault from the stars.

After the villagers left, their lanterns now scattering in various directions toward home, the family broke their silence and cursed her.
"Aiaa, we're going to die. Death is coming. Death is coming. Look
what you've done. You've killed us. Ghost! Dead ghost! Ghost!
You've never been born." She ran out into the fields, far enough
from the house so that she could no longer hear their voices, and
pressed herself against the earth, her own land no more. When she

felt the birth coming, she thought that she had been hurt. Her body seized together. "They've hurt me too much," she thought. "This is gall, and it will kill me." With forehead and knees against the earth, her body convulsed and then relaxed. She turned on her back, lay on the ground. The black well of sky and stars went out and out and out forever; her body and her complexity seemed to disappear. She was one of the stars, a bright dot in blackness, without home, without a companion, in eternal cold and silence. An agoraphobia rose in her, speeding higher and higher, bigger and bigger; she would not be able to contain it; there would no end to fear.

Flayed, unprotected against space, she felt pain return, focusing her body. This pain chilled her—a cold, steady kind of surface pain. Inside, spasmodically, the other pain, the pain of the child, heated her. For hours she lay on the ground, alternately body and space. Sometimes a vision of normal comfort obliterated reality: she saw the family in the evening gambling at the dinner table, the young people massaging their elders' backs. She saw them congratulating one another, high joy on the mornings the rice shoots came up. When these pictures burst, the stars drew yet further apart. Black space opened.

She got to her feet to fight better and remembered that old-fashioned women gave birth in their pigsties to fool the jealous, pain-dealing gods, who do not snatch piglets. Before the next spasms could stop her, she ran to the pigsty, each step a rushing out into emptiness. She climbed over the fence and knelt in the dirt. It was good to have a fence enclosing her, a tribal person alone.

Laboring, this woman who had carried her child as a foreign growth that sickened her every day, expelled it at last. She reached down to touch the hot, wet, moving mass, surely smaller than anything human, and could feel that it was human after all—fingers, toes, nails, nose. She pulled it up on to her belly, and it lay curled there, butt in the air, feet precisely tucked one under the other. She opened her loose shirt and buttoned the child inside. After resting, it squirmed and thrashed and she pushed it up to her breast. It turned its head this way and that until it found her nipple. There, it made little snuffling noises. She clenched her teeth at its preciousness, lovely as a young calf, a piglet, a little dog.

She may have gone to the pigsty as a last act of responsibility: she would protect this child as she had protected its father. It would look after her soul, leaving supplies on her grave. But how would this tiny child without family find her grave when there would be no marker for her anywhere, neither in the earth nor the family hall? No one would give her a family hall name. She had taken the child with her into the wastes. At its birth the two of them had felt the same raw pain of separation, a wound that only the family pressing tight could close. A child with no descent line would not soften her life but only trail after her, ghostlike, begging her to give it purpose. At dawn the villagers on their way to the fields would stand around the fence and look.

Full of milk, the little ghost slept. When it awoke, she hardened her breasts against the milk that crying loosens. Toward morning she picked up the baby and walked to the well.

Carrying the baby to the well shows loving. Otherwise abandon it. Turn its face into the mud. Mothers who love their children take them along. It was probably a girl; there is some hope of forgiveness for boys.

"Don't tell anyone you had an aunt. Your father does not want to hear her name. She has never been born." I have believed that sex was unspeakable and words so strong and fathers so frail that "aunt" would do my father mysterious harm. I have thought that my family, having settled among immigrants who had also been their neighbors in the ancestral land, needed to clean their name, and a wrong word would incite the kinspeople even here. But there is more to this silence: they want me to participate in her punishment. And I have.

In the twenty years since I heard this story I have not asked for details nor said my aunt's name; I do not know it. People who can comfort the dead can also chase after them to hurt them further—a reverse ancestor worship. The real punishment was not the raid swiftly inflicted by the villagers, but the family's deliberately forgetting her. Her betrayal so maddened them, they saw to it that she would suffer forever, even after death. Always hungry, always needing, she would have to beg food from other ghosts, snatch and steal it from those whose living descendants give them gifts. She would have to fight the ghosts massed at crossroads for the buns a few thoughtful citizens leave to decoy her away from village and home so that the ancestral spirits could feast unharassed. At peace, they could act like gods, not ghosts, their descent lines providing them with paper suits and dresses, spirit money, paper houses, paper automobiles, chicken, meat, and rice into eternity—essences delivered up in smoke and flames, steam and incense rising from each rice bowl. In an attempt to make the Chinese care for people outside the family, Chairman Mao[1] encourages us now to give our paper replicas to the spirits of outstanding soldiers and workers, no matter whose ancestors they may be. My aunt remains forever hungry. Goods are not distributed evenly among the dead.

My aunt haunts me—her ghost drawn to me because now, after fifty years of neglect, I alone devote pages of paper to her, though not origamied into houses and clothes. I do not think she always means me well. I am telling on her, and she was a spite suicide, drowning herself in the drinking water. The Chinese are always very frightened of the drowned one, whose weeping ghost, wet hair hanging and skin bloated, waits silently by the water to pull down a substitute.

1976

---

1. Mao Zedong (1893–1976), founder of the People's Republic of China; chief of state, 1949–59; and chairman of the Communist Party until his death.

Jonathan Kozol
b. 1936

> *In 1998, the National Institute for Literacy estimated that 22 percent of adult Americans, about 42 million people, could sign their name to a document but not locate an intersection on a street map or find two pieces of information in a newspaper article. Obviously, we have not solved the problems that Kozol decried during the Reagan era when his book* Illiterate America *was published (1985). This essay, "The Human Cost of an Illiterate Society," is the fourth chapter in Kozol's book, so it is only a small part of a larger argument. The previous chapter calculated that in the mid-seventies illiteracy cost taxpayers about $20 billion per year in welfare, prison costs, workman's compensation, court costs, and so on. This essay attempts to describe the incalculable moral price paid by people individually and by the nation as a whole. Ultimately, Kozol argues that illiteracy in America is not an error or accident: It is a deliberate public policy to protect the interests of people, like you, who are likely to have studied English in college. He tries to turn his audience, the very people he denounces, into allies of America's illiterate underclass. Does he succeed with you?*

The Human Cost of an Illiterate Society

PRECAUTIONS. READ BEFORE USING.
Poison: Contains sodium hydroxide (caustic soda-lye).
Corrosive: Causes severe eye and skin damage, may cause blindness.
Harmful or fatal if swallowed.
If swallowed, give large quantities of milk or water.
Do not induce vomiting.
Important: Keep water out of can at all times to
prevent contents from violently erupting . . .

—warning on a can of Drāno

We are speaking here no longer of the dangers faced by passengers on Eastern Airlines or the dollar costs incurred by U.S. corporations and taxpayers.[1] We are speaking now of human suffering and of the ethical dilemmas that are faced by a society that looks upon such suffering with qualified concern but does not take those actions which its wealth and ingenuity would seemingly demand.

Questions of literacy, in Socrates' belief, must at length be judged as matters of morality.[2] Socrates could not have had in mind the moral compromise peculiar to a nation like our own. Some of our Founding Fathers did, however, have this question in their minds. One of the wisest of those Founding Fathers (one who may not have been most compassionate but surely was more prescient than some of his peers) recognized the special dangers that illiteracy would pose to basic equity in the political construction that he helped to shape.

"A people who mean to be their own governors," James Madison wrote, "must arm themselves with the power knowledge gives. A popular government without popular information or the means of acquiring it, is but a prologue to a farce or a tragedy, or perhaps both."[3]

Tragedy looms larger than farce in the United States today. Illiterate citizens seldom vote. Those who do are forced to cast a vote of questionable worth. They cannot make informed decisions based on serious print information. Sometimes they can be alerted to their interests by aggressive voter education. More frequently, they vote for a face, a smile, or a style, not for a mind or character or body of beliefs.

The number of illiterate adults exceeds by 16 million the entire vote cast for the winner in the 1980 presidential contest. If even one third of all illiterates could vote, and read enough and do sufficient math to vote in their self-interest, Ronald Reagan would not likely have been chosen president. There is, of course, no way to know for sure. We do know this: Democracy is a mendacious term when used by those who are prepared to countenance the forced exclusion of

---

1. Topics discussed in previous chapters.
2. In Plato's *Meno*, Socrates wonders whether virtue, defined as knowledge, can be taught.

3. From a letter to W. T. Barry, August 4, 1882.

one third of our electorate. So long as 60 million people are denied significant participation, the government is neither of, nor for, nor by, the people. It is a government, at best, of those two thirds whose wealth, skin color, or parental privilege allows them opportunity to profit from the provocation and instruction of the written word.

The undermining of democracy in the United States is one "expense" that sensitive Americans can easily deplore because it represents a contradiction that endangers citizens of all political positions. The human price is not so obvious at first.

Since I first immersed myself within this work I have often had the following dream: I find that I am in a railroad station or a large department store within a city that is utterly unknown to me and where I cannot understand the printed words. None of the signs or symbols is familiar. Everything looks strange: like mirror writing of some kind. Gradually I understand that I am in the Soviet Union. All the letters on the walls around me are Cyrillic. I look for my pocket dictionary but I find that it has been mislaid. Where have I left it? Then I recall that I forgot to bring it with me when I packed my bags in Boston. I struggle to remember the name of my hotel. I try to ask somebody for directions. One person stops and looks at me in a peculiar way. I lose the nerve to ask. At last I reach into my wallet for an ID card. The card is missing. Have I lost it? Then I remember that my card was confiscated for some reason, many years before. Around this point, I wake up in a panic.

This panic is not so different from the misery that millions of adult illiterates experience each day within the course of their routine existence in the U.S.A.

Illiterates cannot read the menu in a restaurant.

They cannot read the cost of items on the menu in the *window* of the restaurant before they enter.

Illiterates cannot read the letters that their children bring home from their teachers. They cannot study school department circulars that tell them of the courses that their children must be taking if they hope to pass the SAT exams. They cannot help with homework. They cannot write a letter to the teacher. They are afraid to visit in the classroom. They do not want to humiliate their child or themselves.

Illiterates cannot read instructions on a bottle of prescription medicine. They cannot find out when a medicine is past the year of safe consumption; nor can they read of allergenic risks, warnings to diabetics, or the potential sedative effect of certain kinds of nonprescription pills. They cannot observe preventive health care admonitions. They cannot read about "the seven warning signs of cancer" or the indications of blood-sugar fluctuations or the risks of eating certain foods that aggravate the likelihood of cardiac arrest.

Illiterates live, in more than literal ways, an uninsured existence. They cannot understand the written details on a health insurance form. They cannot read the waivers that they sign preceding surgical procedures. Several women I have known in Boston have entered a slum hospital with the intention of obtaining a tubal ligation and have emerged a few days later after having been subjected to a hysterectomy. Unaware of their rights, incognizant of jargon, intimidated by the unfamiliar air of fear and atmosphere of ether that so many of us find oppressive in the confines even of the most attractive and expensive medical facilities, they have signed their names to documents they could not read and which nobody, in the hectic situation that prevails so often in those overcrowded hospitals that serve the urban poor, had even bothered to explain.

Childbirth might seem to be the last inalienable right of any female citizen within a civilized society. Illiterate mothers, as we shall see, already have been cheated of the power to protect their progeny against the likelihood of demolition in deficient public schools and, as a result, against the verbal servitude within which they themselves exist. Surgical denial of the right to bear that child in the first place represents an ultimate denial, an unspeakable metaphor, a final darkness that denies even the twilight gleamings of our own humanity. What greater violation of our biological, our biblical, our spiritual humanity could possibly exist than that which takes place nightly, perhaps hourly these days, within such overburdened and benighted institutions as the Boston City Hospital? Illiteracy has many costs; few are so irreversible as this.

Even the roof above one's head, the gas or other fuel for heating that protects the residents of northern city slums against the threat of illness in the winter months become uncertain guarantees. Illiterates cannot read the lease that they must sign to live in an apartment which, too often, they cannot afford. They cannot manage check accounts and therefore seldom pay for anything by mail. Hours and entire days of difficult travel (and the cost of bus or other public transit) must be added to the real cost of whatever they consume. Loss of interest on the check accounts they do not have, and could not manage if they did, must be regarded as another of the excess costs paid by the citizen who is excluded from the common instruments of commerce in a numerate[4] society.

"I couldn't understand the bills," a woman in Washington, D.C., reports, "and then I couldn't write the checks to pay them. We signed things we didn't know what they were."

Illiterates cannot read the notices that they receive from welfare offices or from the IRS. They must depend on word-of-mouth instruction from the welfare worker—or from other persons whom they have good reason to mistrust. They do not know what rights they have, what deadlines and requirements they face, what options they might choose to exercise. They are half-citizens. Their rights exist in print but not in fact.

Illiterates cannot look up numbers in a telephone directory. Even if they can find the names of friends, few possess the sorting skills to make use of the yellow pages; categories are bewildering and trade names are beyond decoding capabilities for millions of nonreaders. Even the emergency numbers listed on the first page of the phone book—"Ambulance," "Police," and "Fire"—are too frequently beyond the recognition of nonreaders.

Many illiterates cannot read the admonition on a pack of cigarettes. Neither the Surgeon General's warning nor its reproduction on the package can alert them to the risks. Although most people learn by word of mouth that smoking is related to a number of grave physical disorders, they do not get the chance to read the detailed stories which can document this danger with the vividness that turns concern into determination to resist. They can see the handsome cowboy or the slim Virginia lady lighting up a filter cigarette; they cannot heed the words that tell them that this product is (not "may be") dangerous to their health. Sixty million men and women are condemned to be the unalerted, high-risk candidates for cancer.

Illiterates do not buy "no-name" products in the supermarkets.

4. Numerically literate, able to express onself effectively in quantitative terms.

They must depend on photographs or the familiar logos that are printed on the packages of brand-name groceries. The poorest people, therefore, are denied the benefits of the least costly products.

Illiterates depend almost entirely upon label recognition. Many labels, however, are not easy to distinguish. Dozens of different kinds of Campbell's soup appear identical to the nonreader. The purchaser who cannot read and does not dare to ask for help, out of the fear of being stigmatized (a fear which is unfortunately realistic), frequently comes home with something which she never wanted and her family never tasted.

Illiterates cannot read instructions on a pack of frozen food. Packages sometimes provide an illustration to explain the cooking preparations; but illustrations are of little help to someone who must "boil water, drop the food—*within* its plastic wrapper—in the boiling water, wait for it to simmer, instantly remove."

Even when labels are seemingly clear, they may be easily mistaken. A woman in Detroit brought home a gallon of Crisco for her children's dinner. She thought that she had bought the chicken that was pictured on the label. She had enough Crisco now to last a year—but no more money to go back and buy the food for dinner.

Recipes provided on the packages of certain staples sometimes tempt a semiliterate person to prepare a meal her children have not tasted. The longing to vary the uniform and often starchy content of low-budget meals provided to the family that relies on food stamps commonly leads to ruinous results. Scarce funds have been wasted and the food must be thrown out. The same applies to distribution of food-surplus produce in emergency conditions. Government inducements to poor people to "explore the ways" by which to make a tasty meal from tasteless noodles, surplus cheese, and powdered milk are useless to nonreaders. Intended as benevolent advice, such recommendations mock reality and foster deeper feelings of resentment and of inability to cope. (Those, on the other hand, who cautiously refrain from "innovative" recipes in preparation of their children's meals must suffer the opprobrium of "laziness," "lack of imagination . . .")

Illiterates cannot travel freely. When they attempt to do so, they encounter risks that few of us can dream of. They cannot read traffic signs and, while they often learn to recognize and to decipher symbols, they cannot manage street names which they haven't seen before. The same is true for bus and subway stops. While ingenuity can sometimes help a man or woman to discern directions from familiar landmarks, buildings, cemeteries, churches, and the like, most illiterates are virtually immobilized. They seldom wander past the streets and neighborhoods they know. Geographical paralysis becomes a bitter metaphor for their entire existence. They are immobilized in almost every sense we can imagine. They can't move up. They can't move out. They cannot see beyond. Illiterates may take an oral test for drivers' permits in most sections of America. It is a questionable concession. Where will they go? How will they get there? How will they get home? Could it be that some of us might like it better if they stayed where they belong?

Travel is only one of many instances of circumscribed existence. Choice, in almost all its facets, is diminished in the life of an illiterate adult. Even the printed TV schedule, which provides most people with the luxury of preselection, does not belong within the arsenal of options in illiterate existence. One consequence is that the viewer watches only what appears at moments when he happens to have time to turn the switch. Another consequence, a lot more common, is that the TV set remains in operation night and day. Whatever the program offered at the hour when he walks into the room will be the nutriment that he accepts and swallows. Thus, to passivity, is added frequency—indeed, almost uninterrupted continuity. Freedom to select is no more possible here than in the choice of home or surgery or food.

"You don't choose," said one illiterate woman. "You take your wishes from somebody else." Whether in perusal of a menu, selection of highways, purchase of groceries, or determination of affordable enjoyment, illiterate Americans must trust somebody else: a friend, a relative, a stranger on the street, a grocery clerk, a TV copywriter.

"All of our mail we get, it's hard for her to read. Settin' down and writing a letter, she can't do it. Like if we get a bill . . . we take it over to my sister-in-law . . . My sister-in-law reads it."

Billing agencies harass poor people for the payment of the bills for purchases that might have taken place six months before. Utility companies offer an agreement for a staggered payment schedule on a bill past due. "You have to trust them," one man said. Precisely for this reason, you end up by trusting no one and suspecting everyone of possible deceit. A submerged sense of distrust becomes the corollary to a constant need to trust. "They are cheating me . . . I have been tricked . . . I do not know . . ."

Not knowing: This is a familiar theme. Not knowing the right word for the right thing at the right time is one form of subjugation. Not knowing the world that lies concealed behind those words is a more terrifying feeling. The longitude and latitude of one's existence are beyond all easy apprehension. Even the hard, cold stars within the firmament above one's head begin to mock the possibilities for self-location. Where am I? Where did I come from? Where will I go?

"I've lost a lot of jobs," one man explains. "Today, even if you're a janitor, there's still reading and writing . . . They leave a note saying, 'Go to room so-and-so . . .' You can't do it. You can't read it. You don't know."

"The hardest thing about it is that I've been places where I didn't know where I was. You don't know where you are . . . You're lost."

"Like I said: I have two kids. What do I do if one of my kids starts choking? I go running to the phone . . . I can't look up the hospital phone number. That's if we're at home. Out on the street, I can't read the sign. I get to a pay phone. 'Okay, tell us where you are. We'll send an ambulance.' I look at the street sign. Right there, I can't tell you what it says. I'd have to spell it out, letter for letter. By that time, one of my kids would be dead . . . These are the kinds of fears you go with, every single day . . ."

"Reading directions, I suffer with. I work with chemicals . . . That's scary to begin with . . ."

"You sit down. They throw the menu in front of you. Where do you go from there? Nine times out of ten you say, 'Go ahead. Pick out something for the both of us.' I've eaten some weird things, let me tell you!"

Menus. Chemicals. A child choking while his mother searches for a word she does not know to find assistance that will come too late. Another mother speaks about the inability to help her kids to read: "I can't read to them. Of course that's leaving them out of something they should have. Oh, it matters. You *believe* it matters! I ordered all these books. The kids belong to a book club. Donny wanted me to read a book to him. I told Donny: 'I can't read.' He said: 'Mommy, you sit down. I'll read it to you.' I tried it one day, reading from the pictures. Donny looked at me. He said, 'Mommy, that's not right.' He's only five. He knew I couldn't read . . ."

A landlord tells a woman that her lease allows him to evict her if her baby cries and causes inconvenience to her neighbors. The consequence of challenging his words conveys a danger which appears, unlikely as it seems, even more alarming than the danger of eviction. Once she admits that she can't read, in the desire to maneuver for the time in which to call a friend, she will have defined herself in terms of an explicit impotence that she cannot endure. Capitulation in this case is preferable to self-humiliation. Resisting the definition of oneself in terms of what one cannot do, what others take for granted, represents a need so great that other imperatives (even one so urgent as the need to keep one's home in winter's cold) evaporate and fall away in face of fear. Even the loss of home and shelter, in this case, is not so terrifying as the loss of self.

"I come out of school. I was sixteen. They had their meetings. The directors meet. They said that I was wasting their school paper. I was wasting pencils . . ."

Another illiterate, looking back, believes she was not worthy of her teacher's time. She believes that it was wrong of her to take up space within her school. She believes that it was right to leave in order that somebody more deserving could receive her place.

Children choke. Their mother chokes another way: on more than chicken bones.

People eat what others order, know what others tell them, struggle not to see themselves as they believe the world perceives them. A man in California speaks about his own loss of identity, of self-location, definition:

"I stood at the bottom of the ramp. My car had broke down on the freeway. There was a phone. I asked for the police. They was nice. They said to tell them where I was. I looked up at the signs. There was one that I had seen before. I read it to them: ONE WAY STREET. They thought it was a joke. I told them I couldn't read. There was other signs above the ramp. They told me to try. I looked around for somebody to help. All the cars was going by real fast. I couldn't make them understand that I was lost. The cop was nice. He told me: 'Try once more.' I did my best. I couldn't read. I only knew the sign above my head. The cop was trying to be nice. He knew that I was trapped, 'I can't send out a car to you if you can't tell me where you are.' I felt afraid. I nearly cried. I'm forty-eight years old. I only said: 'I'm on a one-way street . . .' "

The legal problems and the courtroom complications that confront illiterate adults have been discussed above. The anguish that may underlie such matters was brought home to me this year while I was working on this book. I have spoken, in the introduction, of a sudden phone call from one of my former students, now in prison for a criminal offense. Stephen is not a boy today. He is twenty-eight years old. He called to ask me to assist him in his trial, which comes up next fall. He will be on trial for murder. He has just knifed and killed a man who first enticed him to his home, then cheated him, and then insulted him—as "an illiterate subhuman."

Stephen now faces twenty years to life. Stephen's mother was illiterate. His grandparents were illiterate as well. What parental curse did not destroy was killed off finally by the schools. Silent violence is repaid with interest. It will cost us $25,000 yearly to maintain this broken soul in prison. But what is the price that has been paid by Stephen's victim? What is the price that will be paid by Stephen?

Perhaps we might slow down a moment here and look at the realities described above. This is the nation that we live in. This is a society that most of us did not create but which our President and other leaders have been willing to sustain by virtue of malign neglect. Do we possess the character and courage to address a problem which so many nations, poorer than our own, have found it natural to correct?

The answers to these questions represent a reasonable test of our belief in the democracy to which we have been asked in public school to swear allegiance.

1985

Lewis Lapham

b. 1935

Lapham alludes to two important—and controversial—concepts that he does not really define in his essay. The first is the notion of American exceptionalism—that the United States is fundamentally different from most of the other nations of the earth. Exceptionalists give a variety of reasons for this difference. Lapham adheres to the idea that the United States is not a population that naturally coheres because of shared origins or language or culture; instead, Americans are bound by a political ideology they hold in common. Thus the historical education of Americans is particularly crucial to our sense of national identity.

The second is a theory advanced in the last fifty years or so: namely, that the degree to which history is formed into a narrative, into a story, it will be naïve. By turning history into a narrative, this theory suggests, historians must distort the truth, resorting to "master narratives," or grand historical stories. One such story presents history as progress, sometimes slower, sometimes faster, sometimes retrograde but in the long run always tending toward greater political freedom and equality. That was a "master narrative" popular with Enlightenment thinkers of the eighteenth century, including many of the men who founded the American republic. But the fear of "master narratives" has persuaded some historians that they must not make stories out of the past. In the classroom, the conscious attempt to avoid narrative, while escaping the more obvious distortions, can result in a dry, unmemorable recitation of facts. In this essay, Lapham regrets that attempt to escape narrative at all.

Time Lines

Life must be lived forwards, but can only be understood backwards.
—KIERKEGAARD[1]

Assume that the existence of the American democracy requires the existence of an electorate that knows something about American history, and last November's press release from the U.S. Department of Education can be read as a coroner's report. The government's examiners questioned 22,000 schoolchildren in fifty states about their knowledge of the nation's past, and after arranging the answers as a set of charts, they returned a finding of mortal ignorance: more than 50 percent of all high school seniors unaware of the Cold War,[2] nearly six in ten bereft of even a primitive understanding of where America came from, only one in every hundred capable of placing General Custer's last stand on the hill in Montana on the same geopolitical horizon with Colonel Roosevelt's assault, twenty-two years later, on the hill in Cuba.[3] Although the report card showed a better grasp of history among grammar school students than among high school students, it revealed few important differences between students of different genders, races, or economic strata.

It wasn't as if anybody had expected the news to be good. For the last twenty years the ministers of the nation's educational affairs (university deans as well as federal bureaucrats) have been reporting signs of decay—low SAT scores, dwindling verbal aptitudes, a general inability to find Tokyo on a map—and like the falling grades in all the other subjects, the poor marks in history didn't mean that

1. Søren Kierkegaard (1813–1855), Danish philosopher and theologian considered by some to be the father of existentialism.

2. The term "Cold War" refers to the long enmity—that did not erupt into direct warfare—between the Soviet Union and the United States, from the end of World War II to the fall of Russian communism, roughly 1945 to 1989.

3. Lt. Colonel George Armstrong Custer (1839–1976) of the 7th Cavalry died, along with his command, at the Battle of Little Big Horn in Montana, overwhelmed by Sioux, Cheyenne, and Arapaho Indians. Theodore Roosevelt (1858–1919), later U.S. president (1901–09), led a charge of cavalry, the "Rough Riders," up San Juan Hill in Cuba during the Spanish American War in 1898.

Old Glory wouldn't continue to float in the orange-scented breeze over the Rose Bowl. It's a nice flag and a rich country, and nobody expected the stock market to collapse because a lot of high school seniors didn't know the difference between a Federalist and a Pequot Indian.[4] American schoolchildren never have been fond of textbooks, choosing whenever possible to follow Huckleberry Finn south and out of town, and their inattention didn't foretell the sudden disappearance of Revlon, Microsoft, and the professional golf tour.

What the report card did mean was that the schools have lost the thread of the American narrative, and that without that narrative the country cannot long sustain the appearance, much less the substance, of democratic self-government—not because everybody needs to remember the *Maine* or the Alamo but because as Americans we have no other way of knowing ourselves.[5] Unlike every other nation in the world, the United States defines itself as a hypothesis and constitutes itself as an argument. Other nations make do with shared bloodlines, a common store of language, inherited portfolios of ancestral myth reaching backward in time to the first Irishman or the first Korean. But as Americans we have only the dialectic in which we try to frame the opposing principles of liberty and equality into a political architecture that best supports the cause of freedom. The founders of the American republic devoted themselves to the study of history because they knew that they had nothing else on which to build the future except the blueprint of the past. Well aware of both the continuity and contingency of human affairs, Adams and Madison searched the works of Tac-itus and Voltaire and Locke like carpenters rummag-

---

4. The Federalists were one of the first American political parties, generally favoring a strong central government and friendly relations with England. The party was in existence, roughly, from 1792 to 1820. The Pequot Indians are a tribe native to Connecticut.

5. "Remember the *Maine*" and "Remember the Alamo" were battle cries in the Spanish-American War (1898) and the Texas War of Independence (1835–36). The U.S. battleship *Maine* exploded under mysterious circumstances in Havana harbor, precipitating the Spanish-American War. At the Alamo, in San Antonio, a few hundred American settlers fought the Mexican Army commanded by General Santa Anna, until the Mexicans stormed the fort and massacred its defenders.

ing through their assortment of tools, knowing that all the pediments were jury-rigged, all the inscriptions provisional, all the alliances temporary.[6]

If we no longer hold the study of history in such passionate regard, it's because we like to think of our political institutions as monuments or museum pieces, completed works in a past tense, and if American schoolchildren believe that Squanto[7] is a rock group, it's because they live in a society that thinks of history as ornament and stage design—a subject fit for interior decorators and best rendered as a theme park.

The government report card aroused a fair number of the country's newspaper columnists to cries of indignant alarm—America falling behind in the economic competition with Germany and Japan, the schools failing to deliver high-quality product to the infrastructure, etc.—but my own feeling was nearer to sorrow. I sent for the government's report, and behind the bleak walls of institutional prose, I could all too easily imagine cell blocks K through 12 in which history appears as a collection of old stones or a cabinet of dead birds. The government examiners had asked their questions in the stunted language of multiple choice (For five points, which of the following was one of the original thirteen colonies?), and it was clear that even if the children had got the answers right, they had been poorly served, disarmed as citizens and denied their inheritance as the beneficiaries of the whole of the human story.

When taught by a teacher who knows what he or she is about, the imaginative taking up of the experience of the past can be put through as many paces as a well-trained circus horse. The study of history furnishes what Dionysius of Halicarnassus praised as "philosophy learned by example," instills a sense of humor, wards off

6. John Adams (1735–1826), second U.S. president (1797–1801) and James Madison, fourth president (1809–1817), helped design the forms of government framed by the Constitution. Tacitus (c. 56–117), Roman historian and senator; François-Marie Arouet, or Voltaire (1694–1778), French writer; and John Locke (1632–1704), English philosopher—all were political scientists who influenced the founders of the American republic.

7. Squanto, or Tisquantum (c. 1580s–1622), a Patuxet Indian who helped the Pilgrims in the early years of their settlement in Massachusetts.

what Hamlet decried as "the slings and arrows of outrageous fortune," allows the citizens of a democracy to know the difference between their enemies and their friends.[8]

People unfamiliar with the world in time find themselves marooned in the ceaselessly dissolving and therefore terrifying present, divorced from both the future and the past, surrounded by the siege of images in the mirrors of the news. The mass media promote the impression that the urgent questions of the moment (war in Bosnia, corruption in Washington, crime in Los Angeles) arrive like monstrous apparitions, uninvited and unannounced, from the Land of Mordor. The spectators forget how and why events come to pass, and not knowing where to find their place in the human story (in Chapter 12 or on page 438), condemned to a state of constant dread, they become an audience fit for the market in three-day wonders and one-line jokes.

I narrowly escaped recruitment into the same claque. Although I was lucky enough to attend private schools, the higher fees by no means guaranteed a higher order of instruction, and among all the history teachers from whom I took notes over the span of sixteen years, I remember only two who brought to their subject the gifts of passion and talent. In my mind's eye I see them both as clearly as the paper on which I'm writing this sentence. Mr. Mulholland stands at the blackboard in a seventh-grade classroom in San Francisco, a heavy and florid man given to broad gestures and sudden shouts, drawing the line of Hannibal's elephants through the valleys of Cisalpine Gaul.[9] The chalk squeaks, and the annals of ancient Rome come as vividly to life as the sound of the ball game in progress under the windows on Jackson Street. Mr. Mulholland spends a week on the Carthaginian descent into Italy, another week at the bend in the river near Cannae, a month on the Punic Wars, six months on the destruction of the Roman republic and the con-

8. Dionysius of Halicarnassus, 1st century B.C.E., Greek historian and rhetorician; Hamlet is the title character of Shakespeare's famous tragedy.

9. In the Second Punic War (218–201 B.C.E.), between Carthage and Rome, Hannibal (247–c. 183 B.C.E.) invaded Italy from Spain by crossing the Alps and Pyrenees mountains, a singular achievement that took advantage of Rome's undefended border.

trived divinity of Caesar Augustus.[1] Never once does his voice tire or his enthusiasm fail. He tells the story as if it happened yesterday in Golden Gate Park, stringing together a coherent narrative from different phyla of meaning, different kingdoms of fact: a military expedition in Scythia reminds him of something Pliny said about jackals at a dinner party in Pompeii; discussing the logistics of the Egyptian grain trade, he remembers how bitterly Juvenal[2] resented Egyptian barbers; and before the hour ends he has improvised a philippic against Cleopatra and the Ptolemies.[3] On Monday he compares and contrasts the deaths of Cicero and Seneca; on Tuesday he describes Trimalchio's banquet and Ovid's exile on the Black Sea; on Wednesday he draws the moral about how hard it was to tell the truth in Imperial Rome and still dine on plover's eggs.[4]

Mr. Garside, whom I encountered in my third year at boarding school in northwestern Connecticut, paces back and forth in front of the arched windows that overlook the golf course, his voice high and thin and vaguely British, his clothes eccentric, and his manner foppish—a man easily mocked for what at first seemed like the affectations of an actor appearing in a play by Oscar Wilde.[5] His genius for telling stories dispels the suspicion of the class, and by the end of the fall term the muffled witticisms in the back row have given way to awe. Much younger than Mr. Mulholland, Mr. Garside has been engaged to teach modern European literature, but he is also studying for a doctorate at a university from which he has

1. Augustus Caesar, or Octavius (63 B.C.E.–14 C.E.), was the first Roman emperor, eliminating the meaningful rule of the Roman senate and instituting the high prestige, even "divinity," of the emperors.

2. Juvenal, Roman satirist of the late first and early second centuries.

3. Cleopatra (69–30 B.C.E.), Egyptian queen who ruled with her father, husband, and brother, each, in their turn, King Ptolemy.

4. Cicero (106–43 B.C.E.), Roman senator and orator during the tumultuous years after Julius Caesar's assassination, was himself assassinated by agents of Mark Antony and Octavius; Seneca (c. 4 B.C.E.–65 C.E.), Roman playwright and adviser to Nero, fell out of favor with the emperor and, after a failed assassination attempt, committed suicide. Trimalchio is a character in Petronius's *Satyricon*; he attempts to gain status by throwing lavish parties. Ovid (43 B.C.E.–14 C.E.), Roman writer of the *Metamorphoses*, was exiled to Tomis on the Black Sea for reasons that remain mysterious.

5. Oscar Wilde (1854–1900), Irish playwright and celebrity. His comedies often featured elegantly dressed, affected characters.

taken temporary leave, and he cannot suppress the impulse to extend his observations about Dickens or Flaubert to further remarks about Victorian England and the comic-opera empire of Napoleon III.[6] I can still see him, forty years ago on a warm October afternoon, pausing slightly before he makes his customary turn under the window with a broken pane, about to describe Dickens's morbid wandering through the Paris morgue during the same week in June 1863 that the Army of Northern Virginia was moving north toward Gettysburg and the Duke de Morny (the principal conspirator in the coup d'état of 1851 and a mountebank of whom Mr. Garside was particularly fond) was gambling away his wife's fortune at the roulette tables in Biarritz.[7]

At Yale University I entertained but soon abandoned the thought of becoming a historian. Even as long ago as the 1950s the study of history was sinking into the mire of heavily footnoted research, the life and times of Lincoln or Alexander the Great[8] beginning to disappear into a fog of abstract nouns that sounded like translations from a German treatise on postindustrial socioeconomic theory. History is only intelligible as narrative (which is why the Department of Education noticed a better grasp of the subject among very small children), but narrative these days is against the university rules. People who tell stories cannot avoid making judgments—about character, motive, the nature of right and wrong. Judgments imply opinions, which bring up questions of politics, which embarrass the deans and the Development Office.

Given the bias against the telling of stories, I'm astonished that anybody learns anything at all, but I still cannot help thinking of people without a sense of history as orphans. Deprived of the feeling of kinship with a larger whole and a wider self, and unable to fix

---

6. Napoleon III, or Charles Louis-Napoleon Bonaparte (1808–1873), was the nephew of Napoleon Bonaparte, the first emperor of France. Napoleon III ruled from 1848 until 1870, nearly twenty of those years as "emperor," in what many considered a dim reflection of his uncle's career. Charles Dickens (1812–1870), British novelist; Gustave Flaubert (1821–1880), French novelist.

7. Charles Auguste Louis Joseph, Duke

of Morny (1811–1865), was instrumental in the 1851 coup d'état that established Napoleon III, his half-brother, as Emperor of France.

8. Abraham Lincoln (1809–1865), American president from 1861 to 1865; Alexander the Great (356–323 B.C.E.), king of Macedonia and conqueror of most of the world known to ancient Greek civilization.

their position on the map of time, they don't know that the story in the old books is also their own. How, then, do they make sense of what they read in the newspapers, much less heed the counsel of the dead, or marshal the strength of their own minds against what G. K. Chesterton[9] called "the small and arrogant oligarchy of those who merely happen to be walking around"?

Were it not for the gauge of history, I wouldn't know how to measure the emptiness of what now passes for political statement on the television news. On the same day that I read the Department of Education's report card, I came across several orators from the Rocky Mountain states boasting to the CNN cameras of the regional traits of character (self-reliance, rugged individualism, etc.) that allow the cattle to safely roam, and if I hadn't known something about the settling of the trans-Mississippi West I would have missed the joke. The westward course of American empire was conceived and organized as a public-works project, entirely dependent (then as now) on the government dole. By 1845 everybody traveling west on the Oregon or Santa Fe Trails understood that the new country was rich in five primary resources—land, minerals, furs, timber, and government subsidy—and that of these, the last was by far the easiest to reach and exploit. The federal treasury supplied funds for every improvement that anybody could name (railroads, dams, forts, river channels, mining and fishing rights, irrigation canals, orange groves), and the trick (now as then) was to know the right people in Washington or the county courthouse. The West was won less by the force of independent mind than by the lying government contract, the crooked lawsuit, the worthless Indian treaty. The entire chronicle of the western adventure rings with the whining voices of the not-so-sturdy pioneers, blaming their misfortunes on somebody else, never on their own stupidity and greed. The sound was as unpleasant then as it is now, and somehow by knowing that it is not new, I can more easily bear the effrontery of Phil Gramm.[1]

Similarly, when I read in the papers that the mass media have corrupted the American mind with the shows of violence, I remember that in the 1840s prosperous farmers in small midwestern towns

9. G. K. Chesterton (1874–1936), British essayist, novelist, humorist.

1. Phil Gramm (b. 1942), member of the U.S. House of Representatives (1978–85) and U.S. Senator (1985–2002) from Texas.

(i.e., the *fons* and *origo* of Dan Quayle's family values) brought picnics and small children to public hangings.[2] At conferences sponsored by the World Policy Institute or the Council on Foreign Relations,[3] I listen to important newspaper columnists urge the sending of American troops to Bosnia because the Serbian bullies must be punished to discourage other bullies elsewhere in the world, and I think not only of the same important columnists making the same fatuous remarks prior to the American expedition in Vietnam but also of the slaveholding southern gentry in Charleston in April 1861, drinking triumphal toasts on the night before the Confederate artillery fired on Fort Sumter.[4] In Central Park I see Pope John Paul II blessing the crowds gathered in the sheep meadow, and instead of thinking his message as pious and sweet as the sentiment on a Hallmark card, I remember how the flock of the faithful was winnowed by the good shepherds of the Spanish Inquisition.[5]

Because we live in an age demanding of miracles and grand simplifications, I would have thought that the study of history deserved a fairly high place in anybody's curriculum. I'm told that the number of people in the United States at the moment who believe in the literal truth of the biblical Book of Revelation[6] exceeds the number of people who lived in all of medieval Christendom, and in a newspaper the other day I noticed that a voodoo priestess in New Orleans by the name of Sallie Ann Glassman was seeking to rid the

2. James Danforth Quayle (b. 1948), Vice President of the United States (1989–93) under George H. W. Bush. "Family values" was a campaign theme of the Republican party in the 1980s and 1990s; *fons* and *origo* = source and origin.

3. The World Policy Institute is a think tank whose mission is "policy research and advocacy on critical world problems." The Council on Foreign Relations is a nonpartisan institute of scholars researching and promoting public policies since 1921. The Bosnian War (1992–95), during which Serbia perpetrated campaigns of ethnic cleansing against Muslim Bosnians, ended when NATO intervened, defeating Serbia.

4. The Confederate shelling of Fort Sumter, then held by Union troops, started the Civil War.

5. The Spanish Inquisition, from the late 1500s until 1834, was an office of the Catholic Church designed to ensure absolute religious orthodoxy among citizens of Spain by severely punishing dissent. Pope John Paul II (1920–2005) preached in New York's Central Park on October 7, 1995.

6. Book of Revelation, or the Book of the Apocalypse, the last book in the Christian Bible, purported to have been written by St. John the Apostle. As a work of apocalyptic literature, it features a wide range of allegorical figures.

city of crack cocaine through the good offices of Ogoun La Flambeau, a god of war and fire, whom she had summoned from the forests with an offering of rum, gunpowder, and old graveyard dirt. At Harvard University a professor of psychiatry verifies the sighting of intergalactic aliens, and other seers at other microphones speak of Zionist cabals, of balanced budgets and zero debt, of the Trilateral Commission deploying black helicopters to harass the settlements of virtue in eastern Idaho. Across all the world's twenty-four time zones the adherents of one or another of the ancient superstitions wage their furious assaults on what for the last two hundred years has been known as the spirit of the Enlightenment. Against the vivid cries and promises of transcendence, we have little else with which to preserve and extend the work of civilization except the voices of experience. Defined as means rather than end, history defends the future against the past.

1996

Abraham Lincoln
1809–1865

> Lincoln was elected to the presidency in November 1860, and in the four months between the election and his inauguration, on March 4, 1861, six of the states that eventually made up the Confederacy followed South Carolina's lead into secession. Lame duck President Buchanan did little to stop these states from taking over federal property—including forts, weapons, and the like. On the first day of the new administration, the entire nation—North and South—eagerly awaited Lincoln's inaugural address, for no one knew whether the new president would determinedly resist secession or resignedly accept it. When newspapers printed it, Lincoln's address was (in the words of his biographer, Carl Sandburg) "the most widely read and closely scrutinized utterance that had ever come from an American president." His speech had two distinct purposes: to persuade moderate Southerners that he would not threaten their constitutional right to own slaves and to persuade moderate Northerners that they should, if need be, preserve the Union by force of arms. Die-hard secessionists he could persuade of nothing; and he had no need to persuade militant Unionists. Lincoln's resolve probably helped persuade hundreds of thousands of Northerners to join the army when South Carolina bombarded Fort Sumter (April 14, 1861). Some border states—Missouri, Delaware, and Kentucky—never seceded. But Lincoln's first inaugural address was not enough to persuade North Carolina, Arkansas, Virginia, and Tennessee against joining the Confederacy. The ensuing war was far more terrible than anyone had expected. (Eventually, more Americans would die in the Civil War than all other American wars combined.) After two years of disappointing battles, the Union won a decisive victory at Gettysburg, Pennsylvania. The Confederate army that had invaded the North was turned back. Even so, the outcome of the war was still in doubt, largely because it was not clear whether the North had the resolve to see it through to its bloody conclusion. In the 1864 election, for example, Lincoln would face considerable opposition from General George McClellan, who essentially promised to end the war by allowing the South to secede. Lincoln delivered his Gettysburg Address during a cere-

mony dedicating a cemetery at the Gettysburg battlefield. It was widely distributed by newspapers throughout the North.

First Inaugural Address

Fellow-citizens of the United States:

In compliance with a custom as old as the government itself, I appear before you to address you briefly, and to take, in your presence, the oath prescribed by the Constitution of the United States, to be taken by the President "before he enters on the execution of his office."

I do not consider it necessary at present for me to discuss those matters of administration about which there is no special anxiety or excitement.

Apprehension seems to exist among the people of the Southern States, that by the accession of a Republican Administration, their property, and their peace, and personal security, are to be endangered. There has never been any reasonable cause for such apprehension. Indeed, the most ample evidence to the contrary has all the while existed, and been open to their inspection. It is found in nearly all the published speeches of him who now addresses you. I do but quote from one of those speeches when I declare that "I have no purpose, directly or indirectly, to interfere with the institution of slavery in the States where it exists. I believe I have no lawful right to do so, and I have no inclination to do so." Those who nominated and elected me did so with full knowledge that I had made this, and many similar declarations, and had never recanted them. And more than this, they placed in the platform, for my acceptance, and as a law to themselves, and to me, the clear and emphatic resolution which I now read:

"*Resolved*, That the maintenance inviolate of the rights of the States, and especially the right of each State to order and control its own domestic institutions according to its own judgment exclusively, is essential to that balance of power on which the perfection and endurance of our political fabric depend; and we denounce the lawless invasion by armed force of the soil of any State or Territory, no matter under what pretext, as among the gravest of crimes."

I now reiterate these sentiments: and in doing so, I only press upon the public attention the most conclusive evidence of which the case is susceptible, that the property, peace and security of no section are to be in any wise endangered by the now incoming Administration. I add too, that all the protection which, consistently with the Constitution and the laws, can be given, will be cheerfully given to all the States when lawfully demanded, for whatever cause—as cheerfully to one section as to another.

There is much controversy about the delivering up of fugitives from service or labor.[1] The clause I now read is as plainly written in the Constitution as any other of its provisions:

"No person held to service or labor in one State, under the laws thereof, escaping into another, shall, in consequence of any law or regulation therein, be discharged from such service or labor, but shall be delivered up on claim of the party to whom such service or labor may be due."

It is scarcely questioned that this provision was intended by those who made it, for the reclaiming of what we call fugitive slaves; and the intention of the law-giver is the law. All members of Congress swear their support to the whole Constitution—to this provision as much as to any other. To the proposition, then, that slaves whose cases come within the terms of this clause, "shall be delivered up," their oaths are unanimous. Now, if they would make the effort in good temper, could they not, with nearly equal unanimity, frame and pass a law, by means of which to keep good that unanimous oath?

There is some difference of opinion whether this clause should be enforced by national or by state authority; but surely that difference is not a very material one. If the slave is to be surrendered, it can be of but little consequence to him, or to others, by which authority it is done. And should any one, in any case, be content that his oath shall go unkept, on a merely unsubstantial controversy as to *how* it shall be kept?

1. Northerners refused openly or contrived to violate the clause of the Constitution Lincoln quotes here.

Again, in any law upon this subject, ought not all the safeguards of liberty known in civilized and humane jurisprudence to be introduced, so that a free man be not, in any case, surrendered as a slave?[2] And might it not be well, at the same time to provide by law for the enforcement of that clause in the Constitution which guarantees that "the citizens of each State shall be entitled to all privileges and immunities of citizens in the several States"?

I take the official oath to-day, with no mental reservations, and with no purpose to construe the Constitution or laws, by any hypercritical rules. And while I do not choose now to specify particular acts of Congress as proper to be enforced, I do suggest that it will be much safer for all, both in official and private stations, to conform to, and abide by, all those acts which stand unrepealed, than to violate any of them, trusting to find impunity in having them held to be unconstitutional.

It is seventy-two years since the first inauguration of a President under our national Constitution. During that period fifteen different and greatly distinguished citizens, have, in succession, administered the executive branch of the government. They have conducted it through many perils; and, generally, with great success. Yet, with all this scope for precedent, I now enter upon the same task for the brief constitutional term of four years, under great and peculiar difficulty. A disruption of the Federal Union, heretofore only menaced, is now formidably attempted.

I hold, that in contemplation of universal law, and of the Constitution, the Union of these States is perpetual. Perpetuity is implied, if not expressed, in the fundamental law of all national governments. It is safe to assert that no government proper, ever had a provision in its organic law for its own termination. Continue to execute all the express provisions of our national Constitution, and the Union will endure forever—it being impossible to destroy it, except by some action not provided for in the instrument itself.

Again, if the United States be not a government proper, but an association of States in the nature of contract merely, can it, as a contract, be peaceably unmade, by less than all the parties who

2. Free blacks living in the North were often kidnapped and sold into slavery by Southern bounty hunters. Southern states refused to treat such people as "citizens."

made it? One party to a contract may violate it—break it, so to speak; but does it not require all to lawfully rescind it?

Descending from these general principles, we find the proposition that, in legal contemplation, the Union is perpetual, confirmed by the history of the Union itself. The Union is much older than the Constitution. It was formed in fact, by the Articles of Association in 1774. It was matured and continued by the Declaration of Independence in 1776. It was further matured and the faith of all the then thirteen States expressly plighted and engaged that it should be perpetual, by the Articles of Confederation in 1778. And finally, in 1787, one of the declared objects for ordaining and establishing the Constitution, was "*to form a more perfect Union.*"

But if destruction of the Union, by one, or by a part only, of the States, be lawfully possible, the Union is *less* perfect than before the Constitution, having lost the vital element of perpetuity.

It follows from these views that no State, upon its own mere motion, can lawfully get out of the Union,—that *resolves* and *ordinances* to that effect are legally void, and that acts of violence, within any State or States, against the authority of the United States, are insurrectionary or revolutionary, according to circumstances.

I therefore consider that in view of the Constitution and the laws, the Union is unbroken; and to the extent of my ability I shall take care, as the Constitution itself expressly enjoins upon me, that the laws of the Union be faithfully executed in all the States. Doing this I deem to be only a simple duty on my part; and I shall perform it, so far as practicable, unless my rightful masters, the American people, shall withhold the requisite means, or, in some authoritative manner, direct the contrary. I trust this will not be regarded as a menace, but only as the declared purpose of the Union that it will constitutionally defend and maintain itself.

In doing this there needs to be no bloodshed or violence; and there shall be none, unless it be forced upon the national authority. The power confided to me will be used to hold, occupy, and possess the property and places belonging to the government, and to collect the duties and imposts; but beyond what may be necessary for these objects, there will be no invasion—no using of force against or among the people anywhere. Where hostility to the United States, in any interior locality, shall be so great and so universal, as to prevent competent resident citizens from holding the Federal offices, there will be no attempt to force obnoxious strangers among the people for that object. While the strict legal right may exist in the government to enforce the exercise of these offices, the attempt to do so would be so irritating, and so nearly impracticable with all, that I deem it better to forego, for the time, the uses of such offices.

The mails, unless repelled, will continue to be furnished in all parts of the Union. So far as possible, the people everywhere shall have that sense of perfect security which is most favorable to calm thought and reflection. The course here indicated will be followed, unless current events and experience shall show a modification or change to be proper; and in every case and exigency my best discretion will be exercised according to circumstances actually existing, and with a view and a hope of a peaceful solution of the national troubles, and the restoration of fraternal sympathies and affections.

That there are persons in one section or another who seek to destroy the Union at all events, and are glad of any pretext to do it, I will neither affirm or deny; but if there be such, I need address no word to them. To those, however, who really love the Union, may I not speak?

Before entering upon so grave a matter as the destruction of our national fabric, with all its benefits, its memories and its hopes, would it not be wise to ascertain precisely why we do it? Will you hazard so desperate a step, while there is any possibility that any portion of the ills you fly from have no real existence? Will you, while the certain ills you fly to, are greater than all the real ones you fly from? Will you risk the commission of so fearful a mistake?

All profess to be content in the Union, if all constitutional rights can be maintained. Is it true, then, that any right, plainly written in the Constitution, has been denied? I think not. Happily the human mind is so constituted, that no party can reach to the audacity of doing this. Think, if you can, of a single instance in which a plainly written provision of the Constitution has ever been denied. If, by the mere force of numbers, a majority should deprive a minority of any clearly written constitutional right, it might, in a moral point of view, justify revolution—certainly would, if such a right were a vital one. But such is not our case. All the vital rights of minorities, and of individuals, are so plainly assured to them, by affirmations and negations, guarantees and prohibitions, in the Constitution, that controversies never arise concerning them. But no organic law can ever be framed with a provision specifically applicable to every question which may occur in practical administration. No foresight can anticipate, nor any document of reasonable length contain express provisions for all possible questions. Shall fugitives from labor be surrendered by national or by State authority? The Constitution does not expressly say. *May* Congress prohibit slavery in the territories? The Constitution does not expressly say. *Must* Congress protect slavery in the territories? The Constitution does not expressly say.[3]

From questions of this class spring all our constitutional controversies, and we divide upon them into majorities and minorities. If the minority will not acquiesce, the majority must, or the government must cease. There is no other alternative; for continuing the government, is acquiescence on one side or the other. If a minority, in such case, will secede rather than acquiesce, they make a precedent which, in turn, will divide and ruin them; for a minority of their own will secede from them whenever a majority refuses to be controlled by such minority. For instance, why may not any portion of a new confederacy, a year or two hence, arbitrarily secede again, precisely as portions of the present Union now claim to secede from it? All who cherish disunion sentiments, are now being educated to the exact temper of doing this.

Is there such perfect identity of interests among the States to compose a new Union, as to produce harmony only, and prevent renewed secession?

Plainly, the central idea of secession, is the essence of anarchy. A majority, held in restraint by constitutional checks and limitations, and always changing easily with deliberate changes of popular opinions and sentiments is the only true sovereign of a free people. Whoever rejects it, does, of necessity, fly to anarchy or to despotism. Unanimity is impossible; the rule of a minority, as a permanent arrangement, is wholly inadmissible; so that, rejecting the majority principle, anarchy or despotism in some form is all that is left.

---

3. Whether to expand or prohibit slavery in the western territories was debated by Northern and Southern Congressmen.

I do not forget the position assumed by some, that constitutional questions are to be decided by the Supreme Court; nor do I deny that such decisions must be binding in any case, upon the parties to a suit, as to the object of that suit, while they are also entitled to very high respect and consideration in all parallel cases by all other departments of the government. And while it is obviously possible that such decision may be erroneous in any given case, still the evil effect following it, being limited to that particular case, with the chance that it may be over-ruled, and never become a precedent for other cases, can better be borne than could the evils of a different practice. At the same time, the candid citizen must confess that if the policy of the government upon vital questions, affecting the whole people, is to be irrevocably fixed by decisions of the Supreme Court, the instant they are made, in ordinary litigation between parties, in personal actions, the people will have ceased to be their own rulers, having to that extent practically resigned their government into the hands of that eminent tribunal. Nor is there in this view any assault upon the court or the judges. It is a duty from which they may not shrink, to decide cases properly brought before them; and it is no fault of theirs if others seek to turn their decisions to political purposes.

One section of our country believes slavery is *right*, and ought to be extended, while the other believes it is *wrong*, and ought not to be extended. This is the only substantial dispute. The fugitive slave clause of the Constitution, and the law for the suppression of the foreign slave trade, are each as well enforced, perhaps, as any law can ever be in a community where the moral sense of the people imperfectly supports the law itself. The great body of the people abide by the dry legal obligation in both cases, and a few break over in each. This, I think, cannot be perfectly cured; and it would be worse in both cases *after* the separation of the sections, than before. The foreign slave trade, now imperfectly suppressed, would be ultimately revived without restriction, in one section;[4] while fugitive slaves, now only partially surrendered, would not be surrendered at all, by the other.

Physically speaking, we cannot separate. We cannot remove our

---

4. In 1808, as sanctioned by the Constitution, Congress banned the foreign slave trade.

respective sections from each other, nor build an impassable wall between them. A husband and wife may be divorced, and go out of the presence, and beyond the reach of each other; but the different parts of our country cannot do this. They cannot but remain face to face; and intercourse, either amicable or hostile, must continue between them. Is it possible, then, to make that intercourse more advantageous or more satisfactory, *after* separation than *before*? Can aliens make treaties easier than friends can make laws? Can treaties be more faithfully enforced between aliens than laws can among friends? Suppose you go to war, you cannot fight always; and when, after much loss on both sides, and no gain on either, you cease fighting, the identical old questions, as to terms of intercourse, are again upon you.

This country, with its institutions, belongs to the people who inhabit it. Whenever they shall grow weary of the existing government, they can exercise their *constitutional* right of amending it, or their *revolutionary* right to dismember or overthrow it. I cannot be ignorant of the fact that many worthy and patriotic citizens are desirous of having the national Constitution amended. While I make no recommendation of amendments, I fully recognize the rightful authority of the people over the whole subject to be exercised in either of the modes prescribed in the instrument itself; and I should under existing circumstances favor rather than oppose a fair opportunity being afforded the people to act upon it.

I will venture to add that to me the Convention mode seems preferable, in that it allows amendments to originate with the people themselves, instead of only permitting them to take or reject propositions, originated by others, not especially chosen for the purpose, and which might not be precisely such as they would wish to either accept or refuse. I understand a proposed amendment to the Constitution, which amendment, however, I have not seen, has passed Congress, to the effect that the federal government shall never interfere with the domestic institutions of the States, including that of persons held to service. To avoid misconstruction of what I have said, I depart from my purpose not to speak of particular amendments, so far as to say that holding such a provision to now be implied constitutional law, I have no objection to its being made express and irrevocable.

The Chief Magistrate derives all his authority from the people, and they have conferred none upon him to fix terms for the separation of the States. The people themselves can do this also if they choose; but the executive, as such, has nothing to do with it. His duty is to administer the present government, as it came to his hands, and to transmit it, unimpaired by him, to his successor.

Why should there not be a patient confidence in the ultimate justice of the people? Is there any better or equal hope, in the world? In our present differences, is either party without faith of being in the right? If the Almighty Ruler of nations, with his eternal truth and justice, be on your side of the North or on yours of the South, that truth, and that justice, will surely prevail, by the judgment of this great tribunal, the American people.

By the frame of the government under which we live, this same people have wisely given their public servants but little power for mischief; and have, with equal wisdom, provided for the return of that little to their own hands at very short intervals.

While the people retain their virtue and vigilance, no administration, by any extreme of wickedness or folly, can very seriously injure the government in the short space of four years.

My countrymen, one and all, think calmly and *well*, upon this whole subject. Nothing valuable can be lost by taking time. If there be an object to *hurry* any of you, in hot haste, to a step which you would never take *deliberately*, that object will be frustrated by taking time; but no good object can be frustrated by it. Such of you as are now dissatisfied, still have the old Constitution unimpaired, and, on the sensitive point, the laws of your own framing under it; while the new administration will have no immediate power, if it would, to change either. If it were admitted that you who are dissatisfied, hold the right side in the dispute, there still is no single good reason for precipitate action. Intelligence, patriotism, Christianity, and a firm reliance on Him, who has never yet forsaken this favored land, are still competent to adjust, in the best way, all our present difficulty.

In *your* hands, my dissatisfied fellow countrymen, and not in *mine*, is the momentous issue of civil war. The government will not assail *you*. You can have no conflict, without being yourselves the aggressors. *You* have no oath registered in Heaven to destroy the government, while *I* shall have the most solemn one to "preserve, protect and defend" it.

I am loth to close. We are not enemies, but friends. We must not be enemies. Though passion may have strained, it must not break our bonds of affection. The mystic chords of memory, stretching from every battle-field, and patriot grave, to every living heart and hearth-stone, all over this broad land, will yet swell the chorus of the Union, when again touched, as surely they will be, by the better angels of our nature.

1861

The Gettysburg Address

Four score and seven years ago, our fathers brought forth upon this continent a new nation: conceived in liberty, and dedicated to the proposition that all men are created equal.

Now we are engaged in a great civil war, testing whether that nation, or any nation so conceived and so dedicated, can long endure. We are met on a great battlefield of that war.

We have come to dedicate a portion of that field as a final resting-place for those who here gave their lives that this nation might live. It is altogether fitting and proper that we should do this.

But, in a larger sense, we cannot dedicate . . . we cannot consecrate . . . we cannot hallow this ground. The brave men, living and dead, who struggled here have consecrated it, far above our poor power to add or detract. The world will little note, nor long remember, what we say here, but it can never forget what they did here. It is for us the living, rather, to be dedicated here to the unfinished work which they who fought here have thus far so nobly advanced. It is rather for us to be here dedicated to the great task remaining before us . . . that from these honored dead we take increased devotion to that cause for which they gave the last full measure of devotion; that we here highly resolve that these dead shall not have died in vain; that this nation, under God, shall have a new birth of freedom; and that government of the people, by the people, for the people, shall not perish from the earth.

1863

Bret Lott
b. 1958

Lott included this essay in his autobiographical collection Fathers, Sons, and Brothers: The Men in My Family, *an exploration of evolving relationships among three generations. Lott is best known as a novelist, and his essays exploit the techniques of fiction better than most. This piece, for example, can almost be read as a short story. But, as its title suggests, its central theme is more highly defined than is typical in contemporary fiction. Though this short piece does not really try to persuade readers explicitly, it does set out in more or less direct fashion to "essay" the nature of its subject, in this case, "atonement." The common meaning of that word is to propitiate someone you have offended by offering reparations; often, we speak of repairing our relationship to God by atoning for sins. An older use of the word refers to a reconciliation between people after a fight or some other discord. In this sense, the word is synonymous with "harmony" or "accord."*

Atonement

Then there are days like today. We were trying to get out of the house for karate camp this morning, karate camp being a program for kids from eight o'clock to noon for a week at the studio where Zeb has his lessons. Melanie was already gone for work, and the boys, out in the garage, were ready to go. Except for the reefs, those Velcro sandals I'd told Zeb to put on before we ever got outside.

"But Dad," he said, "we're barefoot in the studio. We don't have to wear them."

Then, for all the various and minuscule transgressions that had already been visited upon me this day—when I let the dog out this morning to relieve herself, she made a beeline to the house under construction next door and the discarded chicken bones the framers leave there each day; Zeb and Jake argued, before a single light had been turned on, about who got to use the bathroom first when they woke up; I had to tell Jacob four times to comb his hair; I had to tell Zeb three times to clear the breakfast dishes; the sink was full of pots and pans from the dinner party last night; Melanie was already gone—for all these terrible facts of the day thus far, I blew up at Zeb.

I yelled. I shouted. I threw my hands up in the air, ranted about obeying your father; ranted about the fire ants out there on the grass where we park our old VW Bug, those ants just waiting for bare feet and the opportunity to bite; ranted about never listening to me; ranted about and about and about.

I yelled the first ten minutes of the fifteen-minute drive to the studio, my stomach churned up now about how little writing I'd gotten done the day before, in preparing for the above-mentioned dinner party, about the deadline for a book I'd missed by a month already, about the twenty-two-page story I was about to trash because it had died suddenly the day before yesterday. All of these concerns were translated into a language that involved only words about Velcro sandals, about fire ants, about the idea of obeying your father. My world and its woes boiled down to *Why can't you just listen and obey me without making me yell?*

The last five minutes of the drive we passed in silence, me feeling the stupidity of it all, of my yelling about things that, finally, had very little to do with these two boys. Zeb, next to me, only looked out his window, as did Jacob behind us, the two of them wondering, I imagined, if they dared speak.

But when we parked in front of the studio, Zeb already with his door open, ready to climb out; I reached to him, put my arm around his neck, pulled him to me. I hugged him, said, "I'm sorry I yelled. I shouldn't have done that."

"That's okay," he said into my shoulder.

"Can we go to Wendy's for lunch?" Jacob said from the backseat, sensing this window of opportunity, his father contrite.

Zeb pulled away, smiling, and I turned, looked at Jacob. He was leaning forward, grinning. "Sure," I said. "Wendy's," I said.

Then I looked at Zeb, standing now and pulling forward the seatback to let his brother out. "Zeb," I said, and he looked at me. "You have to wear the reefs so you don't get ant bites. Okay?"

"Okay," he said, and smiled again. By this time Jacob was out.

He slammed shut the door, and they turned, ran along the sidewalk to the glass door of the place, disappeared. Just like that.

There are days like today. Days with no story, really, other than the misstep, the idiot words and gestures, the sincere belief for a moment, however blind, that all this yelling might actually do some good, when the world and Velcro sandals seem somehow malevolently aligned against you. Then the right word, the right gesture. The lunch at Wendy's, atonement after confession.

No story, really, other than of being a father.

2000

Thomas Lynch
b. 1948

Lynch is a special type of essayist: nonprofessional writers whose initial attraction for readers is their primary vocation. Whether the writer tells us what it is like to be a veterinarian, an astronaut, or an undertaker, the daily details of their unusual professions fascinate readers. But such occupational essayists do more than introduce readers to their day jobs. They use their primary professions as a telescope, or a microscope, through which they explore the mysteries that confront us all. Lynch's job naturally leads to ruminations on death and the "Overwhelming Question" of "why oh why oh why?" That phrase alludes to T. S. Eliot's poem, "The Love Song of J. Alfred Prufrock," *about a stuffy, timid man in Boston society who avoids facing the "overwhelming question" by distracting himself with a cocktail party. The elusive question in Eliot's poem is something that Lazarus, back from the dead, could answer: What happens to us after we die?*

Bodies in Motion and at Rest

S
o I'm over at the Hortons' with my stretcher and minivan and my able apprentice, young Matt Sheffler, because they found old George, the cemetery sexton,[1] dead in bed this Thursday morning in ordinary time. And the police have been in to rule out foul play and the EMS team to run a tape so some ER doctor wired to the world can declare him dead at a safe distance. And now it's ours to do—Matt's and mine—to ease George from the bed to the stretcher, negotiate the sharp turn at the top of the stairs, and go out the front door to the dead wagon idling in the driveway and back to the funeral home from whence he'll take his leave—waked and well remembered—a Saturday service in the middle of April, his death observed, his taxes due.

We are bodies in motion and at rest—there in George's master bedroom, in the gray light of the midmorning, an hour or so after his daughter found him because he didn't answer when she called this morning, and he always answers, and she always calls, so she got in the car and drove over and found him exactly as we find him here: breathless, unfettered, perfectly still, manifestly indifferent to all this hubbub. And he is here, assembled on his bed as if nothing had happened, still propped on his left shoulder, his left ear buried in his pillow, his right leg hitched up over the left one, his right hand tucked up under the far pillow his ex-wife used to sleep on, before she left him twenty years ago, and under the former Mrs. Horton's pillow, I lift to show Matt, is a little pearl-handled .22 caliber that George always slept with since he has slept alone. "Security," he called it. He said it helped him sleep.

And really there is nothing out of order, no sign of panic or struggle or pain, and except for the cardiac-blue tinting around his ears, the faint odor of body heat and a little early rigor in his limbs, which makes the moving of him easier, one'd never guess George wasn't just sleeping in this morning—catching the twenty extra winks—because maybe he'd been up late playing poker with the

---

1. Caretaker and supervisor of the cemetery, a lay person who often helps with funeral ceremonies.

boys, or maybe he'd had a late dinner with his woman friend, or maybe he was just a little tired from digging graves and filling them, and anyway, he hadn't a grave to open this morning for one of the locals who was really dead.

But this morning George Horton is really dead and he's really being removed from his premises by Matt and me after we swaddle him in his own bed linens, sidle him on to the stretcher, tip the stretcher up to make the tight turn at the top of the stairs and carefully ease it down, trying to keep the wheels from thumping each time the heavier head end of the enterprise takes a step. And it's really a shame, all things considered, because here's George, more or less in his prime, just south of sixty, his kids raised, his house paid off, a girlfriend still in her thirties with whom he maintained twice-weekly relations—"catch as catch can," he liked to say. And he's a scratch golfer and a small business owner with reliable employees and frequent flier miles that he spends on trips to Vegas twice a year, where he lets himself get a little crazy with the crap tables and showgirls. And he has his money tucked into rental homes and mutual funds, and a host of friends who'd only say good things about him, and a daughter about to make him a grandfather for the first time, and really old George seemed to have it made, and except for our moving him feet first down the stairs this morning, he has everything to live for, everything.

And it is there, on the landing of the first floor, only a few feet from the front door out, that his very pregnant daughter waits in her warmup suit to tender her good-byes to the grandfather of her baby, not yet born. And Matt's face is flushed with the lifting, the huffing and puffing, or the weight of it all, or the sad beauty of the woman as she runs her hand along her father's cheek, and she is catching her breath and her eyes are red and wet and she lifts her face to ask me, "Why?"

"His heart, Nancy . . ." is what I tell her. "It looks like he just slept away. He never felt a thing." These are all the well-tested comforts one learns after twenty-five years of doing these things.

"But *why*?" she asks me, and now it is clear that *how* it happened is not good enough. And here I'm thinking all the usual suspects: the cheeseburgers, the whiskey, the Lucky Strikes, the thirty extra pounds we, some of us, carry, the walks we didn't take, the preventive medicines we all ignore, the work and the worry and the tax man, the luck of the draw, the nature of the beast, the way of the world, the shit that happens because it happens.

But Nancy is not asking for particulars. She wants to know why in the much larger, Overwhelming Question sense: why we don't just live forever. Why are we all eventually orphaned and heartbroken? Why we human beings cease to be. Why our nature won't leave well enough alone. Why we are not all immortal. Why this morning? Why George Horton? Why oh why oh why?

No few times in my life as a funeral director have I been asked this. Schoolchildren, the newly widowed, musing clergy, fellow pilgrims—maybe they think it was my idea. Maybe they just like to see me squirm contemplating a world in which folks wouldn't need caskets and hearses and the likes of me always ready and willing and at their service. Or maybe, like me, sometimes they really wonder.

"Do the math" is what George Horton would say. Or "Bottom line." Or "It's par for the course." Or "It's Biblical." If none of these wisdoms seemed to suit, then "Not my day to watch it" is what he'd say. Pressed on the vast adverbials that come to mind whilst opening or closing graves, George could be counted for tidy answers. Self-schooled in the Ways of the World, he confined his reading to the King James Bible, *The Wall Street Journal*, *Golf Digest*, the *Victoria's Secret* catalog and the Big Book of Alcoholics Anonymous. He watched C-SPAN, The Home Shopping Network, and The Weather Channel. Most afternoons he'd doze off watching Oprah, with whom he was, quite helplessly, in love. On quiet days he'd surf the Web or check his portfolio on-line. On Sundays he watched talking heads and went to dinner and the movies with his woman friend. Weekday mornings he had coffee with the guys at the Summit Café before making the rounds of the half dozen cemeteries he was in charge of. Wednesdays and Saturdays he'd mostly golf.

"Do the math" I heard him give out with once from the cab of his backhoe for no apparent reason. He was backfilling a grave in Milford Memorial. "You gonna make babies, you've gotta make some room; it's Biblical."

Or once, leaning on a shovel, waiting for the priest to finish: "Copulation, population, inspiration, expiration. It's all arithmetic—addition, multiplication, subtraction and long division.

That's all we're doing here, just the math. Bottom line, we're buried a thousand per acre, or burned into two quarts of ashes, give or take."

There was no telling when such wisdoms would come to him.

But it came to me, embalming George later that morning, that the comfort in numbers is that they all add up. There is a balm in the known quantities, however finite. Any given year at this end of the millennium, 2.3 million Americans will die. Ten percent of pregnancies will be unintended. There'll be 60 million common colds. These are numbers you can take to the bank. Give or take, 3.9 million babies will be born. It's Biblical. They'll get a little more or a little less of their 76 years of life expectancy. The boys will grow to just over 69 inches, the girls to just under 64. Of them, 25 percent will be cremated, 35 percent will be overweight, 52 percent will drink. Every year 2 million will get divorced, 4 million will get married and there'll be 30,000 suicides. A few will win the lotto, a few will run for public office, a few will be struck by lightning. And any given day, par for the course, 6,300 of our fellow citizens, just like George, will get breathless and outstretched and spoken of in the past tense; and most will be dressed up the way I dress up George, in his good blue suit, and put him in a casket with Matt Sheffler's help, and assemble the 2 or 3 dozen floral tributes and the 100 or 200 family and friends and the 60 or 70 cars that will follow in the 15 mile per hour procession down through town to grave 4 of lot 17 of section C in Milford Memorial, which will become, in the parlance of our trade, his final resting place, over which a 24-by-12-by-4-inch Barre granite stone will be placed, into which we will have sandblasted his name and dates, one of which, subtracted from the other, will amount, more or less, to his life and times. The corruptible, according to the officiating clergy, will have put on incorruption, the mortal will have put on immortality. "Not my day to watch it" will be among the things we'll never hear George Horton say again.

Nor can we see clearly now, looking into his daughter Nancy's eyes, the blue morning at the end of this coming May when she'll stand, upright as any walking wound, holding her newborn at the graveside of the man, her one and only father, for whom her baby will be named. Nor can we hear the promises she makes to keep him alive, to always remember, forever and ever, in her heart of hearts. Nor is there any math or bottom line or Bible verse that adds or subtracts or in any way accounts for the moment or the mystery she holds there.

2000

Malcolm X
1925–1965

> Malcolm X's father, Earl Little, was a follower of the black nationalist Marcus Garvey, so, when Malcolm was a child, white supremacists burned his house down and may have been responsible for his father's death. A racist high school frustrated Malcolm's aspirations to be a lawyer, and eventually he drifted into crime, was convicted of burglary in 1946, and was sentenced to eight to ten years in prison. The excerpt from his autobiography that follows details his conversion in prison to the Nation of Islam, a religion that restored dignity to many oppressed African Americans and preached separatism; in addition, it tells of his commitment to a rigorous program of self-education. After his release from prison in 1952, Malcolm X rose high enough in the Nation of Islam to rival Elijah Muhammad, its founder and leader. Even so, when Malcolm X began dictating his autobiography to Arthur Haley, he expected to aid Muhammad's evangelism and planned to dedicate the book to Muhammad. The portion included here probably was written with that design. But in 1963, Malcolm X was suspended and later expelled from the Nation of Islam. Muhammad had criticized Malcolm X for the incendiary rhetoric with which he attacked Martin Luther King Jr. and other integrationists and for treating John F. Kennedy's assassination irreverently; Malcolm X had criticized Elijah Muhammad for his lavish lifestyle. Malcolm X made a pilgrimage to Mecca, experienced a powerful conversion to orthodox Islam, changed his name to El-Hajj Malik El-Shabazz, reversed his own racist rhetoric, and began to make amends with leaders of the civil rights movement. So the climax of his autobiography became not his conversion to Muhammad's teachings, but his conversion to

orthodoxy. The book was a best-seller in 1964. In 1965 Malcolm X was assassinated by three Black Muslims who were jealous of his influence. Today Malcolm X's reputation is dominated by the last year of his life, not by the racism of his twelve years in the Nation of Islam. A man of unmatched eloquence, integrity, conviction, and courage, Malcolm X now commands an ethos that rivals even that of Martin Luther King Jr.

A Homemade Education

It was because of my letters that I happened to stumble upon starting to acquire some kind of a homemade education.

I became increasingly frustrated at not being able to express what I wanted to convey in letters that I wrote, especially those to Mr. Elijah Muhammad. In the street, I had been the most articulate hustler out there—I had commanded attention when I said something. But now, trying to write simple English, I not only wasn't articulate, I wasn't even functional. How would I sound writing in slang, the way I would *say* it, something such as "Look, daddy, let me pull your coat about a cat, Elijah Muhammad—"

Many who today hear me somewhere in person, or on television, or those who read something I've said, will think I went to school far beyond the eighth grade. This impression is due entirely to my prison studies.

It had really begun back in the Charlestown Prison, when Bimbi[1] first made me feel envy of his stock of knowledge. Bimbi had always taken charge of any conversation he was in, and I had tried to emulate him. But every book I picked up had few sentences which didn't contain anywhere from one to nearly all of the words that might as well have been in Chinese. When I just skipped those words, of course, I really ended up with little idea of what the book said. So I had come to the Norfolk Prison Colony still going through only book-reading motions. Pretty soon, I would have quit even these motions, unless I had received the motivation that I did.

I saw that the best thing I could do was get hold of a dictio-

---

1. A fellow inmate.

nary—to study, to learn some words. I was lucky enough to reason also that I should try to improve my penmanship. It was sad. I couldn't even write in a straight line. It was both ideas together that moved me to request a dictionary along with some tablets and pencils from the Norfolk Prison Colony school.

I spent two days just riffling uncertainly through the dictionary's pages. I'd never realized so many words existed! I didn't know *which* words I needed to learn. Finally, just to start some kind of action, I began copying.

In my slow, painstaking, ragged handwriting, I copied into my tablet everything printed on that first page, down to the punctuation marks.

I believe it took me a day. Then, aloud, I read back, to myself, everything I'd written on the tablet. Over and over, aloud, to myself, I read my own handwriting.

I woke up the next morning, thinking about those words—immensely proud to realize that not only had I written so much at one time, but I'd written words that I never knew were in the world. Moreover, with a little effort, I also could remember what many of these words meant. I reviewed the words whose meanings I didn't remember. Funny thing, from the dictionary first page right now, that "aardvark" springs to my mind. The dictionary had a picture of it, a long-tailed, long-eared, burrowing African mammal, which lives off termites caught by sticking out its tongue as an anteater does for ants.

I was so fascinated that I went on—I copied the dictionary's next page. And the same experience came when I studied that. With every succeeding page, I also learned of people and places and events from history. Actually the dictionary is like a miniature encyclopedia. Finally the dictionary's A section had filled a whole tablet—and I went on into the B's. That was the way I started copying what eventually became the entire dictionary. It went a lot faster after so much practice helped me to pick up handwriting speed. Between what I wrote in my tablet, and writing letters, during the rest of my time in prison I would guess I wrote a million words.

I suppose it was inevitable that as my word-base broadened, I could for the first time pick up a book and read and now begin to understand what the book was saying. Anyone who has read a great deal can imagine the new world that opened. Let me tell you something: from then until I left that prison, in every free moment I had, if I was not reading in the library, I was reading on my bunk. You couldn't have gotten me out of books with a wedge. Between Mr. Muhammad's teachings, my correspondence, my visitors—usually Ella and Reginald[2]—and my reading of books, months passed without my even thinking about being imprisoned. In fact, up to then, I never had been so truly free in my life.

The Norfolk Prison Colony's library was in the school building. A variety of classes was taught there by instructors who came from such places as Harvard and Boston universities. The weekly debates between inmate teams were also held in the school building. You would be astonished to know how worked up convict debaters and audiences would get over subjects like "Should Babies Be Fed Milk?"

Available on the prison library's shelves were books on just about every general subject. Much of the big private collection that Parkhurst[3] had willed to the prison was still in crates and boxes in the back of the library—thousands of old books. Some of them looked ancient: covers faded, old-time parchment-looking binding. Parkhurst, I've mentioned, seemed to have been principally interested in history and religion. He had the money and the special interest to have a lot of books that you wouldn't have in general circulation. Any college library would have been lucky to get that collection.

As you can imagine, especially in a prison where there was heavy emphasis on rehabilitation, an inmate was smiled upon if he demonstrated an unusually intense interest in books. There was a sizable number of well-read inmates, especially the popular debaters. Some were said by many to be practically walking encyclopedias. They were almost celebrities. No university would ask any student to devour literature as I did when this new world opened to me, of being able to read and *understand*.

I read more in my room than in the library itself. An inmate who

2. His half sister and brother.
3. Charles Henry Parkhurst (1842–1933), American clergyman, reformer, and president of the Society for the Prevention of Crime.

was known to read a lot could check out more than the permitted maximum number of books. I preferred reading in the total isolation of my own room.

When I had progressed to really serious reading, every night at about ten P.M. I would be outraged with the "lights out." It always seemed to catch me right in the middle of something engrossing.

Fortunately, right outside my door was a corridor light that cast a glow into my room. The glow was enough to read by, once my eyes adjusted to it. So when "lights out" came, I would sit on the floor where I could continue reading in that glow.

At one-hour intervals the night guards paced past every room. Each time I heard the approaching footsteps, I jumped into bed and feigned sleep. And as soon as the guard passed, I got back out of bed onto the floor area of that light-glow, where I would read for another fifty-eight minutes—until the guard approached again. That went on until three or four every morning. Three or four hours of sleep a night was enough for me. Often in the years in the streets I had slept less than that.

The teachings of Mr. Muhammad stressed how history had been "whitened"—when white men had written history books, the black man simply had been left out. Mr. Muhammad couldn't have said anything that would have struck me much harder. I had never forgotten how when my class, me and all of those whites, had studied seventh-grade United States history back in Mason,[4] the history of the Negro had been covered in one paragraph, and the teacher had gotten a big laugh with his joke, "Negroes' feet are so big that when they walk, they leave a hole in the ground."

This is one reason why Mr. Muhammad's teachings spread so swiftly all over the United States, among *all* Negroes, whether or not they became followers of Mr. Muhammad. The teachings ring true—to every Negro. You can hardly show me a black adult in America—or a white one, for that matter—who knows from the history books anything like the truth about the black man's role. In my own case, once I heard of the "glorious history of the black

4. Mason, Michigan, ten miles outside Lansing.

man," I took special pains to hunt in the library for books that would inform me on details about black history.

I can remember accurately the very first set of books that really impressed me. I have since bought that set of books and have it at home for my children to read as they grow up. It's called *Wonders of the World*. It's full of pictures of archeological finds, statues that depict, usually, non-European people.

I found books like Will Durant's *Story of Civilization*. I read H. G. Wells' *Outline of History*. *Souls Of Black Folk* by W. E. B. Du Bois gave me a glimpse into the black people's history before they came to this country. Carter G. Woodson's *Negro History* opened my eyes about black empires before the black slave was brought to the United States, and the early Negro struggles for freedom.

J. A. Rogers' three volumes of *Sex and Race* told about race-mixing before Christ's time; about Aesop being a black man who told fables; about Egypt's Pharaohs; about the great Coptic Christian Empires; about Ethiopia, the earth's oldest continuous black civilization, as China is the oldest continuous civilization.

Mr. Muhammad's teaching about how the white man had been created led me to *Findings In Genetics* by Gregor Mendel. (The dictionary's G section was where I had learned what "genetics" meant.) I really studied this book by the Austrian monk. Reading it over and over, especially certain sections, helped me to understand that if you started with a black man, a white man could be produced; but starting with a white man, you never could produce a black man—because the white gene is recessive. And since no one disputes that there was but one Original Man, the conclusion is clear.

During the last year or so, in the *New York Times*, Arnold Toynbee used the word "bleached" in describing the white man. (His words were: "White (i.e. bleached) human beings of North European origin. . . .") Toynbee also referred to the European geographic area as only a peninsula of Asia. He said there is no such thing as Europe. And if you look at the globe, you will see for yourself that America is only an extension of Asia. (But at the same time Toynbee is among those who have helped to bleach history. He has written that Africa was the only continent that produced no history. He won't write that again. Every day now, the truth is coming to light.)

I never will forget how shocked I was when I began reading about slavery's total horror. It made such an impact upon me that it later became one of my favorite subjects when I became a minister of Mr. Muhammad's. The world's most monstrous crime, the sin and the blood on the white man's hands, are almost impossible to believe. Books like the one by Frederick Olmstead opened my eyes to the horrors suffered when the slave was landed in the United States. The European woman, Fannie Kimball, who had married a Southern white slaveowner, described how human beings were degraded. Of course I read *Uncle Tom's Cabin*. In fact, I believe that's the only novel I have ever read since I started serious reading.

Parkhurst's collection also contained some bound pamphlets of the Abolitionist Anti-Slavery Society of New England. I read descriptions of atrocities, saw those illustrations of black slave women tied up and flogged with whips; of black mothers watching their babies being dragged off, never to be seen by their mothers again; of dogs after slaves, and of the fugitive slave catchers, evil white men with whips and clubs and chains and guns. I read about the slave preacher Nat Turner, who put the fear of God into the white slavemaster. Nat Turner wasn't going around preaching pie-in-the-sky and "non-violent" freedom for the black man. There in Virginia one night in 1831, Nat and seven other slaves started out at his master's home and through the night they went from one plantation "big house" to the next, killing, until by the next morning 57 white people were dead and Nat had about 70 slaves following him. White people, terrified for their lives, fled from their homes, locked themselves up in public buildings, hid in the woods, and some even left the state. A small army of soldiers took two months to catch and hang Nat Turner. Somewhere I have read where Nat Turner's example is said to have inspired John Brown to invade Virginia and attack Harper's Ferry nearly thirty years later, with thirteen white men and five Negroes.

I read Herodotus, "the father of History," or, rather, I read about him. And I read the histories of various nations, which opened my eyes gradually, then wider and wider, to how the whole world's white men had indeed acted like devils, pillaging and raping and bleeding and draining the whole world's non-white people. I remember, for instance, books such as Will Durant's story of Oriental civilization, and Mahatma Gandhi's accounts of the struggle to drive the British out of India.

Book after book showed me how the white man had brought upon the world's black, brown, red, and yellow peoples every variety of the sufferings of exploitation. I saw how since the sixteenth century, the so-called "Christian trader" white man began to ply the seas in his lust for Asian and African empires, and plunder, and power. I read, I saw, how the white man never has gone among the non-white peoples bearing the Cross in the true manner and spirit of Christ's teachings—meek, humble, and Christ-like.

I perceived, as I read, how the collective white man had been actually nothing but a piratical opportunist who used Faustian machinations to make his own Christianity his initial wedge in criminal conquests. First, always "religiously," he branded "heathen" and "pagan" labels upon ancient non-white cultures and civilizations. The stage thus set, he then turned upon his non-white victims his weapons of war.

I read how, entering India—half a *billion* deeply religious brown people—the British white man, by 1759, through promises, trickery and manipulations, controlled much of India through Great Britain's East India Company. The parasitical British administration kept tentacling out to half of the subcontinent. In 1857, some of the desperate people of India finally mutinied—and, excepting the African slave trade, nowhere has history recorded any more unnecessary bestial and ruthless human carnage than the British suppression of the non-white Indian people.

Over 115 million African blacks—close to the 1930's population of the United States—were murdered or enslaved during the slave trade. And I read how when the slave market was glutted, the cannibalistic white powers of Europe next carved up, as their colonies, the richest areas of the black continent. And Europe's chancelleries for the next century played a chess game of naked exploitation and power from Cape Horn to Cairo.

Ten guards and the warden couldn't have torn me out of those books. Not even Elijah Muhammad could have been more eloquent than those books were in providing indisputable proof that the collective white man had acted like a devil in virtually every contact he had with the world's collective non-white man. I listen today to the radio, and watch television, and read the headlines about the collective white man's fear and tension concerning China. When the white man professes ignorance about why the Chinese hate him so, my mind can't help flashing back to what I read, there in prison, about how the blood forebears of this same white man raped China at a time when China was trusting and helpless. Those original white "Christian traders" sent into China millions of pounds of opium. By 1839, so many of the Chinese were addicts that China's desperate government destroyed twenty thousand chests of opium. The first Opium War was promptly declared by the white man. Imagine! Declaring *war* upon someone who objects to being narcotized! The Chinese were severely beaten, with Chinese-invented gunpowder.

The Treaty of Nanking made China pay the British white man for the destroyed opium; forced open China's major ports to British trade; forced China to abandon Hong Kong; fixed China's import tariffs so low that cheap British articles soon flooded in, maiming China's industrial development.

After a second Opium War, the Tientsin Treaties legalized the ravaging opium trade, legalized a British-French-American control of China's customs. China tried delaying that Treaty's ratification; Peking was looted and burned.

"Kill the foreign white devils!" was the 1901 Chinese war cry in the Boxer Rebellion. Losing again, this time the Chinese were driven from Peking's choicest areas. The vicious, arrogant white man put up the famous signs, "Chinese and dogs not allowed."

Red China after World War II closed its doors to the Western white world. Massive Chinese agricultural, scientific, and industrial efforts are described in a book that *Life* magazine recently published. Some observers inside Red China have reported that the world never has known such a hate-white campaign as is now going on in this non-white country where, present birth-rates continuing, in fifty more years Chinese will be half the earth's population. And it seems that some Chinese chickens will soon come home to roost, with China's recent successful nuclear tests.

Let us face reality. We can see in the United Nations a new world order being shaped, along color lines—an alliance among the non-white nations. America's U.N. Ambassador Adlai Stevenson complained not long ago that in the United Nations "a skin game" was being played. He was right. He was facing reality. A "skin game" *is* being played. But Ambassador Stevenson sounded like Jesse James accusing the marshal of carrying a gun. Because who in the world's history ever has played a worse "skin game" than the white man?

Mr. Muhammad, to whom I was writing daily, had no idea of what a new world had opened up to me through my efforts to document his teachings in books.

When I discovered philosophy, I tried to touch all the landmarks of philosophical development. Gradually, I read most of the old philosophers, Occidental and Oriental. The Oriental philosophers were the ones I came to prefer; finally, my impression was that most Occidental philosophy had largely been borrowed from the Oriental thinkers. Socrates, for instance, traveled in Egypt. Some sources even say that Socrates was initiated into some of the Egyptian mysteries. Obviously Socrates got some of his wisdom among the East's wise men.

I have often reflected upon the new vistas that reading opened to me. I knew right there in prison that reading had changed forever the course of my life. As I see it today, the ability to read awoke inside me some long dormant craving to be mentally alive. I certainly wasn't seeking any degree, the way a college confers a status symbol upon its students. My homemade education gave me, with every additional book that I read, a little bit more sensitivity to the deafness, dumbness, and blindness that was afflicting the black race in America. Not long ago, an English writer telephoned me from London, asking questions. One was, "What's your alma mater?" I told him, "Books." You will never catch me with a free fifteen minutes in which I'm not studying something I feel might be able to help the black man.

Yesterday I spoke in London, and both ways on the plane across the Atlantic I was studying a document about how the United Nations proposes to insure the human rights of the oppressed minorities of the world. The American black man is the world's most shameful case of minority oppression. What makes the black man think of himself as only an internal United States issue is just a catch-phrase, two words, "civil rights." How is the black man going to get "civil rights" before first he wins his *human* rights? If the American black man will start thinking about his *human* rights, and then start thinking of himself as part of one of the world's great peoples, he will see he has a case for the United Nations.

I can't think of a better case! Four hundred years of black blood and sweat invested here in America, and the white man still has the black man begging for what every immigrant fresh off the ship can take for granted the minute he walks down the gangplank.

But I'm digressing. I told the Englishman that my alma mater was books, a good library. Every time I catch a plane, I have with me a book that I want to read—and that's a lot of books these days. If I weren't out here every day battling the white man, I could spend the rest of my life reading, just satisfying my curiosity—because you can hardly mention anything I'm not curious about. I don't think anybody ever got more out of going to prison than I did. In fact, prison enabled me to study far more intensively than I would have if my life had gone differently and I had attended some college. I imagine that one of the biggest troubles with colleges is there are too many distractions, too much panty-raiding, fraternities, and boola-boola and all of that. Where else but in a prison could I have attacked my ignorance by being able to study intensely sometimes as much as fifteen hours a day?

1964

N. Scott Momaday
b. 1934

In this essay, Momaday provides an example of a land ethic, and this is meant to persuade readers of the truth of his conclusion: "We Americans must come again to a moral comprehension of the earth and air." The essay first appeared in the 1970 Ecotactics: The Sierra Club Handbook for Environmental Activists. *Like Chief Seattle's letter, it helped express the philosophical foundation of the modern environmental movement. Throughout the essay, Momaday refers to his book* The Way to Rainy Mountain, *which is an amalgam of Kiowa mythology, history, and Momaday's personal recollections. Rainy Mountain is in Kiowa County, Oklahoma, not far from Momaday's birthplace, and was a natural landmark and gathering spot for Plains Indians; later, it was within the reservations that constituted most of Oklahoma before the tribal lands were settled by whites. In Momaday's view, it has a deep and mysterious racial connection to the Kiowa.*

An American Land Ethic

I

One night a strange thing happened. I had written the greater part of *The Way to Rainy Mountain*—all of it, in fact, except the epilogue. I had set down the last of the old Kiowa[1] tales, and I had composed both the historical and the autobiographical commentaries for it. I had the sense of being out of breath, of having said what it was in me to say on that subject. The manuscript lay before me in the bright light, small, to be sure, but complete; or nearly so. I had written the second of the two poems in which that book is framed. I had uttered the last word, as it were. And yet a whole, penultimate piece was missing. I began once again to write:

> During the first hours after midnight on the morning of November 13, 1833, it seemed that the world was coming to an end. Suddenly the stillness of the night was broken; there were brilliant flashes of light in the sky, light of such intensity that people were awakened by it. With the speed and density of a driving rain, stars were falling in the universe. Some were brighter than Venus; one was said to be as large as the moon.

I went on to say that that event, the falling of the stars on North America, that explosion of Leonid meteors which occurred 137 years

---

1. The Kiowa are a large tribe of Native Americans who originated in Montana but eventually moved south over the Great Plains, finally allying themselves with the Comanche of Texas and Oklahoma.

ago, is among the earliest entries in the Kiowa calendars. So deeply impressed upon the imagination of the Kiowas is that old phenom-enon that it is remembered still; it has become a part of the racial memory.

"The living memory," I wrote, "and the verbal tradition which transcends it, were brought together for me once and for all in the person of Ko-sahn." It seemed eminently right for me to deal, after all, with that old woman. Ko-sahn is among the most venerable people I have ever known. She spoke and sang to me one summer afternoon in Oklahoma. It was like a dream. When I was born she was already old; she was a grown woman when my grandparents came into the world. She sat perfectly still, folded over on herself. It did not seem possible that so many years—a century of years—could be so compacted and distilled. Her voice shuddered, but it did not fail. Her songs were sad. An old whimsy, a delight in lan-guage and in remembrance, shone in her one good eye. She con-jured up the past, imagining perfectly the long continuity of her being. She imagined the lovely young girl, wild and vital, she had been. She imagined the Sun Dance:

There was an old, old woman. She had something on her back. The boys went out to see. The old woman had a bag full of earth on her back. It was a certain kind of sandy earth. That is what they must have in the lodge. The dancers must dance upon the sandy earth. The old woman held a digging tool in her hand. She turned towards the south and pointed with her lips. It was like a kiss, and she began to sing:

We have brought the earth.
Now it is time to play;
As old as I am, I still have the feeling of play.

That was the beginning of the Sun Dance.

By this time I was back into the book, caught up completely in the act of writing. I had projected myself—imagined myself—out of the room and out of time. I was there with Ko-sahn in the Okla-homa July. We laughed easily together; I felt that I had known her all of my life—all of hers. I did not want to let her go. But I had come to the end. I set down, almost grudgingly, the last sentences:

It was—all of this and more—a quest, a going forth upon the way to Rainy Mountain. Probably Ko-sahn too is dead now. At times, in the quiet of evening, I think she must have wondered, dreaming, who she was. Was she become in her sleep that old purveyor of the sacred earth, perhaps, that ancient one who, old as she was, still had the feeling of play? And in her mind, at times, did she see the falling stars?

For some time I sat looking down at these words on the page, trying to deal with the emptiness that had come about inside of me. The words did not seem real. The longer I looked at them, the more unfamiliar they became. At last I could scarcely believe that they made sense, that they had anything whatsoever to do with meaning. In desperation almost, I went back over the final paragraphs, backward and forward, hurriedly. My eyes fell upon the name Ko-sahn. And all at once everything seemed suddenly to refer to that name. The name seemed to humanize the whole complexity of language. All at once, absolutely, I had the sense of the magic of words and of names. Ko-sahn, I said. And I said again, KO-SAHN.

Then it was that that ancient, one-eyed woman stepped out of the language and stood before me on the page. I was amazed, of course, and yet it seemed to me entirely appropriate that this should happen.

"Yes, grandson," she said. "What is it? What do you want?"

"I was just now writing about you," I replied, stammering. "I thought—forgive me—I thought that perhaps you were . . . That you had . . ."

"No," she said. And she cackled. And she went on. "You have imagined me well, and so I am. You have imagined that I dream, and so I do. I have seen the falling stars."

"But all of this, this *imagining*," I protested, "this has taken place—is taking place in my mind. You are not actually here, not here in this room." It occurred to me that I was being extremely rude, but I could not help myself. She seemed to understand.

"Be careful of your pronouncements, grandson," she answered.

"You imagine that I am here in this room, do you not? This is worth something. You see, I have existence, whole being, in your imagination. It is but one kind of being, to be sure, but it is perhaps the best of all kinds. If I am not here in this room, grandson, then surely neither are you."

"I think I see what you mean," I said. I felt justly rebuked. "Tell me grandmother, how old are you?"

"I do not know," she replied. "There are times when I think that I am the oldest woman on earth. You know, the Kiowas came into the world through a hollow log. In my mind's eye I have seen them emerge, one by one, from the mouth of the log. I have seen them so clearly, how they were dressed, how delighted they were to see the world around them. I *must* have been there. And I must have taken part in that old migration of the Kiowas from the Yellowstone to the southern plains, for I have seen antelope bounding in the tall grass near the Big Horn River, and I have seen the ghost forests in the Black Hills. Once I saw the red cliffs of Palo Duro Canyon. I was with those who were camped in the Wichita Mountains when the stars fell."[2]

"You are indeed very old," I said, "and you have seen many things."

"Yes, I imagine that I have," she replied. Then she turned slowly around, nodding once, and receded into the language I had made. And then I imagined I was alone in the room.

II

Once in his life a man ought to concentrate his mind upon the re-membered earth, I believe. He ought to give himself up to a partic-ular landscape in his experience, to look at it from as many angles as he can, to wonder about it, to dwell upon it. He ought to imagine

2. The Big Horn River is in Montana; a tributary of it was the site of Custer's "Last Stand," the massacre of the 7th Cavalry by the Sioux. This area and the Black Hills of South Dakota were the grounds of the Kiowa before the Sioux drove them further south around 1800. Palo Duro Canyon is in Texas and was the site of one of the last battles between the U.S. Army and the Kiowa and Comanche tribes. The Wichita Mountains in Oklahoma were part of the ancestral Kiowa and Comanche lands, and later part of their reservation.

that he touches it with his hands at every season and listens to the sounds that are made upon it. He ought to imagine the creatures there and all the faintest motions of the wind. He ought to recollect the glare of noon and all the colors of the dawn and dusk.

The Wichita Mountains rise out of the southern plains in a long crooked line that runs from east to west. The mountains are made of red earth, and of rock that is neither red nor blue but some very rare admixture of the two, like the feathers of certain birds. They are not so high and mighty as the mountains of the Far West, and they bear a different relationship to the land around them. One does not imagine that they are distinctive in themselves, or indeed that they exist apart from the plain in any sense. If you try to think of them in the abstract, they lose the look of mountains. They are preeminently an expression of the larger landscape, more perfectly organic than one can easily imagine. To behold these mountains from the plain is one thing; to see the plain from the mountains is something else. I have stood on the top of Mount Scott and seen the earth below, bending out into the whole circle of the sky. The wind runs always close upon the slopes, and there are times when you hear the rush of it like water in the ravines.

Here is the hub of an old commerce. More than a hundred years ago the Kiowas and Comanches[3] journeyed outward from the Wichitas in every direction, seeking after mischief and medicine, horses and hostages. Sometimes they went away for years, but they always returned, for the land had got hold of them. It is a consecrated place, and even now there is something of the wilderness about it. There is a game preserve in the hills. Animals graze away in the open meadows or, closer by, keep to the shadows of the groves: antelope and deer, longhorns and buffalo. It was here, the Kiowas say, that the first buffalo came into the world.

The yellow grassy knoll that is called Rainy Mountain lies a short distance to the north and west. There, on the west side, is the ruin of an old school where my grandmother went as a wild girl in blanket and braids to learn of numbers and of names in English. And there she is buried.

---

3. The Comanche Indians were a South Plains tribe closely allied with the Kiowas.

Most is your name the name of this dark stone.
Deranged in death, the mind to be inheres
Forever in the nominal unknown,
The wake of nothing audible he hears
Who listens here and now to hear your name.
The early sun, red as a hunter's moon,
Runs in the plain. The mountain burns and shines;
And silence is the long approach of noon
Upon the shadow that your name defines—
And death this cold, black density of stone.

III

I am interested in the way that a man looks at a given landscape and takes possession of it in his blood and brain. For this happens, I am certain, in the ordinary motion of life. None of us lives apart from the land entirely; such an isolation is unimaginable. We have sooner or later to come to terms with the world around us—and I mean especially the physical world, not only as it is revealed to us immediately through our senses, but also as it is perceived more truly in the long turn of seasons and of years. And we must come to moral terms. There is no alternative, I believe, if we are to realize and maintain our humanity, for our humanity must consist in part in the ethical as well as in the practical ideal of preservation. And particularly here and now is that true. We Americans need now more than ever before—and indeed more than we know—to imagine who and what we are with respect to the earth and sky. I am talking about an act of the imagination, essentially, and the concept of an American land ethic.

It is no doubt more difficult to imagine the landscape of America now, than it was in, say, 1900. Our whole experience as a nation in this century has been a repudiation of the pastoral ideal which informs so much of the art and literature of the nineteenth century. One effect of the technological revolution has been to uproot us from the soil. We have become disoriented, I believe; we have suffered a kind of psychic dislocation of ourselves in time and space. We may be perfectly sure of where we are in relation to the supermarket and the next coffee break, but I doubt that any of us knows where he is in relation to the stars and to the solstices. Our sense of the natural order has become dull and unreliable. Like the wilderness itself, our sphere of instinct has diminished in proportion as we have failed to imagine truly what it is. And yet I believe that it is possible to formulate an ethical idea of the land—a notion of what it is and must be in our daily lives—and I believe moreover that it is absolutely necessary to do so.

It would seem on the surface of things that a land ethic is something that is alien to, or at least dormant in, most Americans. Most of us have developed an attitude of indifference toward the land. In terms of my own experience, it is difficult to see how such an attitude could ever have come about.

IV

Ko-sahn could remember where my grandmother was born. "It was just there," she said, pointing to a tree, and the tree was like a hundred others that grew up in the broad depression of the Washita River. I could see nothing to indicate that anyone had ever been there, spoken so much as a word, or touched the tips of his fingers to the tree. But in her memory Ko-sahn could see the child. I think she must have remembered my grandmother's voice, for she seemed for a long moment to listen and to hear. There was a still, heavy heat upon that place; I had the sense that ghosts were gathering there.

And in the racial memory, Ko-sahn had seen the falling stars. For her there was no distinction between the individual and the racial experience, even as there was none between the mythical and the historical. Both were realized for her in the one memory, and that was of the land. This landscape, in which she had lived for a hundred years, was the common denominator of everything that she knew and would ever know—and her knowledge was profound. Her roots ran deep into the earth, and from those depths she drew strength enough to hold still against all the forces of chance and disorder. And she drew therefrom the sustenance of meaning and of mystery as well. The falling stars were not for Ko-sahn an isolated or accidental phenomenon. She had a great personal investment in that awful commotion of light in the night sky. For it remained to be imagined. She must at last deal with it in words; she must appropriate it to her understanding of the whole universe. And, again, when she spoke of the Sun Dance, it was an essential expression of her relationship to the life of the earth and to the sun and moon.

In Ko-sahn and in her people we have always had the example of a deep, ethical regard for the land. We had better learn from it. Surely that ethic is merely latent in ourselves. It must now be activated, I believe. We Americans must come again to a moral comprehension of the earth and air. We must live according to the principle of a land ethic. The alternative is that we shall not live at all.

1970

George Orwell
1903–1950

> *This essay tells about an actual event in Orwell's life, although some of the details might have been changed (in reality, for example, he rode an old Ford, not a pony, in search of the elephant). Englishmen had been in parts of India as early as the seventeenth century, but British control was more fully developed by 1858, when Great Britain assumed dominion over most of the subcontinent, including Lower Burma. Orwell's father was part of the colonial administration, and Orwell himself was born in northern India. Though he honestly tried to believe in the nobility of England's paternal attitude toward its possessions, even as a young man Orwell recoiled from the racist injustices the English had to commit to maintain control over these territories. Orwell grew up at the height of the British and other European empires, when England ruled about one-fourth of the world's territory and the major European countries competed with each other for dominion over the natural resources and consumer markets of less powerful peoples across the globe. But World War I (1914–18) helped to begin the end of the European empires. Advocates of Indian independence expanded their ranks after the war, and in 1926, when Orwell killed the elephant, colonial policemen found themselves trying to keep the*

*peace among an increasingly restive population. Eventually, Or-
well's conscience led him to resign his position, and he came back to
England to write. Part of what he explores here is the mentality of
the people who hold the power in a police state. He published this
essay in 1936, after he committed himself to democratic socialism,
which included an anti-imperial philosophy. The British still ruled
India—which would not win its independence until 1947. Orwell
was attempting to influence the debates in England about the future of the British empire. Even so, in its original context, this essay
would have been as much a warning for the English to oppose
Hitler's Germany, Mussolini's Italy, and Stalin's Russia, each of
which erected police states in their home countries that were similar
in many ways to the colonial police states abroad, and each of
which sought to establish new empires of their own.*

Shooting an Elephant

In Moulmein, in Lower Burma, I was hated by large numbers of
people—the only time in my life that I have been important
enough for this to happen to me. I was sub-divisional police officer of the town, and in an aimless, petty kind of way anti-
European feeling was very bitter. No one had the guts to raise a riot,
but if a European woman went through the bazaars alone somebody
would probably spit betel juice[1] over her dress. As a police officer I
was an obvious target and was baited whenever it seemed safe to do
so. When a nimble Burman tripped me up on the football field and
the referee (another Burman) looked the other way, the crowd
yelled with hideous laughter. This happened more than once. In the
end the sneering yellow faces of young men that met me everywhere, the insults hooted after me when I was at a safe distance, got
badly on my nerves. The young Buddhist priests were the worst of
all. There were several thousands of them in the town and none of
them seemed to have anything to do except stand on street corners
and jeer at Europeans.

All this was perplexing and upsetting. For at that time I had

---

1. Indians chew the betel leaf like tobacco.

already made up my mind that imperialism was an evil thing and the sooner I chucked up my job and got out of it the better. Theoretically—and secretly, of course—I was all for the Burmese and all against their oppressors, the British. As for the job I was doing, I hated it more bitterly than I can perhaps make clear. In a job like that you see the dirty work of Empire at close quarters. The wretched prisoners huddling in the stinking cages of the lock-ups, the grey, cowed faces of the long-term convicts, the scarred buttocks of the men who had been flogged with bamboos—all these oppressed me with an intolerable sense of guilt. But I could get nothing into perspective. I was young and ill-educated and I had had to think out my problems in the utter silence that is imposed on every Englishman in the East. I did not even know that the British Empire is dying, still less did I know that it is a great deal better than the younger empires that are going to supplant it. All I knew was that I was stuck between my hatred of the empire I served and my rage against the evil-spirited little beasts who tried to make my job impossible. With one part of my mind I thought of the British Raj[2] as an unbreakable tyranny, as something clamped down, *in saecula saeculorum*,[3] upon the will of prostrate peoples; with another part I thought that the greatest joy in the world would be to drive a bayonet into a Buddhist priest's guts. Feelings like these are the normal by-products of imperialism; ask any Anglo-Indian official, if you can catch him off duty.

One day something happened which in a roundabout way was enlightening. It was a tiny incident in itself, but it gave me a better glimpse than I had had before of the real nature of imperialism— the real motives for which despotic governments act. Early one morning the sub-inspector at a police station the other end of the town rang me up on the phone and said that an elephant was ravaging the bazaar. Would I please come and do something about it? I did not know what I could do, but I wanted to see what was happening and I got on to a pony and started out. I took my rifle, an old .44 Winchester and much too small to kill an elephant, but I

---

2. Literally, British rule or dominion; the term refers to those parts of India directly administered by the British colonials.
3. Forever (Latin).

thought the noise might be useful *in terrorem*.[4] Various Burmans stopped me on the way and told me about the elephant's doings. It was not, of course, a wild elephant, but a tame one which had gone "must." It had been chained up as tame elephants always are when their attack of "must" is due, but on the previous night it had broken its chain and escaped. Its mahout,[5] the only person who could manage it when it was in that state, had set out in pursuit, but he had taken the wrong direction and was now twelve hours' journey away, and in the morning the elephant had suddenly reappeared in the town. The Burmese population had no weapons and were quite helpless against it. It had already destroyed somebody's bamboo hut, killed a cow and raided some fruit-stalls and devoured the stock; also it had met the municipal rubbish van, and, when the driver jumped out and took to his heels, had turned the van over and inflicted violence upon it.

The Burmese sub-inspector and some Indian constables were waiting for me in the quarter where the elephant had been seen. It was a very poor quarter, a labyrinth of squalid bamboo huts, thatched with palm-leaf, winding all over a steep hillside. I remember that it was a cloudy stuffy morning at the beginning of the rains. We began questioning the people as to where the elephant had gone, and, as usual, failed to get any definite information. That is invariably the case in the East; a story always sounds clear enough at a distance, but the nearer you get to the scene of events the vaguer it becomes. Some of the people said that the elephant had gone in one direction, some said that he had gone in another, some professed not even to have heard of any elephant. I had almost made up my mind that the whole story was a pack of lies, when we heard yells a little distance away. There was a loud, scandalised cry of "Go away, child! Go away this instant!" and an old woman with a switch in her hand came round the corner of a hut, violently shooing away a crowd of naked children. Some more women followed, clicking their tongues and exclaiming; evidently there was something there that the children ought not to have seen. I rounded the hut and saw a man's dead body sprawling in the mud. He was an Indian, a black Dravidian

4. To threaten (Latin).   5. The elephant's driver.

coolie,[6] almost naked, and he could not have been dead many minutes. The people said that the elephant had come suddenly upon him round the corner of the hut, caught him with its trunk, put its foot on his back and ground him into the earth. This was the rainy season and the ground was soft, and his face had scored a trench a foot deep and a couple of yards long. He was lying on his belly with arms crucified and head sharply twisted to one side. His face was coated with mud, the eyes wide open, the teeth bared and grinning with an expression of unendurable agony. (Never tell me, by the way, that the dead look peaceful. Most of the corpses I have seen looked devilish.) The friction of the great beast's foot had stripped the skin from his back as neatly as one skins a rabbit. As soon as I saw the dead man I sent an orderly to a friend's house nearby to borrow an elephant rifle. I had already sent back the pony, not wanting it to go mad with fright and throw me if it smelled the elephant.

The orderly came back in a few minutes with a rifle and five cartridges, and meanwhile some Burmans had arrived and told us that the elephant was in the paddy fields below, only a few hundred yards away. As I started forward practically the whole population of the quarter flocked out of their houses and followed me. They had seen the rifle and were all shouting excitedly that I was going to shoot the elephant. They had not shown much interest in the elephant when he was merely ravaging their homes, but it was different now that he was going to be shot. It was a bit of fun to them, as it would be to an English crowd; besides, they wanted the meat. It made me vaguely uneasy. I had no intention of shooting the elephant—I had merely sent for the rifle to defend myself if necessary—and it is always unnerving to have a crowd following you. I marched down the hill, looking and feeling a fool, with the rifle over my shoulder and an ever-growing army of people jostling at my heels. At the bottom, when you got away from the huts, there was a metalled road and beyond that a miry waste of paddy fields a thousand yards across, not yet ploughed but soggy from the first rains and dotted with coarse grass. The elephant was standing eighty yards from the road, his left side towards us. He took not the

---

6. Dravidians are native to southern India and Sri Lanka; *coolie* is derogatory slang for a poor, unskilled laborer.

slightest notice of the crowd's approach. He was tearing up bunches of grass, beating them against his knees to clean them and stuffing them into his mouth.

I had halted on the road. As soon as I saw the elephant I knew with perfect certainty that I ought not to shoot him. It is a serious matter to shoot a working elephant—it is comparable to destroying a huge and costly piece of machinery—and obviously one ought not to do it if it can possibly be avoided. And at that distance, peacefully eating, the elephant looked no more dangerous than a cow. I thought then and I think now that his attack of "must" was already passing off; in which case he would merely wander harmlessly about until the mahout came back and caught him. Moreover, I did not in the least want to shoot him. I decided that I would watch him for a little while to make sure that he did not turn savage again, and then go home.

But at that moment I glanced round at the crowd that had followed me. It was an immense crowd, two thousand at the least and growing every minute. It blocked the road for a long distance on either side. I looked at the sea of yellow faces above the garish clothes—faces all happy and excited over this bit of fun, all certain that the elephant was going to be shot. They were watching me as they would watch a conjuror about to perform a trick. They did not like me, but with the magical rifle in my hands I was momentarily worth watching. And suddenly I realised that I should have to shoot the elephant after all. The people expected it of me and I had got to do it; I could feel their two thousand wills pressing me forward, irresistibly. And it was at this moment, as I stood there with the rifle in my hands, that I first grasped the hollowness, the futility of the white man's dominion in the East. Here was I, the white man with his gun, standing in front of the unarmed native crowd—seemingly the leading actor of the piece; but in reality I was only an absurd puppet pushed to and fro by the will of those yellow faces behind. I perceived in this moment that when the white man turns tyrant it is his own freedom that he destroys. He becomes a sort of hollow, posing dummy, the conventionalised figure of a sahib.[7] For it is the condition of his rule that he shall spend his life in trying to impress

7. Term of respect used by Indians when addressing Europeans.

the "natives" and so in every crisis he has got to do what the "natives" expect of him. He wears a mask, and his face grows to fit it. I had got to shoot the elephant. I had committed myself to doing it when I sent for the rifle. A sahib has got to act like a sahib; he has got to appear resolute, to know his own mind and do definite things. To come all that way, rifle in hand, with two thousand people marching at my heels, and then to trail feebly away, having done nothing—no, that was impossible. The crowd would laugh at me. And my whole life, every white man's life in the East, was one long struggle not to be laughed at.

But I did not want to shoot the elephant. I watched him beating his bunch of grass against his knees, with that preoccupied grandmotherly air that elephants have. It seemed to me that it would be murder to shoot him. At that age I was not squeamish about killing animals, but I had never shot an elephant and never wanted to. (Somehow it always seems worse to kill a *large* animal.) Besides, there was the beast's owner to be considered. Alive, the elephant was worth at least a hundred pounds; dead, he would only be worth the value of his tusks—five pounds, possibly. But I had got to act quickly. I turned to some experienced-looking Burmans who had been there when we arrived, and asked them how the elephant had been behaving. They all said the same thing: he took no notice of you if you left him alone, but he might charge if you went too close to him.

It was perfectly clear to me what I ought to do. I ought to walk up to within, say, twenty-five yards of the elephant and test his behaviour. If he charged I could shoot, if he took no notice of me it would be safe to leave him until the mahout came back. But also I knew that I was going to do no such thing. I was a poor shot with a rifle and the ground was soft mud into which one would sink at every step. If the elephant charged and I missed him, I should have about as much chance as a toad under a steam-roller. But even then I was not thinking particularly of my own skin, only the watchful yellow faces behind. For at that moment, with the crowd watching me, I was not afraid in the ordinary sense, as I would have been if I had been alone. A white man mustn't be frightened in front of "natives"; and so, in general, he isn't frightened. The sole thought in my mind was that if anything went wrong those two thousand Burmans would see me pursued, caught, trampled on and reduced to a grinning corpse like that Indian up the hill. And if that happened it was quite probable that some of them would laugh. That would never do. There was only one alternative. I shoved the cartridges into the magazine and lay down on the road to get a better aim.

The crowd grew very still, and a deep, low, happy sigh, as of people who see the theatre curtain go up at last, breathed from innumerable throats. They were going to have their bit of fun after all. The rifle was a beautiful German thing with cross-hair sights. I did not then know that is shooting an elephant one should shoot to cut an imaginary bar running from ear-hole to ear-hole. I ought therefore, as the elephant was sideways on, to have aimed straight at his ear-hole; actually I aimed several inches in front of this, thinking the brain would be further forward.

When I pulled the trigger I did not hear the bang or feel the kick—one never does when a shot goes home—but I heard the devilish roar of glee that went up from the crowd. In that instant, in too short a time, one would have thought, even for the bullet to get there, a mysterious, terrible change had come over the elephant. He neither stirred nor fell, but every line of his body had altered. He looked suddenly stricken, shrunken, immensely old, as though the frightful impact of the bullet had paralysed him without knocking him down. At last, after what seemed a long time—it might have been five seconds, I dare say—he sagged flabbily to his knees. His mouth slobbered. An enormous senility seemed to have settled upon him. One could have imagined him thousands of years old. I fired again into the same spot. At the second shot he did not collapse but climbed with desperate slowness to his feet and stood weakly upright, with legs sagging and head drooping. I fired a third time. That was the shot that did for him. You could see the agony of it jolt his whole body and knock the last remnant of strength from his legs. But in falling he seemed for a moment to rise, for as his hind legs collapsed beneath him he seemed to tower upwards like a huge rock toppling, his trunk reaching skyward like a tree. He trumpeted, for the first and only time. And then down he came, his belly towards me, with a crash that seemed to shake the ground even where I lay.

I got up. The Burmans were already racing past me across the mud. It was obvious that the elephant would never rise again, but he was not dead. He was breathing very rhythmically with long rattling gasps, his great mound of a side painfully rising and falling. His mouth was wide open—I could see far down into caverns of pale pink throat. I waited a long time for him to die, but his breathing did not weaken. Finally I fired my two remaining shots into the spot where I thought his heart must be. The thick blood welled out of him like red velvet, but still he did not die. His body did not even jerk when the shots hit him, the tortured breathing continued without a pause. He was dying, very slowly and in great agony, but in some world remote from me where not even a bullet could damage him further. I felt that I had got to put an end to that dreadful noise. It seemed dreadful to see the great beast lying there, powerless to move and yet powerless to die, and not even to be able to finish him. I sent back for my small rifle and poured shot after shot into his heart and down his throat. They seemed to make no impression. The tortured gasps continued as steadily as the ticking of a clock.

In the end I could not stand it any longer and went away. I heard later that it took him half an hour to die. Burmans were arriving with dahs[8] and baskets even before I left, and I was told they had stripped his body almost to the bones by the afternoon.

Afterwards, of course, there were endless discussions about the shooting of the elephant. The owner was furious, but he was only an Indian and could do nothing. Besides, legally I had done the right thing, for a mad elephant has to be killed, like a mad dog, if its owner fails to control it. Among the Europeans opinion was divided. The older men said I was right, the younger men said it was a damn shame to shoot an elephant for killing a coolie, because an elephant was worth more than any damn Coringhee coolie.[9] And afterwards I was very glad that the coolie had been killed; it put me legally in the right and it gave me a sufficient pretext for shooting the elephant. I often wondered whether any of the others grasped that I had done it solely to avoid looking a fool.

1936

---

8. Short swords or knives.   9. A laborer from the town of Coringa.

Leonard Pitts
b. 1957

> *It is very easy to interpret the September 11, 2001, terrorist attacks on New York and Washington as a watershed event in American history. Most of those expressing public opinions agreed that America—and the world—after the attacks was fundamentally different than before the attacks. Pitts's assessment five years after the fact was certainly unusual, and, though he does not go into it, his position, should he persuade many readers, would have important consequences for public policy—both domestic and foreign. You might read this essay alongside Lewis Lapham's discussion of American history; essentially, Pitts is trying to persuade readers to interpret American history in a particular way.*

On 9/11, Innocence Was Lost Once Again

On Sept. 10, 2001, this nation was over a quarter century past its last real crisis.

This is not to say the intervening years were uneventful: they were not. Those years saw three attempted presidential assassinations, a shuttle explosion, an impeachment and sundry hostage takings, military actions and political scandals. But there had not, since Watergate, been a true *crisis*, no event of the kind that shakes a nation, that stops it cold and takes its beneath and makes it anxious about its future.

In this, the quarter century that ended five years ago was an aberration. Previous generations of Americans had come of age with reminders of life's true nature breathing close enough to stir the heirs at the nape of the neck. From the Great Depression that put the nation on the skids in the 1930s, to the sneak attack that plunged it into war in the 1940s, from the 1960s when every day seemed to bring fresh outrage—assassinations, riots, a step to the brink of nuclear war—to Watergate and the subsequent fall of a president, and from there to the Cold War that hung over more than forty years of American history like a pall of smoke, we were a nation too frequently made to know that life does not play fair.

By Sept. 10, 2001, we had largely forgotten this truth. Or, more accurately, we had enjoyed the luxury of not being reminded for a very long time.

It was the last day of the good old days and we didn't even know. Not that the days were good and old. Not that they were doomed.

But then, you never know the good old days when you are in them. On Sept. 10, 2001, the Cold War was ten years past, 17-year-olds were becoming Internet millionaires and we thought a crisis was a president receiving oral sex in the Oval Office.

We had not yet seen people jumping from flaming skyscrapers. We had not yet seen office towers crumble to the ground on live television. We had not yet seen dust-caked people wandering the streets of our greatest city. We had not yet seen an airplane sticking out of the Pentagon. We had not yet seen wreckage in a Pennsylvania field. We had not yet seen men and women in badges and uniforms rushing forward into chaos and smoke and a certainty of death.

We had not yet seen. So we could not yet know.

On Sept. 10, 2001, such sights as those—never mind the attendant feelings of fury and terror—were unthinkable. As in, literally unable to be thought, unless in the context of a Steven Spielberg movie, a Tom Clancy book, some artist's artifice by which we gave ourselves the pleasure of a good, hard scare, a shiver up the back in the heat of a summer's day. But real? Not in a million years.

On Sept. 10, 2001, we were innocent. And that seems a purely strange thing to say because innocence is the commodity we were repeatedly assured we had lost. We were told this in 1963, when John F. Kennedy was murdered, in 1974 when Richard Nixon resigned, in 1993, when the World Trade Center was bombed.

But innocence, it turns out, is a renewable commodity. That's heartening. Also troubling, because if you can have it again, it can be stolen again.

No, check that. It *will* be stolen again. That's the lesson of these past five years, that there is no vacation from history, no finish line you cross where you can raise your arms and lower your guard. Chaos is not the aberration. Respite from chaos is. And being human means molding yourself to that reality, finding a way to live in the spaces chaos leaves.

On Sept. 10, 2001, we had forgotten that we once knew this.

That last day, like every day, the sun came to America first on the rugged coast of Maine and began its slow arc across the country. Down below, we worked, watched television, checked homework, got dinner on. The sun left us in the South Pacific, the sky turning dark above a pendant of American islands.

On Sept. 10, 2001, we went to bed. We slept in innocence.

And then the morning came.

2006

Katha Pollitt
b. 1949

Pollitt, an award-winning poet, is also well known as a liberal essayist for The Nation. *She contends that much of her writing argues for "women's entitlement to full human rights," and this essay, "Why Boys Don't Play with Dolls," certainly was written in that vein. She has a well-deserved reputation for dismantling bad arguments by exposing the faulty logic and poor use of evidence of many of today's cultural critics. This piece, first published in the* New York Times Magazine, *is too short for Pollitt's usual detailed examination of evidence. It relies, instead, largely on her reputation as a careful researcher. So Pollitt may not expect to persuade hostile readers to change their minds on the basis of this one essay. But she does expect readers to recognize that what we take for common sense—in this case, the belief that there are innate differences between the sexes—might be ridiculous.*

Why Boys Don't Play with Dolls

It's 28 years since the founding of NOW,[1] and boys still like trucks and girls still like dolls. Increasingly, we are told that the source of these robust preferences must lie outside society—in prenatal hormonal influences, brain chemistry, genes—and that feminism

---

1. National Organization for Women.

has reached its natural limits. What else could possibly explain the love of preschool girls for party dresses or the desire of toddler boys to own more guns than Mark from Michigan.

True, recent studies claim to show small cognitive differences between the sexes: he gets around by orienting himself in space, she does it by remembering landmarks. Time will tell if any deserve the hoopla with which each is invariably greeted, over the protests of the researchers themselves. But even if the results hold up (and the history of such research is not encouraging), we don't need studies of sex-differentiated brain activity in reading, say, to understand why boys and girls still seem so unalike.

The feminist movement has done much for some women, and something for every woman, but it has hardly turned America into a playground free of sex roles. It hasn't even got women to stop dieting or men to stop interrupting them.

Instead of looking at kids to "prove" that differences in behavior by sex are innate, we can look at the ways we raise kids as an index to how unfinished the feminist revolution really is, and how tentatively it is embraced even by adults who fully expect their daughters to enter previously male-dominated professions and their sons to change diapers.

I'm at a children's birthday party. "I'm sorry," one mom silently mouths to the mother of the birthday girl, who has just torn open her present—Tropical Splash Barbie. Now, you can love Barbie or you can hate Barbie, and there are feminists in both camps. But *apologize* for Barbie? Inflict Barbie, against your own convictions, on the child of a friend you know will be none too pleased?

Every mother in that room had spent years becoming a person who had to be taken seriously, not least by herself. Even the most attractive, I'm willing to bet, had suffered over her body's failure to fit the impossible American ideal. Given all that, it seems crazy to transmit Barbie to the next generation. Yet to reject her is to say that what Barbie represents—being sexy, thin, stylish—is unimportant, which is obviously not true, and children know it's not true.

Women's looks matter terribly in this society, and so Barbie, however ambivalently, must be passed along. After all, there are worse toys. The Cut and Style Barbie styling head, for example, a grotesque object intended to encourage "hair play." The grown-ups who give that probably apologize, too.

How happy would most parents be to have a child who flouted sex conventions? I know a lot of women, feminists, who complain in a comical, eyeball-rolling way about their sons' passion for sports: the ruined weekends, obnoxious coaches, macho values. But they would not think of discouraging their sons from participating in this activity they find so foolish. Or do they? Their husbands are sports fans, too, and they like their husbands a lot.

Could it be that even sports-resistant moms see athletics as part of manliness? That if their sons wanted to spend the weekend writing up their diaries, or reading, or baking, they'd find it disturbing? Too antisocial? Too lonely? Too gay?

Theories of innate differences in behavior are appealing. They let parents off the hook—no small recommendation in a culture that holds moms, and sometimes even dads, responsible for their children's every misstep on the road to bliss and success.

They allow grown-ups to take the path of least resistance to the dominant culture, which always requires less psychic effort, even if it means more actual work: just ask the working mother who comes home exhausted and nonetheless finds it easier to pick up her son's socks than make him do it himself. They let families buy for their children, without too much guilt, the unbelievably sexist junk that the kids, who have been watching commercials since birth, understandably crave.

But the thing the theories do most of all is tell adults that the *adult* world—in which moms and dads still play by many of the old rules even as they question and fidget and chafe against them—is the way it's supposed to be. A girl with a doll and a boy with a truck "explain" why men are from Mars and women are from Venus, why wives do housework and husbands just don't understand.

The paradox is that the world of rigid and hierarchal sex roles evoked by determinist theories is already passing away. Three-year-olds may indeed insist that doctors are male and nurses female, even if their own mother is a physician. Six-year-olds know better. These days, something like half of all medical students are female, and male applications to nursing school are inching upward. When tomorrow's 3-year-olds play doctor, who's to say how they'll assign the roles?

With sex roles, as in every area of life, people aspire to what is possible and conform to what is necessary. But these are not fixed, especially today. Biological determinism may reassure some adults about their present, but it is feminism, the ideology of flexible and converging sex roles, that fits our children's future. And the kids, somehow, know this.

That's why, if you look carefully, you'll find that for every kid who fits a stereotype, there's another who's breaking one down. Sometimes it's the same kid—the boy who skateboards *and* takes cooking in his after-school program; the girl who collects stuffed animals *and* A-pluses in science.

Feminists are often accused of imposing their "agenda" on children. Isn't that what adults always do, consciously and unconsciously? Kids aren't born religious, or polite, or kind, or able to remember where they put their sneakers. Inculcating these behaviors, and the values behind them, is a tremendous amount of work, involving many adults. We don't have a choice, really, about *whether* we should give our children messages about what it means to be male and female—they're bombarded with them from morning till night.

The question, as always, is what do we want those messages to be?

1985

Ronald Reagan
1911–2004

> *Ronald Reagan began developing this speech as spokesman for General Electric in the late 1950s. By 1962, he was warning GE's employees against Soviet communists and American liberals. General Electric asked him to stop discussing politics; when he didn't, he was fired. Soon after, he joined the Republican Party and became cochair of California Citizens for Goldwater. He spent 1964 cam-*

paigning for Barry Goldwater in his presidential race against Lyndon Johnson. "A Time for Choosing" was Reagan's stump speech, and Goldwater was so impressed with it that on the eve of the election, October 27, 1964, he broadcast it to a national audience. Reagan's immediate goal was to get Barry Goldwater elected president. He failed in that. But conservatives point to the national broadcast of this speech as the beginning of the "Reagan revolution," so in this wider context "A Time for Choosing" has been very influential. In fact, its attack on big government and communism became the centerpiece of contemporary conservative politics in America, so that conservatives affectionately refer to it simply as "The Speech."

A Time for Choosing

Thank you very much. Thank you, and good evening. The sponsor has been identified, but unlike most television programs, the performer hasn't been provided with a script. As a matter of fact, I have been permitted to choose my own words and discuss my own ideas regarding the choice that we face in the next few weeks.

I have spent most of my life as a Democrat. I recently have seen fit to follow another course. I believe that the issues confronting us cross party lines. Now, one side in this campaign has been telling us that the issues of this election are the maintenance of peace and prosperity. The line has been used "We've never had it so good!"

But I have an uncomfortable feeling that this prosperity isn't something upon which we can base our hopes for the future. No nation in history has ever survived a tax burden that reached a third of its national income. Today thirty-seven cents out of every dollar earned in this country is the tax collector's share, and yet our government continues to spend 17 million dollars a day more than the government takes in. We haven't balanced our budget twenty-eight out of the last thirty-four years. We have raised our debt limit three times in the last twelve months, and now our national debt is one and a half times bigger than all the combined debts of all the nations of the world. We have 15 billion dollars in gold in our treasury—we don't own an ounce. Foreign dollar claims are 27.3 billion dollars, and we have just had announced that the dollar of 1939 will now purchase forty-five cents in its total value.

As for the peace that we would preserve, I wonder who among us would like to approach the wife or mother whose husband or son has died in Vietnam and ask them if they think this is a peace that should be maintained indefinitely. Do they mean peace, or do they mean we just want to be left in peace? There can be no real peace while one American is dying someplace in the world for the rest of us. We are at war with the most dangerous enemy that has ever faced mankind in his long climb from the swamp to the stars, and it has been said if we lose that war, and in so doing lose this way of freedom of ours, history will record with the greatest astonishment that those who had the most to lose did the least to prevent its happening. Well, I think it's time we ask ourselves if we still know the freedoms that were intended for us by the Founding Fathers.

Not too long ago two friends of mine were talking to a Cuban refugee, a businessman who had escaped from Castro,[1] and in the midst of his story one of my friends turned to the other and said, "We don't know how lucky we are." And the Cuban stopped and said, "How lucky you are! I had someplace to escape to." In that sentence he told us the entire story. If we lose freedom here, there is no place to escape to. This is the last stand on earth.

And this idea that government is beholden to the people, that it has no other source of power except the sovereign people, is still the newest and most unique idea in all the long history of man's relation to man. This is the issue of this election. Whether we believe in our capacity for self-government or whether we abandon the American Revolution and confess that a little intellectual elite in a far-distant capital can plan our lives for us better than we can plan them ourselves.

You and I are told increasingly that we have to choose between a left or right, but I would like to suggest that there is no such thing as a left or right. There is only an up or down—up to man's age-old

---

1. Fidel Castro (b. 1926) led the Cuban Revolution against the corrupt dictatorship of Fulgencio Batista in 1959. He established a communist dictatorship, and many well-to-do and middle-class Cubans fled, as their property was confiscated by the regime.

dream—the ultimate in individual freedom consistent with law and order—or down to the ant heap of totalitarianism, and regardless of their sincerity, their humanitarian motives, those who would trade our freedom for security have embarked on this downward course.

In this vote-harvesting time they use terms like the "Great Society,"[2] or as we were told a few days ago by the President, we must accept a "greater government activity in the affairs of the people." But they have been a little more explicit in the past and among themselves—and all of the things that I now will quote have appeared in print. These are not Republican accusations. For example, they have voices that say "the cold war will end through our acceptance of a not undemocratic socialism." Another voice says that the profit motive has become outmoded, it must be replaced by the incentives of the welfare state; or our traditional system of individual freedom is incapable of solving the complex problems of the twentieth century.

Senator Fulbright[3] has said at Stanford University that the Constitution is outmoded. He referred to the president as our moral teacher and our leader, and he said he is hobbled in his task by the restrictions in power imposed on him by this antiquated document. He must be freed so that he can do for us what he knows is best.

And Senator Clark[4] of Pennsylvania, another articulate spokesman, defines liberalism as "meeting the material needs of the masses through the full power of centralized government." Well, I for one resent it when a representative of the people refers to you and me—the free men and women of this country—as "the masses." This is a term we haven't applied to ourselves in America. But beyond that, "the full power of centralized government"—this was the very thing the Founding Fathers sought to minimize. They knew that governments don't control *things*. A government can't control the economy

---

2. Slogan adopted by President Lyndon Johnson to describe the nation that would result from his domestic policies. He aspired to create a prosperous nation that had overcome its racial divisions and poverty. In his first State of the Union address, in 1964, Johnson advocated expanding the federal government's role in domestic affairs to realize these aims.

3. J. William Fulbright, democratic senator from Arkansas, 1945–75, best known for the Fulbright Act (1946), which provides for the exchange of students and teachers between the United States and many other countries.

4. Joseph S. Clark Jr., democratic senator from Pennsylvania, 1957–69.

without controlling people. And they knew when a government sets out to do that, it must use force and coercion to achieve its purpose. They also knew, those Founding Fathers, that outside of its legitimate functions, government does nothing as well or as economically as the private sector of the economy.

Now, we have no better example of this than the government's involvement in the farm economy over the last thirty years. Since 1955 the cost of this program has nearly doubled. One-fourth of farming in America is responsible for 85 percent of the farm surplus. Three-fourths of farming is out on the free market and has known a 21 percent increase in the per capita consumption of all its produce. You see, that one-fourth of farming is regulated and controlled by the federal government. In the last three years we have spent forty-three dollars in the feed grain program for every dollar bushel of corn we don't grow.

Senator Humphrey[5] last week charged that Barry Goldwater as president would seek to eliminate farmers. He should do his homework a little better, because he will find out that we have had a decline of 5 million in the farm population under these government programs. He will also find that the Democratic administration has sought to get from Congress an extension of the farm program to include that three-fourths that is now free. He will find that they have also asked for the right to imprison farmers who wouldn't keep books as prescribed by the federal government. The secretary of agriculture asked for the right to seize farms through condemnation and resell them to other individuals. And contained in that same program was a provision that would have allowed the federal government to remove 2 million farmers from the soil.

At the same time there has been an increase in the Department of Agriculture employees. There is now one for every thirty farms in the United States, and still they can't tell us how sixty-six shiploads of grain headed for Austria disappeared without a trace, and Billie Sol Estes never left shore![6]

---

5. Hubert Humphrey was senator from Minnesota, 1948–65 and 1972–78; Lyndon Johnson's running mate in 1964; and vice president, 1965–69.

6. A reference to the allegedly corrupt federal grain contracts issued during this period. Billie Sol Estes was a friend of Lyndon Johnson's, known for his dishonest practices. He was investigated for fraud and tax evasion and convicted of these crimes in 1963.

Every responsible farmer and farm organization has repeatedly asked the government to free the farm economy, but who are farmers to know what is best for them? The wheat farmers voted against a wheat program. The government passed it anyway. Now the price of bread goes up; the price of wheat to the farmers goes down.

Meanwhile, back in the city, under urban renewal[7] the assault on freedom carries on. Private property rights are so diluted that public interest is almost anything that a few government planners decide it should be. In a program that takes from the needy and gives to the greedy, we see such spectacles as in Cleveland, Ohio, a million-and-a-half-dollar building completed only three years ago must be destroyed to make way for what government officials call a "more compatible use of the land." The President tells us he is now going to start building public housing units in the thousands where heretofore we have only built them in the hundreds. But FHA[8] and the Veterans Administration tell us that they have 120,000 housing units they've taken back through mortgage foreclosures.

For three decades we have sought to solve the problems of unemployment through government planning, and the more the plans fail, the more the planners plan. The latest is the Area Redevelopment Agency.[9] They have just declared Rice County, Kansas, a depressed area. Rice County, Kansas, has two hundred oil wells, and the 14,000 people there have over thirty million dollars on deposit in personal savings in their banks. When the government tells you you are depressed, lie down and be depressed!

We have so many people who can't see a fat man standing beside a thin one without coming to the conclusion that the fat man got that way by taking advantage of the thin one! So they are going to solve all the problems of human misery through government and government planning. Well, now if government planning and welfare had the answer, and they've had almost thirty years of it, shouldn't we expect government to read the score to us once in a

---

7. A program whereby impoverished urban neighborhoods were to be resuscitated by tearing down existing structures and replacing them with publicly owned buildings, such as housing projects for the poor.

8. The Federal Housing Administration

insures mortgage loans to lower-income Americans, providing more people with the opportunity to buy their homes.

9. Established by the Employment Bureau in 1961 to use federal funds for vocational training programs.

while? Shouldn't they be telling us about the decline each year in the number of people needing help? . . . the reduction in the need for public housing?

But the reverse is true. Each year the need grows greater, the program grows greater. We were told four years ago that seventeen million people went to bed hungry each night. Well, that was probably true. They were all on a diet! But now we are told that 9.3 million families in this country are poverty-stricken on the basis of earning less than $3,000 a year. Welfare spending is ten times greater than in the dark depths of the Depression. We are spending 45 billion dollars on welfare. Now do a little arithmetic, and you will find that if we divided the 45 billion dollars up equally among those 9 million poor families, we would be able to give each family $4,600 a year, and this added to their present income should eliminate poverty! Direct aid to the poor, however, is running only about $600 per family. It seems that someplace there must be some overhead.

So now we declare "war on poverty,"[1] or "you, too, can be a Bobby Baker!"[2] How do they honestly expect us to believe that if we add 1 billion dollars to the 45 billion we are spending . . . one more program to the thirty-odd we have—and remember, this new program doesn't replace any, it just duplicates existing programs . . . do they believe that poverty is suddenly going to disappear by magic? Well, in all fairness I should explain that there is one part of the new program that isn't duplicated. This is the youth feature. We are now going to solve the dropout problem, juvenile delinquency, by reinstituting something like the old CCC camps,[3] and we are going to put our young people in camps, but again we do some arithmetic, and we find that we are going to spend each year just on room and board for each young person that we help $4,700 a year! We can send them to Harvard for $2,700! Don't get me wrong. I'm not suggesting that Harvard is the answer to juvenile delinquency!

But seriously, what are we doing to those we seek to help? Not

1. From President Johnson's 1964 State of the Union address.

2. Robert Baker (b. 1929), longtime aid and political operative of Lyndon Johnson.

3. The Civilian Conservation Corps, an organization established in 1933 by Franklin Delano Roosevelt to employ hundreds of thousands of young men during the Great Depression. Living in military-style camps, the men in the CCC worked on outdoor construction projects, including many of the improvements to the national parks.

too long ago, a judge called me here in Los Angeles. He told me of a young woman who had come before him for a divorce. She had six children, was pregnant with her seventh. Under his questioning, she revealed her husband was a laborer earning $250 a month. She wanted a divorce so that she could get an $80 raise. She is eligible for $330 a month in the Aid to Dependent Children Program. She got the idea from two women in her neighborhood who had already done that very thing.

Yet anytime you and I question the schemes of the do-gooders, we are denounced as being against their humanitarian goals. They say we are always "against" things, never "for" anything. Well, the trouble with our liberal friends is not that they are ignorant, but that they know so much that isn't so! We are for a provision that destitution should not follow unemployment by reason of old age, and to that end we have accepted social security as a step toward meeting the problem.

But we are against those entrusted with this program when they practice deception regarding its fiscal shortcomings, when they charge that any criticism of the program means that we want to end payments to those people who depend on them for a livelihood. They have called it insurance to us in a hundred million pieces of literature. But then they appeared before the Supreme Court and they testified that it was a welfare program. They only use the term "insurance" to sell it to the people. And they said social security dues are a tax for the general use of the government, and the government has used that tax. There is no fund, because Robert Byers, the actuarial head, appeared before a congressional committee and admitted that social security as of this moment is $298 billion in the hole! But he said there should be no cause for worry because as long as they have the power to tax, they could always take away from the people whatever they needed to bail them out of trouble! And they are doing just that.

A young man, twenty-one years of age, working at an average salary . . . his social security contribution would, in the open market, buy him an insurance policy that would guarantee $220 a month at age sixty-five. The government promises 127! He could live it up until he is thirty-one and then take out a policy that would pay more than social security. Now, are we so lacking in business sense that we can't put this program on a sound basis so that people who do require those payments will find that they can get them when they are due . . . that the cupboard isn't bare? Barry Goldwater thinks we can.

At the same time, can't we introduce voluntary features that would permit a citizen to do better on his own, to be excused upon presentation of evidence that he had made provisions for the non-earning years? Should we not allow a widow with children to work, and not lose the benefits supposedly paid for by her deceased husband? Shouldn't you and I be allowed to declare who our beneficiaries will be under these programs, which we cannot do? I think we are for telling our senior citizens that no one in this country should be denied medical care because of a lack of funds. But I think we are against forcing all citizens, regardless of need, into a compulsory government program, especially when we have such examples, as announced last week, when France admitted that their medicare program was now bankrupt. They've come to the end of the road.

In addition, was Barry Goldwater so irresponsible when he suggested that our government give up its program of deliberate planned inflation so that when you do get your social security pension, a dollar will buy a dollar's worth, and not forty-five cents' worth?

I think we are for the international organization,[4] where the nations of the world can seek peace. But I think we are against subordinating American interests to an organization that has become so structurally unsound that today you can muster a two-thirds vote on the floor of the General Assembly among nations that represent less than 10 percent of the world's population. I think we are against the hypocrisy of assailing our allies because here and there they cling to a colony, while we engage in a conspiracy of silence and never open our mouths about the millions of people enslaved in Soviet colonies in the satellite nations.

I think we are for aiding our allies by sharing of our material blessings with those nations which share in our fundamental beliefs, but we are against doling out money government to government, creating bureaucracy, if not socialism, all over the world. We set out

4. The United Nations.

to help 19 countries. We are helping 107. We spent $146 billion. With that money, we bought a 2-million-dollar yacht for Haile Selassie.[5] We bought dress suits for Greek undertakers, extra wives for Kenya government officials. We bought a thousand TV sets for a place where they have no electricity. In the last six years, fifty-two nations have bought $7 billion of our gold, and all fifty-two are receiving foreign aid from us. No government ever voluntarily reduces itself in size. Government programs, once launched, never disappear. Actually, a government bureau is the nearest thing to eternal life we'll ever see on this earth!

Federal employees number 2.5 million, and federal, state, and local, one out of six of the nation's work force is employed by government. These proliferating bureaus with their thousands of regulations have cost us many of our constitutional safeguards. How many of us realize that today federal agents can invade a man's property without a warrant? They can impose a fine without a formal hearing, let alone a trial by jury, and they can seize and sell his property in auction to enforce the payment of that fine. In Chicot County, Arkansas, James Wier overplanted his rice allotment. The government obtained a $17,000 judgment, and a U.S. marshal sold his 950-acre farm at auction. The government said it was necessary as a warning to others to make the system work! Last February 19th, at the University of Minnesota, Norman Thomas, six times candidate for president on the Socialist Party ticket, said, "If Barry Goldwater became president, he would stop the advance of socialism in the United States." I think that's exactly what he will do!

As a former Democrat, I can tell you Norman Thomas isn't the only man who has drawn this parallel to socialism with the present administration. Back in 1936, Mr. Democrat himself, Al Smith,[6] the great American, came before the American people and charged that the leadership of his party was taking the party of Jefferson, Jackson, and Cleveland down the road under the banners of Marx, Lenin, and Stalin. And he walked away from his party, and he never re-

---

5. Emperor of Ethiopia (1930–74).

6. Governor of New York, 1919–20, 1923–28; Democratic presidential nominee, 1928. Smith's opposition to FDR's pro-Russian policy during World War II made him shift his allegiance; he voted for the Republican candidate for the presidency when Roosevelt was elected to a third term in office.

turned to the day he died, because to this day, the leadership of that party has been taking that party, that honorable party, down the road in the image of the labor socialist party of England. Now it doesn't require expropriation or confiscation of private property or business to impose socialism upon a people. What does it mean whether you hold the deed or the title to your business or property if the government holds the power of life and death over that business or property? Such machinery already exists. The government can find some charge to bring against any concern it chooses to prosecute. Every businessman has his own tale of harassment. Somewhere a perversion has taken place. Our natural, inalienable rights are now considered to be a dispensation from government, and freedom has never been so fragile, so close to slipping from our grasp as it is at this moment. Our Democratic opponents seem unwilling to debate these issues. They want to make you and I think that this is a contest between two men . . . that we are to choose just between two personalities. Well, what of this man they would destroy . . . and in destroying, they would destroy that which he represents, the ideas that you and I hold dear.

Is he the brash and shallow and trigger-happy man they say he is? Well, I have been privileged to know him "when." I knew him long before he ever dreamed of trying for high office, and I can tell you personally I have never known a man in my life I believe so incapable of doing a dishonest or dishonorable thing.

This is a man who in his own business, before he entered politics, instituted a profit-sharing plan, before unions had ever thought of it. He put in health and medical insurance for all his employees. He took 50 percent of the profits before taxes and set up a retirement plan, and a pension plan for all his employees. He sent monthly checks for life to an employee who was ill and couldn't work. He provided nursing care for the children of mothers who work in the stores. When Mexico was ravaged by the floods from the Rio Grande, he climbed in his airplane and flew medicine and supplies down there.

An ex-GI told me how he met him. It was the week before Christmas during the Korean War, and he was at the Los Angeles airport trying to get a ride home to Arizona, and he said that there were a lot of servicemen there and no seats available on the planes.

Then a voice came over the loudspeaker and said, "Any men in uniform wanting a ride to Arizona, go to runway such-and-such," and they went down there, and there was a fellow named Barry Goldwater sitting in his plane. Every day in the weeks before Christmas, all day long, he would load up the plane, fly to Arizona, fly them to their homes, then fly back over to get another load.

During the hectic split-second timing of a campaign, this is a man who took time out to sit beside an old friend who was dying of cancer. His campaign managers were understandably impatient, but he said, "There aren't many left who care what happens to her. I'd like her to know that I care." This is a man who said to his nineteen-year-old son, "There is no foundation like the rock of honesty and fairness, and when you begin to build your life upon that rock, with the cement of the faith in God that you have, then you have a real start!" This is not a man who could carelessly send other people's sons to war. And that is the issue of this campaign that makes all of the other problems I have discussed academic, unless we realize that we are in a war that must be won.

Those who would trade our freedom for the soup kitchen of the welfare state have told us that they have a utopian solution of peace without victory. They call their policy "accommodation." And they say if we only avoid any direct confrontation with the enemy, he will forget his evil ways and learn to love us. All who oppose them are indicted as warmongers. They say we offer simple answers to complex problems. Well, perhaps there is a simple answer . . . not an easy one . . . but a simple one, if you and I have the courage to tell our elected officials that we want our *national* policy based upon what we know in our hearts is morally right.

We cannot buy our security, our freedom from the threat of the bomb by committing an immortality so great as saying to a billion human beings now in slavery behind the Iron Curtain, "Give up your dreams of freedom because to save our own skin, we are willing to make a deal with your slave-masters." Alexander Hamilton[7] said, "A nation which can prefer disgrace to danger is pre-

---

7. Among his many accomplishments, Hamilton (1757–1804) advocated the cause of revolution in pamphlets and speeches, was confidential secretary to George Washington during the Revolutionary War, contributed half of the essays collected in *The Federalist,* and was Secretary of the Treasury, 1789–95.

pared for a master, and deserves one!" Let's set the record straight. There is no argument over the choice between peace and war, but there is only one guaranteed way you can have peace . . . and you can have it in the next second . . . surrender!

Admittedly there is a risk in any course we follow other than this, but every lesson in history tells us that the greater risk lies in appeasement, and this is the specter our well-meaning liberal friends refuse to face . . . that their policy of accommodation is appeasement, and it gives no choice between peace and war, only between fight or surrender. If we continue to accommodate, continue to back and retreat, eventually we have to face the final demand—the ultimatum. And what then? When Nikita Khrushchev has told his people he knows what our answer will be? He has told them that we are retreating under the pressure of the cold war, and someday, when the time comes to deliver the ultimatum, our surrender will be voluntary because by that time we will have been weakened from within spiritually, morally, and economically. He believes this because from our side he has heard voices pleading for "peace at any price" or "better Red than dead," or as one commentator put it, he would rather "live on his knees than die on his feet." And therein lies the road to war, because those voices don't speak for the rest of us. You and I know and do not believe that life is so dear and peace so sweet as to be purchased at the price of chains and slavery. If nothing in life is worth dying for, when did this begin—just in the face of this enemy?—or should Moses have told the children of Israel to live in slavery under the pharaohs? Should Christ have refused the cross? Should the patriots at Concord Bridge have thrown down their guns and refused to fire the shot heard round the world?[8] The martyrs of history were not fools, and our honored dead who gave their lives to stop the advance of the Nazis didn't die in vain! Where, then, is the road to peace? Well, it's a simple answer after all.

You and I have the courage to say to our enemies, "There is a price we will not pay." There is a point beyond which they must not

---

8. On April 19, 1775, America militiamen opposed the British army in the villages of Lexington and Concord, Massachusetts. News of this battle sparked the American Revolution.

advance! This is the meaning in the phrase of Barry Goldwater's "peace through strength!" Winston Churchill said that "the destiny of man is not measured by material computation. When great forces are on the move in the world, we learn we are spirits—not animals." And he said, "There is something going on in time and space, and beyond time and space, which, whether we like it or not, spells duty." You and I have a rendezvous with destiny. We will preserve for our children this, the last best hope of man on earth, or we will sentence them to take the last step into a thousand years of darkness.

We will keep in mind and remember that Barry Goldwater has faith in us. He has faith that you and I have the ability and the dignity and the right to make our own decisions and determine our own destiny.

Thank you.

1964

Richard Rodriguez
b. 1944

On January 31, 1972, the Racial Data Committee of the Office of Management and Budget decided that all Puerto Ricans, Mexican Americans, Cubans, Central and South Americans, and others of "Spanish descent" would constitute one racial/ethnic category. Though "Spanish descent" or "Hispanic" suggests a blood relation between these various populations, we now know that there is very little meaningful biological distinction between any of the "races." Generally speaking, biological diversity within a race is as great as biological diversity among races. "Race," as it is used by government agencies and in common parlance, is a socially constructed category. Rodriguez suggests there are two ways of defining American society, the Mexican way and the Canadian way, the mestizaje and the multicultural. Rodriguez first published this essay in the Chronicle of Higher Education, *the trade magazine of college and university professors, so he was writing to a fairly liberal audience that has, for the last generation or so, looked favorably upon multiculturalism.*

"Blaxicans" and Other Reinvented Americans

There is something unsettling about immigrants because . . . well, because they chatter incomprehensibly, and they get in everyone's way. Immigrants seem to be bent on undoing America. Just when Americans think we know who we are—we are Protestants, culled from Western Europe, are we not?—then new immigrants appear from Southern Europe or from Eastern Europe. We—we who are already here—we don't know exactly what the latest comers will mean to our community. How will they fit in with us? Thus we—we who were here first—we begin to question our own identity.

After a generation or two, the grandchildren or the great-grandchildren of immigrants to the United States and the grandchildren of those who tried to keep immigrants out of the United States will romanticize the immigrant, will begin to see the immigrant as the figure who teaches us most about what it means to be an American. The immigrant, in mythic terms, travels from the outermost rind of America to the very center of American mythology. None of this, of course, can we admit to the Vietnamese immigrant who served us our breakfast at the hotel this morning. In another forty years, we will be prepared to say to the Vietnamese immigrant that he, with his breakfast tray, with his intuition for travel, with his memory of tragedy, with his recognition of peerless freedoms, he fulfills the meaning of America.

In 1997, Gallup[1] conducted a survey on race relations in America, but the poll was concerned only with white and black Americans. No question was put to the aforementioned Vietnamese man. There was certainly no question for the Chinese grocer, none for the Guatemalan barber, none for the tribe of Mexican Indians who reroofed your neighbor's house.

The American conversation about race has always been a black-and-white conversation, but the conversation has become as bloodless as badminton.

---

1. The Gallup Organization uses statistical analyses of surveys to determine public opinion on a wide range of issues.

I have listened to the black-and-white conversation for most of my life. I was supposed to attach myself to one side or the other, without asking the obvious questions: What is this perpetual dialectic between Europe and Africa? Why does it admit so little reference to anyone else?

I am speaking to you in American English that was taught me by Irish nuns—immigrant women. I wear an Indian face; I answer to a Spanish surname as well as this California first name, Richard. You might wonder about the complexity of historical factors, the collision of centuries, that creates Richard Rodriguez. My brownness is the illustration of that collision, or the bland memorial of it. I stand before you as an Impure-American, an Ambiguous-American.

In the nineteenth century, Texans used to say that the reason Mexicans were so easily defeated in battle was because we were so dilute, being neither pure Indian nor pure Spaniard. Yet, at the same time, Mexicans used to say that Mexico, the country of my ancestry, joined two worlds, two competing armies. José Vasconcelos, the Mexican educator and philosopher, famously described Mexicans as *la raza cósmica*, the cosmic race. In Mexico what one finds as early as the eighteenth century is a predominant population of mixed-race people. Also, once the slave had been freed in Mexico, the incidence of marriage between Indian and African people there was greater than in any other country in the Americas and has not been equaled since.

Race mixture has not been a point of pride in America. Americans speak more easily about "diversity" than we do about the fact that I might marry your daughter; you might become we; we might become us. America has so readily adopted the Canadian notion of multiculturalism because it preserves our preference for thinking ourselves separate—our elbows need not touch, thank you. I would prefer *that* table. I can remain Mexican, whatever that means, in the United States of America.

I would propose that instead of adopting the Canadian model of multiculturalism, America might begin to imagine the Mexican alternative—that of a *mestizaje* society.

Because of colonial Mexico, I am *mestizo*. But I was reinvented by President Richard Nixon. In the early 1970s, Nixon instructed the Office of Management and Budget to identify the major racial and ethnic groups in the United States. OMB came up with five major ethnic or racial groups. The groups are white, black, Asian/Pacific Islander, American Indian/Eskimo, and Hispanic.

It's what I learned to do when I was in college: to call myself a Hispanic. At my university we even had separate cafeteria tables and "theme houses," where the children of Nixon could gather—of a feather. Native Americans united. African Americans. Casa Hispanic.[2]

The interesting thing about Hispanics is that you will never meet us in Latin America. You may meet Chileans and Peruvians and Mexicans. You will not meet Hispanics. If you inquire in Lima or Bogotá about Hispanics, you will be referred to Dallas. For "Hispanic" is a gringo contrivance, a definition of the world according to European patterns of colonization. Such a definition suggests I have more in common with Argentine-Italians than with American Indians; that there is an ineffable union between the white Cuban and the mulatto Puerto Rican because of Spain. Nixon's conclusion has become the basis for the way we now organize and understand American society.

The Census Bureau foretold that by the year 2003, Hispanics would outnumber blacks to become the largest minority in the United States. And, indeed, the year 2003 has arrived and the proclamation of Hispanic ascendancy has been published far and wide. While I admit a competition has existed—does exist—in America between Hispanic and black people, I insist that the comparison of Hispanics with blacks will lead, ultimately, to complete nonsense. For there is no such thing as a Hispanic race. In Latin America, one sees every race of the world. One sees white Hispanics, one sees black Hispanics, one sees brown Hispanics who are Indians, many of whom do not speak Spanish because they resist Spain. One sees Asian-Hispanics. To compare blacks and Hispanics, therefore, is to construct a fallacious equation.

Some Hispanics have accepted the fiction. Some Hispanics have too easily accustomed themselves to impersonating a third race, a great new third race in America. But Hispanic is an ethnic term. It is a term denoting culture. So when the Census Bureau says by the

2. Hispanic House. A building on campus serving the Hispanic community.

year 2060 one-third of all Americans will identify themselves as Hispanic, the Census Bureau is not speculating in pigment or quantifying according to actual historical narratives, but rather is predicting how by the year 2060 one-third of all Americans will identify themselves culturally. For a country that traditionally has taken its understandings of community from blood and color, the new circumstance of so large a group of Americans identifying themselves by virtue of language or fashion or cuisine or literature is an extraordinary change, and a revolutionary one.

People ask me all the time if I envision another Quebec forming in the United States because of the large immigrant movement from the south. Do I see a Quebec forming in the Southwest, for example? No, I don't see that at all. But I do notice the Latin American immigrant population is as much as 10 years younger than the U.S. national population. I notice the Latin American immigrant population is more fertile than the U.S. national population. I see the movement of the immigrants from south to north as a movement of youth—like approaching spring!—into a country that is growing middle-aged. I notice immigrants are the archetypal Americans at a time when we—U.S. citizens—have become post-Americans, most concerned with subsidized medications.

I was at a small Apostolic Assembly in East Palo Alto a few years ago—a mainly Spanish-speaking congregation in an area along the freeway, near the heart of the Silicon Valley. This area used to be black East Palo Alto, but it is quickly becoming an Asian and Hispanic Palo Alto neighborhood. There was a moment in the service when newcomers to the congregation were introduced. Newcomers brought letters of introduction from sister evangelical churches in Latin America. The minister read out the various letters and pronounced the names and places of origin to the community. The congregation applauded. And I thought to myself: It's over. The border is over. These people were not being asked whether they had green cards. They were not being asked whether they arrived here legally or illegally. They were being welcomed within a new community for reasons of culture. There is now a north-south line that is theological, a line that cannot be circumvented by the U.S. Border Patrol.

I was on a British Broadcasting Corporation interview show, and a woman introduced me as being "in favor" of assimilation. I am not in favor of assimilation any more than I am in favor of the Pacific Ocean or clement weather. If I had a bumper sticker on the subject, it might read something like ASSIMILATION HAPPENS. One doesn't get up in the morning, as an immigrant child in America, and think to oneself, "How much of an American shall I become today?" One doesn't walk down the street and decide to be forty percent Mexican and sixty percent American. Culture is fluid. Culture is smoke. You breathe it. You eat it. You can't help hearing it—Elvis Presley goes in your ear, and you cannot get Elvis Presley out of your mind.

I am in favor of assimilation. I am not in favor of assimilation. I recognize assimilation. A few years ago, I was in Merced, California—a town of about 75,000 people in the Central Valley where the two largest immigrant groups at that time (California is so fluid, I believe this is no longer the case) were Laotian Hmong and Mexicans. Laotians have never in the history of the world, as far as I know, lived next to Mexicans. But there they were in Merced, and living next to Mexicans. They don't like each other. I was talking to the Laotian kids about why they don't like the Mexican kids. They were telling me that the Mexicans do this and the Mexicans don't do that, when I suddenly realized that they were speaking English with a Spanish accent.

On his interview show, Bill Moyers once asked me how I thought of myself. As an American? Or Hispanic? I answered that I am Chinese, and that is because I live in a Chinese city and because I want to be Chinese. Well, why not? Some Chinese-American people in the Richmond and Sunset districts of San Francisco sometimes paint their houses (so many qualifiers!) in colors I would once have described as garish: lime greens, rose reds, pumpkin. But I have lived in a Chinese city for so long that my eye has taken on that palette, has come to prefer lime greens and rose reds and all the inventions of this Chinese Mediterranean. I see photographs in magazines or documentary footage of China, especially rural China, and I see what I recognize as home. Isn't that odd?

I do think distinctions exist. I'm not talking about an America tomorrow in which we're going to find that black and white are no longer the distinguishing marks of separateness. But many young people I meet tell me they feel like Victorians when they identify themselves as black or white. They don't think of themselves in those terms. And they're already moving into a world in which tattoo or ornament or movement or commune or sexuality or drug or rave or electronic bombast are the organizing principles of their identity. The notion that they are white or black simply doesn't occur.

And increasingly, of course, one meets children who really don't know how to say what they are. They simply are too many things. I met a young girl in San Diego at a convention of mixed-race children, among whom the common habit is to define one parent over the other—black over white, for example. But this girl said that her mother was Mexican and her father was African. The girl said "Blaxican." By reinventing language, she is reinventing America.

America does not have a vocabulary like the vocabulary the Spanish empire evolved to describe the multiplicity of racial possibilities in the New World. The conversation, the interior monologue of America cannot rely on the old vocabulary—black, white. We are no longer a black-white nation.

So, what myth do we tell ourselves? The person who got closest to it was Karl Marx. Marx predicted that the discovery of gold in California would be a more central event to the Americas than the discovery of the Americas by Columbus—which was only the meeting of two tribes, essentially, the European and the Indian. But when gold was discovered in California in the 1840s, the entire world met. For the first time in human history, all of the known world gathered. The Malaysian stood in the gold fields alongside the African, alongside the Chinese, alongside the Australian, alongside the Yankee.

That was an event without parallel in world history and the beginning of modern California—why California today provides the mythological structure for understanding how we might talk about the American experience: not as biracial, but as the re-creation of the known world in the New World.

Sometimes truly revolutionary things happen without regard. I mean, we may wake up one morning and there is no black race. There is no white race either. There are mythologies, and—as I am in the business, insofar as I am in any business at all, of demythologizing such identities as black and white—I come to you as a man of many cultures. I come to you as Chinese. Unless you understand that I am Chinese, then you have not understood anything I have said.

2003

Richard Rorty

1941–2007

Multiculturalism, as a mode of conceiving one's nation, began to spread in Western democracies in the 1970s. It offers an alternative to an older nationalist ideology, that conceived of a nation as a people growing out of a particular single, unified, rooted culture. Such a view of the nation was largely discredited in World War II because it was the foundation of fascist states, like Italy and Germany, in which citizenship was guaranteed by racial, almost even tribal, homogeneity. But multiculturalism also disputes the "melting pot" identity of immigrant nations like the United States. The metaphor "melting pot" suggests that a single unique American culture emerges from the mix of the various immigrant and native cultures living within the borders of the nation. In this model, the nation still is defined by a common, homogeneous culture, which is modified as each new cultural group assimilates to it. Multiculturalism sees this assimilation as tyrannical, and conceives of a nation as a multiplicity of cultures living together in polity. The cultures are not "melted" together into a new single, distinctive culture: they each retain their differences from one another. If multiculturalism never influenced American public policy as dramatically as it did European, it did hold sway in academia. In this essay, Rorty is reacting to the ascendance of multiculturalism among professors in American colleges, and, though a liberal himself, he is arguing from a minority position. It is important to place this essay in this historical context. It is part of a book, Philosophy and Social Hope, *which was published two years before 9/11 (and subsequent events, such as the passing of the "Patriot Act" made patriotism, once again, nearly compulsory in American life).*

The Unpatriotic Academy

Most of us, despite the outrage we may feel about governmental cowardice or corruption, and despite our despair over what is being done to the weakest and poorest among us, still identify with our country. We take pride in being citizens of a self-invented, self-reforming, enduring constitutional democracy. We think of the United States as having glorious—if tarnished—national traditions.

Many of the exceptions to this rule are found in colleges and universities, in the academic departments that have become sanctuaries for left-wing political views. I am glad there are such sanctuaries, even though I wish we had a left more broadly based, less self-involved and less jargon-ridden than our present one. But any left is better than none, and this one is doing a great deal of good for people who have a raw deal in our society: women, African Americans, gay men and lesbians. This focus on marginalized groups will, in the long run, help to make our country much more decent, more tolerant and more civilized.

But there is a problem with this left: it is unpatriotic. In the name of "the politics of difference," it refuses to rejoice in the country it inhabits. It repudiates the idea of a national identity, and the emotion of national pride. This repudiation is the difference between traditional American pluralism and the new movement called multiculturalism. Pluralism is the attempt to make America what the philosopher John Rawls call "a social union of social unions," a community of communities, a nation with far more room for difference that most. Multiculturalism is turning into the attempt to keep these communities at odds with one another.

Academic leftists who are enthusiastic about multiculturalism distrust the proposal made by Sheldon Hackney, chairman of the National Endowment for the Humanities, to hold televised town meetings to "explore the meaning of American identity." Criticizing Mr. Hackney in the *New York Times* on January 30, 1994, Richard Sennett, a distinguished social critic, wrote that the idea of such an identity is just "the gentlemanly face of nationalism," and speaks of "the evil of a shared national identity."

It is too early to say now [February 1994] whether the conversations Mr. Hackney proposes will be fruitful. But whether they are or not, it is important to insist that a sense of shared national identity is not an evil. It is an absolutely essential component of citizenship, of any attempt to take our country and its problems seriously. There is no incompatibility between respect for cultural differences and American patriotism.

Like every other country, ours has a lot to be proud of and a lot to be ashamed of. But a nation cannot reform itself unless it takes pride in itself—unless it has an identity, rejoices in it, reflects upon it and tries to live up to it. Such pride sometimes takes the form of arrogant, bellicose nationalism. But it often takes the form of a yearning to live up to the nation's professed ideals.

That is the desire to which the Rev. Dr. Martin Luther King Jr. appealed, and he is somebody every American can be proud of. It is just as appropriate for white Americans to take pride in Dr. King and in his (limited) success as for black Americans to take pride in Ralph Waldo Emerson and John Dewey and their (limited) successes.[1] Cornel West[2] wrote a book—*The American Evasion of Philosophy*—about the connections between Emerson, Dewey, W. E. B. Du Bois[3] and his own preaching in African-American churches. The late Irving Howe[4] whose "World of Our Fathers" did much to make us aware that we are a nation of immigrants, also tried to persuade us (in "The American Newness: Culture and Politics in the Age of Emerson") to cherish a distinctively American, distinctively Emersonian, hope.

Mr. Howe was able to rejoice in a country that had only in his lifetime started to allow Jews to be fully fledged members of society. Cornel West can still identify with a country that, by denying them

1. Emerson (1803–1882), white essayist and philosopher, leader of the Transcendental movement, and abolitionist. Among other things, Emerson preached "self-reliance" and a distinctively American ethic of individualism. Dewey (1859–1952), white philosopher and educator whose "pragmatism" led a revolution in American schools, which began to emphasize problem-solving skills over the memorization of facts.

2. West (b. 1953), black professor of religion at Princeton University.

3. Du Bois (1868–1963), black scholar and social activist whose disgust with American racism led to his emigration to Ghana.

4. Howe (1920–1993), white, leftist, literary and social critic.

decent schools and jobs, keeps so many black Americans humiliated and wretched.

There is no contradiction between such identification and shame at the greed, the intolerance and the indifference to suffering that is widespread in the United States. On the contrary, you can feel shame over your country's behavior only to the extent to which you feel it is your country. If we fail in such identification, we fail in national hope. If we fail in national hope, we shall no longer even try to change our ways. If American leftists cease to be proud of being the heirs of Emerson, Lincoln and King, Irving Howe's prophecy that "the newness will come again"—that we shall once again experience the joyous self-confidence which fills Emerson's "American Scholar"—is unlikely to come true.

If in the interests of ideological purity, or out of the need to stay as angry as possible, the academic left insists on a "politics of difference," it will become increasingly isolated and ineffective. An unpatriotic left has never achieved anything. A left that refuses to take pride in its country will have no impact on that country's politics, and will eventually become an object of contempt.

1994

Salman Rushdie

b. 1947

Over a billion people live in India. That is just over three times the population of the United States living in an area roughly one-third the size of the United States. Overpopulation has been a problem for generations, so in 1971 the government legalized abortion. But most attempts to limit births were hampered by families' hopes to have at least two boys. A number of cultural factors—both religious and economic—encourage parents to prefer boys to girls, and, because of low childhood survival rates, to have only one boy was risky. In the 1980s ultrasounds became widely available, and parents for the first time could identify the sex of a fetus before birth. (An ultrasound uses noninvasive sound waves to make X-raylike images of internal anatomy. According to the Boston Globe, *an ultrasound cannot accurately identify sex until the fourth or fifth month of pregnancy.) So many families used ultrasounds to select boys for birth and girls for abortions that India outlawed the practice in 1994. Nevertheless, the law is commonly ignored by doctors and parents alike. Rushdie first published this article in the British paper* The Guardian *in 2001; in 2006 the British medical journal,* The Lancet, *estimated that between 1985 and 2005, ten million fetuses were aborted because they were female. In the Punjab region, for example, before ultrasounds, there were 925 girls for every 1,000 boys. The first ultrasound machine arrived in 1979; twelve years later, the ratio had fallen to 875 girls for every 1,000 boys; by 2001 there were only 793 girls for every 1,000 boys.*

Abortion in India

I have always believed myself fortunate to have come from a sprawling Indian family dominated by women. I have no brothers but plenty of sisters (three: believe me, that's plenty). My mother's sisters are a pair of aunts as formidable and irresistible as Bertie Wooster's Aunt Dahlia and Aunt Agatha.[1] In my generation of cousins, girls outnumber boys by two to one. While I was growing up, the family's houses, in India and Pakistan, were full of the instructions, quarrels, laughter, and ambitions of these women, few of whom resemble the stereotype of the demure, self-effacing Indian woman. These are opinionated, voluble, smart, funny, arm-waving persons—lawyers, educators, radicals, movers, shakers, matriarchs—and to be heard in their company you must not only raise your voice but also have something interesting to say. If you aren't worth listening to, you will most certainly not be heard.

As a result, I feel, to this day, most at home in the company of women. Among my close friends the girls far outnumber the boys. In my writing, I have repeatedly sought to create female characters as rich and powerful as those I have known. The men in my books

---

1. Characters in a series of satiric novels by the British author P. G. Wodehouse (1881–1975).

are rarely as flamboyant as the women. This is as it should be: or at least, in my experience, how it has been, more often than not.

It is therefore worrying, to say the least, that these women, or rather their potential successors in the Indian generation presently being conceived, are rapidly becoming an endangered species. In spite of the illegality of the practice—and under cover of spurious health checks—ultrasound tests to determine the gender of unborn children are increasingly being used all over India to identify, and then abort, obscene quantities of healthy female fetuses. The population is rapidly becoming lopsided, skewed toward male numerical dominance to a genuinely alarming degree.

Here's a tough nut for the pro-choice lobby on abortion, of which I've always been a fully paid-up member. What should be done when a woman uses her power over her own body to discriminate against female fetuses? Many Indian commentators say that if these sex-discriminatory abortions are to end, the refusals must come from Indian women. But Indian women want male children as much as their husbands do. In part this is because of the myriad pressures of a male-centered society, including the expenses of the dowry system. But fundamentally it's the result of modern technology being placed at the service of medieval social attitudes. Clearly not all Indian women are as emancipated as those among whom I was lucky enough to be raised. Traditional India still exists, and its values are still powerful. Women beware women: an old story, given a chilling new gynecological twist.

Ever since Indira and Sanjay Gandhi's attempt to introduce birth control by diktat[2] during the forced-vasectomy excesses of the mid-seventies, it has been very hard to get the Indian masses to accept the idea of family planning. Mother Teresa's hardline attack on contraception didn't help. Lately, Hindu nationalists have made things even harder by suggesting that the country's Muslims are breeding faster than Hindus, thus placing Hinduism "under threat." (This, even though the Hindu majority makes up a whopping 85 percent of the population.)

Abortion, along with contraception, has up to now been anathe-

2. Dictatorial decree.

matized by Indian religious leaders. As a result India's population has soared past the one billion mark, and is projected to overtake China's within a decade or so. But now, suddenly, terminations of pregnancies have become acceptable to many Indians, for the most reprehensible of reasons; and the argument over the urgent issues of population control gets even murkier. There are those who claim that the new wave of abortions is actually beneficial, because the bias toward boys means that Indian couples who have girl children will tend to go on having daughters until they have a son, thus contributing to overpopulation. Allowing them to make the choice, the argument continues, will not result in a scarcity of girl children but rather make sure there isn't a glut of them. The trouble with this theory is that the statistical evidence suggests that in a generation's time there will indeed be a girl shortage. Then what? Will girls become more valued than they are today, or will the masculinism of Indian society, reinforced by the weight of numbers, simply create more and more macho men, and increasingly downtrodden women?

Not all problems are capable of instant solution. Even though the nation imagines itself as a woman—Bharat-Mata, Mother India—and even though, in Hinduism, the dynamic principle of the godhead—shakti—is female, the scandal of the missing girls of India will end only when and if modern India succeeds in overturning centuries of prejudice against girl children.

This doesn't mean that nothing can be done. The government can and should crack down hard on the ultrasound clinics that are allowing people to defy the law. It should provide state benefits for families with girl children and perhaps even, for a time, impose tax penalties on families with boys. Politicians, educators, activist groups, even newspaper columnists can and should batter away at the ingrained prejudices that are at the heart of the trouble. In the end it all boils down to this: is today's India prepared to be seen as the country that gets rid of its daughters because it believes them inferior to men? The parents who are doing this may one day face questions from the children they allowed to live. "Where are my sisters?" What will they answer then?

2001

Chief Seattle
c. 1790–1866

> *This work has a curious history. Although it and similar versions are attributed to Chief Seattle (as here), he didn't actually write it. When Isaac Stevens, commissioner of Indian Affairs for the Washington Territory, offered a treaty to various tribes of the Northwest in 1854, Seattle did, indeed, rise and deliver a powerful speech, which was translated into English by another Native American. But it was Henry Smith, a witness to the event, who took notes and, thirty-three years later, in 1887, used them to reconstruct the speech for his column, a series of ten "Early Reminiscences," published in the* Seattle Sunday Star. *And that was only the beginning. In 1969, William Arrowsmith, a professor of classics at the University of Texas, "translated" Smith's account from its Victorian idiom into contemporary English. Based on Arrowsmith's "translation," Ted Perry wrote a script for a television special that aired on ABC in 1972. Modifications of Perry's script found their way into various popular venues, from Joseph Campbell's television series* The Power of Myth, *to children's books, political pamphlets, and even monuments and essay anthologies—all purporting to be the authentic words of Chief Seattle. These modern versions are only vaguely similar to Smith's 1887 account, which itself is highly suspect. In fact, the speech no longer has anything to do with relations between whites and Native Americans. And in some places the modern versions say the opposite of what appeared in Smith's account, and so they represent neither the words nor the sentiments of Chief Seattle. Instead, they express the sentiments of environmentalists in the 1970s, who romanticized and stereotyped Native Americans in their fight against pollution. You should think of the speech's audience, then, as citizens of industrialized nations in the 1970s (European environmentalists distributed the letter widely, especially in Germany) and its authors as white Americans from the same era. The version below comes from the first edition of a 1978 anthology of Native American speeches and writing; it was dropped from the 1991 edition of the anthology, presumably because the editors discovered its inauthenticity. I include the "Letter to President Pierce" here to provide an interesting example of ethical arguments,*

the effectiveness of which depends, obviously, on the reader's mistaken belief that these are Chief Seattle's words.

Letter to President Pierce

We know that the white man does not understand our ways. One portion of the land is the same to him as the next, for he is a stranger who comes in the night and takes from the land whatever he needs. The earth is not his brother, but his enemy, and when he has conquered it, he moves on. He leaves his fathers' graves, and his children's birthright is forgotten. The sight of your cities pains the eyes of the red man. But perhaps it is because the red man is a savage and does not understand.

There is no quiet place in the white man's cities. No place to hear the leaves of spring or the rustle of insect's wings. But perhaps because I am a savage and do not understand, the clatter only seems to insult the ears. The Indian prefers the soft sound of the wind darting over the face of the pond, the smell of the wind itself cleansed by a mid-day rain, or scented with the piñon pine. The air is precious to the red man. For all things share the same breath—the beasts, the trees, the man. Like a man dying for many days, he is numb to the stench.

What is man without the beasts? If all the beasts were gone, men would die from great loneliness of spirit, for whatever happens to the beasts also happens to man. All things are connected. Whatever befalls the earth befalls the sons of the earth.

It matters little where we pass the rest of our days; they are not many. A few more hours, a few more winters, and none of the children of the great tribes that once lived on this earth, or that roamed in small bands in the woods, will be left to mourn the graves of a people once as powerful and hopeful as yours.

The whites, too, shall pass—perhaps sooner than other tribes. Continue to contaminate your bed, and you will one night suffocate in your own waste. When the buffalo are all slaughtered, the wild horses all tamed, the secret corners of the forest heavy with the scent of many men, and the view of the ripe hills blotted by talking wires,[1] where is the thicket? Gone. Where is the eagle? Gone. And what is it to say goodby to the swift and the hunt, the end of living and the beginning of survival? We might understand if we knew what it was that the white man dreams, what he describes to his children on the long winter nights, what visions he burns into their minds, so they will wish for tomorrow. But we are savages. The white man's dreams are hidden from us.

c. 1972

David Sedaris
b. 1956

Sedaris regularly reads his work on National Public Radio and is often published in leading magazines, such as Esquire *and* The New Yorker. *His essays are almost exclusively autobiographical, often exposing emotionally painful and funny incidents from his family life growing up in Raleigh, North Carolina. This essay recounts his move to France, where he and his partner live. Sedaris is noted for the way his stories mix humor and poignancy. His personal essays are, perhaps, even further from persuasive purpose than most. Often they are compared to stories; indeed, Sedaris, when asked how he could expose the intimacies of his personal life, replies that when he writes he thinks of himself as a character.*

Me Talk Pretty One Day

At the age of forty-one, I am returning to school and have to think of myself as what my French textbook calls "a true debutant." After paying my tuition, I was issued a student ID, which allows me a discounted entry fee at movie theaters, puppet shows, and Festyland, a farflung amusement park that advertises with billboards picturing a cartoon stegosaurus sitting in a canoe and eating what appears to be a ham sandwich.

---

1. Telegraph wires.

I've moved to Paris with hopes of learning the language. My school is an easy ten-minute walk from my apartment, and on the first day of class I arrived early, watching as the returning students greeted one another in the school lobby. Vacations were recounted, and questions were raised concerning mutual friends with names like Kang and Vlatnya. Regardless of their nationalities, everyone spoke in what sounded to me like excellent French. Some accents were better than others, but the students exhibited an ease and confidence I found intimidating. As an added discomfort, they were all young, attractive, and well dressed, causing me to feel not unlike Pa Kettle[1] trapped backstage after a fashion show.

The first day of class was nerve-racking because I knew I'd be expected to perform. That's the way they do it here—it's everybody into the language pool, sink or swim. The teacher marched in, deeply tanned from a recent vacation, and proceeded to rattle off a series of administrative announcements. I've spent quite a few summers in Normandy, and I took a monthlong French class before leaving New York. I'm not completely in the dark, yet I understood only half of what this woman was saying.

"If you have not *meimslsxp* or *lgpdmurct* by this time, then you should not be in this room. Has everyone *apzkiubjxow*? Everyone? Good, we shall begin." She spread out her lesson plan and sighed, saying, "All right, then, who knows the alphabet?"

It was startling because (a) I hadn't been asked that question in a while and (b) I realized, while laughing, that I myself did *not* know the alphabet. They're the same letters, but in France they're pronounced differently. I know the shape of the alphabet but had no idea what it actually sounded like.

"Ahh." The teacher went to the board and sketched the letter *a*. "Do we have anyone in the room whose first name commences with an *ahh*?"

Two Polish Annas raised their hands, and the teacher instructed them to present themselves by stating their names, nationalities, occupations, and a brief list of things they liked and disliked in this world. The first Anna hailed from an industrial town outside of War-

---

1. Character in a series of comic movies from the 1940s and 1950s. Pa Kettle was a likeable, slow-thinking country bumpkin who often found himself in preposterous, fish-out-of-water situations.

saw and had front teeth the size of tombstones. She worked as a seam-stress, enjoyed quiet times with friends, and hated the mosquito.

"Oh, really," the teacher said. "How very interesting. I thought that everyone loved the mosquito, but here, in front of all the world, you claim to detest him. How is it that we've been blessed with someone as unique and original as you? Tell us, please."

The seamstress did not understand what was being said but knew that this was an occasion for shame. Her rabbity mouth huffed for breath, and she stared down at her lap as though the appropriate comeback were stitched somewhere alongside the zipper of her slacks.

The second Anna learned from the first and claimed to love sun-shine and detest lies. It sounded like a translation of one of those Playmate of the Month data sheets, the answers always written in the same loopy handwriting: "Turn-ons: Mom's famous five-alarm chili! Turnoffs: insecurity and guys who come on too strong!!!!"

The two Polish Annas surely had clear notions of what they loved and hated, but like the rest of us, they were limited in terms of vo-cabulary, and this made them appear less than sophisticated. The teacher forged on, and we learned that Carlos, the Argentine ban-donion player, loved wine, music, and, in his words, "making sex with the womens of the world." Next came a beautiful young Yu-goslav who identified herself as an optimist, saying that she loved everything that life had to offer.

The teacher licked her lips, revealing a hint of the saucebox we would later come to know. She crouched low for her attack, placed her hands on the young woman's desk, and leaned close, saying, "Oh yeah? And do you love your little war?"

While the optimist struggled to defend herself, I scrambled to think of an answer to what had obviously become a trick question. How often is one asked what he loves in this world? More to the point, how often is one asked and then publicly ridiculed for his an-swer? I recalled my mother, flushed with wine, pounding the table-top late one night, saying, "Love? I love a good steak cooked rare. I love my cat, and I love . . ." My sisters and I leaned forward, wait-ing to hear our names. "Tums,"[2] our mother said. "I love Tums."

---

2. Brand of flavored antacid tablets.

The teacher killed some time accusing the Yugoslavian girl of masterminding a program of genocide, and I jotted frantic notes in the margins of my pad. While I can honestly say that I love leafing through medical textbooks devoted to severe dermatological conditions, the hobby is beyond the reach of my French vocabulary, and acting it out would only have invited controversy.

When called upon, I delivered an effortless list of things that I detest: blood sausage, intestinal pâtés, brain pudding. I'd learned these words the hard way. Having given it some thought, I then declared my love for IBM typewriters, the French word for *bruise*, and my electric floor waxer. It was a short list, but still I managed to mispronounce *IBM* and assign the wrong gender to both the floor waxer and the typewriter. The teacher's reaction led me to believe that these mistakes were capital crimes in the country of France.

"Were you always this *palicmkrexis*?" she asked. "Even a *fiuscrzsa ticiwelmun* knows that a typewriter is feminine."

I absorbed as much of her abuse as I could understand, thinking—but not saying—that I find it ridiculous to assign a gender to an inanimate object incapable of disrobing and making an occasional fool of itself. Why refer to crack pipe or Good Sir Dishrag when these things could never live up to all that their sex implied?

The teacher proceeded to belittle everyone from German Eva, who hated laziness, to Japanese Yukari, who loved paintbrushes and soap. Italian, Thai, Dutch, Korean, and Chinese—we all left class foolishly believing that the worst was over. She'd shaken us up a little, but surely that was just an act designed to weed out the deadweight. We didn't know it then, but the coming months would teach us what it was like to spend time in the presence of a wild animal, something completely unpredictable. Her temperament was not based on a series of good and bad days but, rather, good and bad moments. We soon learned to dodge chalk and protect our heads and stomachs whenever she approached us with a question. She hadn't yet punched anyone, but it seemed wise to protect ourselves against the inevitable.

Though we were forbidden to speak anything but French, the teacher would occasionally use us to practice any of her five fluent languages.

"I hate you," she said to me one afternoon. Her English was

flawless. "I really, really hate you." Call me sensitive, but I couldn't help but take it personally.

After being singled out as a lazy *kfdtinvfm*, I took to spending four hours a night on my homework, putting in even more time whenever we were assigned an essay. I suppose I could have gotten by with less, but I was determined to create some sort of identity for myself: David the hard worker, David the cut-up. We'd have one of those "complete this sentence" exercises, and I'd fool with the thing for hours, invariably settling on something like "A quick run around the lake? I'd love to! Just give me a moment while I strap on my wooden leg." The teacher, through word and action, conveyed the message that if this was my idea of an identity, she wanted nothing to do with it.

My fear and discomfort crept beyond the borders of the classroom and accompanied me out onto the wide boulevards. Stopping for a coffee, asking directions, depositing money in my bank account: these things were out of the question, as they involved having to speak. Before beginning school, there'd been no shutting me up, but now I was convinced that everything I said was wrong. When the phone rang, I ignored it. If someone asked me a question, I pretended to be deaf. I knew my fear was getting the best of me when I started wondering why they don't sell cuts of meat in vending machines.

My only comfort was the knowledge that I was not alone. Huddled in the hallways and making the most of our pathetic French, my fellow students and I engaged in the sort of conversations commonly overheard in refugee camps.

"Sometime me cry alone at night."

"That be common for I, also, but be more strong, you. Much work and someday you talk pretty. People start love you soon. Maybe tomorrow, okay."

Unlike the French class I had taken in New York, here there was no sense of competition. When the teacher poked a shy Korean in the eyelid with a freshly sharpened pencil, we took no comfort in the fact that, unlike Hyeyoon Cho, we all knew the irregular past tense of the verb *to defeat*. In all fairness, the teacher hadn't meant to stab the girl, but neither did she spend much time apologizing, saying only, "Well, you should have been *ukkdyo* more *kdeynfulh*."

Over time it became impossible to believe that any of us would ever improve. Fall arrived and it rained every day, meaning we would now be scolded for the water dripping from our coats and umbrellas. It was mid-October when the teacher singled me out, saying, "Every day spent with you is like having a cesaran section." And it struck me that, for the first time since arriving in France, I could understand every word that someone was saying.

Understanding doesn't mean that you can suddenly speak the language. Far from it. It's a small step, nothing more, yet its rewards are intoxicating and deceptive. The teacher continued her diatribe and I settled back, bathing in the subtle beauty of each new curse and insult.

"You exhaust me with your foolishness and reward my efforts with nothing but pain, do you understand me?"

The world opened up, and it was with great joy that I responded, "I know the thing that you speak exact now. Talk me more, you, plus, please, plus."

2000

Elizabeth Cady Stanton
1815–1902

> *In 1848, Stanton, Lucretia Mott, and three other women organized the first woman's rights convention in the small, upstate New York town of Seneca Falls, where Stanton lived. They announced it only in a local newspaper, but over three hundred people attended, many of whom were already leaders in the abolitionist movement, such as Frederick Douglass and Mott's husband, James. The five organizers drafted this declaration, paraphrasing Jefferson's Declaration of Independence, and Stanton read it aloud. The convention adopted the declaration. Each of the resolutions passed unanimously, except for the claim to a woman's right to vote, which passed by only a small margin. A hundred attendees signed the document (thirty-two of these were men). The declaration, like its model, addresses a "candid world," but its main target was women discontented with their second-class status in American society. Stanton indicated her purpose when she addressed the convention: "I should feel exceed-*

*ingly diffident to appear before you at this time, having never be-
fore spoken in public, were I not nerved by a sense of right and
duty, did I not feel that the time had come for the question of
woman's wrongs to be laid before the public, did I not believe that
woman herself must do this work." The Seneca Falls convention
and the declaration that came from it served as the rallying cry for
the nascent women's movement.*

Declaration of Sentiments and Resolutions

When, in the course of human events, it becomes necessary for one portion of the family of man to assume among the people of the earth a position different from that which they have hitherto occupied, but one to which the laws of nature and of nature's God entitle them, a decent respect to the opinions of mankind requires that they should declare the causes that impel them to such a course.

We hold these truths to be self-evident: that all men and women are created equal; that they are endowed by their Creator with certain inalienable rights; that among these are life, liberty, and the pursuit of happiness; that to secure these rights governments are instituted, deriving their just powers from the consent of the governed. Whenever any form of government becomes destructive of these ends, it is the right of those who suffer from it to refuse allegiance to it, and to insist upon the institution of a new government, laying its foundation on such principles, and organizing its powers in such form, as to them shall seem most likely to effect their safety and happiness. Prudence indeed, will dictate that governments long established should not be changed for light and transient causes; and accordingly all experience hath shown that mankind are more disposed to suffer, while evils are sufferable, than to right themselves by abolishing the forms to which they were accustomed. But when a long train of abuses and usurpations, pursuing invariably the same object evinces a design to reduce them under absolute despotism, it is their duty to throw off such government, and to provide new guards for their future security. Such has been the patient sufferance of the women under this government, and such is now the necessity which constrains them to demand the equal station to which they are entitled.

The history of mankind is a history of repeated injuries and usurpations on the part of man toward woman, having in direct object the establishment of an absolute tyranny over her. To prove this, let facts be submitted to a candid world.

He has never permitted her to exercise her inalienable right to the elective franchise.

He has compelled her to submit to laws, in the formation of which she had no voice.

He has withheld from her rights which are given to the most ignorant and degraded men—both natives and foreigners.

Having deprived her of this first right of a citizen, the elective franchise, thereby leaving her without representation in the halls of legislation, he has oppressed her on all sides.

He has made her, if married, in the eye of the law, civilly dead.

He has taken from her all right in property, even to the wages she earns.

He has made her, morally, an irresponsible being, as she can commit many crimes with impunity, provided they be done in the presence of her husband. In the covenant of marriage, she is compelled to promise obedience to her husband, he becoming, to all intents and purposes, her master—the law giving him power to deprive her of her liberty, and to administer chastisement.

He has so framed the laws of divorce, as to what shall be the proper causes, and in case of separation, to whom the guardianship of the children shall be given, as to be wholly regardless of the happiness of women—the law, in all cases, going upon a false supposition of the supremacy of man, and giving all power into his hands.

After depriving her of all rights as a married woman, if single, and the owner of property, he has taxed her to support a government which recognizes her only when her property can be made profitable to it.

He has monopolized nearly all the profitable employments, and from those she is permitted to follow, she receives but a scanty remuneration. He closes against her all the avenues to wealth and distinction which he considers most honorable to himself. As a teacher of theology, medicine, or law, she is not known.

He has denied her the facilities for obtaining a thorough education, all colleges being closed against her.

He allows her in Church, as well as State, but a subordinate position, claiming Apostolic authority for her exclusion from the ministry, and, with some exceptions, from any public participation in the affairs of the Church.

He has created a false public sentiment by giving to the world a different code of morals for men and women, by which moral delinquencies which exclude women from society, are not only tolerated, but deemed of little account in man.

He has usurped the prerogative of Jehovah himself, claiming it as his right to assign for her a sphere of action, when that belongs to her conscience and to her God.

He has endeavored, in every way that he could, to destroy her confidence in her own powers, to lessen her self-respect, and to make her willing to lead a dependent and abject life.

Now, in view of this entire disfranchisement of one-half the people of this country, their social and religious degradation—in view of the unjust laws above mentioned, and because women do feel themselves aggrieved, oppressed, and fraudulently deprived of their most sacred rights, we insist that they have immediate admission to all the rights and privileges which belong to them as citizens of the United States.

In entering upon the great work before us, we anticipate no small amount of misconception, misrepresentation, and ridicule; but we shall use every instrumentality within our power to effect our object. We shall employ agents, circulate tracts, petition the State and National legislatures, and endeavor to enlist the pulpit and the press in our behalf. We hope this Convention will be followed by a series of Conventions embracing every part of the country.

1848

Brent Staples
b. 1951

Staples wrote this essay in 1986 for a special issue of Ms. *magazine devoted to men. It appeared under the ironic title "Just Walk on By," which must have sounded like a rebuke to the magazine's readers, most of whom were middle-class white women who, presumably, viewed black men as dangers to be avoided. Staples probably expected his readers to recognize themselves in the opening portrait of his "first victim," a woman who feels herself threatened by the presence of a black man behind her on a Chicago street. On the streets of New York, Staples persuades frightened pedestrians that he is no danger by whistling classical music, his taste for Beethoven and Vivaldi supposedly proving that he is no mugger. This essay uses a similar technique: It offers tokens of a shared economic status and culture to the readers of* Ms. *Staples adroitly establishes and exploits this ethos.*

Black Men and Public Space

My first victim was a woman—white, well dressed, probably in her early twenties. I came upon her late one evening on a deserted street in Hyde Park, a relatively affluent neighborhood in an otherwise mean, impoverished section of Chicago. As I swung onto the avenue behind her, there seemed to be a discreet, uninflammatory distance between us. Not so. She cast back a worried glance. To her, the youngish black man—a broad six feet two inches with a beard and billowing hair, both hands shoved into the pockets of a bulky military jacket—seemed menacingly close. After a few more quick glimpses, she picked up her pace and was soon running in earnest. Within seconds she disappeared into a cross street.

That was more than a decade ago, I was twenty-two years old, a graduate student newly arrived at the University of Chicago. It was in the echo of that terrified woman's footfalls that I first began to know the unwieldy inheritance I'd come into—the ability to alter public space in ugly ways. It was clear that she thought herself the quarry of a mugger, a rapist, or worse. Suffering a bout of insomnia, however, I was stalking sleep, not defenseless wayfarers. As a softy who is scarcely able to take a knife to a raw chicken—let alone hold one to a person's throat—I was surprised, embarrassed, and dismayed all at once. Her flight made me feel like an accomplice in tyranny. It also made it clear that I was indistinguishable from the muggers who occasionally seeped into the area from the surrounding ghetto. That first encounter, and those that followed, signified that a vast, unnerving gulf lay between nighttime pedestrians—particularly women—and me. And I soon gathered that being perceived as dangerous is a hazard in itself. I only needed to turn a corner into a dicey situation, or crowd some frightened, armed person in a foyer somewhere, or make an errant move after being pulled over by a policeman. Where fear and weapons meet—and they often do in urban America—there is always the possibility of death.

In that first year, my first away from my hometown, I was to become thoroughly familiar with the language of fear. At dark, shadowy intersections, I could cross in front of a car stopped at a traffic light and elicit the *thunk, thunk, thunk, thunk* of the driver—black, white, male, or female—hammering down the door locks. On less traveled streets after dark, I grew accustomed to but never comfortable with people crossing to the other side of the street rather than pass me. Then there were the standard unpleasantries with policemen, doormen, bouncers, cabdrivers, and others whose business it is to screen out troublesome individuals *before* there is any nastiness.

I moved to New York nearly two years ago and I have remained an avid night walker. In central Manhattan, the near-constant crowd cover minimizes tense one-on-one street encounters. Elsewhere—in SoHo, for example, where sidewalks are narrow and tightly spaced buildings shut out the sky—things can get very taut indeed.

After dark, on the warrenlike streets of Brooklyn where I live, I often see women who fear the worst from me. They seem to have set their faces on neutral, and with their purse straps strung across their chests bandolier-style, they forge ahead as though bracing themselves against being tackled. I understand, of course, that the danger they perceive is not a hallucination. Women are particularly vulnerable to street violence, and young black males are drastically overrepresented among the perpetrators of that violence. Yet these truths are no solace against the kind of alienation that comes of being ever the suspect, a fearsome entity with whom pedestrians avoid making eye contact.

It is not altogether clear to me how I reached the ripe old age of twenty-two without being conscious of the lethality nightime pedestrians attributed to me. Perhaps it was because in Chester, Pennsylvania, the small, angry industrial town where I came of age in the 1960s, I was scarcely noticeable against a backdrop of gang warfare, street knifings, and murders. I grew up one of the good boys, had perhaps a half-dozen fistfights. In retrospect, my shyness of combat has clear sources.

As a boy, I saw countless tough guys locked away; I have since buried several, too. They were babies, really—a teenage cousin, a brother of twenty-two, a childhood friend in his mid-twenties—all gone down in episodes of bravado played out in the streets. I came to doubt the virtues of intimidation early on. I chose, perhaps unconciously, to remain a shadow—timid, but a survivor.

The fearsomeness mistakenly attributed to me in public places often has a perilous flavor. The most frightening of these confusions occurred in the late 1970s and early 1980s, when I worked as a journalist in Chicago. One day, rushing into the office of a magazine I was writing for with a deadline story in hand, I was mistaken for a burglar. The office manager called security and, with an ad hoc posse, pursued me through the labyrinthine halls, nearly to my editor's door. I had no way of proving who I was. I could only move briskly toward the company of someone who knew me.

Another time I was on assignment for a local paper and killing time before an interview. I entered a jewelry store on the city's affluent Near North Side. The proprietor excused herself and returned with an enormous red Doberman pinscher straining at the end of a leash. She stood, the dog extended toward me, silent to my questions, her eyes bulging nearly out of her head. I took a cursory look around, nodded, and bade her good night.

Relatively speaking, however, I never fared as badly as another black male journalist. He went to nearby Waukegan, Illinois, a couple of summers ago to work on a story about a murderer who was born there. Mistaking the reporter for the killer, police officers hauled him from his car at gunpoint and but for his press credentials would probably have tried to book him. Such episodes are not uncommon. Black men trade tales like this all the time.

Over the years, I learned to smother the rage I felt at so often being taken for a criminal. Not to do so would surely have led to madness. I now take precautions to make myself less threatening. I move about with care, particularly late in the evening. I give a wide berth to nervous people on subway platforms during the wee hours, particularly when I have exchanged business clothes for jeans. If I happen to be entering a building behind some people who appear skittish, I may walk by, letting them clear the lobby before I return, so as not to seem to be following them. I have been calm and extremely congenial on those rare occasions when I've been pulled over by the police.

And on late-evening constitutionals I employ what has proved to be an excellent tension-reducing measure: I whistle melodies from Beethoven and Vivaldi and the more popular classical composers. Even steely New Yorkers hunching toward nighttime destinations seem to relax, and occasionally they even join in the tune. Virtually everybody seems to sense that a mugger wouldn't be warbling bright, sunny selections from Vivaldi's *Four Seasons*. It is my equivalent of the cowbell that hikers wear when they know they are in bear country.

1986

Jonathan Swift
1667–1745

Swift, the dean of St. Patrick's Cathedral in Dublin, was a minister of the Anglican Church and a member of the English ruling class of Ireland. He thought it his responsibility "to tell the People what is their Duty; and then to convince them that it is so." "A Modest Proposal," which Swift published anonymously in 1729, is written in the style typical of eighteenth-century "projectors," writers (usually economists) who project what will happen if their proposed reforms are put into practice. This pamphlet crowned ten years of Swift's own determined effort to persuade all classes

—Catholic peasants, middle-class shopkeepers, and Protestant landlords—to adopt higher morals and patriotism. (The projector's list of the other "expedients" for solving Ireland's ills is a fair summary of these efforts.) No particular event precipitated "A Modest Proposal," but Swift wrote it in the midst of intense, ineffectual parliamentary debate over how to end a famine and economic depression in Ireland that had been worsening for years. He criticizes the landowning ruling class, the shopkeepers, the peasants, Protestants and Catholics alike who feel greed more keenly than kinship to their fellow countrymen. "A Modest Proposal"'s argument is a famous example of irony, of saying the opposite of what you mean. Obviously, Swift does not really believe that the Irish poor should fatten their babies for the tables of the Irish rich. Rather, Swift's point is that the Irish already act as if they are beasts: The poor are idle, thieving, and promiscuous; the middle class is greedy and cheating; while the rich, uninspired by patriotism, are content. The irony establishes common ground with readers who have been unmoved by Swift's earlier, more direct appeals. Recoiling from the projector's rational but inhumane solution and uneasy with the suspicion that they already are (at least metaphorically) cannibalizing their nation, readers will view the other "expedients" as all the more attractive, urgent, and right.

A Modest Proposal

For Preventing the Children of Poor People in Ireland from Being a Burden to Their Parents or Country, and for Making Them Beneficial to the Public

It is a melancholy object to those who walk through this great town[1] or travel in the country, when they see the streets, the roads, and cabin doors, crowded with beggars of the female-sex, followed by three, four, or six children, all in rags and importuning every passenger for an alms. These mothers, instead of being able to work for their honest livelihood, are forced to employ all their time

---

1. Dublin.

in strolling to beg sustenance for their helpless infants, who, as they grow up, either turn thieves for want of work, or leave their dear native country to fight for the Pretender[2] in Spain, or sell themselves to the Barbadoes.[3]

I think it is agreed by all parties that this prodigious number of children in the arms, or on the backs, or at the heels of their mothers, and frequently of their fathers, is in the present deplorable state of the kingdom a very great additional grievance; and therefore whoever could find out a fair, cheap, and easy method of making these children sound, useful members of the commonwealth would deserve so well of the public as to have his statue set up for a preserver of the nation.

But my intention is very far from being confined to provide only for the children of professed beggars; it is of a much greater extent, and shall take in the whole number of infants at a certain age who are born of parents in effect as little able to support them as those who demand our charity in the streets.

As to my own part, having turned my thoughts for many years upon this important subject, and maturely weighed the several schemes of other projectors, I have always found them grossly mistaken in their computation. It is true, a child just dropped from its dam may be supported by her milk for a solar year, with little other nourishment; at most not above the value of two shillings,[4] which the mother may certainly get, or the value in scraps, by her lawful occupation of begging; and it is exactly at one year old that I propose to provide for them in such a manner as instead of being a charge upon their parents or the parish, or wanting food and raiment for the rest of their lives, they shall on the contrary contribute to the feeding, and partly to the clothing, of many thousands.

There is likewise another great advantage in my scheme, that it

---

2. The Pretender, son of King James II, who was dethroned in a Protestant revolution, was barred from succeeding to the British crown; many Irish Catholics supported his claim as rightful heir, joined him in exile, and tried to further his unsuccessful efforts at counterrevolution.

3. Many of the poor in Ireland emigrated as indentured servants, for they were unable to pay for their own passage. Such bargains made them virtual slaves for a fixed period of time, usually about seven years.

4. There were twelve shillings to the British pound, and a pound in 1729 would have bought approximately one hundred fifty dollars worth of goods in today's money.

will prevent those voluntary abortions, and that horrid practice of women murdering their bastard children, alas, too frequent among us, sacrificing the poor innocent babes, I doubt,[5] more to avoid the expense than the shame, which would move tears and pity in the most savage and inhuman breast.

The number of souls in this kingdom being usually reckoned one million and a half, of these I calculate there may be about two hundred thousand couple whose wives are breeders; from which number I subtract thirty thousand couples who are able to maintain their own children, although I apprehend there cannot be so many under the present distresses of the kingdom; but this being granted, there will remain an hundred and seventy thousand breeders. I again subtract fifty thousand for those women who miscarry, or whose children die by accident or disease within the year. There only remain an hundred and twenty thousand children of poor parents annually born. The question therefore is, how this number shall be reared and provided for, which, as I have already said, under the present situation of affairs, is utterly impossible by all the methods hitherto proposed. For we can neither employ them in handicraft or agriculture; we neither build houses (I mean in the country) nor cultivate land. They can very seldom pick up a livelihood by stealing till they arrive at six years old, except where they are of towardly parts;[6] although I confess they learn the rudiments much earlier, during which time they can however be looked upon only as probationers, as I have been informed by a principal gentleman in the county of Cavan, who protested to me that he never knew above one or two instances under the age of six, even in a part of the kingdom so renowned for the quickest proficiency in that art.

I am assured by our merchants that a boy or a girl before twelve years old is no salable commodity; and even when they come to this age they will not yield above three pounds, or three pounds and half a crown[7] at most on the Exchange; which cannot turn to account either to the parents or the kingdom, the charge of nutriment and rags having been at least four times that value.

---

5. "Expect" or "believe."
6. Show talent.

7. A crown was one-fourth of a pound.

I shall now therefore humbly propose my own thoughts, which I hope will not be liable to the least objection.

I have been assured by a very knowing American of my acquaintance in London, that a young healthy child well nursed is at a year old a most delicious, nourishing, and wholesome food, whether stewed, roasted, baked, or boiled; and I make no doubt that it will equally serve in a fricassee or a ragout.

I do therefore humbly offer it to public consideration that of the hundred and twenty thousand children, already computed, twenty thousand may be reserved for breed, whereof only one fourth part to be males, which is more than we allow to sheep, black cattle, or swine; and my reason is that these children are seldom the fruits of marriage, a circumstance not much regarded by our savages, therefore one male will be sufficient to serve four females. That the remaining hundred thousand may at a year old be offered in sale to the persons of quality and fortune through the kingdom, always advising the mother to let them suck plentifully in the last month, so as to render them plump and fat for a good table. A child will make two dishes at an entertainment for friends; and when the family dines alone, the fore or hind quarter will make a reasonable dish, and seasoned with a little pepper or salt will be very good boiled on the fourth day, especially in winter.

I have reckoned upon a medium that a child just born will weigh twelve pounds, and in a solar year if tolerably nursed increaseth to twenty-eight pounds.

I grant this food will be somewhat dear, and therefore very proper for landlords, who, as they have already devoured most of the parents, seem to have the best title to the children.

Infant's flesh will be in season throughout the year, but more plentiful in March, and a little before and after. For we are told by a grave author, an eminent French physician,[8] that fish being a prolific diet, there are more children born in Roman Catholic countries about nine months after Lent than at any other season; therefore, reckoning a year after Lent, the markets will be more glutted than usual, because the number of popish infants is at least three to one

8. François Rabelais (1483–1553), a comic writer.

in this kingdom; and therefore it will have one other collateral advantage, by lessening the number of Papists among us.[9]

I have already computed the charge of nursing a beggar's child (in which list I reckon all cottagers, laborers, and four fifths of the farmers) to be about two shillings per annum, rags included; and I believe no gentleman would repine to give ten shillings for the carcass of a good fat child, which, as I have said, will make four dishes of excellent nutritive meat, when he hath only some particular friend or his own family to dine with him. Thus the squire will learn to be a good landlord, and grow popular among the tenants; the mother will have eight shillings net profit, and be fit for work till she produces another child.

Those who are more thrifty (as I must confess the times require) may flay the carcass; the skin of which artificially[1] dressed will make admirable gloves for ladies, and summer boots for fine gentlemen.

As to our city of Dublin, shambles[2] may be appointed for this purpose in the most convenient parts of it, and butchers we may be assured will not be wanting; although I rather recommend buying the children alive, and dressing them hot from the knife as we do roasting pigs.

A very worthy person, a true lover of his country, and whose virtues I highly esteem, was lately pleased in discoursing on this matter to offer a refinement upon my scheme. He said that many gentlemen of this kingdom, having of late destroyed their deer, he conceived that the want of venison might be well supplied by the bodies of young lads and maidens, not exceeding fourteen years of age nor under twelve, so great a number of both sexes in every county being now ready to starve for want of work and service; and these to be disposed of by their parents, if alive, or otherwise by their nearest relations. But with due deference to so excellent a friend and so deserving a patriot, I cannot be altogether in his sentiments; for as to the males, my American acquaintance assured me from frequent experience that their flesh was generally tough and lean, like that of our schoolboys, by continual exercise, and their

---

9. Swift's audience would have been Anglo-Irish Protestants. Papists are Roman Catholics.

1. Skillfully.
2. Slaughterhouses.

taste disagreeable; and to fatten them would not answer the charge. Then as to the females, it would, I think with humble submission, be a loss to the public, because they soon would become breeders themselves: and besides, it is not improbable that some scrupulous people might be apt to censure such a practice (although indeed very unjustly) as a little bordering upon cruelty; which, I confess, hath always been with me the strongest objection against any project, how well soever intended.

But in order to justify my friend, he confessed that this expedient was put into his head by the famous Psalmanazar, a native of the island Formosa,[3] who came from thence to London above twenty years ago, and in conversation told my friend that in his country when any young person happened to be put to death, the executioner sold the carcass to persons of quality as a prime dainty; and that in his time the body of a plump girl of fifteen, who was crucified for an attempt to poison the emperor, was sold to his Imperial Majesty's prime minister of state, and other great mandarins of the court, in joints from the gibbet, at four hundred crowns. Neither indeed can I deny that if the same use were made of several plump young girls in this town, who without one single groat[4] to their fortunes cannot stir abroad without a chair,[5] and appear at the playhouse and assemblies in foreign fineries which they never will pay for, the kingdom would not be the worse.

Some persons of a desponding spirit are in great concern about that vast number of poor people who are aged, diseased, or maimed, and I have been desired to employ my thoughts what course may be taken to ease the nation of so grievous an encumbrance. But I am not in the least pain upon that matter, because it is very well known that they are every day dying and rotting by cold and famine, and filth and vermin, as fast as can be reasonably expected. And as to the younger laborers, they are now in almost as hopeful a condition. They cannot get work, and consequently pine away for want of nourishment to a degree that if at any time they are accidentally

3. George Psalmanazar, a Frenchman who pretended to be from Formosa (now Taiwan), had written a book about his supposed homeland that described human sacrifice and cannibalism.

4. Worth about four English pence; there were 240 pence to the pound in 1729.

5. A chair, often covered, carried on poles by two people; akin to a taxi.

hired to common labor, they have not strength to perform it; and thus the country and themselves are happily delivered from the evils to come.

I have too long digressed, and therefore shall return to my subject. I think the advantages by the proposal which I have made are obvious and many, as well as of the highest importance.

For first, as I have already observed, it would greatly lessen the number of Papists, with whom we are yearly overrun, being the principal breeders of the nation as well as our most dangerous enemies; and who stay at home on purpose to deliver the kingdom to the Pretender, hoping to take their advantage by the absence of so many good Protestants, who have chosen rather to leave their country than to stay at home and pay tithes against their conscience to an Episcopal curate.

Secondly, the poorer tenants will have something valuable of their own, which by law may be made liable to distress,[6] and help to pay their landlord's rent, their corn and cattle being already seized and money a thing unknown.

Thirdly, whereas the maintenance of an hundred thousand children, from two years old and upwards, cannot be computed at less than ten shillings a piece per annum, the nation's stock will be thereby increased fifty thousand pounds per annum, besides the profit of a new dish introduced to the tables of all gentlemen of fortune in the kingdom who have any refinement in taste. And the money will circulate among ourselves, the goods being entirely of our own growth and manufacture.

Fourthly, the constant breeders, besides the gain of eight shillings sterling per annum by the sale of their children, will be rid of the charge of maintaining them after the first year.

Fifthly, this food would likewise bring great custom to taverns, where the vintners will certainly be so prudent as to procure the best receipts[7] for dressing it to perfection, and consequently have their houses frequented by all the fine gentlemen, who justly value themselves upon their knowledge in good eating; and a skillful cook, who understands how to oblige his guests, will contrive to make it as expensive as they please.

6. Seizure in payment of debts.   7. Recipes.

Sixthly, this would be a great inducement to marriage, which all wise nations have either encouraged by rewards or enforced by laws and penalties. It would increase the care and tenderness of mothers toward their children, when they were sure of a settlement for life to the poor babes, provided in some sort by the public, to their annual profit instead of expense. We should see an honest emulation among the married women, which of them could bring the fattest child to the market. Men would become as fond of their wives during the time of their pregnancy as they are now of their mares in foal, their cows in calf, or sows when they are ready to farrow; nor offer to beat or kick them (as is too frequent a practice) for fear of a miscarriage.

Many other advantages might be enumerated. For instance, the addition of some thousand carcasses in our exportation of barreled beef, the propagation of swine's flesh, and improvement in the art of making good bacon, so much wanted among us by the great destruction of pigs, too frequent at our tables, which are no way comparable in taste or magnificence to a well-grown, fat, yearling child, which roasted whole will make a considerable figure at a lord mayor's feast or any other public entertainment. But this and many others I omit, being studious of brevity.

Supposing that one thousand families in this city would be constant customers for infants' flesh, besides others who might have it at merry meetings, particularly weddings and christenings, I compute that Dublin would take off annually about twenty thousand carcasses, and the rest of the kingdom (where probably they will be sold somewhat cheaper) the remaining eighty thousand.

I can think of no one objection that will possibly be raised against this proposal, unless it should be urged that the number of people will be thereby much lessened in the kingdom. This I freely own, and it was indeed one principal design in offering it to the world. I desire the reader will observe, that I calculate my remedy for this one individual kingdom of Ireland and for no other that ever was, is, or I think ever can be upon earth. Therefore let no man talk to me of other expedients: of taxing our absentees at five shillings a pound: of using neither clothes nor household furniture except what is of our own growth and manufacture: of utterly rejecting the materials and instruments that promote foreign luxury: of curing the expensiveness of pride, vanity, idleness, and gaming in our women: of introducing a vein of parsimony, prudence, and temperance: of learning to love our country, in the want of which we differ even from Laplanders and the inhabitants of Topinamboo[8]: of quitting our animosities and factions, nor acting any longer like the Jews, who were murdering one another at the very moment their city was taken: of being a little cautious not to sell our country and conscience for nothing: of teaching landlords to have at least one degree of mercy toward their tenants: lastly, of putting a spirit of honesty, industry, and skill into our shopkeepers; who, if a resolution could now be taken to buy only our native goods, would immediately unite to cheat and exact upon us in the price, the measure, and the goodness, nor could ever yet be brought to make one fair proposal of just dealing, though often and earnestly invited to it.

Therefore I repeat, let no man talk to me of these and the like expedients, till he hath at least some glimpse of hope that there will ever be some hearty and sincere attempt to put them in practice.

But as to myself, having been wearied out for many years with offering vain, idle, visionary thoughts, and at length utterly despairing of success, I fortunately fell upon this proposal, which, as it is wholly new, so it hath something solid and real, of no expense and little trouble, full in our own power, and whereby we can incur no danger in disobliging England. For this kind of commodity will not bear exportation, the flesh being of too tender a consistence to admit a long continuance in salt, although perhaps I could name a country[9] which would be glad to eat up our whole nation without it.

After all, I am not so violently bent upon my own opinion as to reject any offer proposed by wise men, which shall be found equally innocent, cheap, easy, and effectual. But before something of that kind shall be advanced in contradiction to my scheme, and offering a better, I desire the author or authors will be pleased maturely to consider two points. First, as things now stand, how they will be able to find food and raiment for an hundred thousand useless mouths and backs. And secondly, there being a round million of creatures in human figure throughout this kingdom, whose sole

8. In Brazil.   9. England.

subsistence put into a common stock would leave them in debt two millions of pounds sterling, adding those who are beggars by profession to the bulk of farmers, cottagers, and laborers, with their wives and children who are beggars in effect; I desire those politicians who dislike my overture, and may perhaps be so bold to attempt an answer, that they will first ask the parents of these mortals whether they would not at this day think it a great happiness to have been sold for food at a year old in the manner I prescribe, and thereby have avoided such a perpetual scene of misfortunes as they have since gone through by the oppression of landlords, the impossibility of paying rent without money or trade, the want of common sustenance, with neither house nor clothes to cover them from the inclemencies of the weather, and the most inevitable prospect of entailing the like or greater miseries upon their breed forever.

I profess, in the sincerity of my heart, that I have not the least personal interest in endeavoring to promote this necessary work, having no other motive than the public good of my country, by advancing our trade, providing for infants, relieving the poor, and giving some pleasure to the rich. I have no children by which I can propose to get a single penny; the youngest being nine years old, and my wife past childbearing.

1729

Amy Tan

b. 1952

Tan wrote "Mother Tongue" for the Threepenny Review *in 1989, the same year that her best-selling novel* The Joy Luck Club *was published. Although the* Threepenny Review *is published in Berkeley, California, it has a national audience used to cosmopolitan fare. So Tan's intention is not to liberalize her readers' attitudes toward women like her mother: Her readers are not like the hospital workers and the stockbroker in the essay. Her intent is more discursive and less persuasive. It concerns the influence her mother and her mother's language have had on Tan's writing. The point of the essay is wrapped up in the final anecdote.*

Mother Tongue

I am not a scholar of English or literature. I cannot give you much more than personal opinions on the English language and its variations in this country or others.

I am a writer. And by that definition, I am someone who has always loved language. I am fascinated by language in daily life. I spend a great deal of my time thinking about the power of language—the way it can evoke an emotion, a visual image, a complex idea, or a simple truth. Language is the tool of my trade. And I use them all—all the Englishes I grew up with.

Recently, I was made keenly aware of the different Englishes I do use. I was giving a talk to a large group of people, the same talk I had already given to half a dozen other groups. The nature of the talk was about my writing, my life, and my book, *The Joy Luck Club*. The talk was going along well enough, until I remembered one major difference that made the whole talk sound wrong. My mother was in the room. And it was perhaps the first time she had heard me give a lengthy speech—using the kind of English I have never used with her. I was saying things like, "The intersection of memory upon imagination" and "There is an aspect of my fiction that relates to thus-and-thus"—a speech filled with carefully wrought grammatical phrases, burdened, it suddenly seemed to me, with nominalized forms, past perfect tenses, conditional phrases—all the forms of standard English that I had learned in school and through books, the forms of English I did not use at home with my mother.

Just last week, I was walking down the street with my mother, and I again found myself conscious of the English I was using, the English I do use with her. We were talking about the price of new and used furniture and I heard myself saying this: "Not waste money that way." My husband was with us as well, and he didn't notice any switch in my English. And then I realized why. It's because over the twenty years we've been together I've often used that same kind of English with him, and sometimes he even uses it with me. It has become our language of intimacy, a different sort of English that relates to family talk, the language I grew up with.

So you'll have some idea of what this family talk I heard sounds like, I'll quote what my mother said during a recent conversation which I videotaped and then transcribed. During this conversation, my mother was talking about a political gangster in Shanghai who had the same last name as her family's, Du, and how the gangster in his early years wanted to be adopted by her family which was rich by comparison. Later, the gangster became more powerful, far richer than my mother's family, and one day showed up at my mother's wedding to pay his respects. Here's what she said in part:

"Du Yusong having business like fruit stand. Like off the street kind. He is Du like Du Zong—but not Tsung-ming Island people. The local people call putong, the river east side, he belong to that side local people. That man want to ask Du Zong father take him in like become own family. Du Zong father wasn't look down on him, but didn't take seriously, until that man big like become a mafia. Now important person, very hard to inviting him. Chinese way, came only to show respect, don't stay for dinner. Respect for making big celebration, he shows up. Mean gives lots of respect. Chinese custom. Chinese social life that way. If too important won't have to stay too long. He come to my wedding. I didn't see, I heard it. I gone to boy's side, they have YMCA dinner. Chinese age I was 19."

You should know that my mother's expressive command of English belies how much she actually understands. She reads the Forbes report, listens to Wall Street Week, converses daily with her stockbroker, reads all of Shirley MacLaine's books with ease—all kinds of things I can't begin to understand. Yet some of my friends tell me they understand fifty percent of what my mother says. Some say they understand eighty to ninety percent. Some say they understand none of it, as if she were speaking pure Chinese. But to me, my mother's English is perfectly clear, perfectly natural. It's my mother tongue. Her language, as I hear it, is vivid, direct, full of observation and imagery. That was the language that helped shape the way I saw things, expressed things, made sense of the world.

Lately, I've been giving more thought to the kind of English my mother speaks. Like others, I have described it to people as "broken" or "fractured" English. But I wince when I say that. It has always bothered me that I can think of no way to describe it other than "broken," as if it were damaged and needed to be fixed, as if it lacked a certain wholeness and soundness. I've heard other terms used, "limited English," for example. But they seem just as bad, as if everything is limited, including people's perception of the limited English speaker.

I know this for a fact, because when I was growing up, my mother's "limited" English limited *my* perception of her. I was ashamed of her English. I believed that her English reflected the quality of what she had to say. That is, because she expressed them imperfectly her thoughts were imperfect. And I had plenty of empirical evidence to support me: the fact that people in department stores, at banks, and at restaurants did not take her seriously, did not give her good service, pretended not to understand her, or even acted as if they did not hear her.

My mother has long realized the limitations of her English as well. When I was fifteen, she used to have me call people on the phone to pretend I was she. In this guise, I was forced to ask for information or even to complain and yell at people who had been rude to her. One time it was a call to her stockbroker in New York. She had cashed out her small portfolio and it just so happened we were going to go to New York the next week, our very first trip outside California. I had to get on the phone and say in an adolescent voice that was not very convincing, "This is Mrs. Tan."

And my mother was standing in the back whispering loudly,

"Why he don't send me check, already two weeks late. So mad he lie to me, losing me money."

And then I said in perfect English, "Yes, I'm getting rather concerned. You had agreed to send the check two weeks ago, but it hasn't arrived."

Then she began to talk more loudly, "What he want, I come to New York tell him front of his boss, you cheating me?" And I was trying to calm her down, make her be quiet, while telling the stockbroker, "I can't tolerate any more excuses. If I don't receive the check immediately, I am going to have to speak to your manager when I'm in New York next week." And sure enough, the following week there we were in front of this astonished stockbroker, and I was sitting there red-faced and quiet, and my mother, the real Mrs. Tan, was shouting at his boss in her impeccable broken English.

We used a similar routine just five days ago, for a situation that was far less humorous. My mother had gone to the hospital for an appointment, to find out about a benign brain tumor a CAT scan had revealed a month ago. She said she had spoken very good English, her best English, no mistakes. Still, she said, the hospital did not apologize when they said they had lost the CAT scan and she had come for nothing. She said they did not seem to have any sympathy when she told them she was anxious to know the exact diagnosis since her husband and son had both died of brain tumors. She said they would not give her any more information until the next time and she would have to make another appointment for that. So she said she would not leave until the doctor called her daughter. She wouldn't budge. And when the doctor finally called her daughter, me, who spoke in perfect English—lo and behold—we had assurances the CAT scan would be found, promises that a conference call on Monday would be held, and apologies for any suffering my mother had gone through for a most regrettable mistake.

I think my mother's English almost had an effect on limiting my possibilities in life as well. Sociologists and linguists probably will tell you that a person's developing language skills are more influenced by peers. But I do think that the language spoken in the family, especially in immigrant families which are more insular, plays a large role in shaping the language of the child. And I believe that it affected my results on achievement tests, IQ tests, and the SAT.

While my English skills were never judged as poor, compared to math, English could not be considered my strong suit. In grade school, I did moderately well, getting perhaps Bs, sometimes B+s in English, and scoring perhaps in the sixtieth or seventieth percentile on achievement tests. But those scores were not good enough to override the opinion that my true abilities lay in math and science, because in those areas I achieved As and scored in the ninetieth percentile or higher.

This was understandable. Math is precise; there is only one correct answer. Whereas, for me at least, the answers on English tests were always a judgment call, a matter of opinion and personal experience. Those tests were constructed around items like fill-in-the-blank sentence completion, such as "Even though Tom was _____, Mary thought he was _____." And the correct answer always seemed to be the most bland combinations of thoughts, for example, "Even though Tom was shy, Mary thought he was charming," with the grammatical structure "even though" limiting the correct answer to some sort of semantic opposites, so you wouldn't get answers like "Even though Tom was foolish, Mary thought he was ridiculous." Well, according to my mother, there were very few limitations as to what Tom could have been, and what Mary might have thought of him. So I never did well on tests like that.

The same was true with word analogies, pairs of words, in which you were supposed to find some sort of logical, semantic relationship—for example, "sunset" is to "nightfall" as _____ is to _____." And here, you would be presented with a list of four possible pairs, one of which showed the same kind of relationship: "red" is to "stoplight," "bus" is to "arrival," "chills" is to "fever," "yawn" is to "boring." Well, I could never think that way. I knew what the tests were asking, but I could not block out of my mind the images already created by the first pair, "sunset is to nightfall"— and I would see a burst of colors against a darkening sky, the moon rising, the lowering of a curtain of stars. And all the other pairs of words—red, bus, stoplight, boring—just threw up a mass of confusing images, making it impossible for me to sort out something as logical as saying: "A sunset precedes nightfall" is the same as "a chill precedes a fever." The only way I would have gotten that answer right would have been to imagine an associative situation, for example, my being disobedient and staying out past sunset, catching a chill at night, which turns into feverish pneumonia as punishment, which indeed did happen to me.

I have been thinking about all this lately, about my mother's English, about achievement tests. Because lately I've been asked, as a writer, why there are not more Asian-Americans represented in American literature. Why are there few Asian-Americans enrolled in creative writing programs? Why do so many Chinese students go into engineering? Well, these are broad sociological questions I can't begin to answer. But I have noticed in surveys—in fact, just last week—that Asian students, as a whole, always do significantly better on math achievement tests than in English. And this makes me think that there are other Asian-American students whose English spoken in the home might also be described as "broken" or "limited." And perhaps they also have teachers who are steering them away from writing and into math and science, which is what happened to me.

Fortunately, I happen to be rebellious in nature, and enjoy the challenge of disproving assumptions made about me. I became an English major my first year in college after being enrolled as premed. I started writing non-fiction as a freelancer the week after I was told by my former boss that writing was my worst skill and I should hone my talents toward account management.

But it wasn't until 1985 that I finally began to write fiction. And at first I wrote using what I thought to be wittily crafted sentences, sentences that would finally prove I had mastery over the English language. Here's an example from the first draft of a story that later made its way into *The Joy Luck Club*, but without this line: "That was my mental quandary in its nascent state." A terrible line, which I can barely pronounce.

Fortunately, for reasons I won't get into today, I later decided I should envision a reader for the stories I would write. And the reader I decided upon was my mother, because these were stories about mothers. So with this reader in mind—and in fact, she did read my early drafts—I began to write stories using all the Englishes I grew up with: the English I spoke to my mother, which for lack of a better term, might be described as "simple"; the English she used with me, which for lack of a better term might be described as "bro-ken"; my translation of her Chinese, which could certainly be described as "watered down"; and what I imagined to be her trans-lation of her Chinese if she could speak in perfect English, her in-ternal language, and for that I sought to preserve the essence, but not either an English or a Chinese structure. I wanted to capture what language ability tests can never reveal: her intent, her passion, her imagery, the rhythms of her speech and the nature of her thoughts.

Apart from what any critic had to say about my writing, I knew I had succeeded where it counted when my mother finished reading my book, and gave me her verdict: "So easy to read."

1989

Deborah Tannen
b. 1945

Tannen, a linguist teaching at Georgetown University, published You Just Don't Understand! Men and Women in Conversation *in 1990. The following year she published "Conversational Styles" in the* Chronicle of Higher Education, *the national weekly news-paper for college teachers. So this essay's thesis, that "small-group in-teraction should be part of any class," was immediately relevant to the essay's audience. The essay offers none of the evidence that you might expect to find if it had been published in a journal of the so-cial sciences: Tannen doesn't try to meet the criteria of a valid in-ductive argument. Instead, she relies on anecdotal evidence (her experience in one class of twenty-one students) and her reputation as an expert on how men and women speak in public. Few readers would demand more from an article in the* Chronicle. *Most would approach this essay as they would an informal conversation over lunch: They would look for insights into their own students and helpful, practical advice about how to improve their own teaching. The "proof" would be in how closely their own experiences con-firmed Tannen's conclusions. As a student, you have plenty of expe-rience from which to make a similar judgment.*

Conversational Styles

When I researched and wrote my latest book, *You Just Don't Understand! Women and Men in Conversation*, the furthest thing from my mind was reevaluating my teaching strategies. But that has been one of the direct benefits of having written the book.

The primary focus of my linguistic research always has been the language of everyday conversation. One facet of this is conversational style: how different regional, ethnic, and class backgrounds, as well as age and gender, result in different ways of using language to communicate. *You Just Don't Understand* is about the conversational styles of women and men. As I gained more insight into typically male and female ways of using language, I began to suspect some of the causes of the troubling facts that women who go to single-sex schools do better in later life, and that when young women sit next to young men in classrooms, the males talk more. This is not to say that all men talk in class, nor that no women do. It is simply that a greater percentage of discussion time is taken by men's voices.

The research of sociologists and anthropologists such as Janet Lever, Marjorie Harness Goodwin, and Donna Eder has shown that girls and boys learn to use language differently in their sex-separate peer groups. Typically, a girl has a best friend with whom she sits and talks, frequently telling secrets. It's the telling of secrets, the fact and the way that they talk to each other, that makes them best friends. For boys, activities are central: Their best friends are the ones they do things with. Boys also tend to play in larger groups that are hierarchical. High-status boys give orders and push low-status boys around. So boys are expected to use language to seize center stage: by exhibiting their skill, displaying their knowledge, and challenging and resisting challenges.

These patterns have stunning implications for classroom interaction. Most faculty members assume that participating in class discussion is a necessary part of successful performance. Yet speaking in a classroom is more congenial to boys' language experience than to girls', since it entails putting oneself forward in front of a large group of people, many of whom are strangers and at least one of whom is sure to judge speakers' knowledge and intelligence by their verbal display.

Another aspect of many classrooms that makes them more hospitable to most men than to most women is the use of debate-like formats as a learning tool. Our educational system, as Walter Ong argues persuasively in his book *Fighting for Life* (Cornell University Press, 1981), is fundamentally male in that the pursuit of knowledge is believed to be achieved by ritual opposition: public display followed by argument and challenge. Father Ong demonstrates that ritual opposition—what he calls "adversativeness" or "agonism"—is fundamental to the way most males approach almost any activity. (Consider, for example, the little boy who shows he likes a little girl by pulling her braids and shoving her.) But ritual opposition is antithetical to the way most females learn and like to interact. It is not that females don't fight, but that they don't fight for fun. They don't *ritualize* opposition.

Anthropologists working in widely disparate parts of the world have found contrasting verbal rituals for women and men. Women in completely unrelated cultures (for example, Greece and Bali) engage in ritual laments: spontaneously produced rhyming couplets that express their pain, for example, over the loss of loved ones. Men do not take part in laments. They have their own, very different verbal ritual: a contest, a war of words in which they vie with each other to devise clever insults.

When discussing these phenomena with a colleague, I commented that I see these two styles in American conversation: Many women bond by talking about troubles, and many men bond by exchanging playful insults and put-downs, and other sorts of verbal sparring. He exclaimed: "I never thought of this, but that's the way I teach: I have students read an article, and then I invite them to tear it apart. After we've torn it to shreds, we talk about how to build a better model."

This contrasts sharply with the way I teach: I open the discussion of readings by asking, "What did you find useful in this? What can we use in our own theory building and our own methods?" I note what I see as weaknesses in the author's approach, but I also point out that the writer's discipline and purposes might be different from ours. Finally, I offer personal anecdotes illustrating the phenomena under discussion and praise students' anecdotes as well as their critical acumen.

These different teaching styles must make our classrooms wildly different places and hospitable to different students. Male students are more likely to be comfortable attacking the readings and might find the inclusion of personal anecdotes irrelevant and "soft." Women are more likely to resist discussion they perceive as hostile, and, indeed, it is women in my classes who are most likely to offer personal anecdotes.

A colleague who read my book commented that he had always taken for granted that the best way to deal with students' comments is to challenge them; this, he felt it was self-evident, sharpens their minds and helps them develop debating skills. But he had noticed that women were relatively silent in his classes, so he decided to try beginning discussion with relatively open-ended questions and letting comments go unchallenged. He found, to his amazement and satisfaction, that more women began to speak up.

Though some of the women in his class clearly liked this better, perhaps some of the men liked it less. One young man in my class wrote in a questionnaire about a history professor who gave students questions to think about and called on people to answer them: "He would then play devil's advocate . . . *i.e.,* he debated us. . . . That class *really* sharpened me intellectually. . . . We as students do need to know how to defend ourselves." This young man valued the experience of being attacked and challenged publicly. Many, if not most, women would shrink from such "challenge," experiencing it as public humiliation.

A professor at Hamilton College told me of a young man who was upset because he felt his class presentation had been a failure. The professor was puzzled because he had observed that class members had listened attentively and agreed with the student's observations. It turned out that it was this very agreement that the student interpreted as failure: Since no one had engaged his ideas by arguing with him, he felt they had found them unworthy of attention.

So one reason men speak in class more than women is that many of them find the "public" classroom setting more conducive to speaking, whereas most women are more comfortable speaking in private to a small group of people they know well. A second reason is that men are more likely to be comfortable with the debate-like form that discussion may take. Yet another reason is the different attitudes toward speaking in class that typify women and men.

Students who speak frequently in class, many of whom are men, assume that it is their job to think of contributions and try to get the floor to express them. But many women monitor their participation not only to get the floor but to avoid getting it. Women students in my class tell me that if they have spoken up once or twice, they hold back for the rest of the class because they don't want to dominate. If they have spoken a lot one week, they will remain silent the next. These different ethics of participation are, of course, unstated, so those who speak freely assume that those who remain silent have nothing to say, and those who are reining themselves in assume that the big talkers are selfish and hoggish.

When I looked around my classes, I could see these differing ethics and habits at work. For example, my graduate class in analyzing conversation had 20 students, 11 women and 9 men. Of the men, four were foreign students: two Japanese, one Chinese, and one Syrian. With the exception of the three Asian men, all the men spoke in class at least occasionally. The biggest talker in the class was a woman, but there were also five women who never spoke at all, only one of whom was Japanese. I decided to try something different.

I broke the class into small groups to discuss the issues raised in the readings and to analyze their own conversational transcripts. I devised three ways of dividing the students into groups: one by the degree program they were in, one by gender, and one by conversational style, as closely as I could guess it. This meant that when the class was grouped according to conversational style, I put Asian students together, fast talkers together, and quiet students together. The class split into groups six times during the semester, so they met in each grouping twice. I told students to regard the groups as examples of interactional data and to note the different ways they participated in the different groups. Toward the end of the term, I gave them a questionnaire asking about their class and group participation.

I could see plainly from my observation of the groups at work that women who never opened their mouths in class were talking away in the small groups. In fact, the Japanese woman commented that she found it particularly hard to contribute to the all-woman group she was in because "I was overwhelmed by how talkative the female students were in the female-only group." This is particularly revealing because it highlights that the same person who can be "oppressed" into silence in one context can become the talkative "oppressor" in another. No one's conversational style is absolute; everyone's style changes in response to the context and others' styles.

Some of the students (seven) said they preferred the same-gender groups; others preferred the same-style groups. In answer to the question "Would you have liked to speak in class more than you did?" six of the seven who said Yes were women; the one man was Japanese. Most startlingly, this response did not come only from quiet women; it came from women who had indicated they had spoken in class never, rarely, sometimes, and often. Of the 11 students who said the amount they had spoken was fine, 7 were men. Of the four women who checked "fine," two added qualifications indicating it wasn't completely fine: One wrote in "maybe more," and one wrote, "I have an urge to participate but often feel I should have something more interesting/relevant/wonderful/intelligent to say!!"

I counted my experiment a success. Everyone in the class found the small groups interesting, and no one indicated he or she would have preferred that the class not break into groups. Perhaps most instructive, however, was the fact that the experience of breaking into groups, and of talking about participation in class, raised everyone's awareness about classroom participation. After we had talked about it, some of the quietest women in the class made a few voluntary contributions, though sometimes I had to insure their participation by interrupting the students who were exuberantly speaking out.

Americans are often proud that they discount the significance of cultural differences: "We are all individuals," many people boast. Ignoring such issues as gender and ethnicity becomes a source of pride: "I treat everyone the same." But treating people the same is not equal treatment if they are not the same.

The classroom is a different environment for those who feel comfortable putting themselves forward in a group than it is for those who find the prospect of doing so chastening, or even terrifying. When a professor asks, "Are there any questions?," students who can formulate statements the fastest have the greatest opportunity to respond. Those who need significant time to do so have not really been given a chance at all, since by the time they are ready to speak, someone else has the floor.

In a class where some students speak out without raising hands, those who feel they must raise their hands and wait to be recognized do not have equal opportunity to speak. Telling them to feel free to jump in will not make them feel free; one's sense of timing, of one's rights and obligations in a classroom, are automatic, learned over years of interaction. They may be changed over time, with motivation and effort, but they cannot be changed on the spot. And everyone assumes his or her own way is best. When I asked my students how the class could be changed to make it easier for them to speak more, the most talkative woman said she would prefer it if no one had to raise hands, and a foreign student said he wished people would raise their hands and wait to be recognized.

My experience in this class has convinced me that small-group interaction should be part of any class that is not a small seminar. I also am convinced that having the students become observers of their own interaction is a crucial part of their education. Talking about ways of talking in class makes students aware that their ways of talking affect other students, that the motivations they impute to others may not truly reflect others' motives, and that the behaviors they assume to be self-evidently right are not universal norms.

The goal of complete equal opportunity in class may not be attainable, but realizing that one monolithic classroom-participation structure is not equal opportunity is itself a powerful motivation to find more-diverse methods to serve diverse students—and every classroom is diverse.

1991

Henry David Thoreau
1817–1862

In the summer of 1846, when Thoreau was in the midst of his experimental hermitage on Walden Pond, the United States invaded Mexico. The Mexican War divided the nation. Southerners and empire-minded Northerners welcomed it, for it secured Texas (as a slave state) and won for the United States the spoils of Utah, New Mexico, Arizona, Nevada, and California, which Southerners expected to be admitted as slave states to balance the admittance of new states in the North. Abolitionists opposed it, as did anti-imperialists, for obvious reasons. Thoreau's opposition to the war and his opposition to slavery compelled him to protest by refusing to pay his annual poll tax, for which he was jailed in 1846. He was putting into practice the principle of nonviolent protest advocated by abolitionists for years. He described his night in jail and the principles behind his civil disobedience to the Concord Lyceum in 1848. Later, after the war was over, he published the lecture in the first and only issue of Aesthetic Papers. *That journal mustered only fifty subscribers and sold just as poorly in bookstores, so Thoreau's original audience was only the clique of radicals we have come to know as the Transcendentalists. In short, he was preaching to the choir: people who already regarded the Mexican War and slavery as evils. So he didn't need to persuade these like-minded people to reject slavery. Instead, he needed to persuade his readers to act on their beliefs. Although the Mexican War was over by the time this essay was published, an occasion to accept or reject Thoreau's advice would soon be pressed on the citizens of Massachusetts, for in 1850 Congress passed the second Fugitive Slave Act, which reinforced the Constitutional stipulation that Northern states return to their oppressors black men and women who had escaped from slavery in the South and also penalized any individuals who helped slaves escape. "Civil Disobedience" was intended to challenge Thoreau's readers to defy this law and the Constitution.*

Civil Disobedience

I heartily accept the motto,—"That government is best which governs least;" and I should like to see it acted up to more rapidly and systematically. Carried out, it finally amounts to this, which also I believe,—"That government is best which governs not at all;" and when men are prepared for it, that will be the kind of government which they will have. Government is at best but an expedient; but most governments are usually, and all governments are sometimes, inexpedient. The objections which have been brought against a standing army, and they are many and weighty, and deserve to prevail, may also at last be brought against a standing government. The standing army is only an arm of the standing government. The government itself, which is only the mode which the people have chosen to execute their will, is equally liable to be abused and perverted before the people can act through it. Witness the present Mexican war, the work of comparatively a few individuals using the standing government as their tool; for, in the outset, the people would not have consented to this measure.

This American government,—what is it but a tradition, though a recent one, endeavoring to transmit itself unimpaired to posterity, but each instant losing some of its integrity? It has not the vitality and force of a single living man; for a single man can bend it to his will. It is a sort of wooden gun to the people themselves; and, if ever they should use it in earnest as a real one against each other, it will surely split. But it is not the less necessary for this; for the people must have some complicated machinery or other, and hear its din, to satisfy that idea of government which they have. Governments show thus how successfully men can be imposed on, even impose on themselves, for their own advantage. It is excellent, we must all allow; yet this government never of itself furthered any enterprise, but by the alacrity with which it got out of its way. *It* does not keep the country free. *It* does not settle the West. *It* does not educate. The character inherent in the American people has done all that has been accomplished; and it would have done somewhat more, if the government had not sometimes got in its way. For government is an expedient by which men would fain succeed in letting one another alone; and, as has been said, when it is most expedient, the governed are most let alone by it. Trade and commerce, if they were not made of India rubber, would never manage to bounce over the obstacles which legislators are continually putting in their way; and, if one were to judge these men wholly by the effects of their actions, and not partly by their intentions, they would deserve to be classed and punished with those mischievous persons who put obstructions on the railroads.

But, to speak practically and as a citizen, unlike those who call themselves no-government men, I ask for, not at once no government, but *at once* a better government. Let every man make known what kind of government would command his respect, and that will be one step toward obtaining it.

After all, the practical reason why, when the power is once in the hands of the people, a majority are permitted, and for a long period continue, to rule, is not because they are most likely to be in the right, nor because this seems fairest to the minority, but because they are physically the strongest. But a government in which the majority rule in all cases cannot be based on justice, even as far as men understand it. Can there not be a government in which majorities do not virtually decide right and wrong, but conscience?— in which majorities decide only those questions to which the rule of expediency is applicable? Must the citizen ever for a moment, or in the least degree, resign his conscience to the legislator? Why has every man a conscience, then? I think that we should be men first, and subjects afterward. It is not desirable to cultivate a respect for the law, so much as for the right. The only obligation which I have a right to assume, is to do at any time what I think right. It is truly enough said, that a corporation has no conscience; but a corporation of conscientious men is a corporation *with* a conscience. Law never made men a whit more just; and, by means of their respect for it, even the well-disposed are daily made the agents of injustice. A common and natural result of an undue respect for law is, that you may see a file of soldiers, colonel, captain, corporal, privates, powder-monkeys and all, marching in admirable order over hill and dale to the wars, against their wills, aye, against their common sense and consciences, which makes it very steep marching indeed, and produces a palpitation of the heart. They have no doubt that it is a

damnable business in which they are concerned; they are all peaceably inclined. Now, what are they? Men at all? or small moveable
forts and magazines, at the service of some unscrupulous man in
power? Visit the Navy Yard, and behold a marine, such a man as an
American government can make, or such as it can make a man with
its black arts, a mere shadow and reminiscence of humanity, a man
laid out alive and standing, and already, as one may say, buried under arms with funeral accompaniments, though it may be

"Not a drum was heard, nor a funeral note,
    As his corse to the ramparts we hurried;
Not a soldier discharged his farewell shot
    O'er the grave where our hero we buried." [1]

The mass of men serve the State thus, not as men mainly, but as
machines, with their bodies. They are the standing army, and the
militia, jailers, constables, *posse comitatus,* &c. In most cases there is
no free exercise whatever of the judgment or of the moral sense; but
they put themselves on a level with wood and earth and stones; and
wooden men can perhaps be manufactured that will serve the purpose as well. Such command no more respect than men of straw, or
a lump of dirt. They have the same sort of worth only as horses
and dogs. Yet such as these even are commonly esteemed good citizens. Others, as most legislators, politicians, lawyers, ministers, and
office-holders, serve the State chiefly with their heads; and, as they
rarely make any moral distinctions, they are as likely to serve the
devil, without intending it, as God. A very few, as heroes, patriots,
martyrs, reformers in the great sense, and *men,* serve the State with
their consciences also, and so necessarily resist it for the most part;
and they are commonly treated by it as enemies. A wise man will
only be useful as a man, and will not submit to be "clay," and "stop
a hole to keep the wind away," but leave that office to his dust at
least:—

"I am too high-born to be propertied,
    To be a secondary at control,

1. "The Burial of Sir John Moore at Corunna," lines 1–4, by Charles Wolfe.

Or useful serving-man and instrument
To any sovereign state throughout the world."[2]

He who gives himself entirely to his fellow-men appears to them useless and selfish; but he who gives himself partially to them is pronounced a benefactor and philanthropist.

How does it become a man to behave toward this American government to-day? I answer that he cannot without disgrace be associated with it. I cannot for an instant recognize that political organization as *my* government which is the *slave's* government also.

All men recognize the right of revolution; that is, the right to refuse allegiance to and to resist the government, when its tyranny or its inefficiency are great and unendurable. But almost all say that such is not the case now. But such was the case, they think, in the Revolution of '75. If one were to tell me that this was a bad government because it taxed certain foreign commodities brought to its ports, it is most probable that I should not make an ado about it, for I can do without them: all machines have their friction; and possibly this does enough good to counterbalance the evil. At any rate, it is a great evil to make a stir about it. But when the friction comes to have its machine, and oppression and robbery are organized, I say, let us not have such a machine any longer. In other words, when a sixth of the population of a nation which has undertaken to be the refuge of liberty are slaves, and a whole country is unjustly overrun and conquered by a foreign army, and subjected to military law, I think that it is not too soon for honest men to rebel and revolutionize. What makes this duty the more urgent is the fact, that the country so overrun is not our own, but ours is the invading army.

Paley, a common authority with many on moral questions, in his chapter on the "Duty of Submission to Civil Government,"[3] resolves all civil obligation into expediency; and he proceeds to say, "that so long as the interest of the whole society requires it, that is, so long as the established government cannot be resisted or changed without public inconveniency, it is the will of God that the estab-

---

2. *The Life and Death of King John*, Act V, Scene ii, lines 83–86, by William Shakespeare.

3. William Paley (1743–1805), English theologian. "Duty of Submission to Civil Government" appears in *Principles of Moral and Political Philosophy* (1785).

lished government be obeyed, and no longer."—"This principle being admitted, the justice of every particular case of resistance is reduced to a computation of the quantity of the danger and grievance
on the one side, and of the probability and expense of redressing it
on the other." Of this, he says, every man shall judge for himself.
But Paley appears never to have contemplated those cases to which
the rule of expediency does not apply, in which a people, as well as
an individual, must do justice, cost what it may. If I have unjustly
wrested a plank from a drowning man, I must restore it to him
though I drown myself. This, according to Paley, would be inconve-
nient. But he that would save his life, in such a case, shall lose it.
This people must cease to hold slaves, and to make war on Mexico,
though it cost them their existence as a people.

In their practice, nations agree with Paley; but does any one
think that Massachusetts does exactly what is right at the present
crisis?

"A drab of state, a cloth-o'-silver slut,
   To have her train borne up, and her soul trail in the dirt."[4]

Practically speaking, the opponents to a reform in Massachusetts are
not a hundred thousand politicians at the South, but a hundred
thousand merchants and farmers here, who are more interested in
commerce and agriculture than they are in humanity, and are not
prepared to do justice to the slave and to Mexico, *cost what it may.* I
quarrel not with far-off foes, but with those who, near at home, co-
operate with, and do the bidding of those far away, and without
whom the latter would be harmless. We are accustomed to say, that
the mass of men are unprepared; but improvement is slow, because
the few are not materially wiser or better than the many. It is not so
important that many should be as good as you, as that there be
some absolute goodness somewhere; for that will leaven the whole
lump. There are thousands who are *in opinion* opposed to slavery
and to the war, who yet in effect do nothing to put an end to them;
who, esteeming themselves children of Washington and Franklin,
sit down with their hands in their pockets, and say that they know

4. *The Revengers Tragadie*, Act IV, Scene iv, lines 77–78, by Cyril Tourneur.

not what to do, and do nothing; who even postpone the question of freedom to the question of free-trade, and quietly read the prices-current along with the latest advices from Mexico, after dinner, and, it may be, fall asleep over them both. What is the price-current of an honest man and patriot today? They hesitate, and they regret, and sometimes they petition; but they do nothing in earnest and with effect. They will wait, well disposed, for others to remedy the evil, that they may no longer have it to regret. At most, they give only a cheap vote, and a feeble countenance and Godspeed, to the right, as it goes by them. There are nine hundred and ninety-nine patrons of virtue to one virtuous man; but it is easier to deal with the real possessor of a thing than with the temporary guardian of it.

All voting is a sort of gaming, like chequers or backgammon, with a slight moral tinge to it, a playing with right and wrong, with moral questions; and betting naturally accompanies it. The character of the voters is not staked. I cast my vote, perchance, as I think right; but I am not vitally concerned that that right should prevail. I am willing to leave it to the majority. Its obligation, therefore, never exceeds that of expediency. Even voting *for the right* is *doing* nothing for it. It is only expressing to men feebly your desire that it should prevail. A wise man will not leave the right to the mercy of chance, nor wish it to prevail through the power of the majority. There is but little virtue in the action of masses of men. When the majority shall at length vote for the abolition of slavery, it will be because they are indifferent to slavery, or because there is but little slavery left to be abolished by their vote. *They* will then be the only slaves. Only *his* vote can hasten the abolition of slavery who asserts his own freedom by his vote.

I hear of a convention to be held at Baltimore, or elsewhere, for the selection of a candidate for the Presidency, made up chiefly of editors, and men who are politicians by profession; but I think, what is it to any independent, intelligent, and respectable man what decision they may come to, shall we not have the advantage of his wisdom and honesty, nevertheless? Can we not count upon some independent votes? Are there not many individuals in the country who do not attend conventions? But no: I find that the respectable man, so called, has immediately drifted from his position, and despairs of his country, when his country has more reason to despair of him. He forthwith adopts one of the candidates thus selected as the only *available* one, thus proving that he is himself *available* for any purposes of the demagogue. His vote is of no more worth than that of any unprincipled foreigner or hireling native, who may have been bought. Oh for a man who is a *man*, and, as my neighbor says, has a bone in his back which you cannot pass your hand through! Our statistics are at fault: the population has been returned too large. How many *men* are there to a square thousand miles in this country? Hardly one. Does not America offer any inducement for men to settle here? The American has dwindled into an Odd Fellow,[5]—one who may be known by the development of his organ of gregariousness, and a manifest lack of intellect and cheerful self-reliance; whose first and chief concern, on coming into the world, is to see that the alms-houses are in good repair; and, before yet he has lawfully donned the virile garb, to collect a fund for the support of the widows and orphans that may be; who, in short, ventures to live only by the aid of the mutual insurance company, which has promised to bury him decently.

It is not a man's duty, as a matter of course, to devote himself to the eradication of any, even the most enormous wrong; he may still properly have other concerns to engage him; but it is his duty, at least, to wash his hands of it, and, if he gives it no thought longer, not to give it practically his support. If I devote myself to other pursuits and contemplations, I must first see, at least, that I do not pursue them sitting upon another man's shoulders. I must get off him first, that he may pursue his contemplations too. See what gross inconsistency is tolerated: I have heard some of my townsmen say, "I should like to have them order me out to help put down an insurrection of the slaves, or to march to Mexico,—see if I would go;" and yet these very men have each, directly by their allegiance, and so indirectly, at least, by their money, furnished a substitute. The soldier is applauded who refuses to serve in an unjust war by those who do not refuse to sustain the unjust government which makes the war; is applauded by those whose own act and authority he disregards and sets at nought; as if the State were penitent to that de-

5. A member of the Independent Order of Odd Fellows, a fraternal and benevolent secret society.

gree that it hired one to scourge it while it sinned, but not to that degree that it left off sinning for a moment. Thus, under the name of order and civil government, we are all made at last to pay homage to and support our own meanness. After the first blush of sin, comes its indifference; and from immoral it becomes, as it were, *un*moral, and not quite unnecessary to that life which we have made.

The broadest and most prevalent error requires the most disinterested virtue to sustain it. The slight reproach to which the virtue of patriotism is commonly liable, the noble are most likely to incur. Those who, while they disapprove of the character and measures of a government, yield to it their allegiance and support, are undoubtedly its most conscientious supporters, and so frequently the most serious obstacles to reform. Some are petitioning the State to dissolve the Union, to disregard the requisitions of the President. Why do they not dissolve it themselves,—the union between themselves and the State,—and refuse to pay their quota into its treasury? Do not they stand in the same relation to the State, that the State does to the Union? And have not the same reasons prevented the State from resisting the Union, which have prevented them from resisting the State?

How can a man be satisfied to entertain an opinion merely, and enjoy *it*? Is there any enjoyment in it, if his opinion is that he is aggrieved? If you are cheated out of a single dollar by your neighbor, you do not rest satisfied with knowing that you are cheated, or with saying that you are cheated, or even with petitioning him to pay you your due; but you take effectual steps at once to obtain the full amount, and see that you are never cheated again. Action from principle,—the perception and the performance of right,—changes things and relations; it is essentially revolutionary, and does not consist wholly with any thing which was. It not only divides states and churches, it divides families; aye, it divides the *individual*, separating the diabolical in him from the divine.

Unjust laws exist: shall we be content to obey them, or shall we endeavor to amend them, and obey them until we have succeeded, or shall we transgress them at once? Men generally, under such a government as this, think that they ought to wait until they have persuaded the majority to alter them. They think that if they should resist, the remedy would be worse than the evil. But it is the fault of the government itself that the remedy *is* worse than the evil. *It* makes it worse. Why is it not more apt to anticipate and provide for reform? Why does it not cherish its wise minority? Why does it cry and resist before it is hurt? Why does it not encourage its citizens to be on the alert to point out its faults, and *do* better than it would have them? Why does it always crucify Christ, and excommunicate Copernicus and Luther, and pronounce Washington and Franklin rebels?

One would think, that a deliberate and practical denial of its authority was the only offence never contemplated by government; else, why has it not assigned its definite, its suitable and proportionate penalty? If a man who has no property refuses but once to earn nine shillings for the State, he is put in prison for a period unlimited by any law that I know, and determined only by the discretion of those who placed him there; but if he should steal ninety times nine shillings from the State, he is soon permitted to go at large again.

If the injustice is part of the necessary friction of the machine of government, let it go, let it go: perchance it will wear smooth,—certainly the machine will wear out. If the injustice has a spring, or a pulley, or a rope, or a crank, exclusively for itself, then perhaps you may consider whether the remedy will not be worse than the evil; but if it is of such a nature that it requires you to be the agent of injustice to another, then, I say, break the law. Let your life be a counter friction to stop the machine. What I have to do is to see, at any rate, that I do not lend myself to the wrong which I condemn.

As for adopting the ways which the State has provided for remedying the evil, I know not of such ways. They take too much time, and a man's life will be gone. I have other affairs to attend to. I came into this world, not chiefly to make this a good place to live in, but to live in it, be it good or bad. A man has not every thing to do, but something; and because he cannot do *every thing*, it is not necessary that he should do *something* wrong. It is not my business to be petitioning the governor or the legislature any more than it is theirs to petition me; and, if they should not hear my petition, what should I do then? But in this case the State has provided no way: its very Constitution is the evil. This may seem to be harsh and stubborn and unconciliatory; but it is to treat with the utmost kindness and consideration the only spirit that can appreciate or deserves it. So is all change for the better, like birth and death which convulse the body.

I do not hesitate to say, that those who call themselves abolitionists should at once effectually withdraw their support, both in person and property, from the government of Massachusetts, and not wait till they constitute a majority of one, before they suffer the right to prevail through them. I think that it is enough if they have God on their side, without waiting for that other one. Moreover, any man more right than his neighbors, constitutes a majority of one already.

I meet this American government, or its representative the State government, directly, and face to face, once a year, no more, in the person of its tax-gatherer; this is the only mode in which a man situated as I am necessarily meets it; and it then says distinctly, Recognize me; and the simplest, the most effectual, and, in the present posture of affairs, the indispensablest mode of treating with it on this head, of expressing your little satisfaction with and love for it, is to deny it then. My civil neighbor, the tax-gatherer, is the very man I have to deal with,—for it is, after all, with men and not with parchment that I quarrel,—and he has voluntarily chosen to be an agent of the government. How shall he ever know well what he is and does as an officer of the government, or as a man, until he is obliged to consider whether he shall treat me, his neighbor, for whom he has respect, as a neighbor and well-disposed man, or as a maniac and disturber of the peace, and see if he can get over this obstruction to his neighborliness without a ruder and more impetuous thought or speech corresponding with his action? I know this well, that if one thousand, if one hundred, if ten men whom I could name,—if ten *honest* men only,—aye, if *one* HONEST man, in this State of Massachusetts, *ceasing to hold slaves*, were actually to withdraw from this copartnership, and be locked up in the county jail therefore, it would be the abolition of slavery in America. For it matters not how small the beginning may seem to be: what is once well done is done for ever. But we love better to talk about it: that we say is our mission. Reform keeps many scores of newspapers in its service, but not one man. If my esteemed neighbor, the State's ambassador, who will devote his days to the settlement of the question of human rights in the Council Chamber, instead of being threatened with the prisons of Carolina, were to sit down the prisoner of Massachusetts, that State which is so anxious to foist the sin of slavery upon her sister,—though at present she can discover only an act of inhospitality to be the ground of a quarrel with her,—the Legislature would not wholly waive the subject the following winter.

Under a government which imprisons any unjustly, the true place for a just man is also a prison. The proper place to-day, the only place which Massachusetts has provided for her freer and less desponding spirits, is in her prisons, to be put out and locked out of the State by her own act, as they have already put themselves out by their principles. It is there that the fugitive slave, and the Mexican prisoner on parole, and the Indian come to plead the wrongs of his race, should find them; on that separate, but more free and honorable ground, where the State places those who are not *with* her but *against* her,—the only house in a slave-state in which a free man can abide with honor. If any think that their influence would be lost there, and their voices no longer afflict the ear of the State, that they would not be as an enemy within its walls, they do not know by how much truth is stronger than error, nor how much more eloquently and effectively he can combat injustice who has experienced a little in his own person. Cast your whole vote, not a strip of paper merely, but your whole influence. A minority is powerless while it conforms to the majority; it is not even a minority then; but it is irresistible when it clogs by its whole weight. If the alternative is to keep all just men in prison, or give up war and slavery, the State will not hesitate which to choose. If a thousand men were not to pay their tax-bills this year, that would not be a violent and bloody measure, as it would be to pay them, and enable the State to commit violence and shed innocent blood. This is, in fact, the definition of a peaceable revolution, if any such is possible. If the tax-gatherer, or any other public officer, asks me, as one has done, "But what shall I do?" my answer is, "If you really wish to do any thing, resign your office." When the subject has refused allegiance, and the officer has resigned his office, then the revolution is accomplished. But even suppose blood should flow. Is there not a sort of blood shed when the conscience is wounded? Through this wound a man's real manhood and immortality flow out, and he bleeds to an everlasting death. I see this blood flowing now.

I have contemplated the imprisonment of the offender, rather than the seizure of his goods,—though both will serve the same purpose,—because they who assert the purest right, and consequently are most dangerous to a corrupt State, commonly have not spent much time in accumulating property. To such the State renders comparatively small service, and a slight tax is wont to appear exorbitant, particularly if they are obliged to earn it by special labor with their hands. If there were one who lived wholly without the use of money, the State itself would hesitate to demand it of him. But the rich man—not to make any invidious comparison—is always sold to the institution which makes him rich. Absolutely speaking, the more money, the less virtue; for money comes between a man and his objects, and obtains them for him; and it was certainly no great virtue to obtain it. It puts to rest many questions which he would otherwise be taxed to answer; while the only new question which it puts is the hard but superfluous one, how to spend it. Thus his moral ground is taken from under his feet. The opportunities of living are diminished in proportion as what are called the "means" are increased. The best thing a man can do for his culture when he is rich is to endeavour to carry out those schemes which he entertained when he was poor. Christ answered the Herodians according to their condition. "Show me the tribute-money," said he;—and one took a penny out of his pocket;—If you use money which has the image of Cæsar on it, and which he has made current and valuable, that is, *if you are men of the State*, and gladly enjoy the advantages of Cæsar's government, then pay him back some of his own when he demands it; "Render therefore to Cæsar that which is Cæsar's, and to God those things which are God's,"[6]—leaving them no wiser than before as to which was which; for they did not wish to know.

When I converse with the freest of my neighbors, I perceive that, whatever they may say about the magnitude and seriousness of the question, and their regard for the public tranquillity, the long and the short of the matter is, that they cannot spare the protection of

6. Mark 12.17.

the existing government, and they dread the consequences of disobedience to it to their property and families. For my own part, I should not like to think that I ever rely on the protection of the State. But, if I deny the authority of the State when it presents its tax-bill, it will soon take and waste all my property, and so harass me and my children without end. This is hard. This makes it impossible for a man to live honestly and at the same time comfortably in outward respects. It will not be worth the while to accumulate property; that would be sure to go again. You must hire or squat somewhere, and raise but a small crop, and eat that soon. You must live within yourself, and depend upon yourself, always tucked up and ready for a start, and not have many affairs. A man may grow rich in Turkey even, if he will be in all respects a good subject of the Turkish government. Confucius said,—"If a State is governed by the principles of reason, poverty and misery are subjects of shame; if a State is not governed by the principles of reason, riches and honors are the subjects of shame." No: until I want the protection of Massachusetts to be extended to me in some distant southern port, where my liberty is endangered, or until I am bent solely on building up an estate at home by peaceful enterprise, I can afford to refuse allegiance to Massachusetts, and her right to my property and life. It costs me less in every sense to incur the penalty of disobedience to the State, than it would to obey. I should feel as if I were worth less in that case.

Some years ago, the State met me in behalf of the church, and commanded me to pay a certain sum toward the support of a clergyman whose preaching my father attended, but never I myself. "Pay it," it said, "or be locked up in the jail." I declined to pay. But, unfortunately, another man saw fit to pay it. I did not see why the schoolmaster should be taxed to support the priest, and not the priest the schoolmaster; for I was not the State's schoolmaster, but I supported myself by voluntary subscription. I did not see why the lyceum should not present its tax-bill, and have the State to back its demand, as well as the church. However, at the request of the selectmen, I condescended to make some such statement as this in writing:—"Know all men by these presents, that I, Henry Thoreau, do not wish to be regarded as a member of any incorporated society which I have not joined." This I gave to the town-clerk; and he has it. The State, having thus learned that I did not wish to be regarded as a member of that church, has never made a like demand on me since; though it said that it must adhere to its original presumption that time. If I had known how to name them, I should then have signed off in detail from all the societies which I never signed on to; but I did not know where to find a complete list.

I have paid no poll-tax for six years. I was put into a jail once on this account, for one night; and, as I stood considering the walls of solid stone, two or three feet thick, the door of wood and iron, a foot thick, and the iron grating which strained the light, I could not help being struck with the foolishness of that institution which treated me as if I were mere flesh and blood and bones, to be locked up. I wondered that it should have concluded at length that this was the best use it could put me to, and had never thought to avail itself of my services in some way. I saw that, if there was a wall of stone between me and my townsmen, there was a still more difficult one to climb or break through, before they could get to be as free as I was. I did not for a moment feel confined, and the walls seemed a great waste of stone and mortar. I felt as if I alone of all my townsmen had paid my tax. They plainly did not know how to treat me, but behaved like persons who are underbred. In every threat and in every compliment there was a blunder; for they thought that my chief desire was to stand the other side of that stone wall. I could not but smile to see how industriously they locked the door on my meditations, which followed them out again without let or hinderance, and *they* were really all that was dangerous. As they could not reach me, they had resolved to punish my body; just as boys, if they cannot come at some person against whom they have a spite, will abuse his dog. I saw that the State was half-witted, that it was timid as a lone woman with her silver spoons, and that it did not know its friends from its foes, and I lost all my remaining respect for it, and pitied it.

Thus the State never intentionally confronts a man's sense, intellectual or moral, but only his body, his senses. It is not armed with superior wit or honesty, but with superior physical strength. I was not born to be forced. I will breathe after my own fashion. Let us see who is the strongest. What force has a multitude? They only can force me who obey a higher law than I. They force me to become like themselves. I do not hear of *men* being *forced* to live this way or that by masses of men. What sort of life were that to live? When I meet a government which says to me, "Your money or your life," why should I be in haste to give it my money? It may be in a great strait, and not know what to do: I cannot help that. It must help itself; do as I do. It is not worth the while to snivel about it. I am not responsible for the successful working of the machinery of society. I am not the son of the engineer. I perceive that, when an acorn and a chestnut fall side by side, the one does not remain inert to make way for the other, but both obey their own laws, and spring and grow and flourish as best they can, till one, perchance, overshadows and destroys the other. If a plant cannot live according to its nature, it dies; and so a man.

The night in prison was novel and interesting enough. The prisoners in their shirt-sleeves were enjoying a chat and the evening air in the door-way, when I entered. But the jailer said, "Come, boys, it is time to lock up;" and so they dispersed, and I heard the sound of their steps returning into the hollow apartments. My room-mate was introduced to me by the jailer, as "a first-rate fellow and a clever man." When the door was locked, he showed me where to hang my hat, and how he managed matters there. The rooms were whitewashed once a month; and this one, at least, was the whitest, most simply furnished, and probably the neatest apartment in the town. He naturally wanted to know where I came from, and what brought me there; and, when I had told him, I asked him in my turn how he came there, presuming him to be an honest man, of course; and, as the world goes, I believe he was. "Why," said he, "they accuse me of burning a barn; but I never did it." As near as I could discover, he had probably gone to bed in a barn when drunk, and smoked his pipe there; and so a barn was burnt. He had the reputation of being a clever man, had been there some three months waiting for his trial to come on, and would have to wait as much longer; but he was quite domesticated and contented, since he got his board for nothing, and thought that he was well treated.

He occupied one window, and I the other; and I saw, that, if one stayed there long, his principal business would be to look out the window. I had soon read all the tracts that were left there, and examined where former prisoners had broken out, and where a grate had been sawed off, and heard the history of the various occupants of that room; for I found that even here there was a history and a gossip which never circulated beyond the walls of the jail. Probably this is the only house in the town where verses are composed, which are afterward printed in a circular form, but not published. I was shown quite a long list of verses which were composed by some young men who had been detected in an attempt to escape, who avenged themselves by singing them.

I pumped my fellow-prisoner as dry as I could, for fear I should never see him again; but at length he showed me which was my bed, and left me to blow out the lamp.

It was like travelling into a far country, such as I had never expected to behold, to lie there for one night. It seemed to me that I never had heard the town-clock strike before, nor the evening sounds of the village; for we slept with the windows open, which were inside the grating. It was to see my native village in the light of the middle ages, and our Concord was turned into a Rhine stream, and visions of knights and castles passed before me. They were the voices of old burghers that I heard in the streets. I was an involuntary spectator and auditor of whatever was done and said in the kitchen of the adjacent village-inn,—a wholly new and rare experience to me. It was a closer view of my native town. I was fairly inside of it. I never had seen its institutions before. This is one of its peculiar institutions; for it is a shire town.[7] I began to comprehend what its inhabitants were about.

In the morning, our breakfasts were put through the hole in the door, in small oblong-square tin pans, made to fit, and holding a pint of chocolate, with brown bread, and an iron spoon. When they called for the vessels again, I was green enough to return what bread I had left; but my comrade seized it, and said that I should lay that up for lunch or dinner. Soon after, he was let out to work at haying in a neighboring field, whither he went every day, and would not be back till noon; so he bade me goodday, saying that he doubted if he should see me again.

7. County seat.

When I came out of prison,—for some one interfered, and paid the tax,—I did not perceive that great changes had taken place on the common, such as he observed who went in a youth, and emerged a tottering and gray-headed man; and yet a change had to my eyes come over the scene,—the town, and State, and country,—greater than any that mere time could effect. I saw yet more distinctly the State in which I lived. I saw to what extent the people among whom I lived could be trusted as good neighbors and friends; that their friendship was for summer weather only; that they did not greatly purpose to do right; that they were a distinct race from me by their prejudices and superstitions, as the Chinamen and Malays are; that, in their sacrifices to humanity, they ran no risks, not even to their property; that, after all, they were not so noble but they treated the thief as he had treated them, and hoped, by a certain outward observance and a few prayers, and by walking in a particular straight though useless path from time to time, to save their souls. This may be to judge my neighbors harshly; for I believe that most of them are not aware that they have such an institution as the jail in their village.

It was formerly the custom in our village, when a poor debtor came out of jail, for his acquaintances to salute him, looking through their fingers, which were crossed to represent the grating of a jail window, "How do ye do?" My neighbors did not thus salute me, but first looked at me, and then at one another, as if I had returned from a long journey. I was put into jail as I was going to the shoemaker's to get a shoe which was mended. When I was let out the next morning, I proceeded to finish my errand, and, having put on my mended shoe, joined a huckleberry party, who were impatient to put themselves under my conduct; and in half an hour,—for the horse was soon tackled[8]—was in the midst of a huckleberry field, on one of our highest hills, two miles off; and then the State was nowhere to be seen.

This is the whole history of "My Prisons."

I have never declined paying the highway tax, because I am as desirous of being a good neighbor as I am of being a bad subject; and,

8. In harness.

as for supporting schools, I am doing my part to educate my fellow-countrymen now. It is for no particular item in the tax-bill that I refuse to pay it. I simply wish to refuse allegiance to the State, to withdraw and stand aloof from it effectually. I do not care to trace the course of my dollar, if I could, till it buys a man, or a musket to shoot one with,—the dollar is innocent,—but I am concerned to trace the effects of my allegiance. In fact, I quietly declare war with the State, after my fashion, though I will still make what use and get what advantage of her I can, as is usual in such cases.

If others pay the tax which is demanded of me, from a sympathy with the State, they do but what they have already done in their own case, or rather they abet injustice to a greater extent than the State requires. If they pay the tax from a mistaken interest in the individual taxed, to save his property or prevent his going to jail, it is because they have not considered wisely how far they let their private feelings interfere with the public good.

This, then, is my position at present. But one cannot be too much on his guard in such a case, lest his action be biassed by obstinacy, or an undue regard for the opinions of men. Let him see that he does only what belongs to himself and to the hour.

I think sometimes, Why, this people mean well; they are only ignorant; they would do better if they knew how: why give your neighbors this pain to treat you as they are not inclined to? But I think, again, this is no reason why I should do as they do, or permit others to suffer much greater pain of a different kind. Again, I sometimes say to myself, When many millions of men, without heat, without ill-will, without personal feeling of any kind, demand of you a few shillings only, without the possibility, such is their constitution, of retracting or altering their present demand, and without the possibility, on your side, of appeal to any other millions, why expose yourself to this overwhelming brute force? You do not resist cold and hunger, the winds and the waves, thus obstinately; you quietly submit to a thousand similar necessities. You do not put your head into the fire. But just in proportion as I regard this as not wholly a brute force, but partly a human force, and consider that I have relations to those millions as to so many millions of men, and not of mere brute or inanimate things, I see that appeal is possible, first and instantaneously, from them to the Maker of them, and, secondly, from them to themselves. But, if I put my head deliberately into the fire, there is no appeal to fire or to the Maker of fire, and I have only myself to blame. If I could convince myself that I have any right to be satisfied with men as they are, and to treat them accordingly, and not according, in some respects, to my requisitions and expectations of what they and I ought to be, then, like a good Mussulman[9] and fatalist, I should endeavor to be satisfied with things as they are, and say it is the will of God. And, above all, there is this difference between resisting this and a purely brute or natural force, that I can resist this with some effect; but I cannot expect, like Orpheus, to change the nature of the rocks and trees and beasts.[1]

I do not wish to quarrel with any man or nation. I do not wish to split hairs, to make fine distinctions, or set myself up as better than my neighbors. I seek rather, I may say, even an excuse for conforming to the laws of the land. I am but too ready to conform to them. Indeed I have reason to suspect myself on this head; and each year, as the tax-gatherer comes round, I find myself disposed to review the acts and position of the general and state governments, and the spirit of the people, to discover a pretext for conformity. I believe that the State will soon be able to take all my work of this sort out of my hands, and then I shall be no better a patriot than my fellow-countrymen. Seen from a lower point of view, the Constitution, with all its faults, is very good; the law and the courts are very respectable; even this State and this American government are, in many respects, very admirable and rare things, to be thankful for, such as a great many have described them; but seen from a point of view a little higher, they are what I have described them; seen from a higher still, and the highest, who shall say what they are, or that they are worth looking at or thinking of at all?

However, the government does not concern me much, and I shall bestow the fewest possible thoughts on it. It is not many moments that I live under a government, even in this world. If a man is thought-free, fancy-free, imagination-free, that which *is not* never

---

9. Muslim.
1. In Greek mythology, the music of Orpheus's lyre was so beautiful that it charmed wild beasts, caused trees to dance and rivers to stand still.

for a long time appearing *to be* to him, unwise rulers or reformers cannot fatally interrupt him.

I know that most men think differently from myself; but those whose lives are by profession devoted to the study of these or kindred subjects, content me as little as any. Statesmen and legislators, standing so completely within the institution, never distinctly and nakedly behold it. They speak of moving society, but have no resting-place without it. They may be men of a certain experience and discrimination, and have no doubt invented ingenious and even useful systems, for which we sincerely thank them; but all their wit and usefulness lie within certain not very wide limits. They are wont to forget that the world is not governed by policy and expediency. Webster never goes behind government, and so cannot speak with authority about it. His words are wisdom to those legislators who contemplate no essential reform in the existing government; but for thinkers, and those who legislate for all time, he never once glances at the subject. I know of those whose serene and wise speculations on this theme would soon reveal the limits of his mind's range and hospitality. Yet, compared with the cheap professions of most reformers, and the still cheaper wisdom and eloquence of politicians in general, his are almost the only sensible and valuable words, and we thank Heaven for him. Comparatively, he is always strong, original, and, above all, practical. Still his quality is not wisdom, but prudence. The lawyer's truth is not Truth, but consistency, or a consistent expediency. Truth is always in harmony with herself, and is not concerned chiefly to reveal the justice that may consist with wrong-doing. He well deserves to be called, as he has been called, the Defender of the Constitution. There are really no blows to be given by him but defensive ones. He is not a leader, but a follower. His leaders are the men of '87.[2] "I have never made an effort," he says, "and never propose to make an effort; I have never countenanced an effort, and never mean to countenance an effort, to disturb the arrangement as originally made, by which the various States came into the Union." Still thinking of the sanction which

---

2. Those who passed the Ordinance of 1787, frequently called the Northwest Ordinance, which created the Northwest Territory and prohibited the introduction of slavery there, but not the retention of those already enslaved.

the Constitution gives to slavery, he says, "Because it was a part of the original compact,—let it stand." Notwithstanding his special acuteness and ability, he is unable to take a fact out of its merely political relations, and behold it as it lies absolutely to be disposed of by the intellect,—what, for instance, it behoves a man to do here in America to-day with regard to slavery, but ventures, or is driven, to make some such desperate answer as the following, while professing to speak absolutely, and as a private man,—from which what new and singular code of social duties might be inferred?—"The manner," says he, "in which the government of those States where slavery exists are to regulate it, is for their own consideration, under their responsibility to their constituents, to the general laws of priority, humanity, and justice, and to God. Associations formed elsewhere, springing from a feeling of humanity, or any other cause, have nothing whatever to do with it. They have never received any encouragement from me, and they never will."[3]

They who know of no purer sources of truth, who have traced up its stream no higher, stand, and wisely stand, by the Bible and the Constitution, and drink at it there with reverence and humility; but they who behold where it comes trickling into this lake or that pool, gird up their loins once more, and continue their pilgrimage toward its fountain-head.

No man with a genius for legislation has appeared in America. They are rare in the history of the world. There are orators, politicians, and eloquent men, by the thousand; but the speaker has not yet opened his mouth to speak, who is capable of settling the much-vexed questions of the day. We love eloquence for its own sake, and not for any truth which it may utter, or any heroism it may inspire. Our legislators have not yet learned the comparative value of free-trade and of freedom, of union, and of rectitude, to a nation. They have no genius or talent for comparatively humble questions of taxation and finance, commerce and manufactures and agriculture. If we were left solely to the wordy wit of legislators in Congress for our guidance, uncorrected by the seasonable experience and the effectual complaints of the people, America would not long retain her rank among the nations. For eighteen hundred years, though per-

3. These extracts have been inserted since the Lecture was read [Thoreau's note].

chance I have no right to say it, the New Testament has been written; yet where is the legislator who has wisdom and practical talent
enough to avail himself of the light which it sheds on the science of
legislation?

The authority of government, even such as I am willing to submit to,—for I will cheerfully obey those who know and can do better than I, and in many things even those who neither know nor can
do so well,—is still an impure one: to be strictly just, it must have
the sanction and consent of the governed. It can have no pure right
over my person and property but what I concede to it. The progress
from an absolute to a limited monarchy, from a limited monarchy
to a democracy, is a progress toward a true respect for the individual. Is a democracy, such as we know it, the last improvement possible in government? Is it not possible to take a step further towards
recognizing and organizing the rights of man? There will never be a
really free and enlightened State, until the State comes to recognize
the individual as a higher and independent power, from which all
its own power and authority are derived, and treats him accordingly.
I please myself with imagining a State at last which can afford to be
just to all men, and to treat the individual with respect as a neighbor; which even would not think it inconsistent with its own re-
pose, if a few were to live aloof from it, not meddling with it, nor
embraced by it, who fulfilled all the duties of neighbors and fellow-
men. A State which bore this kind of fruit, and suffered it to drop
off as fast as it ripened, would prepare the way for a still more perfect and glorious State, which also I have imagined, but not yet anywhere seen.

1848, 1849

James Thurber
1894–1961

> *Thurber's autobiographical essay might seem less focused than even
> the other memoirlike essays in this volume—Bret Lott's for instance,
> or Maya Angelou's, which have more obvious themes. That is often
> the case when a writer's goal is, at least partially, to make readers
> laugh. While we are used to ascribing deep intentions to essays that*

make us feel pity or sorrow or regret or urgency, we typically dismiss comedy as meaningless. Unless it is satire, comedy can seem to fulfill its purpose only if we laugh. Nevertheless, we should not dismiss comedy as lightweight just because the essay has a light tone. Thurber gives an interesting picture of the character of higher education in the United States in the early twentieth century, one you might put alongside Zinsser's, for instance. The "land grant university" is a distinctly American phenomenon, which began in 1863, when the federal government gave land to the individual states to fund the establishment of public schools of higher education. Most of the flagship state universities, such as The Ohio State University, were established by land grants. These schools were fairly new when Thurber went to college (Ohio State was founded in 1870), and they offered a curriculum quite different from that of traditional universities, like Harvard and Yale, which had their roots in religion and the medieval curricula of Cambridge and Oxford. The botany, economics, and gym classes described here were part of a new type of curriculum designed to prepare large numbers of people—generally young men—for jobs in an expanding industrial nation. It was a particularly democratic enterprise. The course of study Thurber describes was supposed to have a direct practical application to the careers of its students. The older curriculum was less obviously applicable to the immediate needs of businessmen, engineers, etc. These different philosophies about education are still roughly preserved in the differences between small liberal arts colleges and the large state universities.

University Days

I passed all the other courses that I took at my University, but I could never pass botany. This was because all botany students had to spend several hours a week in a laboratory looking through a microscope at plant cells, and I could never see through a microscope. I never once saw a cell through a microscope. This used to enrage my instructor. He would wander around the laboratory pleased with the progress all the students were making in drawing the involved and, so I am told, interesting structure of flower cells, until he came to me. I would just be standing there. "I can't see anything," I would say. He would begin patiently enough, explaining how anybody can see through a microscope, but he would always end up in a fury, claiming that I could *too* see through a microscope but just pretended that I couldn't. "It takes away from the beauty of flowers anyway," I used to tell him. "We are not concerned with beauty in this course," he would say. "We are concerned solely with what I may call the *mechanics* of flars." "Well," I'd say, "I can't see anything." "Try it just once again," he'd say, and I would put my eye to the microscope and see nothing at all, except now and again a nebulous milky substance—a phenomenon of maladjustment. You were supposed to see a vivid, restless clockwork of sharply defined plant cells. "I see what looks like a lot of milk," I would tell him. This, he claimed, was the result of my not having adjusted the microscope properly, so he would readjust it for me, or rather, for himself. And I would look again and see milk.

I finally took a deferred pass, as they called it, and waited a year and tried again. (You had to pass one of the biological sciences or you couldn't graduate.) The professor had come back from vacation brown as a berry, bright-eyed, and eager to explain cell structure again to his classes. "Well," he said to me, cheerily, when we met in the first laboratory hour of the semester, "we're going to see cells this time, aren't we?" "Yes, sir," I said. Students to right of me and to left of me and in front of me were seeing cells; what's more, they were quietly drawing pictures of them in their notebooks. Of course, I didn't see anything.

"We'll try it," the professor said to me, grimly, "with every adjustment of the microscope known to man. As God is my witness, I'll arrange this glass so that you see cells through it or I'll give up teaching. In twenty-two years of botany, I—" He cut off abruptly for he was beginning to quiver all over, like Lionel Barrymore,[1] and he genuinely wished to hold onto his temper; his scenes with me had taken a great deal out of him.

So we tried it with every adjustment of the microscope known to man. With only one of them did I see anything but blackness or the

---

1. Barrymore (1878–1954), stage and then film actor, often typecast as a grumpy but genial old man.

familiar lacteal opacity, and that time I saw, to my pleasure and amazement, a variegated constellation of flecks, specks, and dots. These I hastily drew. The instructor, noting my activity, came back from an adjoining desk, a smile on his lips and his eyebrows high in hope. He looked at my cell drawing. "What's that?" he demanded, with a hint of a squeal in his voice. "That's what I saw," I said. "You didn't, you didn't, you *did*n't!" he screamed, losing control of his temper instantly, and he bent over and squinted into the microscope. His head snapped up. "That's your eye!" he shouted. "You've fixed the lens so that it reflects! You've drawn your eye!"

Another course that I didn't like, but somehow managed to pass, was economics. I went to that class straight from the botany class, which didn't help me any in understanding either subject. I used to get them mixed up. But not as mixed up as another student in my economics class who came there direct from a physics laboratory. He was a tackle on the football team, named Bolenciecwcz. At that time Ohio State University had one of the best football teams in the country, and Bolenciecwcz was one of its outstanding stars. In order to be eligible to play it was necessary for him to keep up in his studies, a very difficult matter, for while he was not dumber than an ox he was not any smarter. Most of his professors were lenient and helped him along. None gave him more hints, in answering questions, or asked him simpler ones than the economics professor, a thin, timid man named Bassum. One day when we were on the subject of transportation and distribution, it came Bolenciecwcz's turn to answer a question. "Name one means of transportation," the professor said to him. No light came into the big tackle's eyes. "Just any means of transportation," said the professor. Bolenciecwcz sat staring at him. "That is," pursued the professor, "any medium, agency, or method of going from one place to another." Bolenciecwcz had the look of a man who is being led into a trap. "You may choose among steam, horse-drawn, or electrically propelled vehicles," said the instructor. "I might suggest the one which we commonly take in making long journeys across land." There was a profound silence in which everybody stirred uneasily, including Bolenciecwcz and Mr. Bassum. Mr. Bassum abruptly broke this silence in an amazing manner. "Choo-choo-choo," he said, in a low voice, and turned instantly scarlet. He glanced appealingly around the room. All of us, of course, shared Mr. Bassum's desire that Bolenciecwcz should stay abreast of the class in economics, for the Illinois game, one of the hardest and most important of the season, was only a week off. "Toot, toot, too-toooooot!" some student with a deep voice moaned, and we all looked encouragingly at Bolenciecwcz. Somebody else gave a fine imitation of a locomotive letting off steam. Mr. Bassum himself rounded off the little show. "Ding, dong, ding, dong," he said, hopefully. Bolenciecwcz was staring at the floor now, trying to think, his great brow furrowed, his huge hands rubbing together, his face red.

"How did you come to college this year, Mr. Bolenciecwcz?" asked the professor. "*Chuf*fa chuffa, *chuf*fa chuffa."

"M'father sent me," said the football player.

"What on?" asked Bassum.

"I git an 'lowance," said the tackle, in a low, husky voice, obviously embarrassed.

"No, no," said Bassum. "Name a means of transportation. What did you *ride* here on?"

"Train," said Bolenciecwcz.

"Quite right," said the professor. "Now, Mr. Nugent, will you tell us—"

If I went through anguish in botany and economics—for different reasons—gymnasium work was even worse. I don't even like to think about it. They wouldn't let you play games or join in the exercises with your glasses on and I couldn't see with mine off. I bumped into professors, horizontal bars, agricultural students, and swinging iron rings. Not being able to see, I could take it but I couldn't dish it out. Also, in order to pass gymnasium (and you had to pass it to graduate) you had to learn to swim if you didn't know how. I didn't like the swimming pool, I didn't like swimming, and I didn't like the swimming instructor, and after all these years I still don't. I never swam but I passed my gym work anyway, by having another student give my gymnasium number (978) and swim across the pool in my place. He was a quiet, amiable blonde youth, number 473, and he would have seen through a microscope for me if we could have got away with it, but we couldn't get away with it. Another thing I didn't like about gymnasium work was that they made you strip the day you registered. It is impossible for me to be happy when I am stripped and being asked a lot of questions. Still, I did better than a lanky agricultural student who was cross-examined just before I was. They asked each student what college he was in— that is, whether Arts, Engineering, Commerce, or Agriculture. "What college are you in?" the instructor snapped at the youth in front of me. "Ohio State University," he said promptly.

It wasn't that agricultural student but it was another a whole lot like him who decided to take up journalism, possibly on the ground that when farming went to hell he could fall back on newspaper work. He didn't realize, of course, that that would be very much like falling back full-length on a kit of carpenter's tools. Haskins didn't seem cut out for journalism, being too embarrassed to talk to anybody and unable to use a typewriter, but the editor of the college paper assigned him to the cow barns, the sheep house, the horse pavilion, and the animal husbandry department generally. This was a genuinely big "beat," for it took up five times as much ground and got ten times as great a legislative appropriation as the College of Liberal Arts. The agricultural student knew animals, but nevertheless his stories were dull and colorlessly written. He took all afternoon on each of them, on account of having to hunt for each letter on the typewriter. Once in a while he had to ask somebody to help him hunt. "C" and "L," in particular, were hard letters for him to find. His editor finally got pretty much annoyed at the farmer-journalist because his pieces were so uninteresting. "See here, Haskins," he snapped at him one day, "Why is it we never have anything hot from you on the horse pavilion? Here we have two hundred head of horses on this campus—more than any other university in the Western Conference except Purdue—and yet you never get any real low down on them. Now shoot over to the horse barns and dig up something lively." Haskins shambled out and came back in about an hour; he said he had something. "Well, start it off snappily," said the editor. "Something people will read." Haskins set to work and in a couple of hours brought a sheet of typewritten paper to the desk; it was a two-hundred-word story about some disease that had broken out among the horses. Its opening sentence was simple but arresting. It read: "Who has noticed the sores on the tops of the horses in the animal husbandry building?"

Ohio State was a land grant university and therefore two years of military drill was compulsory. We drilled with old Springfield rifles and studied the tactics of the Civil War even though the World War was going on at the time. At 11 o'clock each morning thousands of freshmen and sophomores used to deploy over the campus, moodily creeping up on the old chemistry building. It was good training for the kind of warfare that was waged at Shiloh but it had no connection with what was going on in Europe. Some people used to think there was German money behind it, but they didn't dare say so or they would have been thrown in jail as German spies. It was a period of muddy thought and marked, I believe, the decline of higher education in the Middle West.

As a soldier I was never any good at all. Most of the cadets were glumly indifferent soldiers, but I was no good at all. Once General Littlefield, who was commandant of the cadet corps, popped up in front of me during regimental drill and snapped, "You are the main trouble with this university!" I think he meant that my type was the main trouble with the university but he may have meant me individually. I was mediocre at drill, certainly—that is, until my senior year. By that time I had drilled longer than anybody else in the Western Conference, having failed at military at the end of each preceding year so that I had to do it all over again. I was the only senior still in uniform. The uniform which, when new, had made me look like an interurban railway conductor, now that it had become faded and too tight made me look like Bert Williams in his bellboy act. This had a definitely bad effect on my morale. Even so, I had become by sheer practise little short of wonderful at squad manoeuvres.

One day General Littlefield picked our company out of the whole regiment and tried to get it mixed up by putting it through one movement after another as fast as we could execute them: squads right, squads left, squads on right into line, squads right about, squads left front into line, etc. In about three minutes one hundred and nine men were marching in one direction and I was marching away from them at an angle of forty degrees, all alone. "Company, halt!" shouted General Littlefield, "That man is the only man who has it right!" I was made a corporal for my achievement.

The next day General Littlefield summoned me to his office. He was swatting flies when I went in. I was silent and he was silent too, for a long time. I don't think he remembered me or why he had sent for me, but he didn't want to admit it. He swatted some more flies, keeping his eyes on them narrowly before he let go with the swatter. "Button up your coat!" he snapped. Looking back on it now I can see that he meant me although he was looking at a fly, but I just stood there. Another fly came to rest on a paper in front of the general and began rubbing its hind legs together. The general lifted the swatter cautiously. I moved restlessly and the fly flew away. "You startled him!" barked General Littlefield, looking at me severely. I said I was sorry. "That won't help the situation!" snapped the General, with cold military logic. I didn't see what I could do except offer to chase some more flies toward his desk, but I didn't say anything. He stared out the window at the faraway figures of co-eds crossing the campus toward the library. Finally, he told me I could go. So I went. He either didn't know which cadet I was or else he forgot what he wanted to see me about. It may have been that he wished to apologize for having called me the main trouble with the university; or maybe he had decided to compliment me on my brilliant drilling of the day before and then at the last minute decided not to. I don't know. I don't think about it much any more.

1933

Alice Walker
b. 1944

This essay exemplifies the recuperation of not only Phillis Wheatley but of many women writers in the 1970s, based more on the insights provided by the feminist movement than on those of the civil rights movement. Ironically, many men working for civil rights in the 1960s perpetuated the second-class citizenship of women even in their own progressive organizations, and it was not really until the 1970s that American women began to reap the benefits of the liberalization of American society that began in the early 1960s. Ms. magazine was only three years old when Walker published this article in its pages, and apart from a few exceptions like Zora Neale Hurston, America celebrated few women artists, let alone black women artists. The section of Virginia Woolf's A Room of One's

> Own *included in this volume makes an apt companion piece to
> Walker's essay, which applies Woolf's principles to the characters in
> Jean Toomer's* Cane, *to Phillis Wheatley, and to her own mother.*

In Search of Our Mothers' Gardens

> I described her own nature and temperament. Told how they
> needed a larger life for their expression . . . . I pointed out that in
> lieu of proper channels, her emotions had overflowed into paths
> that dissipated them. I talked, beautifully I thought, about an art
> that would be born, an art that would open the way for women
> the likes of her. I asked her to hope, and build up an inner life
> against the coming of that day. . . . I sang, with a strange quiver
> in my voice, a promise song.
>
> > *—Jean Toomer, "Avey,"*
> > CANE[1]

The poet speaking to a prostitute who falls asleep while he's
talking—

When the poet Jean Toomer walked through the South in the early
twenties, he discovered a curious thing: black women whose spiritually was so intense, so deep, so *unconscious*, that they were themselves
unaware of the richness they held. They stumbled blindly through
their lives: creatures so abused and mutilated in body, so dimmed and
confused by pain, that they considered themselves unworthy even of
hope. In the selfless abstractions their bodies became to the men who
used them, they became more than "sexual objects," more even than
mere women: they became "Saints." Instead of being perceived as
whole persons, their bodies became shrines: what was thought to be
their minds became temples suitable for worship. These crazy Saints
stared out at the world, wildly, like lunatics—or quietly, like suicides;
and the "God" that was in their gaze was as mute as a great stone.

---

1. Jean Toomer was a black writer of mixed racial heritage. His book *Cane* was published
in 1923, during the height of the "Harlem Renaissance," one of the richest flowerings of art in
American history. *Cane* is a mix of sketches, poems, and short stories depicting especially the
lives and struggles of black women.

Who were these Saints? These crazy, loony, pitiful women?

Some of them, without a doubt, were our mothers and grand-mothers.

In the still heat of the post-Reconstruction South,[2] this is how they seemed to Jean Toomer: exquisite butterflies trapped in an evil honey, toiling away their lives in an era, a century, that did not ac-knowledge them, except as "the *mule* of the world." They dreamed dreams that no one knew—not even themselves, in any coherent fashion—and saw visions no one could understand. They wandered or sat about the countryside crooning lullabies to ghosts, and draw-ing the mother of Christ in charcoal on courthouse walls.

They forced their minds to desert their bodies and their striving spirits sought to rise, like frail whirlwinds from the hard red clay. And when those frail whirlwinds fell, in scattered particles, upon the ground, no one mourned. Instead, men lit candles to celebrate the emptiness that remained, as people do who enter a beautiful but vacant space to resurrect a God.

Our mothers and grandmothers, some of them: moving to music not yet written. And they waited.

They waited for a day when the unknown thing that was in them would be made known; but guessed, somehow in their darkness, that on the day of their revelation they would be long dead. There-fore to Toomer they walked, and even ran, in slow motion. For they were going nowhere immediate, and the future was not yet within their grasp. And men took our mothers and grandmothers, "but got no pleasure from it." So complex was their passion and their calm.

To Toomer, they lay vacant and fallow as autumn fields, with harvest time never in sight: and he saw them enter loveless mar-riages, without joy; and become prostitutes, without resistance; and become mothers of children, without fulfillment.

For these grandmothers and mothers of ours were not Saints, but Artists; driven to a numb and bleeding madness by the springs of creativity in them for which there was no release. They were Cre-ators, who lived lives of spiritual waste, because they were so rich in

2. Reconstruction was the period after the Civil War, from 1865 to 1877, when Union troops occupied the South and attempted to enforce racial justice. After sovereignty was re-stored to the South, southern whites forced blacks back into second-class status.

spirituality—which is the basis of Art—that the strain of enduring their unused and unwanted talent drove them insane. Throwing away this spirituality was their pathetic attempt to lighten the soul to a weight their work-worn, sexually abused bodies could bear.

What did it mean for a black woman to be an artist in our grandmothers' time? In our great-grandmothers' day? It is a question with an answer cruel enough to stop the blood.

Did you have a genius of a great-great-grandmother who died under some ignorant and depraved white overseer's lash? Or was she required to bake biscuits for a lazy backwater tramp, when she cried out in her soul to paint watercolors of sunsets, or the rain falling on the green and peaceful pasturelands? Or was her body broken and forced to bear children (who were more often than not sold away from her)—eight, ten, fifteen, twenty children—when her one joy was the thought of modeling heroic figures of rebellion, in stone or clay?

How was the creativity of the black woman kept alive, year after year and century after century, when for most of the years black people have been in America, it was a punishable crime for a black person to read or write? And the freedom to paint, to sculpt, to expand the mind with action did not exist. Consider, if you can bear to imagine it, what might have been the result if singing, too, had been forbidden by law. Listen to the voices of Bessie Smith, Billie Holiday, Nina Simone, Roberta Flack, and Aretha Franklin,[3] among others, and imagine those voices muzzled for life. Then you may begin to comprehend the lives of our "crazy," "Sainted" mothers and grandmothers. The agony of the lives of women who might have been Poets, Novelists, Essayists, and Short-Story Writers (over a period of centuries), who died with their real gifts stifled within them.

And, if this were the end of the story, we would have cause to cry out in my paraphrase of Okot p'Bitek's[4] great poem:

---

3. Bessie Smith (c. 1892–1937), Billie Holiday (1915–1959), Nina Simone (1933–2003), Roberta Flack (b. 1939), and Aretha Franklin (b. 1942) are recording artists, known especially for their blues, jazz, and soul singing.

4. Okot p'Bitek (1931–1982), Ugandan poet whose Song of Lawino (1966) explores the clash of western colonial and African cultures.

O, my clanswomen
Let us all cry together!
Come,
Let us mourn the death of our mother,
The death of a Queen
The ash that was produced
By a great fire!
O, this homestead is utterly dead
Close the gates
With lacari *thorns,*
For our mother
The creator of the Stool is lost!
And all the young women
Have perished in the wilderness!

But this is not the end of the story, for all the young women—our mothers and grandmothers, *ourselves*—have not perished in the wilderness. And if we ask ourselves why, and search for and find the answer, we will know beyond all efforts to erase it from our minds, just exactly who, and of what, we black American women are.

One example, perhaps the most pathetic, most misunderstood one, can provide a backdrop for our mothers' work: Phillis Wheatley, a slave in the 1700s.

Virginia Woolf, in her book *A Room of One's Own*, wrote that in order for a woman to write fiction she must have two things, certainly: a room of her own (with key and lock) and enough money to support herself.

What then are we to make of Phillis Wheatley, a slave, who owned not even herself? This sickly, frail black girl who required a servant of her own at times—her health was so precarious—and who, had she been white, would have been easily considered the intellectual superior of all the women and most of the men in the society of her day.

Virginia Woolf wrote further, speaking of course not of our Phillis, that "any woman born with a great gift in the sixteenth century [insert "eighteenth century," insert "black woman," insert "born or made a slave"] would certainly have gone crazed, shot herself, or ended her days in some lonely cottage outside the village, half witch, half wizard [insert "Saint"], feared and mocked at. For it needs little skill and psychology to be sure that a highly gifted girl who had tried to use her gift for poetry would have been so thwarted and hindered by contrary instincts [add "chains, guns, the lash, the ownership of one's body by someone else, submission to an alien religion"], that she must have lost her health and sanity to a certainty."

The key words, as they relate to Phillis, are "contrary instincts." For when we read the poetry of Phillis Wheatley—as when we read the novels of Nella Larsen[5] or the oddly false-sounding autobiography of that freest of all black women writers, Zora Hurston—evidence of "contrary instincts" is everywhere. Her loyalties were completely divided, as was, without question, her mind.

But how could this be otherwise? Captured at seven, a slave of wealthy, doting whites who instilled in her the "savagery" of the Africa they "rescued" her from . . . one wonders if she was even able to remember her homeland as she had known it, or as it really was.

Yet, because she did try to use her gift for poetry in a world that made her a slave, she was "so thwarted and hindered by . . . contrary instincts, that she . . . lost her health . . ." In the last years of her brief life, burdened not only with the need to express her gift but also with a penniless, friendless "freedom" and several small children for whom she was forced to do strenuous work to feed, she lost her health, certainly. Suffering from malnutrition and neglect and who knows what mental agonies, Phillis Wheatley died.

So torn by "contrary instincts" was black, kidnapped, enslaved Phillis that her description of "the Goddess"—as she poetically called the Liberty she did not have—is ironically, cruelly humorous. And, in fact, has held Phillis up to ridicule for more than a century. It is usually read prior to hanging Phillis's memory as that of a fool. She wrote:

The Goddess comes, she moves divinely fair,
Olive and laurel binds her golden hair.
Wherever shines this native of the skies,
Unnumber'd charms and recent graces rise. [My emphasis]

5. Larsen (1893–1964), African American novelist.

It is obvious that Phillis, the slave, combed the "Goddess's" hair every morning; prior, perhaps, to bringing in the milk, or fixing her mistress's lunch. She took her imagery from the one thing she saw elevated above all others.

With the benefit of hindsight we ask, "How could she?"

But at last, Phillis, we understand. No more snickering when your stiff, struggling, ambivalent lines are forced on us. We know now that you were not an idiot or a traitor; only a sickly little black girl, snatched from your home and country and made a slave; a woman who still struggled to sing the song that was your gift, although in a land of barbarians who praised you for your bewildered tongue. It is not so much what you sang, as that you kept alive, in so many of our ancestors, *the notion of song*.

Black women are called, in the folklore that so aptly identifies one's status in society, "the *mule* of the world," because we have been handed the burdens that everyone else—*everyone* else—refused to carry. We have also been called "Matriarchs," "Superwomen," and "Mean and Evil Bitches." Not to mention "Castraters" and "Sapphire's Mama." When we have pleaded for understanding, our character has been distorted; when we have asked for simple caring, we have been handed empty inspirational appellations, then stuck in the farthest corner. When we have asked for love, we have been given children. In short, even our plainer gifts, our labors of fidelity and love, have been knocked down our throats. To be an artist and a black woman, even today, lowers our status in many respects, rather than raises it: and yet, artists we will be.

Therefore we must fearlessly pull out of ourselves and look at and identify with our lives the living creativity some of our great-grandmothers were not allowed to know. I stress *some* of them because it is well known that the majority of our great-grandmothers knew, even without "knowing" it, the reality of their spirituality, even if they didn't recognize it beyond what happened in the singing at church—and they never had any intention of giving it up.

How they did it—those millions of black women who were not Phillis Wheatley, or Lucy Terry or Frances Harper or Zora Hurston or Nella Larsen or Bessie Smith; or Elizabeth Catlett, or Katherine

Dunham,[6] either—brings me to the title of this essay, "In Search of Our Mothers' Gardens," which is a personal account that is yet shared, in its theme and its meaning, by all of us. I found, while thinking about the far-reaching world of the creative black woman, that often the truest answer to a question that really matters can be found very close.

In the late 1920s my mother ran away from home to marry my father. Marriage, if not running away, was expected of seventeen-year-old girls. By the time she was twenty, she had two children and was pregnant with a third. Five children later, I was born. And this is how I came to know my mother: she seemed a large, soft, loving-eyed woman who was rarely impatient in our home. Her quick, violent temper was on view only a few times a year, when she battled with the white landlord who had the misfortune to suggest to her that her children did not need to go to school.

She made all the clothes we wore, even my brother's overalls. She made all the towels and sheets we used. She spent the summers canning vegetables and fruits. She spent the winter evenings making quilts enough to cover all our beds.

During the "working" day, she labored beside—not behind—my father in the fields. Her day began before sunup, and did not end until late at night. There was never a moment for her to sit down, undisturbed, to unravel her own private thoughts; never a time free from interruption—by work or the noisy inquiries of her many children. And yet, it is to my mother—and all our mothers who were not famous—that I went in search of the secret of what has fed that muzzled and often mutilated, but vibrant, creative spirit that the black woman has inherited, and that pops out in wild and unlikely places to this day.

But when, you will ask, did my overworked mother have time to know or care about feeding the creative spirit?

The answer is so simple that many of us have spent years discov-

6. Lucy Terry (1724–1821), poet whose only extant work was preserved orally until 1855, when it was first published; Frances Harper (1825–1911), poet and novelist; Elizabeth Catlett (b. 1915), sculptor and print maker; Katherine Dunham (1909–2006), choreographer, dancer, songwriter.

ering it. We have constantly looked high, when we should have looked high—and low.

For example: in the Smithsonian Institution in Washington, D.C., there hangs a quilt unlike any other in the world. In fanciful, inspired, and yet simple and identifiable figures, it portrays the story of the Crucifixion. It is considered rare, beyond price. Though it follows no known pattern of quilt-making, and though it is made of bits and pieces of worthless rags, it is obviously the work of a person of powerful imagination and deep spiritual feeling. Below this quilt I saw a note that says it was made by "an anonymous Black woman in Alabama, a hundred years ago."

If we could locate this "anonymous" black woman from Alabama, she would turn out to be one of our grandmothers—an artist who left her mark in the only materials she could afford, and in the only medium her position in society allowed her to use.

As Virginia Woolf wrote further, in *A Room of One's Own*:

> Yet genius of a sort must have existed among women as it must have existed among the working class. [Change this to "slaves" and "the wives and daughters of sharecroppers."] Now and again an Emily Brontë or a Robert Burns [change this to "a Zora Hurston or a Richard Wright"] blazes out and proves its presence. But certainly it never got itself on to paper. When, however, one reads of a witch being ducked, of a woman possessed by devils [or "Sainthood"], of a wise woman selling herbs [our root workers], or even a very remarkable man who had a mother, then I think we are on the track of a lost novelist, a suppressed poet, of some mute and inglorious Jane Austen. . . . Indeed, I would venture to guess that Anon, who wrote so many poems without signing them, was often a woman. . . .

And so our mothers and grandmothers have, more often than not anonymously, handed on the creative spark, the seed of the flower they themselves never hoped to see: or like a sealed letter they could not plainly read.

And so it is, certainly, with my own mother. Unlike "Ma" Rainey's songs, which retained their creator's name even while blasting forth from Bessie Smith's mouth, no song or poem will bear my mother's name. Yet so many of the stories that I write, that we all write, are my mother's stories. Only recently did I fully realize this: that through years of listening to my mother's stories of her life, I have absorbed not only the stories themselves, but something of the manner in which she spoke, something of the urgency that involves the knowledge that her stories—like her life—must be recorded. It is probably for this reason that so much of what I have written is about characters whose counterparts in real life are so much older than I am.

But the telling of these stories, which came from my mother's lips as naturally as breathing, was not the only way my mother showed herself as an artist. For stories, too, were subject to being distracted, to dying without conclusion. Dinners must be started, and cotton must be gathered before the big rains. The artist that was and is my mother showed itself to me only after many years. This is what I finally noticed:

Like Mem, a character in *The Third Life of Grange Copeland*,[7] my mother adorned with flowers whatever shabby house we were forced to live in. And not just your typical straggly country stand of zinnias, either. She planted ambitious gardens—and still does—with over fifty different varieties of plants that bloom profusely from early March until late November. Before she left home for the fields, she watered her flowers, chopped up the grass, and laid out new beds. When she returned from the fields she might divide clumps of bulbs, dig a cold pit, uproot and replant roses, or prune branches from her taller bushes or trees—until night came and it was too dark to see.

Whatever she planted grew as if by magic, and her fame as a grower of flowers spread over three counties. Because of her creativity with her flowers, even my memories of poverty are seen through a screen of blooms—sunflowers, petunias, roses, dahlias, forsythia, spirea, delphiniums, verbena . . . and on and on.

And I remember people coming to my mother's yard to be given cuttings from her flowers; I hear again the praise showered on her because whatever rocky soil she landed on, she turned into a garden. A garden so brilliant with colors, so original in its design, so magnificent with life and creativity, that to this day people drive by our

7. Walker's first novel, published in 1970.

house in Georgia—perfect strangers and imperfect strangers—and ask to stand or walk among my mother's art.

I notice that it is only when my mother is working in her flowers that she is radiant, almost to the point of being invisible—except as Creator: hand and eye. She is involved in work her soul must have. Ordering the universe in the image of her personal conception of Beauty.

Her face, as she prepares the Art that is her gift, is a legacy of respect she leaves to me, for all that illuminates and cherishes life. She has handed down respect for the possibilities—and the will to grasp them.

For her, so hindered and intruded upon in so many ways, being an artist has still been a daily part of her life. This ability to hold on, even in very simple ways, is work black women have done for a very long time.

This poem is not enough, but it is something, for the woman who literally covered the holes in our walls with sunflowers:

They were women then
My mama's generation
Husky of voice—Stout of
Step
With fists as well as
Hands
How they battered down
Doors
And ironed
Starched white
Shirts
How they led
Armies
Headragged Generals
Across mined
Fields
Booby-trapped
Kitchens
To discover books
Desks

A place for us
How they knew what we
Must *know*
Without knowing a page
Of it
Themselves.

Guided by my heritage of a love of beauty and a respect for strength—in search of my mother's garden, I found my own.

And perhaps in Africa over two hundred years ago, there was just such a mother; perhaps she painted vivid and daring decorations in oranges and yellows and greens on the walls of her hut; perhaps she sang—in a voice like Roberta Flack's—*sweetly* over the compounds of her village; perhaps she wove the most stunning mats or told the most ingenious stories of all the village storytellers. Perhaps she was herself a poet—though only her daughter's name is signed to the poems that we know.

Perhaps Phillis Wheatley's mother was also an artist.

Perhaps in more than Phillis Wheatley's biological life is her mother's signature made clear.

1974

Eudora Welty

1909–2001

Welty was already one of the most prominent fiction writers in the United States when she was invited to give a series of lectures at Harvard University in 1983. With most of her creative work behind her, the lectures gave her an opportunity to re-view her own life as an accomplished writer. Together, the three lectures are a literary autobiography, and they were immediately published as a book, One Writer's Beginnings *(1984). Although the book is more imaginative than persuasive, Welty selects and arranges her reminiscences with purpose, as if she were proving something by the example of her life. The book concludes with these sentences: "As you have seen, I am a writer who came of a sheltered life. A sheltered life can be a daring life as well. For all serious daring starts*

from within." This excerpt comes from the first lecture, "Listening."
The final paragraphs express how important "reader-voice" was to
Welty as a writer.

Listening

I learned from the age of two or three that any room in our
house, at any time of day, was there to read in, or to be read to.
My mother read to me. She'd read to me in the big bedroom in
the mornings, when we were in her rocker together, which ticked in
rhythm as we rocked, as though we had a cricket accompanying the
story. She'd read to me in the diningroom on winter afternoons in
front of the coal fire, with our cuckoo clock ending the story with
"Cuckoo," and at night when I'd got in my own bed. I must have
given her no peace. Sometimes she read to me in the kitchen while
she sat churning, and the churning sobbed along with *any* story. It
was my ambition to have her read to me while *I* churned; once she
granted my wish, but she read off my story before I brought her
butter. She was an expressive reader. When she was reading "Puss in
Boots," for instance, it was impossible not to know that she dis-
trusted *all* cats.

It had been startling and disappointing to me to find out that
story books had been written by *people*, that books were not natural
wonders, coming up of themselves like grass. Yet regardless of where
they came from, I cannot remember a time when I was not in love
with them—with the books themselves, cover and binding and the
paper they were printed on, with their smell and their weight and
with their possession in my arms, captured and carried off to myself. Still illiterate, I was ready for them, committed to all the reading I could give them.

Neither of my parents had come from homes that could afford to
buy many books, but though it must have been something of a
strain on his salary, as the youngest officer in a young insurance
company, my father was all the while carefully selecting and ordering away for what he and Mother thought we children should grow
up with. They bought first for the future.

Besides the bookcase in the livingroom, which was always called "the library," there were the encyclopedia tables and dictionary stand under windows in our diningroom. Here to help us grow up arguing around the diningroom table were the Unabridged Webster, the Columbia Encyclopedia, Compton's Pictured Encyclopedia, the Lincoln Library of Information, and later the Book of Knowledge. And the year we moved into our new house, there was room to celebrate it with the new 1925 edition of the Britannica, which my father, his face always deliberately turned toward the future, was of course disposed to think better than any previous edition.

In "the library," inside the mission-style bookcase with its three diamond-latticed glass doors, with my father's Morris chair[1] and the glass-shaded lamp on its table beside it, were books I could soon begin on—and I did, reading them all alike and as they came, straight down their rows, top shelf to bottom. There was the set of Stoddard's Lectures,[2] in all its late nineteenth-century vocabulary and vignettes of peasant life and quaint beliefs and customs, with matching halftone illustrations: Vesuvius[3] erupting, Venice by moonlight, gypsies glimpsed by their campfires. I didn't know then the clue they were to my father's longing to see the rest of the world. I read straight through his other love-from-afar: the Victrola Book of the Opera, with opera after opera in synopsis, with portraits in costume of Melba, Caruso, Galli-Curci, and Geraldine Farrar, some of whose voices we could listen to on our Red Seal records.

My mother read secondarily for information; she sank as a hedonist into novels. She read Dickens in the spirit in which she would have eloped with him. The novels of her girlhood that had stayed on in her imagination, besides those of Dickens and Scott and Robert Louis Stevenson, were *Jane Eyre, Trilby, The Woman in White, Green Mansions, King Solomon's Mines*. Marie Corelli's name would crop up but I understood she had gone out of favor with my

---

1. A semireclining chair, often accompanied by a footrest.

2. A ten-volume set of books published in the 1890s and 1900s; John L. Stoddard traveled extensively and published his observations of the world's cultures in his *Lectures*.

3. Mount Vesuvius, a volcano near Naples, Italy, erupted in 79 C.E., burying the town of Pompeii in ash. The town was rediscovered in 1748 and immediately became the richest archeological source of the Roman Empire.

mother, who had only kept *Ardath* out of loyalty. In time she absorbed herself in Galsworthy, Edith Wharton, above all in Thomas Mann of the *Joseph* volumes.

St. Elmo was not in our house; I saw it often in other houses. This wildly popular Southern novel is where all the Edna Earles in our population started coming from. They're all named for the heroine, who succeeded in bringing a dissolute, sinning roué and atheist of a lover (St. Elmo) to his knees. My mother was able to forgo it. But she remembered the classic advice given to rose growers on how to water their bushes long enough: "Take a chair and *St. Elmo.*"

To both my parents I owe my early acquaintance with a beloved Mark Twain. There was a full set of Mark Twain and a short set of Ring Lardner in our bookcase, and those were the volumes that in time united us all, parents and children.

Reading everything that stood before me was how I came upon a worn old book without a back that had belonged to my father as a child. It was called *Sanford and Merton.* Is there anyone left who recognizes it, I wonder? It is the famous moral tale written by Thomas Day in the 1780s, but of him no mention is made on the title page of *this* book; here it is *Sanford and Merton in Words of One Syllable* by Mary Godolphin. Here are the rich boy and the poor boy and Mr. Barlow, their teacher and interlocutor, in long discourses alternating with dramatic scenes—danger and rescue allotted to the rich and the poor respectively. It may have only words of one syllable, but one of them is "quoth." It ends with not one but two morals, both engraved on rings: "Do what you ought, come what may," and "If we would be great, we must first learn to be good."

This book was lacking its front cover, the back held on by strips of pasted paper, now turned golden, in several layers, and the pages stained, flecked, and tattered around the edges; its garish illustrations had come unattached but were preserved, laid in. I had the feeling even in my heedless childhood that this was the only book my father as a little boy had had of his own. He had held onto it, and might have gone to sleep on its coverless face: he had lost his mother when he was seven. My father had never made any mention to his own children of the book, but he had brought it along with him from Ohio to our house and shelved it in our bookcase.

My mother had brought from West Virginia that set of Dickens; those books looked sad, too—they had been through fire and water before I was born, she told me, and there they were, lined up—as I later realized, waiting for *me*.

I was presented, from as early as I can remember, with books of my own, which appeared on my birthday and Christmas morning. Indeed, my parents could not give me books enough. They must have sacrificed to give me on my sixth or seventh birthday—it was after I became a reader for myself—the ten-volume set of *Our Wonder World*. These were beautifully made, heavy books I would lie down with on the floor in front of the diningroom hearth, and more often than the rest volume 5, *Every Child's Story Book*, was under my eyes. There were the fairy tales—Grimm, Andersen, the English, the French, "Ali Baba and the Forty Thieves"; and there was Aesop and Reynard the Fox; there were the myths and legends, Robin Hood, King Arthur, and St. George and the Dragon, even the history of Joan of Arc; a whack of *Pilgrim's Progress* and a long piece of *Gulliver*. They all carried their classic illustrations. I located myself in these pages and could go straight to the stories and pictures I loved; very often "The Yellow Dwarf" was first choice, with Walter Crane's Yellow Dwarf in full color making his terrifying appearance flanked by turkeys. Now that volume is as worn and backless and hanging apart as my father's poor *Sanford and Merton*. The precious page with Edward Lear's "Jumblies" on it has been in danger of slipping out for all these years. One measure of my love for Our Wonder World was that for a long time I wondered if I would go through fire and water for it as my mother had done for Charles Dickens; and the only comfort was to think I could ask my mother to do it for me.

I believe I'm the only child I know of who grew up with this treasure in the house. I used to ask others, "Did you have Our Wonder World?" I'd have to tell them The Book of Knowledge could not hold a candle to it.

I live in gratitude to my parents for initiating me—and as early as I begged for it, without keeping me waiting—into knowledge of the word, into reading and spelling, by way of the alphabet. They taught it to me at home in time for me to begin to read before starting to school. I believe the alphabet is no longer considered an essential piece of equipment for traveling through life. In my day it was the keystone to knowledge. You learned the alphabet as you learned to count to ten, as you learned "Now I lay me" and the Lord's Prayer and your father's and mother's name and address and telephone number, all in case you were lost.

My love for the alphabet, which endures, grew out of reciting it but, before that, out of seeing the letters on the page. In my own story books, before I could read them for myself, I fell in love with various winding, enchanted-looking initials drawn by Walter Crane at the heads of fairy tales. In "Once upon a time," an "O" had a rabbit running it as a treadmill, his feet upon flowers. When the day came, years later, for me to see the Book of Kells,[4] all the wizardry of letter, initial, and word swept over me a thousand times over, and the illumination, the gold, seemed a part of the word's beauty and holiness that had been there from the start.

Learning stamps you with its moments. Childhood's learning is made up of moments. It isn't steady. It's a pulse.

In a children's art class, we sat in a ring on kindergarten chairs and drew three daffodils that had just been picked out of the yard; and while I was drawing, my sharpened yellow pencil and the cup of the yellow daffodil gave off whiffs just alike. That the pencil doing the drawing should give off the same smell as the flower it drew seemed part of the art lesson—as shouldn't it be? Children, like animals, use all their senses to discover the world. Then artists come along and discover it the same way, all over again. Here and there, it's the same world. Or now and then we'll hear from an artist who's never lost it.

In my sensory education I include my physical awareness of the *word*. Of a certain word, that is; the connection it has with what it stands for. At around age six, perhaps, I was standing by myself in our front yard waiting for supper, just at that hour in a late summer day when the sun is already below the horizon and the risen full

---

4. A beautifully illuminated medieval manuscript of the Latin Gospels.

moon in the visible sky stops being chalky and begins to take on light. There comes the moment, and I saw it then, when the moon goes from flat to round. For the first time it met my eyes as a globe. The word "moon" came into my mouth as though fed to me out of a silver spoon. Held in my mouth the moon became a word. It had the roundness of a Concord grape Grandpa took off his vine and gave me to suck out of its skin and swallow whole, in Ohio.

This love did not prevent me from living for years in foolish error about the moon. The new moon just appearing in the west was the rising moon to me. The new should be rising. And in early childhood the sun and moon, those opposite reigning powers, I just as easily assumed rose in east and west respectively in their opposite sides of the sky, and like partners in a reel they advanced, sun from the east, moon from the west, crossed over (when I wasn't looking) and went down on the other side. My father couldn't have known I believed that when, bending behind me and guiding my shoulder, he positioned me at our telescope in the front yard and, with careful adjustment of the focus, brought the moon close to me.

The night sky over my childhood Jackson was velvety black. I could see the full constellations in it and call their names; when I could read, I knew their myths. Though I was always waked for eclipses, and indeed carried to the window as an infant in arms and shown Halley's Comet in my sleep, and though I'd been taught at our diningroom table about the solar system and knew the earth revolved around the sun, and our moon around us, I never found out the moon didn't come up in the west until I was a writer and Herschel Brickell, the literary critic, told me after I misplaced it in a story. He said valuable words to me about my new profession: "Always be sure you get your moon in the right part of the sky."

My mother always sang to her children. Her voice came out just a little bit in the minor key. "Wee Willie Winkie's" song was wonderfully sad when she sang the lullabies.

"Oh, but now there's a record. She could have her own record to listen to," my father would have said. For there came a Victrola record of "Bobby Shafftoe" and "Rock-a-Bye Baby", all of Mother's lullabies, which could be played to take her place. Soon I was able to play her my own lullabies all day long.

Our Victrola stood in the diningroom. I was allowed to climb onto the seat of a diningroom chair to wind it, start the record turning, and set the needle playing. In a second I'd jumped to the floor, to spin or march around the table as the music called for—now there were all the other records I could play too. I skinned back onto the chair just in time to lift the needle at the end, stop the record and turn it over, then change the needle. That brass receptacle with a hole in the lid gave off a metallic smell like human sweat, from all the hot needles that were fed it. Winding up, dancing, being cocked to start and stop the record, was of course all in one the act of *listening*—to "Overture to *Daughter of the Regiment*," "Selections from *The Fortune Teller*," "Kiss Me Again," "Gypsy Dance from *Carmen*," "Stars and Stripes Forever," "When the Midnight Choo-Choo Leaves for Alabam," or whatever came next. Movement must be at the very heart of listening.

Ever since I was first read to, then started reading to myself, there has never been a line read that I didn't *hear*. As my eyes followed the sentence, a voice was saying it silently to me. It isn't my mother's voice, or the voice of any person I can identify, certainly not my own. It is human, but inward, and it is inwardly that I listen to it. It is to me the voice of the story or the poem itself. The cadence, whatever it is that asks you to believe, the feeling that resides in the printed word, reaches me through the reader-voice. I have supposed, but never found out, that this is the case with all readers—to read as listeners—and with all writers, to write as listeners. It may be part of the desire to write. The sound of what falls on the page begins the process of testing it for truth, for me. Whether I am right to trust so far I don't know. By now I don't know whether I could do either one, reading or writing, without the other.

My own words, when I am at work on a story, I hear too as they go, in the same voice that I hear when I read in books. When I write and the sound of it comes back to my ears, then I act to make my changes. I have always trusted this voice.

1983

E. B. White
1899–1985

White, a writer and contributing editor for The New Yorker, *abandoned New York City in 1938 for a coastal farm, where he mended fences, doctored sick sheep, and wrote. He sent reports of his life and his thoughts to* Harper's *Magazine, where he published a monthly column (1938–43). "Once More to the Lake" was written in August 1941 (the month before he submitted the article, he had taken his son on a visit to the Belgrade Lakes, Maine, where he had vacationed as a boy) and published first in* Harper's *in September and then again in 1942 when the monthly reports of his farm life were gathered in a book. This essay is one chapter in a long personal journal written for public consumption. To his* Harper's *readers, the pastoral peace of "Once More to the Lake" must have seemed a celebration of the isolation and retirement that were threatened by the war in Europe. (Three months after the piece appeared, Japan bombed Pearl Harbor.) To readers who first read the essay in the 1942 book, it was an elegy, and its final line would have had a greater immediacy to them than it has for most of us today. In his foreword to the second edition (1944), White explained that he "wrote from a salt water farm in Maine while engaged in trivial, peaceable pursuits, knowing all the time that the world hadn't arranged any true peace or granted anyone the privilege of indulging himself for long in trivialities. . . . I see no harm in preserving [these essays], the more so since I have begun to receive letters from soldiers overseas assuring me that there is a positive value to them in the memory of peace and of home." In the words of Henry S. Canby, a contemporary critic, White continued the work of America's "cracker-box tree-stump philosophers" like Benjamin Franklin, Henry David Thoreau, Abraham Lincoln, and Mark Twain.*

Once More to the Lake

One summer, along about 1904, my father rented a camp on a lake in Maine and took us all there for the month of August. We all got ringworm from some kittens and had to rub Pond's Extract on our arms and legs night and morning, and my father rolled over in a canoe with all his clothes on; but outside of that the vacation was a success, and from then on none of us ever thought there was any place in the world like that lake in Maine. We returned summer after summer—always on August 1st for one month. I have since become a salt-water man, but sometimes in summer there are days when the restlessness of the tides and the fearful cold of the sea water and the incessant wind that blows across the afternoon and into the evening make me wish for the placidity of a lake in the woods. A few weeks ago this feeling got so strong I bought myself a couple of bass hooks and a spinner and returned to the lake where we used to go, for a week's fishing and to revisit old haunts.

I took along my son, who had never had any fresh water up his nose and who had seen lily pads only from train windows. On the journey over to the lake I began to wonder what it would be like. I wondered how time would have marred this unique, this holy spot—the coves and streams, the hills that the sun set behind, the camps and the paths behind the camps. I was sure that the tarred road would have found it out, and I wondered in what other ways it would be desolated. It is strange how much you can remember about places like that once you allow your mind to return into the grooves that lead back. You remember one thing, and that suddenly reminds you of another thing. I guess I remembered clearest of all the early mornings, when the lake was cool and motionless, remembered how the bedroom smelled of the lumber it was made of and of the wet woods whose scent entered through the screen. The partitions in the camp were thin and did not extend clear to the top of the rooms, and as I was always the first up I would dress softly so as not to wake the others, and sneak out into the sweet outdoors and start out in the canoe, keeping close along the shore in the long shadows of the pines. I remembered being very careful never to rub my paddle against the gunwale for fear of disturbing the stillness of the cathedral.

The lake had not been what you would call a wild lake. There were cottages sprinkled around the shores, and it was in farming country although the shores of the lake were quite heavily wooded. Some of the cottages were owned by nearby farmers, and you would live at the shore and eat your meals at the farmhouse. That's what our family did. But although it wasn't wild, it was a fairly large and undisturbed lake and there were places in it that, to a child at least, seemed infinitely remote and primeval.

I was right about the tar: it led to within half a mile of the shore. But when I got back there, with my boy, and we settled into a camp near a farmhouse and into the kind of summertime I had known, I could tell that it was going to be pretty much the same as it had been before—I knew it, lying in bed the first morning, smelling the bedroom, and hearing the boy sneak quietly out and go off along the shore in a boat. I began to sustain the illusion that he was I, and therefore, by simple transposition, that I was my father. This sensation persisted, kept cropping up all the time we were there. It was not an entirely new feeling, but in this setting it grew much stronger. I seemed to be living a dual existence. I would be in the middle of some simple act, I would be picking up a bait box or laying down a table fork, or I would be saying something, and suddenly it would be not I but my father who was saying the words or making the gesture. It gave me a creepy sensation.

We went fishing the first morning. I felt the same damp moss covering the worms in the bait can, and saw the dragonfly alight on the tip of my rod as it hovered a few inches from the surface of the water. It was the arrival of this fly that convinced me beyond any doubt that everything was as it always had been, that the years were a mirage and there had been no years. The small waves were the same, chucking the rowboat under the chin as we fished at anchor, and the boat was the same boat, the same color green and the ribs broken in the same places, and under the floor-boards the same fresh-water leavings and débris—the dead hellgrammite, the wisps of moss, the rusty discarded fishhook, the dried blood from yesterday's catch. We stared silently at the tips of our rods, at the dragonflies that came and went. I lowered the tip of mine into the water, tentatively, pensively dislodging the fly, which darted two feet away, poised, darted two feet back, and came to rest again a little farther up the rod. There had been no years between the ducking of this dragonfly and the other one—the one that was part of memory. I looked at the boy, who was silently watching his fly, and it was my hands that held his rod, my eyes watching. I felt dizzy and didn't know which rod I was at the end of.

We caught two bass, hauling them in briskly as though they were mackerel, pulling them over the side of the boat in a businesslike manner without any landing net, and stunning them with a blow on the back of the head. When we got back for a swim before lunch, the lake was exactly where we had left it, the same number of inches from the dock, and there was only the merest suggestion of a breeze. This seemed an utterly enchanted sea, this lake you could leave to its own devices for a few hours and come back to, and find that it had not stirred, this constant and trustworthy body of water. In the shallows, the dark, watersoaked sticks and twigs, smooth and old, were undulating in clusters on the bottom against the clean ribbed sand, and the track of the mussel was plain. A school of minnows swam by, each minnow with its small individual shadow, doubling the attendance, so clear and sharp in the sunlight. Some of the other campers were in swimming, along the shore, one of them with a cake of soap, and the water felt thin and clear and unsubstantial. Over the years there had been this person with the cake of soap, this cultist, and here he was. There had been no years.

Up to the farmhouse to dinner through the teeming, dusty field, the road under our sneakers was only a two-track road. The middle track was missing, the one with the marks of the hooves and the splotches of dried, flaky manure. There had always been three tracks to choose from in choosing which track to walk in; now the choice was narrowed down to two. For a moment I missed terribly the middle alternative. But the way led past the tennis court, and something about the way it lay there in the sun reassured me; the tape had loosened along the backline, the alleys were green with plantains and other weeds, and the net (installed in June and removed in September) sagged in the dry noon, and the whole place steamed with midday heat and hunger and emptiness. There was a choice of pie for dessert, and one was blueberry and one was apple, and the waitresses were the same country girls, there having been no passage of time, only the illusion of it as in a dropped curtain—the waitresses were still fifteen; their hair had been washed, that was the only difference—they had been to the movies and seen the pretty girls with the clean hair.

Summertime, oh summertime, pattern of life indelible, the fade-proof lake, the woods unshatterable, the pasture with the sweetfern and the juniper forever and ever, summer without end; this was the background, and the life along the shore was the design, the cottages with their innocent and tranquil design, their tiny docks with the flagpole and the American flag floating against the white clouds in the blue sky, the little paths over the roots of the trees leading from camp to camp and the paths leading back to the outhouses and the can of lime for sprinkling, and at the souvenir counters at the store the miniature birch-bark canoes and the post cards that showed things looking a little better than they looked. This was the American family at play, escaping the city heat, wondering whether the newcomers in the camp at the head of the cove were "common" or "nice," wondering whether it was true that the people who drove up for Sunday dinner at the farmhouse were turned away because there wasn't enough chicken.

It seemed to me, as I kept remembering all this, that those times and those summers had been infinitely precious and worth saving. There had been jollity and peace and goodness. The arriving (at the beginning of August) had been so big a business in itself, at the railway station the farm wagon drawn up, the first smell of the pine-laden air, the first glimpse of the smiling farmer, and the great importance of the trunks and your father's enormous authority in such matters, and the feel of the wagon under you for the long ten-mile haul, and at the top of the last long hill catching the first view of the lake after eleven months of not seeing this cherished body of water. The shouts and cries of the other campers when they saw you, and the trunks to be unpacked, to give up their rich burden. (Arriving was less exciting nowadays, when you sneaked up in your car and parked it under a tree near the camp and took out the bags and in five minutes it was all over, no fuss, no loud wonderful fuss about trunks.)

Peace and goodness and jollity. The only thing that was wrong now, really, was the sound of the place, an unfamiliar nervous sound of the outboard motors. This was the note that jarred, the one thing that would sometimes break the illusion and set the years moving. In those other summertimes all motors were inboard; and when they were at a little distance, the noise they made was a sedative, an ingredient of summer sleep. They were one-cylinder and two-cylinder engines, and some were make-and-break and some were jump-spark, but they all made a sleepy sound across the lake. The one-lungers throbbed and fluttered, and the twin-cylinder ones purred and purred, and that was a quiet sound too. But now the campers all had outboards. In the daytime, in the hot mornings, these motors made a petulant, irritable sound; at night, in the still evening when the afterglow lit the water, they whined about one's ears like mosquitoes. My boy loved our rented outboard, and his great desire was to achieve singlehanded mastery over it, and authority, and he soon learned the trick of choking it a little (but not too much), and the adjustment of the needle valve. Watching him I would remember the things you could do with the old one-cylinder engine with the heavy flywheel, how you could have it eating out of your hand if you got really close to it spiritually. Motor boats in those days didn't have clutches, and you would make a landing by shutting off the motor at the proper time and coasting in with a dead rudder. But there was a way of reversing them, if you learned the trick, by cutting the switch and putting it on again exactly on the final dying revolution of the flywheel, so that it would kick back against compression and begin reversing. Approaching a dock in a strong following breeze, it was difficult to slow up sufficiently by the ordinary coasting method, and if a boy felt he had complete mastery over his motor, he was tempted to keep it running beyond its time and then reverse it a few feet from the dock. It took a cool nerve, because if you threw the switch a twentieth of a second too soon you would catch the flywheel when it still had speed enough to go up past center, and the boat would leap ahead, charging bull-fashion at the dock.

We had a good week at the camp. The bass were biting well and the sun shone endlessly, day after day. We would be tired at night and lie down in the accumulated heat of the little bedrooms after the long hot day and the breeze would stir almost imperceptibly outside and the smell of the swamp drift in through the rusty screens. Sleep would come easily and in the morning the red squirrel would be on the roof, tapping out his gay routine. I kept remembering everything, lying in bed in the mornings—the small steamboat that had a long rounded stern like the lip of a Ubangi, and how quietly she ran on the moonlight sails, when the older boys played their mandolins and the girls sang and we ate doughnuts dipped in sugar, and how sweet the music was on the water in the shining night, and what it had felt like to think about girls then. After breakfast we would go up to the store and the things were in the same place—the minnows in a bottle, the plugs and spinners disarranged and pawed over by the youngsters from the boys' camp, the fig newtons and the Beeman's gum. Outside, the road was tarred and cars stood in front of the store. Inside, all was just as it had always been, except there was more Coca-Cola and not so much Moxie and root beer and birch beer and sarsaparilla. We would walk out with a bottle of pop apiece and sometimes the pop would backfire up our noses and hurt. We explored the streams, quietly, where the turtles slid off the sunny logs and dug their way into the soft bottom; and we lay on the town wharf and fed worms to the tame bass. Everywhere we went I had trouble making out which was I, the one walking at my side, the one walking in my pants.

One afternoon while we were there at that lake a thunderstorm came up. It was like the revival of an old melodrama that I had seen long ago with childish awe. The second-act climax of the drama of the electrical disturbance over a lake in America had not changed in any important respect. This was the big scene, still the big scene. The whole thing was so familiar, the first feeling of oppression and heat and a general air around camp of not wanting to go very far away. In midafternoon (it was all the same) a curious darkening of the sky, and a lull in everything that had made life tick; and then the way the boats suddenly swung the other way at their moorings with the coming of a breeze out of the new quarter, and the premonitory rumble. Then the kettle drum, then the snare, then the bass drum and cymbals, then crackling light against the dark, and the gods grinning and licking their chops in the hills. Afterward the calm, the rain steadily rustling in the calm lake, the return of light and hope and spirits, and the campers running out in joy and relief to go swimming in the rain, their bright cries perpetuating the deathless joke about how they were getting simply drenched, and the children screaming with delight at the new sensation of bathing in the rain, and the joke about getting drenched linking the generations in a strong indestructible chain. And the comedian who waded in carrying an umbrella.

When the others went swimming my son said he was going in too. He pulled his dripping trunks from the line where they had hung all through the shower, and wrung them out. Languidly, and with no thought of going in, I watched him, his hard little body, skinny and bare, saw him wince slightly as he pulled up around his vitals the small, soggy, icy garment. As he buckled the swollen belt, suddenly my groin felt the chill of death.

1941

George Will
b. 1941

> *George Will delivered this speech during graduation ceremonies at Lafayette College in Easton, Pennsylvania, in 2000. He does not explicitly define "values" and "virtues," so an important part of understanding this speech is to figure out what are the differences between them. Will, a political columnist, is consistently conservative in his writing and was an ardent supporter of Ronald Reagan. It would be tempting to assume that this is a partisan complaint against liberals, who often speak of "values" and tend to be more cautious than conservatives when tempted to erect hierarchies, to say one culture's or one person's values are better than another's. Nevertheless, when Will alludes to politics at the end of the speech, he may be referring to an intramural battle between Republicans. When Will wrote this essay, George W. Bush had just defeated John McCain in the Republican primary. (Though the official convention would not be held until that summer, it was clear by May that Bush had secured the Republican nomination.) One of Bush's key strategies was to appeal to religious conservatives, whose political mantra was "family values."*

Virtues Versus Values

Mr. President, members of the Board of Trustees, distinguished faculty, proud parents—proud and somewhat-lighter-in-the-wallet parents—and especially members of the Class of 2000—make that "fellow members of the Class of 2000."

What I say *may* come too late to do you a lick of good, you who today take your leave of this fine institution, but I will say it anyway: I think I have finally figured out the purpose of higher education. I have acquired this sunburst of understanding, if such it truly is, by thinking long and hard about an offensive—at least to me—aspect of American politics just now. I refer to the incessant and ubiquitous talk about "values."

Today our nation is enjoying peace and unprecedented prosperity. These happy circumstances allow, even seem to *demand*, a preoccupation with the teaching of what are nowadays called "values." The word "values" is a relatively new, and I believe regrettable, vocabulary for discussing a recurring American preoccupation: the possible decay of our national character.

When the Marquis de Lafayette[1] returned to America for a hero's tour in 1824—which tour led to the naming of this college—his extended visit catalyzed the young republic's unease about what it sensed was a decline from the pinnacle achieved by the revolutionary generation, which by then had largely passed from the scene.

Then, as now, the nation was feeling its oats economically but was also feeling queasy about whether its character was as strong as its economy. Indeed, it worried that the *process* by which it was becoming rich—the banking, industrialization, speculation, and urbanization of early capitalism—was leading it away from the sturdy virtues of a yeoman's republic.

However, the anxiety of that day was not voiced in talk about

---

1. Lafayette (1757–1834), French aristocrat who, at the age of twenty, volunteered his services to Congress, who conferred upon him the rank of Major-General; he served much of the Revolutionary War on the staff of George Washington, who was a life-long friend.

values. Instead, Americans talked then as the Founders had talked: of *virtues*. You may well wonder: values, virtues, what's the difference? Consider. I think the difference is large.

Historian Gertrude Himmelfarb rightly says that political talk about values is now so ubiquitous we forget how new such talk is. It began, Himmelfarb says, just seventeen years ago, during Britain's 1983 general election campaign, when Prime Minister Margaret Thatcher jauntily embraced the accusation—and it was an accusation—that she favored "*Victorian values*." Except, of course, that the Victorians themselves, those muscular moralists, never spoke of values but of virtues.

Once upon a time the word "values" was used most as a verb, meaning "to esteem," as in "I value your friendship." It was also a singular noun, such as in "inflation hurts the value of the currency." However in today's political discourse, "value" is becoming a *plural* noun denoting beliefs and attitudes of individuals and societies. And what this means is that Friedrich Nietzsche's[2] nihilistic intent, the *de*-moralization of society, is advancing.

The de-moralization of society is advanced when the word "values" supplants the word "virtues" in political and ethical contexts. When we move beyond talk of good and evil, when the categories virtue and vice are transcended, we are left with the thin gruel of values-talk.

Oh, but how very democratic values-talk is. Unlike virtues, *everyone* has *lots* of values; *everyone* has as many as he or she chooses. Hitler had *scads* of values. George Washington had *virtues*. Who among those who knew him—surely not the Marquis de Lafayette—would have spoken of George Washington's values? No one.

Values-talk, alas, suits today's zeitgeist. It is the talk of a nonjudgmental age. Ours is an age judgmental *only* about the sin of being judgmental. Today it is mark of broad-mindedness to say, "Oh, one person's values are as good as another's." But it is, of course, nonsense to say, "One person's virtues are as good as another's."

---

2. Nietzsche (1844–1900), German philosopher in whose *The Gay Science* (1882) can be found the famous phrase "God is dead." Most of Nietzsche's work challenged orthodox standards of morality.

Values are an equal-opportunity business. They are mere *choices*. In contrast, virtues are habits, difficult to develop and therefore not accessible to all. Therefore, speaking of virtues rather than values is elitist, offensive to democracy's egalitarian, leveling ethos, which I say is precisely *why* talk of virtues *should* be revived and talk of values *should* be abandoned.

Another great Frenchman, Alexis de Tocqueville,[3] who toured America not long after Lafayette did, noted that although much is gained by replacing aristocratic institutions and suppositions with democratic ones, something valuable is often lost. What is lost is the ability to recognize and the hunger to honor hierarchies of achievement and character. Therefore, democracy requires the cultivation of preventive virtues. Preventive virtues are those that counter certain unhealthy tendencies in democracies.

Let us hear about this from a man who is currently completing a new translation of de Tocqueville's magnificent *Democracy in America*. I refer to Harvey Mansfield. Harvey C. Mansfield, because of his opposition to grade inflation, is known at Harvard as "Harvey C-minus Mansfield." He is Harvard's conservative.

He notes that a theme of American literature, writ large, for example, in the works of Mark Twain, is the effect of democracy on the higher qualities of human beings. To counter democracy's leveling ethos, with its tinge of envy of those who possess scarce excellence, universities, Harvey Mansfield says, should teach students to *praise*.

Students, that is, should learn to look up, up to the heroic in thought and action, in politics and history and literature, in science and faith. After all, the few men and women who become heroes do so by looking up, by being *pulled up* by some vision of nobility, which makes a hero quite unlike, something quite different from, a role model. The concept of "role model" is also a very democratic notion. A role model is someone anyone can successfully choose to emulate.

Here, then, is higher education's special purpose in a democratic culture: to turn young people toward what is high.

A wit has said that in the nineteenth century England's ruling

3. Tocqueville (1805–1859), French political scientist whose *Democracy in America* (1835 and 1840) analyzed American culture and government.

class developed its system of elite secondary schools for the purpose of making sure that Byron and Shelley could never happen again. The purpose of American higher education is *not* to serve as a values cafeteria where young people are encouraged to pick whichever strikes their fancy. Rather, the purpose of higher education for citizens of a democracy should be to help them identify excellence in its various realms and to understand what virtues make it so.

This message for a commencement season is also perennially germane to our political seasons. When you hear, as you frequently will this year, politicians speaking of their values and America's values, values here and values there, understand that you are in the presence of America's problem, not America's solution.

There, that is my message. I have said elsewhere that no matter *what* columnists say, they *must* say it briefly. Brevity is not among the columnist's *values*. Rather, brevity is a columnist's necessary *virtue*.

Again I thank this college for giving me the privilege of delivering the last lecture to the Class of 2000. I thank you all for the courtesy of your attentiveness. Now go forth and have fun, you've earned it. You have earned it by meeting the high standards of this college, a college worthy of its basketball team, a college whose founders named it for the Marquis de Lafayette, and who did that, they said, because of their respect for—listen to this language, I'm quoting the founders of your college—Lafayette's "talents, *virtues*, and signal services . . . [to] the great cause of freedom."

Virtues, not values. Thank you.

2000

Virginia Woolf
1882–1941

In October 1928, Virginia Woolf gave two lectures on women and literature at Cambridge University. Just ten years earlier, women in England had won for themselves the right to vote, but they were still largely excluded from the professions. In fact, the old belief that men are naturally smarter than women was coming back in vogue. One contemporary reviewer remarked that Woolf was brave to pub-

lish her lectures, because "anti-feminism is so strikingly the correct fashion of the day among the intellectuals." Her immediate audience was a vanguard of young, well-educated women eager to demand an equal place in the public sphere. The women's colleges that hosted the lectures, Girton (founded in 1869) and Newnham (founded in 1871), impressed Woolf with their poverty, especially when she compared them with the posh men's colleges. These are not trivial matters, she argues, for material conditions determine intellectual capacity. If you have to slave away at menial jobs, you'll never have the time to think deeply. According to Woolf, before you can write well, you need a room in which to sequester yourself and enough money to buy food and clothing. These were denied women through most of history, and even in the 1920s, Woolf tells her audience, they are hard to come by. She revised the two lectures, combined them with a slightly fictionalized account of her experiences on the campuses of Cambridge, and published the whole as A Room of One's Own in 1929. The book was an inspiration to the second feminist movement, that of the 1960s and 1970s.

In Search of a Room of One's Own

It was disappointing not to have brought back[1] in the evening some important statement, some authentic fact. Women are poorer than men because—this or that. Perhaps now it would be better to give up seeking for the truth, and receiving on one's head an avalanche of opinion hot as lava, discoloured as dish-water. It would be better to draw the curtains; to shut out distractions; to light the lamp; to narrow the enquiry and to ask the historian, who records not opinions but facts, to describe under what conditions women lived, not throughout the ages, but in England, say in the time of Elizabeth.

For it is a perennial puzzle why no woman wrote a word of that extraordinary literature when every other man, it seemed, was capable of song or sonnet. What were the conditions in which women

---

1. From the British Museum (now British Library), where she was researching her lectures.

lived, I asked myself; for fiction, imaginative work that is, is not dropped like a pebble upon the ground, as science may be; fiction is like a spider's web, attached ever so lightly perhaps, but still attached to life at all four corners. Often the attachment is scarcely perceptible; Shakespeare's plays, for instance, seem to hang there complete by themselves. But when the web is pulled askew, hooked up at the edge, torn in the middle, one remembers that these webs are not spun in midair by incorporeal creatures, but are the work of suffering human beings, and are attached to grossly material things, like health and money and the houses we live in.

I went, therefore, to the shelf where the histories stand and took down one of the latest, Professor Trevelyan's *History of England*. Once more I looked up Women, found "position of," and turned to the pages indicated. "Wife-beating," I read, "was a recognised right of man, and was practised without shame by high as well as low. . . . Similarly," the historian goes on, "the daughter who refused to marry the gentleman of her parents' choice was liable to be locked up, beaten and flung about the room, without any shock being inflicted on public opinion. Marriage was not an affair of personal affection, but of family avarice, particularly in the 'chivalrous' upper classes. . . . Betrothal often took place while one or both of the parties was in the cradle, and marriage when they were scarcely out of the nurses' charge." That was about 1470, soon after Chaucer's time. The next reference to the position of women is some two hundred years later, in the time of the Stuarts. "It was still the exception for women of the upper and middle class to choose their own husbands, and when the husband had been assigned, he was lord and master, so far at least as law and custom could make him. Yet even so," Professor Trevelyan concludes, "neither Shakespeare's women nor those of authentic seventeenth-century memoirs, like the Verneys and the Hutchinsons, seem wanting in personality and character." Certainly, if we consider it, Cleopatra must have had a way with her; Lady Macbeth, one would suppose, had a will of her own; Rosalind, one might conclude, was an attractive girl. Professor Trevelyan is speaking no more than the truth when he remarks that Shakespeare's women do not seem wanting in personality and character. Not being a historian, one might go even further and say that women have burnt like beacons in all the works of all the poets from the beginning of time—Clytemnestra, Antigone, Cleopatra, Lady Macbeth, Phèdre, Cressida, Rosalind, Desdemona, the Duchess of Malfi, among the dramatists; then among the prose writers: Millamant, Clarissa, Becky Sharp, Anna Karenina, Emma Bovary, Madame de Guermantes—the names flock to mind, nor do they recall women "lacking in personality and character." Indeed, if woman had no existence save in the fiction written by men, one would imagine her a person of the utmost importance; very various; heroic and mean; splendid and sordid; infinitely beautiful and hideous in the extreme; as great as a man, some think even greater.[2] But this is woman in fiction. In fact, as Professor Trevelyan points out, she was locked up, beaten and flung about the room.

A very queer, composite being thus emerges. Imaginatively she is of the highest importance; practically she is completely insignificant. She pervades poetry from cover to cover; she is all but absent from history. She dominates the lives of kings and conquerors in fiction; in fact she was the slave of any boy whose parents forced a ring upon her finger. Some of the most inspired words, some of the most profound thoughts in literature fall from her lips; in real life she could hardly read, could scarcely spell, and was the property of her husband.

It was certainly an odd monster that one made up by reading the historians first and the poets afterwards—a worm winged like an eagle; the spirit of life and beauty in a kitchen chopping up suet. But these monsters, however amusing to the imagination, have no existence in fact. What one must do to bring her to life was to think poetically and prosaically at one and the same moment, thus keeping

2. "It remains a strange and almost inexplicable fact that in Athena's city, where women were kept in almost Oriental suppression as odalisques or drudges, the stage should yet have produced figures like Clytemnestra and Cassandra, Atossa and Antigone, Phèdre and Medea, and all the other heroines who dominate play after play of the 'misogynist' Euripides. But the paradox of this world where in real life a respectable woman could hardly show her face alone in the street, and yet on the stage woman equals or surpasses man, has never been satisfactorily explained. In modern tragedy the same predominance exists. At all events, a very cursory survey of Shakespeare's work (similarly with Webster, though not with Marlowe or Jonson) suffices to reveal how this dominance, this initiative of women, persists from Rosalind to Lady Macbeth. So too in Racine; six of his tragedies bear their heroines' names; and what male characters of his shall we set against Hermione and Andromaque, Bérénice and Roxane, Phèdre and Athalie? So again with Ibsen; what men shall we match with Solveig and Nora, Hedda and Hilda Wangel and Rebecca West?"—F. L. Lucas, Tragedy, pp. 114–15 [Woolf's note].

in touch with fact—that she is Mrs. Martin, aged thirty-six, dressed in blue, wearing a black hat and brown shoes; but not losing sight of fiction either—that she is a vessel in which all sorts of spirits and forces are coursing and flashing perpetually. The moment, however, that one tries this method with the Elizabethan woman, one branch of illumination fails; one is held up by the scarcity of facts. One knows nothing detailed, nothing perfectly true and substantial about her. History scarcely mentions her. And I turned to Professor Trevelyan again to see what history meant to him. I found by looking at his chapter headings that it meant—

"The Manor Court and the Methods of Open-field Agriculture . . . The Cistercians and Sheep-farming . . . The Crusades . . . The University . . . The House of Commons . . . The Hundred Years' War . . . The Wars of the Roses . . . The Renaissance Scholars . . . The Dissolution of the Monasteries . . . Agrarian and Religious Strife . . . The Origin of English Seapower . . . The Armada . . ." and so on. Occasionally an individual woman is mentioned, an Elizabeth, or a Mary; a queen or a great lady. But by no possible means could middle-class women with nothing but brains and character at their command have taken part in any one of the great movements which, brought together, constitute the historian's view of the past. Nor shall we find her in any collection of anecdotes. Aubrey[3] hardly mentions her. She never writes her own life and scarcely keeps a diary; there are only a handful of her letters in existence. She left no plays or poems by which we can judge her. What one wants, I thought—and why does not some brilliant student at Newnham or Girton supply it?—is a mass of information; at what age did she marry; how many children had she as a rule; what was her house like; had she a room to herself; did she do the cooking; would she be likely to have a servant? All these facts lie somewhere, presumably, in parish registers and account books; the life of the average Elizabethan woman must be scattered about somewhere, could one collect it and make a book of it. It would be ambitious beyond my daring, I thought, looking about the shelves for books that were not there, to suggest to the students of those famous colleges that they should re-write history, though I own that it often

3. John Aubrey (1626–1697), author of *Brief Lives*, published posthumously.

seems a little queer as it is, unreal, lop-sided; but why should they not add a supplement to history? calling it, of course, by some inconspicuous name so that women might figure there without impropriety? For one often catches a glimpse of them in the lives of the great, whisking away into the background, concealing, I sometimes think, a wink, a laugh, perhaps a tear. And, after all, we have lives enough of Jane Austen; it scarcely seems necessary to consider again the influence of the tragedies of Joanna Baillie upon the poetry of Edgar Allan Poe; as for myself, I should not mind if the homes and haunts of Mary Russell Mitford[4] were closed to the public for a century at least. But what I find deplorable, I continued, looking about the bookshelves again, is that nothing is known about women before the eighteenth century. I have no model in my mind to turn about this way and that. Here am I asking why women did not write poetry in the Elizabethan age, and I am not sure how they were educated; whether they were taught to write; whether they had sitting-rooms to themselves; how many women had children before they were twenty-one; what, in short, they did from eight in the morning till eight at night. They had no money evidently; according to Professor Trevelyan they were married whether they liked it or not before they were out of the nursery, at fifteen or sixteen very likely. It would have been extremely odd, even upon this showing, had one of them suddenly written the plays of Shakespeare, I concluded, and I thought of that old gentleman, who is dead now, but was a bishop, I think, who declared that it was impossible for any woman, past, present, or to come, to have the genius of Shakespeare. He wrote to the papers about it. He also told a lady who applied to him for information that cats do not as a matter of fact go to heaven, though they have, he added, souls of a sort. How much thinking those old gentlemen used to save one! How the borders of ignorance shrank back at their approach! Cats do not go to heaven. Women cannot write the plays of Shakespeare.

Be that as it may, I could not help thinking, as I looked at the works of Shakespeare on the shelf, that the bishop was right at least in this; it would have been impossible, completely and entirely, for

---

4. Jane Austen (1775–1817), English novelist; Joanna Baillie (1762–1851), Scottish playwright and poet; Mary Russell Mitford (1787–1855), English novelist, poet, and playwright.

any woman to have written the plays of Shakespeare in the age of Shakespeare. Let me imagine, since facts are so hard to come by, what would have happened had Shakespeare had a wonderfully gifted sister, called Judith, let us say. Shakespeare himself went, very probably—his mother was an heiress—to the grammar school, where he may have learnt Latin—Ovid, Virgil and Horace—and the elements of grammar and logic. He was, it is well known, a wild boy who poached rabbits, perhaps shot a deer, and had, rather sooner than he should have done, to marry a woman in the neighbourhood, who bore him a child rather quicker than was right. That escapade sent him to seek his fortune in London. He had, it seemed, a taste for the theatre; he began by holding horses at the stage door. Very soon he got work in the theatre, became a successful actor, and lived at the hub of the universe, meeting everybody, knowing everybody, practising his art on the boards, exercising his wits in the streets, and even getting access to the palace of the queen. Meanwhile his extraordinarily gifted sister, let us suppose, remained at home. She was as adventurous, as imaginative, as agog to see the world as he was. But she was not sent to school. She had no chance of learning grammar and logic, let alone of reading Horace and Virgil. She picked up a book now and then, one of her brother's perhaps, and read a few pages. But then her parents came in and told her to mend the stockings or mind the stew and not moon about with books and papers. They would have spoken sharply but kindly, for they were substantial people who knew the conditions of life for a woman and loved their daughter—indeed, more likely than not she was the apple of her father's eye. Perhaps she scribbled some pages up in an apple loft on the sly, but was careful to hide them or set fire to them. Soon, however, before she was out of her teens, she was to be betrothed to the son of a neighbouring wool-stapler. She cried out that marriage was hateful to her, and for that she was severely beaten by her father. Then he ceased to scold her. He begged her instead not to hurt him, not to shame him in this matter of her marriage. He would give her a chain of beads or a fine petticoat, he said; and there were tears in his eyes. How could she disobey him? How could she break his heart? The force of her own gift alone drove her to it. She made up a small parcel of her belongings, let herself down by a rope one summer's night and took the road to London. She was not seventeen. The birds that sang in the hedge were not more musical than she was. She had the quickest fancy, a gift like her brother's, for the tune of words. Like him, she had a taste for the theatre. She stood at the stage door; she wanted to act, she said. Men laughed in her face. The manager—a fat, loose-lipped man—guffawed. He bellowed something about poodles dancing and women acting—no woman, he said, could possibly be an actress.[5] He hinted—you can imagine what. She could get no training in her craft. Could she even seek her dinner in a tavern or roam the streets at midnight? Yet her genius was for fiction and lusted to feed abundantly upon the lives of men and women and the study of their ways. At last—for she was very young, oddly like Shakespeare the poet in her face, with the same grey eyes and rounded brows—at last Nick Greene the actor-manager took pity on her; she found herself with child by that gentleman and so—who shall measure the heat and violence of the poet's heart when caught and tangled in a woman's body?—killed herself one winter's night and lies buried at some cross-roads where the omnibuses now stop outside the Elephant and Castle.

That, more or less, is how the story would run, I think, if a woman in Shakespeare's day had had Shakespeare's genius. But for my part, I agree with the deceased bishop, if such he was—it is unthinkable that any woman in Shakespeare's day should have had Shakespeare's genius. For genius like Shakespeare's is not born among labouring, uneducated, servile people. It was not born in England among the Saxons and the Britons. It is not born today among the working classes. How, then, could it have been born among women whose work began, according to Professor Trevelyan, almost before they were out of the nursery, who were forced to it by their parents and held to it by all the power of law and custom? Yet genius of a sort must have existed among women as it must have existed among the working classes. Now and again an Emily Brontë or a Robert Burns blazes out and proves its presence.[6] But certainly it never got itself on to paper. When, however, one reads of a witch

5. Women were not allowed to act in the Elizabethan theater; instead, boys played women's parts.

6. Emily Brontë (1818–1848), English novelist and clergyman's daughter; Robert Burns (1759–1796), Scottish poet and farmer's son.

being ducked, of a woman possessed by devils, of a wise woman selling herbs, or even of a very remarkable man who had a mother, then I think we are on the track of a lost novelist, a suppressed poet, of some mute and inglorious Jane Austen,[7] some Emily Brontë who dashed her brains out on the moor or mopped and mowed about the highways crazed with the torture that her gift had put her to. Indeed, I would venture to guess that Anon, who wrote so many poems without signing them, was often a woman. It was a woman Edward Fitzgerald,[8] I think, suggested who made the ballads and the folk-songs, crooning them to her children, beguiling her spinning with them, or the length of the winter's night.

This may be true or it may be false—who can say?—but what is true in it, so it seemed to me, reviewing the story of Shakespeare's sister as I had made it, is that any woman born with a great gift in the sixteenth century would certainly have gone crazed, shot herself, or ended her days in some lonely cottage outside the village, half witch, half wizard, feared and mocked at. For it needs little skill in psychology to be sure that a highly gifted girl who had tried to use her gift for poetry would have been so thwarted and hindered by other people, so tortured and pulled asunder by her own contrary instincts, that she must have lost her health and sanity to a certainty. No girl could have walked to London and stood at a stage door and forced her way into the presence of actor-managers without doing herself a violence and suffering an anguish which may have been irrational—for chastity may be a fetish invented by certain societies for unknown reasons—but were none the less inevitable. Chastity had then, it has even now, a religious importance in a woman's life, and has so wrapped itself round with nerves and instincts that to cut it free and bring it to the light of day demands courage of the rarest. To have lived a free life in London in the sixteenth century would have meant for a woman who was poet and playwright a nervous stress and dilemma which might well have killed her. Had she survived, whatever she had written would have been twisted and deformed, issuing from a strained and morbid imagination. And un-

---

7. An allusion to Thomas Gray's "Elegy Written in a Country Churchyard": "Some mute inglorious Milton here may rest" (line 59).

8. Edward FitzGerald (1809–1883), English poet and translator of *The Rubáiyát of Omar Khayyám.*

doubtedly, I thought, looking at the shelf where there are no plays by women, her work would have gone unsigned. That refuge she would have sought certainly. It was the relic of the sense of chastity that dictated anonymity to women even so late as the nineteenth century. Currer Bell, George Eliot, George Sand,[9] all the victims of inner strife as their writings prove, sought ineffectively to veil themselves by using the name of a man. Thus they did homage to the convention, which if not implanted by the other sex was liberally encouraged by them (the chief glory of a woman is not to be talked of, said Pericles,[1] himself a much-talked-of man), that publicity in women is detestable. Anonymity runs in their blood. The desire to be veiled still possesses them. They are not even now as concerned about the health of their fame as men are, and, speaking generally, will pass a tombstone or a signpost without feeling an irresistible desire to cut their names on it, as Alf, Bert or Chas. must do in obedience to their instinct, which murmurs if it sees a fine woman go by, or even a dog, Ce chien est à moi.[2] And, of course, it may not be a dog, I thought, remembering Parliament Square, the Sieges Allee and other avenues; it may be a piece of land or a man with curly black hair. It is one of the great advantages of being a woman that one can pass even a very fine negress without wishing to make an Englishwoman of her.

That woman, then, who was born with a gift of poetry in the sixteenth century, was an unhappy woman, a woman at strife against herself. All the conditions of her life, all her own instincts, were hostile to the state of mind which is needed to set free whatever is in the brain. But what is the state of mind that is most propitious to the act of creation, I asked. Can one come by any notion of the state that furthers and makes possible that strange activity? Here I opened the volume containing the Tragedies of Shakespeare. What was Shakespeare's state of mind, for instance, when he wrote *Lear* and *Antony and Cleopatra*? It was certainly the state of mind most favourable to poetry that there has ever existed. But Shakespeare himself said nothing about it. We

---

9. The pseudonyms of Charlotte Brontë (1816–1855), English novelist; Mary Ann Evans (1819–1880), English novelist; and Amandine Aurore Lucie Dupin, Baronne Dudevant (1804–1876), French novelist.

1. Athenian statesman, died 439 B.C.E.
2. That dog is mine (French).

only know casually and by chance that he "never blotted a line."[3] Nothing indeed was ever said by the artist himself about his state of mind until the eighteenth century perhaps. Rousseau[4] perhaps began it. At any rate, by the nineteenth century self-consciousness had developed so far that it was the habit for men of letters to describe their minds in confessions and autobiographies. Their lives also were written, and their letters were printed after their deaths. Thus, though we do not know what Shakespeare went through when he wrote *Lear*, we do know what Carlyle[5] went through when he wrote the *French Revolution*; what Flaubert went through when he wrote *Madame Bovary*; what Keats was going through when he tried to write poetry against the coming of death and the indifference of the world.

And one gathers from this enormous modern literature of confession and self-analysis that to write a work of genius is almost always a feat of prodigious difficulty. Everything is against the likelihood that it will come from the writer's mind whole and entire. Generally material circumstances are against it. Dogs will bark; people will interrupt; money must be made; health will break down. Further, accentuating all these difficulties and making them harder to bear is the world's notorious indifference. It does not ask people to write poems and novels and histories; it does not need them. It does not care whether Flaubert finds the right word or whether Carlyle scrupulously verifies this or that fact. Naturally, it will not pay for what it does not want. And so the writer, Keats, Flaubert, Carlyle, suffers, especially in the creative years of youth, every form of distraction and discouragement. A curse, a cry of agony, rises from those books of analysis and confession. "Mighty poets in their misery dead"[6]—that is the burden of their song. If anything comes through in spite of all this, it is a miracle, and probably no book is born entire and uncrippled as it was conceived.

But for women, I thought, looking at the empty shelves, these

3. According to the English playwright Ben Jonson (1573–1637) in *Timber: Or Discoveries Made Upon Men and Matter*.

4. Jean-Jacques Rousseau (1712–1778), with his *Confessions*, which were published posthumously.

5. Thomas Carlyle (1795–1881), Scottish essayist.

6. Line 116 from the poem "Resolution and Independence" by William Wordsworth (1770–1850), English poet.

difficulties were infinitely more formidable. In the first place, to have a room of her own, let alone a quiet room or a sound-proof room, was out of the question, unless her parents were exceptionally rich or very noble, even up to the beginning of the nineteenth century. Since her pin money, which depended on the good will of her father, was only enough to keep her clothed, she was debarred from such alleviations as came even to Keats or Tennyson or Carlyle, all poor men, from a walking tour, a little journey to France, from the separate lodging which, even if it were miserable enough, sheltered them from the claims and tyrannies of their families. Such material difficulties were formidable; but much worse were the immaterial. The indifference of the world which Keats and Flaubert and other men of genius have found so hard to bear was in her case not indifference but hostility. The world did not say to her as it said to them, Write if you choose; it makes no difference to me. The world said with a guffaw, Write? What's the good of your writing? Here the psychologists of Newnham and Girton might come to our help, I thought, looking again at the blank spaces on the shelves. For surely it is time that the effect of discouragement upon the mind of the artist should be measured, as I have seen a dairy company measure the effect of ordinary milk and Grade A milk upon the body of the rat. They set two rats in cages side by side, and of the two one was furtive, timid and small, and the other was glossy, bold and big. Now what food do we feed women as artists upon? I asked, remembering, I suppose, that dinner of prunes and custard.[7] To answer that question I had only to open the evening paper and to read that Lord Birkenhead is of opinion—but really I am not going to trouble to copy out Lord Birkenhead's opinion upon the writing of women. What Dean Inge says I will leave in peace. The Harley Street specialist may be allowed to rouse the echoes of Harley Street with his vociferations without raising a hair on my head.[8] I will quote, however, Mr. Oscar Browning, because Mr. Oscar Browning

7. In contrast with the lavish dinner—partridge and wine—Woolf ate as a guest in a men's college at Cambridge University described in Chapter 1.

8. Lord Birkenhead's, Dean Inge's, and Mr. Oscar Browning's opinions of women are alluded to but not discussed in Chapter 2. Fashionable London doctors have their offices in Harley Street.

was a great figure in Cambridge at one time, and used to examine the students at Girton and Newnham.[9] Mr. Oscar Browning was wont to declare "that the impression left on his mind, after looking over any set of examination papers, was that, irrespective of the marks he might give, the best woman was intellectually the inferior of the worst man." After saying that Mr. Browning went back to his rooms—and it is this sequel that endears him and makes him a human figure of some bulk and majesty—he went back to his rooms and found a stable-boy lying on the sofa—"a mere skeleton, his cheeks were cavernous and sallow, his teeth were black, and he did not appear to have the full use of his limbs. . . . 'That's Arthur' [said Mr. Browning]. 'He's a dear boy really and most high-minded.' " The two pictures always seem to me to complete each other. And happily in this age of biography the two pictures often do complete each other, so that we are able to interpret the opinions of great men not only by what they say, but by what they do.

But though this is possible now, such opinions coming from the lips of important people must have been formidable enough even fifty years ago. Let us suppose that a father from the highest motives did not wish his daughter to leave home and become writer, painter or scholar. "See what Mr. Oscar Browning says," he would say; and there was not only Mr. Oscar Browning; there was the *Saturday Review*; there was Mr. Greg[1]—the "essentials of a woman's being," said Mr. Greg emphatically, "are that *they are supported by, and they minister to, men*"—there was an enormous body of masculine opinion to the effect that nothing could be expected of women intellectually. Even if her father did not read out loud these opinions, any girl could read them for herself; and the reading, even in the nineteenth century, must have lowered her vitality, and told profoundly upon her work. There would always have been that assertion—you cannot do this, you are incapable of doing that—to protest against, to overcome. Probably for a novelist this germ is no longer of much effect; for there have been women novelists of merit. But for painters it must still have some sting in it; and for musicians, I imagine, is

9. Oscar Browning (1837–1923) was a historian and lecturer at King's College, Cambridge.

1. Sir W. W. Greg (1875–1959), literary scholar.

even now active and poisonous in the extreme. The women composer stands where the actress stood in the time of Shakespeare. Nick Greene, I thought, remembering the story I had made about Shakespeare's sister, said that a woman acting put him in mind of a dog dancing. Johnson repeated the phrase two hundred years later of women preaching.[2] And here, I said, opening a book about music, we have the very words used again in this year of grace, 1928, of women who try to write music. "Of Mlle. Germaine Tailleferre one can only repeat Dr. Johnson's dictum concerning a woman preacher, transposed into terms of music. "Sir, a woman's composing is like a dog's walking on his hind legs. It is not done well, but you are surprised to find it done at all.' "[3] So accurately does history repeat itself.

Thus, I concluded, shutting Mr. Oscar Browning's life and pushing away the rest, it is fairly evident that even in the nineteenth century a woman was not encouraged to be an artist. On the contrary, she was snubbed, slapped, lectured and exhorted. Her mind must have been strained and her vitality lowered by the need of opposing this, of disproving that. For here again we come within range of that very interesting and obscure masculine complex which has had so much influence upon the woman's movement; that deep-seated desire, not so much that *she* shall be inferior as that *he* shall be superior, which plants him wherever one looks, not only in front of the arts, but barring the way to politics too, even when the risk to himself seems infinitesimal and the suppliant humble and devoted. Even Lady Bessborough, I remembered, with all her passion for politics, must humbly bow herself and write to Lord Granville Leveson-Gower[4]: " . . . notwithstanding all my violence in politics and talking so much on that subject, I perfectly agree with you that no woman has any business to meddle with that or any other serious business, farther than giving her opinion (if she is ask'd)." And so she goes on to spend her enthusiasm where it meets with no obsta-

2. Samuel Johnson (1709–1784), oft-quoted English writer; the quote appears in James Boswell's *Life of Samuel Johnson, L.L.D.*

3. *A Survey of Contemporary Music*, Cecil Gray, p. 246 [Woolf's note].

4. The correspondence of Lady Bessborough (1761–1821) and Lord Granville Leveson-Gower was published in 1916 as his *Private Correspondence, 1781 to 1821.*

cle whatsoever upon that immensely important subject, Lord Granville's maiden speech in the House of Commons. The spectacle is certainly a strange one, I thought. The history of men's opposition to women's emancipation is more interesting perhaps than the story of that emancipation itself. An amusing book might be made of it if some young student at Girton or Newnham would collect examples and deduce a theory—but she would need thick gloves on her hands, and bars to protect her of solid gold.

But what is amusing now, I recollected, shutting Lady Bessborough, had to be taken in desperate earnest once. Opinions that one now pastes in a book labelled cock-a-doodle-dum and keeps for reading to select audiences on summer nights once drew tears, I can assure you. Among your grandmothers and great-grandmothers there were many that wept their eyes out. Florence Nightingale shrieked aloud in her agony.[5] Moreover, it is all very well for you, who have got yourselves to college and enjoy sitting-rooms—or is it only bed-sitting-rooms?—of your own to say that genius should disregard such opinions; that genius should be above caring what is said of it. Unfortunately, it is precisely the men or women of genius who mind most what is said of them. Remember Keats. Remember the words he had cut on his tombstone.[6] Think of Tennyson;[7] think— but I need hardly multiply instances of the undeniable, if very unfortunate, fact that it is the nature of the artist to mind excessively what is said about him. Literature is strewn with the wreckage of men who have minded beyond reason the opinions of others.

And this susceptibility of theirs is doubly unfortunate, I thought, returning again to my original enquiry into what state of mind is most propitious for creative work, because the mind of an artist, in order to achieve the prodigious effort of freeing whole and entire the work that is in him, must be incandescent, like Shakespeare's mind, I conjectured, looking at the book which lay open at *Antony and Cleopatra*. There must be no obstacle in it, no foreign matter unconsumed.

5. See *Cassandra*, by Florence Nightingale, printed in *The Cause*, by R. Strachey [Woolf's note]. Florence Nightingale (1820–1910), English nurse and philanthropist.

6. Keats's epitaph reads "Here lies one whose name was writ in water."

7. Alfred, Lord Tennyson (1809–1892), English poet, was highly sensitive to reviews of his poetry.

For though we say that we know nothing about Shakespeare's state of mind, even as we say that, we are saying something about Shakespeare's state of mind. The reason perhaps why we know so little of Shakespeare—compared with Donne or Ben Jonson or Milton—is that his grudges and spites and antipathies are hidden from us. We are not held up by some "revelation" which reminds us of the winter. All desire to protest, to preach, to proclaim an injury, to pay off a score, to make the world the witness of some hardship or grievance was fired out of him and consumed. Therefore his poetry flows from him free and unimpeded. If ever a human being got his work expressed completely, it was Shakespeare. If ever a mind was incandescent, unimpeded, I thought, turning again to the bookcase, it was Shakespeare's mind.

1928

William Zinsser

b. 1922

Zinsser had an early career as a journalist and only began teaching English at Yale University in 1970, when he was forty-eight. He is most famous for his book On Writing Well *(1976), which dispenses practical advice on the craft and has sold nearly a million copies. This essay was first published in* Blair and Ketchum's Country Journal, *an odd monthly that included articles on a wide range of topics, mostly on practical living. His original audience was probably closer in age and outlook to the parents of the college students he describes than to the students themselves, so you might consider whether Zinsser is trying to persuade his readers to take action or just to inform them about what the next generation is going through. This essay was written in 1979, following a severe recession in 1974–75 and during a period of high inflation and unemployment. Since then, the cost of a college education has risen more than twice as fast as inflation.*

College Pressures

Dear Carlos: I desperately need a dean's excuse for my chem midterm which will begin in about 1 hour. All I can say is that I totally blew it this week. I've fallen incredibly, inconceivably behind.

Carlos: Help! I'm anxious to hear from you. I'll be in my room and won't leave it until I hear from you. Tomorrow is the last day for . . .

Carlos: I left town because I started bugging out again. I stayed up all night to finish a take-home make-up exam & am typing it to hand in on the 10th. It was due on the 5th. P.S. I'm going to the dentist. Pain is pretty bad.

Carlos: Probably by Friday I'll be able to get back to my studies. Right now I'm going to take a long walk. This whole thing has taken a lot out of me.

Carlos: I'm really up the proverbial creek. The problem is I really *bombed* the history final. Since I need that course for my major I . . .

Carlos: Here follows a tale of woe. I went home this weekend, had to help my Mom, & caught a fever so didn't have much time to study. My professor . . .

Carlos: Aargh! Trouble. Nothing original but everything's piling up at once. To be brief, my job interview . . .

Hey Carlos, good news! I've got mononucleosis.

Who are these wretched supplicants, scribbling notes so laden with anxiety, seeking such miracles of postponement and balm? They are men and women who belong to Branford College, one of the twelve residential colleges at Yale University, and the messages are just a few of the hundreds that they left for their dean, Carlos Hortas—often slipped under his door at 4 A.M.—last year.

But students like the ones who wrote those notes can also be found on campuses from coast to coast—especially in New England and at many other private colleges across the country that have high academic standards and highly motivated students. Nobody could doubt that the notes are real. In their urgency and their gallows humor they are authentic voices of a generation that is panicky to succeed.

My own connection with the message writers is that I am master of Branford College. I live in its Gothic quadrangle and know the students well. (We have 485 of them.) I am privy to their hopes and fears—and also to their stereo music and their piercing cries in the dead of night ("Does anybody *ca-a-are?*"). If they went to Carlos to ask how to get through tomorrow, they come to me to ask how to get through the rest of their lives.

Mainly I try to remind them that the road ahead is a long one and that it will have more unexpected turns than they think. There will be plenty of time to change jobs, change careers, change whole attitudes and approaches. They don't want to hear such liberating news. They want a map—right now—that they can follow unswervingly to career security, financial security, Social Security and, presumably, a prepaid grave.

What I wish for all students is some release from the clammy grip of the future. I wish them a chance to savor each segment of their education as an experience in itself and not as a grim preparation for the next step. I wish them the right to experiment, to trip and fall, to learn that defeat is as instructive as victory and is not the end of the world.

My wish, of course, is naive. One of the few rights that America does not proclaim is the right to fail. Achievement is the national god, venerated in our media—the million-dollar athlete, the wealthy executive—and glorified in our praise of possessions. In the presence of such a potent state religion, the young are growing up old.

I see four kinds of pressure working on college students today: economic pressure, parental pressure, peer pressure, and self-induced pressure. It is easy to look around for villains—to blame the colleges for charging too much money, the professors for assigning too much work, the parents for pushing their children too far, the students for driving themselves too hard. But there are no villains; only victims.

"In the late 1960s," one dean told me, "the typical question that I got from students was 'Why is there so much suffering in the world?' or 'How can I make a contribution?' Today it's 'Do you think it would look better for getting into law school if I did a double major in history and political science, or just majored in one of them?' " Many other deans confirmed this pattern. One said: "They're trying to find an edge—the intangible something that will look better on paper if two students are about equal."

Note the emphasis on looking better. The transcript has become a sacred document, the passport to security. How one appears on paper is more important than how one appears in person. *A* is for Admirable and *B* is for Borderline, even though, in Yale's official system of grading, *A* means "excellent" and *B* means "very good." Today, looking very good is no longer good enough, especially for students who hope to go on to law school or medical school. They know that entrance into the better schools will be an entrance into the better law firms and better medical practices where they will make a lot of money. They also know that the odds are harsh. Yale

Law School, for instance, matriculates 170 students from an applicant pool of 3,700; Harvard enrolls 550 from a pool of 7,000.

It's all very well for those of us who write letters of recommendation for our students to stress the qualities of humanity that will make them good lawyers or doctors. And it's nice to think that admission officers are really reading our letters and looking for the extra dimension of commitment or concern. Still, it would be hard for a student not to visualize these officers shuffling so many transcripts studded with *A*s that they regard a *B* as positively shameful.

The pressure is almost as heavy on students who just want to graduate and get a job. Long gone are the days of the "gentleman's C," when students journeyed through college with a certain relaxation, sampling a wide variety of courses—music, art, philosophy, classics, anthropology, poetry, religion—that would send them out as liberally educated men and women. If I were an employer I would rather employ graduates who have this range and curiosity than those who narrowly pursued safe subjects and high grades. I know countless students whose inquiring minds exhilarate me. I like to hear the play of their ideas. I don't know if they are getting *A*s or *C*s, and I don't care. I also like them as people. The country needs them, and they will find satisfying jobs. I tell them to relax. They can't.

Nor can I blame them. They live in a brutal economy. Tuition, room, and board at most private colleges now comes to at least $7,000, not counting books and fees. This might seem to suggest that the colleges are getting rich. But they are equally battered by inflation. Tuition covers only 60 percent of what it costs to educate a student, and ordinarily the remainder comes from what colleges receive in endowments, grants, and gifts. Now the remainder keeps being swallowed by the cruel costs—higher every year—of just opening the doors. Heating oil is up. Insurance is up. Postage is up. Health-premium costs are up. Everything is up. Deficits are up. We are witnessing in America the creation of a brotherhood of paupers—colleges, parents, and students, joined by the common bond of debt.

Today it is not unusual for a student, even if he works part time at college and full time during the summer, to accrue $5,000 in loans after four years—loans that he must start to repay within one year after graduation. Exhorted at commencement to go forth into the world, he is already behind as he goes forth. How could he not feel under pressure throughout college to prepare for this day of reckoning? I have used "he," incidentally, only for brevity. Women at Yale are under no less pressure to justify their expensive education to themselves, their parents, and society. In fact, they are probably under more pressure. For although they leave college superbly equipped to bring fresh leadership to traditionally male jobs, society hasn't yet caught up with this fact.

Along with economic pressure goes parental pressure. Inevitably, the two are deeply intertwined.

I see many students taking pre-medical courses with joyless tenacity. They go off to their labs as if they were going to the dentist. It saddens me because I know them in other corners of their life as cheerful people.

"Do you want to go to medical school?" I ask them.

"I guess so," they say, without conviction, or "Not really."

"Then why are you going?"

"Well, my parents want me to be a doctor. They're paying all this money and . . ."

Poor students, poor parents. They are caught in one of the oldest webs of love and duty and guilt. The parents mean well; they are trying to steer their sons and daughters toward a secure future. But the sons and daughters want to major in history or classics or philosophy—subjects with no "practical" value. Where's the payoff on the humanities? It's not easy to persuade such loving parents that the humanities do indeed pay off. The intellectual faculties developed by studying subjects like history and classics—an ability to synthesize and relate, to weigh cause and effect, to see events in perspective—are just the faculties that make creative leaders in business or almost any general field. Still, many fathers would rather put their money on courses that point toward a specific profession—courses that are pre-law, pre-medical, pre-business, or, as I sometimes heard it put, "pre-rich."

But the pressure on students is severe. They are truly torn. One part of them feels obligated to fulfill their parents' expectations; after all, their parents are older and presumably wiser. Another part tells them that the expectations that are right for their parents are not right for them.

I know a student who wants to be an artist. She is very obviously an artist and will be a good one—she has already had several modest local exhibits. Meanwhile she is growing as a well-rounded person and taking humanistic subjects that will enrich the inner resources out of which her art will grow. But her father is strongly opposed. He thinks that an artist is a "dumb" thing to be. The student vacillates and tries to please everybody. She keeps up with her art somewhat furtively and takes some of the "dumb" courses her father wants her to take—at least they are dumb courses for her. She is a free spirit on a campus of tense students—no small achievement in itself—and she deserves to follow her muse.

Peer pressure and self-induced pressure are also intertwined, and they begin almost at the beginning of freshman year.

"I had a freshman student I'll call Linda," one dean told me, "who came in and said she was under terrible pressure because her roommate, Barbara, was much brighter and studied all the time. I couldn't tell her that Barbara had come in two hours earlier to say the same thing about Linda."

The story is almost funny—except that it's not. It's symptomatic of all the pressures put together. When every student thinks every other student is working harder and doing better, the only solution is to study harder still. I see students going off to the library every night after dinner and coming back when it closes at midnight. I wish they would sometimes forget about their peers and go to a movie. I hear the clacking of typewriters in the hours before dawn. I see the tension in their eyes when exams are approaching and papers are due: *"Will I get everything done?"*

Probably they won't. They will get sick. They will get "blocked." They will sleep. They will oversleep. They will bug out. *Hey Carlos, help!*

Part of the problem is that they do more than they are expected to do. A professor will assign five-page papers. Several students will start writing ten-page papers to impress him. Then more students will write ten-page papers, and a few will raise the ante to fifteen. Pity the poor student who is still just doing the assignment.

"Once you have twenty or thirty percent of the student population deliberately overexerting," one dean points out, "it's bad for everybody. When a teacher gets more and more effort from his class, the student who is doing normal work can be perceived as not doing well. The tactic works, psychologically."

Why can't the professor just cut back and not accept longer papers? He can, and he probably will. But by then the term will be half over and the damage done. Grade fever is highly contagious and not easily reversed. Besides, the professor's main concern is with his course. He knows his students only in relation to the course and doesn't know that they are also overexerting in their other courses. Nor is it really his business. He didn't sign up for dealing with the student as a whole person and with all the emotional baggage the student brought along from home. That's what deans, masters, chaplains, and psychiatrists are for.

To some extent this is nothing new: a certain number of professors have always been self-contained islands of scholarship and shyness, more comfortable with books than with people. But the new pauperism has widened the gap still further, for professors who actually like to spend time with students don't have as much time to spend. They also are overexerting. If they are young, they are busy trying to publish in order not to perish, hanging by their finger nails onto a shrinking profession. If they are old and tenured, they are buried under the duties of administering departments—as departmental chairmen or members of committees—that have been thinned out by the budgetary axe.

Ultimately it will be the students' own business to break the circles in which they are trapped. They are too young to be prisoners of their parents' dreams and their classmates' fears. They must be jolted into believing in themselves as unique men and women who have the power to shape their own future.

"Violence is being done to the undergraduate experience," says Carlos Hortas. "College should be open-ended: at the end it should open many, many roads. Instead, students are choosing their goal in advance, and their choices narrow as they go along. It's almost as if they think that the country has been codified in the type of jobs that exist—that they've got to fit into certain slots. Therefore, fit into the best-paying slot.

"They ought to take chances. Not taking chances will lead to a life of colorless mediocrity. They'll be comfortable. But something in the spirit will be missing."

I have painted too drab a portrait of today's students, making them seem a solemn lot. That is only half of their story; if they were so dreary I wouldn't so thoroughly enjoy their company. The other half is that they are easy to like. They are quick to laugh and to offer friendship. They are not introverts. They are unusually kind and are more considerate of one another than any student generation I have known.

Nor are they so obsessed with their studies that they avoid sports and extracurricular activities. On the contrary, they juggle their crowded hours to play on a variety of teams, perform with musical and dramatic groups, and write for campus publications. But this in turn is one more cause of anxiety. There are too many choices. Academically, they have 1,300 courses to select from; outside class they have to decide how much spare time they can spare and how to spend it.

This means that they engage in fewer extracurricular pursuits than their predecessors did. If they want to row on the crew and play in the symphony they will eliminate one; in the '60s they would have done both. They also tend to choose activities that are self-limiting. Drama, for instance, is flourishing in all twelve of Yale's residential colleges as it never has before. Students hurl themselves into these productions—as actors, directors, carpenters, and technicians—with a dedication to create the best possible play, knowing that the day will come when the run will end and they can get back to their studies.

They also can't afford to be the willing slave of organizations like the *Yale Daily News*. Last spring at the one-hundredth anniversary banquet of that paper—whose past chairmen include such once and future kings as Potter Stewart, Kingman Brewster, and William F. Buckley, Jr.[1]—much was made of the fact that the editorial staff used to be small and totally committed and that "Newsies" routinely

1. Potter Stewart (1915–1985), associate justice of the U.S. Supreme Court, 1958–81; Kingman Brewster (1919–1988), president of Yale University, 1963–77, and ambassador to Great Britain, 1977–81; William F. Buckley Jr. (1925–), founder and former editor-in-chief of the conservative journal *National Review*, syndicated columnist, and host of the television program "Firing Line" from its inception in 1966 unil it went off the air in 1999.

worked fifty hours a week. In effect they belonged to a club; Newsies is how they defined themselves at Yale. Today's student will write one or two articles a week, when he can, and he defines himself as a student. I've never heard the word Newsie except at the banquet.

If I have described the modern undergraduate primarily as a driven creature who is largely ignoring the blithe spirit inside who keeps trying to come out and play, it's because that's where the crunch is, not only at Yale but throughout American education. It's why I think we should all be worried about the values that are nurturing a generation so fearful of risk and so goal-obsessed at such an early age.

I tell students that there is no one "right" way to get ahead—that each of them is a different person, starting from a different point and bound for a different destination. I tell them that change is a tonic and that all the slots are not codified nor the frontiers closed. One of my ways of telling them is to invite men and women who have achieved success outside the academic world to come and talk informally with my students during the year. They are heads of companies or ad agencies, editors of magazines, politicians, public officials, television magnates, labor leaders, business executives, Broadway producers, artists, writers, economists, photographers, scientists, historians—a mixed bag of achievers.

I ask them to say a few words about how they got started. The students assume that they started in their present profession and knew all along that it was what they wanted to do. Luckily for me, most of them got into their field by a circuitous route, to their surprise, after many detours. The students are startled. They can hardly conceive of a career that was not pre-planned. They can hardly imagine allowing the hand of God or chance to nudge them down some unforeseen trail.

1979

Biographical Sketches

Maya Angelou (*b. 1928*)   Poet, playwright, director, actress, dancer, Angelou was born Maguerite Johnson and grew up in Stamps, Arkansas, and San Francisco. When she moved to New York in the late 1950s, she joined the Harlem Writers Guild. In 1961 she moved to Cairo, Egypt, to work for the *Arab Observer*, and later to Ghana, to work for the *African Review*. She returned to the United States in 1966 to write for television and work for the Southern Christian Leadership Conference. Her autobiographical *I Know Why the Caged Bird Sings* (1970) was on the *New York Times* best-seller list for two years. She is now Reynolds Professor of American Studies at Wake Forest University in North Carolina and is one of the few U.S. poets to have written and delivered a poem at a presidential inauguration.

Anne Applebaum (*b. 1964*)   Applebaum graduated from Yale University before she took a job in 1988 as a correspondent for the London *Economist*, reporting from Warsaw, Poland. She filed stories on the fall of communism for a number of periodicals and, in 1992, became foreign editor of the London *Spectator* magazine. Her first book was the acclaimed *Between East and West: Across the Border-*

lands of Europe. Now she is a columnist and editor at the Washington *Post.*

Nicholson Baker (*b. 1957*) Born in Rochester, New York, Baker studied at both the Eastman School of Music and Haverford College. He published his first novel, *The Mezzanine,* in 1988. He has published half a dozen novels and three books of nonfiction, including *U and I,* a tribute to John Updike. His distinctive style uses stream of consciousness to explode time; most of his novels cover very little real time and action, spending most of their energy on memories, ponderings, musings, that go on in the mind of his main characters. Most of his nonfiction writing follows disgressions so assiduously that the main thread of an argument is completely obscured. Baker has taken on the task of preserving the physical artifact of books and newspapers in the electronic age. He founded the American Newspaper Repository in 1999 in the hopes of conserving hard copies of past newspapers; most libraries now convert the physical papers to microfilm and destroy the originals.

James Baldwin (*1924–1987*) Baldwin was born in poverty in Harlem, the eldest of nine children. At seventeen, he left home and began writing seriously, ultimately publishing reviews and essays in magazines like *The Nation* and *The Partisan Review* and winning the Rosenwald Fellowship (1948). Baldwin moved to Europe in 1948 and lived largely in Paris for the next ten years. In 1957, he returned to the United States to take part in the civil rights movement. In 1983, Baldwin became Five College Professor of Afro-American Studies at the University of Massachusetts. His most successful novel, *Go Tell It on the Mountain* (1953), treats his early experience as an evangelical preacher. His later works often deal with issues of racism and homosexuality.

Michael Bérubé (*b. 1961*) Bérubé earned his BA from Columbia University in 1982, and a PhD from the University of Virginia in 1989. Now he teaches cultural studies at Penn State University, where he is the Paterno Family Professor in Literature. An expert on postmodern American literature, in dozens of essays and half a dozen books he has become one of the chief proponents of American academe. The conservative intellectual David Horowitz pronounced him among the "101 most dangerous professors in America," a badge Bérubé wears with good humor. Between 2004 and 2007 he authored an award-winning and popular blog focusing on issues of higher education. One of his books, the 1996 *Life as We Know It: A Father, A Family, and an Exceptional Child*, is an account of his raising his son Jamie, a child with Down syndrome.

Judy Brady (*b. 1937*)   Brady was born in San Francisco. When she received her bachelor's degree from the University of Iowa in painting in 1962, she'd already been married for two years. After a divorce, she raised her two daughters on her own, working as a secretary while taking classes at night. Her work for women's rights involved her in political activism, and in 1973 she visited Cuba (which was then nearly off-limits to American citizens) to study the effects of class on social change. Brady is best known for "Why I Want a Wife" and has not published other work widely.

William F. Buckley Jr. (*b. 1925*)   Buckley, born and raised in New York City, served three years in the army during World War II. After the war, he attended Yale University, where he was chairman of the Yale *Daily News*. He founded the *National Review*, a conservative political journal, in 1955 and served as its editor-in-chief until 1990. Besides writing a syndicated newspaper column and hosting the public affairs television show "Firing Line" until it went off the air in 1999, he has written spy novels and books on sailing. Buckley served on the U.S. Information Agency Advisory Commission, 1969–72, and as delegate to the United Nations, 1973 (under Richard Nixon).

Rachel Carson (*1907–1964*)   Born in Springdale, Pennsylvania, Carson studied at Woods Hole Marine Biological Laboratory and received her master's degree in zoology from Johns Hopkins (1932). In 1936, she became the first woman to pass the civil service test and joined the Bureau of Fisheries as a junior biologist. Over the next fifteen years she rose to become editor-in-chief of all publications for the U.S. Fish and Wildlife Service. In her free time, Carson wrote lyrical prose about marine life, publishing two prize-winning books, *The Sea Around Us* and *The Edge of the Sea*. In 1952 Carson resigned from government service to devote herself to her writing. Her most famous work is *Silent Spring* (1962), which exposed the dangers of pesticides, particularly DDT.

Jerry Coyne (*b. 1949*)   Coyne graduated with a BS in biology from the College of William and Mary in 1971 and earned his PhD from Harvard in 1978. Since 1991, he has been a professor of ecology and evolution at the University of Chicago. His 2004 book, *Speciation*, cowritten with Allen Orr, is the standard text on that subject.

Richard Dawkins (*b. 1941*)   Dawkins was born in Kenya and moved with his family to England when he was eight. Between 1962 and 1989, he has earned four degrees from Balliol College, Oxford. His 1976 book *The Selfish Gene* helped to explain the role of genetics in evolution. Currently, he holds the Charles Simonyi Chair for the Public Understanding of Science at Oxford University.

Joan Didion (*b. 1934*)   Born in Sacramento to a fifth-generation California family, Didion wrote her first story at age five and has continued to write fiction and nonfiction ever since. She graduated from the University of California, Berkeley, in 1956 and moved to New York, where she went to work at *Vogue* magazine. In 1963 she published her first novel, *Run River*, and in 1968, *Slouching Towards Bethlehem*, an essay collection that demonstrates her interest in social disorder and individual dysfunction. Didion continues to write essays and novels on this theme.

Annie Dillard (*b. 1945*)   Dillard was born and raised in Pittsburgh and went to college at Hollins in Roanoke, Virginia, where she earned both a BA (1967) and an MA (1968). She married her writing teacher, and, while recovering from an illness in Roanoke, she penned a reflective, Thoreau-like book on her observations of the natural world surrounding her as they changed through the seasons. This volume, *Pilgrim at Tinker Creek*, won the Pulitzer Prize, among other awards, in 1975 and instantly launched Dillard into the forefront of American essayists. From 1974 through 1985, she was a contributing editor to *Harper's* magazine. Most of her dozen books she describes as "nonfiction narratives," but she has also published poetry and fiction. One critic has suggested that her writing expresses "the mystic's wonder at the physical world . . . in beautiful, near-biblical prose."

Frederick Douglass (*c. 1817–1895*) Douglass, the son of an unknown white man and Sarah Bailey (a slave of African and Native American ancestry), was born Frederick Augustus Washington Bailey near Easton, Maryland, and spent his childhood and early adult years as a slave. He unsuccessfully tried to escape, was jailed, worked as a ship's calker, and finally, on September 3, 1838, succeeded in fleeing the South. He assumed the name Douglass to elude recapture. Impressed by his speaking skills, William Garrison, the great abolitionist, hired Douglass as an agent of the Massachusetts Anti-Slavery Society. Douglass published his autobiography in 1845 and shortly thereafter left America for England and Ireland to avoid claims made upon him by his former master. When he returned in 1847 he bought his freedom legally and started his own abolitionist paper, *North Star.* He fled to Canada when his association with the militant abolitionist John Brown became known but returned to the United States after the Civil War started. He helped raise black regiments in Massachusetts and advised Lincoln during the war. After the war, he worked for the rights of freed slaves. He was a longtime supporter of women's rights, and he died while attending a conference on women's suffrage.

Barbara Ehrenreich (*b. 1941*) Ehrenreich, a feminist and socialist, received her PhD in biology and published initially on inequities in health care; she now frequently writes on the politics of class and gender. She has published many books, including the *New York Times* best-seller *Nickle and Dimed*, and writes regularly for *Harper's* magazine, *Time*, and *The Nation.* She is also an honorary co-chair of the Democratic Socialists of America's National Political Committee.

Louise Erdrich (*b. 1954*) Part Chippewa and part German-American, Erdrich entered Dartmouth College the same year that it opened its now famous Native American Studies department, headed by her future husband and collaborator, Michael Dorris. She earned an MA from Johns Hopkins, and published her first novel, *Love Medicine*, in 1984. She's published nine other novels, three books of poetry, and children's stories, including the novel *The Birchbark House*, a sort of response to *Little House on the Prairie*.

Stephen Jay Gould (*1941–2002*)   Born in New York, Gould spent his entire career as a professor and curator at Harvard University, beginning in 1967. As a professional paleontologist, he is best known for contributing the idea of "punctuated equilibrium" to the theory of evolution. According to Gould, species tend to remain mostly in a state of equilibrium over time, and evolutionary changes occur in quick, short bursts. He published many highly regarded academic studies, but is best remembered for his essays, most of which were written for his monthly column in the magazine *Natural History*. In these, Gould explored a few themes so persistently that they have come to be associated with him. The first is the general messiness of the universe, the odd, unfitting, gerrymandered nature of the world. Another is the recognition that science is embedded in culture; that it arises from and manifests itself according to the cultural parameters of its gestation. Also, perhaps most important, Gould is justly known for combating the misuse of science in promoting injustices, such as racism and sexism. He was diagnosed with cancer in 1982 and, despite a poor prognosis, was cured of the disease. He died in 2002 of a different type of cancer.

Angelina Grimké (*1805–1879*)   Although born to a wealthy slave-holding family in Charleston, South Carolina, Grimké abhorred slavery and moved to Philadelphia in 1829, where she wrote a number of pamphlets urging Southerners to abolish the institution. Through the American Anti-Slavery Society, she began meeting with small groups of women and eventually giving lectures on abolition to large audiences. A persuasive speaker, Grimké was one of the first American women to speak publicly on the issues of slavery and women's rights. In 1838, she married a fellow abolitionist and retired from public life.

Sam Harris (*b. 1967*)   Harris, who has a BA in philosophy from Stanford University, is currently at work on his PhD in neuroscience, a study of the brain. After 9/11, he began writing down his criticisms of religion, which he considered largely responsible for that event, and in 2004 he published *The End of Faith: Religion, Terror, and the Future of Reason*. The book argues that even moderate religiosity creates an atmosphere that makes it impossible to successfully oppose radical, violent Islam. The controversial book spent thirty-three weeks on the *New York Times* Best-Seller list, and Harris followed it up with the 2006 *Letter to a Christian Nation*.

S. I. Hayakawa (*1906–1992*)   Born in Vancouver, Canada, of Japanese parents, Hayakawa received his PhD in English and American literature in 1935. He published a popular treatment of semantics, *Language in Thought and Action*, in 1939 and subsequently wrote and lectured widely on this topic. In the midst of student protests, he became president of San Francisco State College (1968) and gained a reputation for his uncompromising opposition to leftist student activism. He was elected to the U.S. Senate in 1986 as a Republican and served one term.

Jim Hightower (*b. 1943*)   Born in Denison, Texas, Hightower graduated from North Texas State University in 1965 and then studied for two years at Columbia University. After a number of jobs in the 1970s, including editor of the alternative paper the *Texas Observer*, he was elected to the position of Commissioner of the Department of Agriculture in Texas, where he remained until 1991, shortly before George W. Bush won the gubernatorial race. Absenting himself from America's two main political parties, Hightower calls himself a populist, and in that capacity he publishes political books and a newsletter, travels the lecture circuit, and hosts his own radio show.

Zora Neale Hurston (*1903–1960*)   Hurston was raised in the all-black town of Eatonville, Florida. At sixteen, she joined a traveling theater company and made her way to New York City. She graduated from Barnard College (1928), where she had studied anthropology with Franz Boaz, and then pursued a graduate degree at Columbia and did field work on African American folklore in the South. After collaborating with Langston Hughes on a play that was never finished, she published her first novel, *Jonah's Gourd Vine*

(1934), which offered an unsentimental treatment of life among black Americans. She continued to write fiction (including *Their Eyes Were Watching God*, 1937) and anthropological studies. Hurston's work was neglected for many years (she died in obscurity in Florida), but since the late 1970s there has been a resurgence of interest in and a renewed appreciation of her contribution to literature and her role in the Harlem Renaissance.

Molly Ivins (*1944–2007*)　Ivins was born in California, grew up in Houston, graduated from Smith College then earned a master's in journalism from Columbia University. She also spent a year studying in Paris before she took her first job at the *Houston Chronicle*. While writing for the *Texas Observer*, she was hired by the *New York Times*, where she was the Rocky Mountain bureau chief until 1982. She wrote for the *Dallas Times-Herald* and the *Fort Worth Star-Telegram* before becoming an independent columnist, circulated in hundreds of newspapers nationwide. Most of her books are collections of her best columns, and she was known for her characteristic down-home, no-nonsense style of humorous commentary, which made famous a number of Texas aphorisms, such as *You Got to Dance With Them What Brung You*, the title of one of her popular books. She died of breast cancer in 2007 after an eight-year battle with the disease.

Thomas Jefferson (*1743–1826*)　In 1776, Thomas Jefferson, Virginia's delegate to the Second Continental Congress, drafted the Declaration of Independence. He was elected governor of Virginia in 1779 and in 1784 was appointed minister to France. He became George Washington's secretary of state on his return (1790–93), served as vice president under John Adams (1797–1801), and was elected president in 1800, after a rancorous campaign against his rival, Aaron Burr. His greatest act as president (1801–1809) was probably the successful conclusion of the Louisiana Purchase (1803), which doubled the size of the nation. After two terms as president, he retired to Monticello, the home he had designed in Virginia, where he made continual improvements to his estate, entertained widely, and kept up a voluminous correspondence. His extravagant habits led him to incur enormous debt, and on his death his belongings were all absorbed by creditors, except for his extensive library, which was purchased by the federal government and forms the foundation for the collection of the Library of Congress. Jefferson's legacy is contradictory. He vigorously opposed the national debt but was responsible for a huge increase through the Louisiana Purchase and was himself personally profligate; and while enlightened for his time on the issue of slavery, he was himself a slaveholder and freed only five slaves, his children by Sally Hemings, his slave and mistress.

Robert F. Kennedy (*1925–1968*)   Born into the wealthy and powerful Kennedy family in Massachusetts, Robert was the seventh of nine children, the younger brother of the promising Joe and John Kennedy, and older brother of Ted Kennedy, now a U.S. Senator. He left Harvard to join the navy in 1944 during World War II, eventually graduating from Harvard and then the University of Virginia Law School in 1951. He worked first for the Department of Justice and then for the Senate, a position he resigned in protest of Senator Joseph McCarthy's notorious methods of pursuing communists. Again working for the Senate, he prosecuted leaders of the Teamsters Union, including Jimmy Hoffa, in 1957. He chaired John Kennedy's presidential campaign and was appointed attorney general by his brother when he was elected. A year after John Kennedy was assassinated in 1963, Robert was elected to the Senate by the State of New York. He ran for president himself in 1968 and was assassinated shortly after winning the California Democratic primary.

Martin Luther King Jr. (*1929–1968*)   King, leader of the civil rights movement in the 1950s and 1960s, was born in Atlanta, Georgia, the son and grandson of Baptist ministers. He entered Morehouse College at fifteen and studied theology at Crozer Theological Seminary, where he became acquainted with Mohandas Gandhi's philosophy of nonviolent protest. He was ordained for the ministry and earned a PhD in theology at Boston University. In 1954, he moved to his wife Coretta Scott's home state of Alabama, where he became pastor of the Dexter Avenue Baptist Church in Montgomery. With Rosa Parks's 1955 arrest for refusing to give up her seat on a bus to a white rider and the bus boycott that followed, King was catapulted to the forefront of the civil rights movement. He founded the Southern Christian Leadership Conference; worked for the passage of the 1964 Civil Rights Act, the 1965 Voting Rights Act, and the 1968 Open Housing Act; and was awarded the Nobel Peace Prize in 1964 for his civil rights work. On April 4, 1968, he was assassinated in Memphis, Tennessee.

Maxine Hong Kingston (*b. 1940*)   Born in Stockton, California, the daughter of Chinese immigrants, Kingston spoke Cantonese before she spoke English, but by the age of nine she was writing poems and stories in her adopted tongue. At the University of California, Berkeley, Kingston first studied engineering but soon switched to English literature. In 1964 she married Earl Kingston, an aspiring actor, and they moved to Hawaii, where Kingston held a series of teaching jobs. In 1976, while teaching creative writing at the Mid-Pacific Institute, Kingston published her first book, *The Woman Warrior*, which won the 1976 National Book Critics Circle Award for nonfiction. Her next book, *China Men* (1980), won the American Book Award for nonfiction. Kingston has published four other books, *Hawaii One Summer* (1987), *Tripmaster Monkey: His Fake Book* (1989), *To Be the Poet* (2002), and *The Fifth Book of Peace* (2006).

Jonathan Kozol (*b. 1936*)   A Rhodes scholar and Harvard graduate, Kozol moved to a poor black neighborhood in Boston in 1964 to become a fourth-grade teacher in the public schools. He was fired in 1967 for reading a poem by Langston Hughes to his class. His book *Death at an Early Age* (1967), which gives an account of this experience, was awarded a National Book Award in 1968. In 1980 he designed a literacy program for the Cleveland Public Library that became a model for the state library system of California. Kozol continues to write widely on social inequality and illiteracy, publishing such books as *Rachel and Her Children* (1988), *Savage Inequalities* (1991), *Amazing Grace* (1995), *Ordinary Resurrections* (2000), and *The Shame of the Nation* (2005).

Lewis Lapham (*b. 1935*)   Lapham is the great-grandson of one of the founders of Texaco, and his grandfather was mayor of San Francisco. He attended Yale University (BA in 1956) and Cambridge before working for the *San Francisco Chronicle*, the *New York Herald-Tribune*, and the *Saturday Evening Post*. He became a managing editor of *Harper's* magazine in 1971, then editor in 1975, a post that he held until his semiretirement thirty years later. During that span he wrote a monthly column for the magazine and numerous books on public affairs. Now he edits a history journal, *Lapham's Quarterly*, which is scheduled to be launched in fall 2007.

Abraham Lincoln (*1809–1865*) Lincoln was born to barely literate parents in Kentucky, which was then the frontier. He attended school only sporadically but studied on his own and developed a passion for reading. He passed the Illinois bar in 1836 and served in the Illinois state legislature for four terms, before being elected in 1846 to one term in the U.S. House of Representataives. Lincoln became the candidate for the U.S. Senate in Illinois's newly formed Republican Party, and although he lost that campaign, he gained national recognition for his oratory in the Lincoln-Douglas debates. He was elected president in 1860, and by the time he took office, seven southern states had seceded from the Union. As president, he waged the Civil War to reunite the nation and issued the Emancipation Proclamation (1863), which freed the slaves. He was assassinated on April 15, 1865, by John Wilkes Booth, a fanatical advocate of slavery.

Bret Lott (*b. 1958*) Lott was born in California, earned degrees from California State University and the University of Massachusetts, Amherst (MFA in 1984). He is best known as a fiction writer, and published his first novel, *The Man Who Owned Vermont*, in 1987. His third novel, *Jewel*, first published in 1991, was chosen by Oprah Winfrey for her book club. All of Lott's fiction is characterized by attention to the minute details of human relations, especially within the family, and the sometimes oblique symbolic gestures by which people—even intimates—communicate with each other. He is the editor of *The Southern Review* and teaches creative writing at the College of Charleston.

Thomas Lynch (*b. 1948*)   Lynch, born in Detroit, earned a certificate in mortuary science from Wayne State University. He is an undertaker in Milford, Michigan, and he is also a poet and essayist. His first volume, *Skating with Heather Grace*, was published in 1986 and was followed by two other books of poems. His first book of essays, *The Undertaking: Life Studies from the Dismal Trade* (1998), won the American Book Award and was nominated for the National Book Award. Lynch travels often to County Clare, Ireland, and that country and his native Roman Catholicism are diffused throughout his work, nearly as thoroughly as his unusual perspective as a mortician. *Bodies in Motion and at Rest: On Metaphor and Mortality* was published in 2000.

Malcolm X (*1925–1965*)   Born Malcolm Little in Lansing, Michigan, Malcolm X was the son of an outspoken critic of racism whose house was burned down by the Ku Klux Klan and who was likely murdered for his views. After his mother was institutionalized for mental illness, Malcolm spent time in detention homes and in 1946 moved to Boston to live with his sister. In Boston, he was arrested for burglary and sent to prison, where he embarked upon a campaign of self-education and joined the Nation of Islam. On his release in 1952, he became a key figure in the Nation of Islam, lecturing widely on white exploitation of blacks and calling for black self-dependence, black separatism, and black pride. He left the Nation of Islam in 1964, after making disparaging comments about Martin Luther King Jr. A pilgrimage to Mecca in 1964 inspired him to convert to orthodox Islam and to recant his more virulent antiwhite positions. He was shot to death at a rally in Harlem by three Black Muslims, members of a rival group.

N. Scott Momaday (*b. 1934*)   Navarre Scott Momaday, of the Kiowa tribe, was born in Oklahoma but was raised on reservations in Arizona. His parents were teachers and, after earning his BA from the University of New Mexico, he followed them into that profession. Eventually, he returned to school to earn a PhD in literature from Stanford University. In 1969, his first novel, *House Made of Dawn*, won the Pulitzer Prize, and led to an appointment teaching Native American literature at the University of California, Berkeley.

He followed his initial novel with books of essays, Kiowa tales, poetry, and memoirs. He is also a painter and printmaker.

George Orwell (*1903–1950*)   Orwell was born Eric Arthur Blair, the
son of a minor British official in the India service. After being educated at Eton as a scholarship pupil, Blair went out to Burma (1922)
as a policeman. That experience informs his first novel, *Burmese
Days* (1934), and one of his most famous essays, "Shooting an Elephant" (1936). Disgusted by British imperialism, he returned to
England, where he resigned his commission and dropped out, living
with the poor in cheap lodgings and on the road, from which experience he produced *Down and Out in London and Paris* (1933). Like
many in the 1930s, Orwell embraced socialism, which he advocated
for the rest of his life. But his experiences during the Spanish Civil
War—he went to report on the war and remained to fight on the
side of the Republicans—left him disenchanted with the Communists, who had attempted to squeeze out their rivals in the Republican forces. His disgust with Soviet communism informs his two
most popular works, the novels *Animal Farm* (1945) and *1984*
(1949). He died of tuberculosis shortly after the publication of *1984*.

Leonard Pitts (*b. 1957*)   Pitts grew up in South Central Los Angeles. He entered the University of Southern California at the age of
fifteen, and graduated in 1977 with a degree in English. He embarked on a career as a freelance writer, often writing music criticism for a variety of periodicals, and even wrote for Casey Kasem's
popular radio show, *American Top 40*. In 1991, he went to work as
music critic for the *Miami Herald*, winning numerous awards, until,
in 1995, he was promoted to columnist. A series of columns he
wrote from his own experience was published as a book, *Becoming
Dad: Black Men and the Journey to Fatherhood*, in 1999. His column
was syndicated by Knight-Ridder, and he rocketed to national
prominence because of his widely acclaimed essay the day after 9/11.
Today, his column is circulated in 150 newspapers throughout the
country. He won the Pulitzer Prize for Commentary in 2004.

Katha Pollitt (*b. 1949*)   Born in New York City and educated at
Harvard College and the Columbia School for the Arts, Pollitt is a

poet and a witty, incisive, and outspoken critic of rightist politics and social policy. She has taught poetry at Barnard College and the 92nd Street Y in New York, writes a regular column—"Subject to Debate"—for *The Nation*, and contributes poetry and prose to national magazines like *The New Yorker*, *The Atlantic*, *The New Republic*, and *Mother Jones*. Both her essays and her poetry have won many awards, including the National Book Critics Circle Award (for her 1982 book *Antarctic Traveler*) and the National Magazine Award (for her 1992 essay "Why We Read: Canon to the Right of Me").

Ronald Reagan (*1911–2004*)   Born in Tampico, Illinois, and raised in nearby Dixon, Reagan grew up in near poverty, the son of an unsuccessful and alcoholic shoe salesman. He attended Eureka College and after graduation (in 1932) worked as a radio announcer and sportscaster. In 1937, he had a successful screen test and was thereafter cast in a series of movies as a wholesome, genial fellow. During World War II, Reagan served at an army film unit in California and never saw active duty. He was president of the Screen Actors' Guild from 1947 to 1952. Initially a Democrat, he supported the California senatorial campaign of Richard Nixon (1950) and the presidential candidacies of Dwight Eisenhower (1952, 1956) and Richard Nixon (1960) before registering as a Republican in 1962. He was elected governor of California (1966, 1970) on a promise to make government more efficient and accountable and was elected president (1980, 1984) on a platform both fiscally and socially conservative. In 1994, Reagan announced that he had been diagnosed with Alzheimer's disease and withdrew from public life.

Richard Rodriguez (*b. 1944*)   Rodriguez was born in San Francisco to Mexican immigrants. He did not speak English when he entered grammar school, and the course of his education, which he details in the autobiographical *Hunger of Memory: The Education of Richard Rodriguez*, was also a deracination. By the time he was studying at Stanford University (BA 1967), he was largely severed from the culture of his parents. He earned an MA from Columbia in 1969, and began work on his doctorate at the University of California, Berkeley that same year, where he was studying English Renaissance literature. He became disillusioned with the university profession while in London on a Fulbright fellowship; and eventually he refused numerous job offers at colleges in order to pursue his lost ethnicity and a freelance writing career. He wrote *Hunger of Memory*, which launched his successful career as an essayist/memoirist, and much of his writing since is grounded in his own ethnic experiences, especially regarding language. *Days of Obligation: An Argument with My Mexican Father* appeared in 1992, and ten years later his *Brown: The Last Discovery of America* was published.

Richard Rorty (*1931–2007*) Rorty was born in New York to parents politically committed to Leon Trotsky's Marxist views. He was a precocious scholar, enrolling in the University of Chicago at fifteen and graduating from Yale with a PhD in philosophy at twenty-five. Teaching at Wellesley and Princeton, he established a reputation in the Anglo-American school of analytic philosophy, but eventually he developed much more into a philosopher of the continental tradition, a man of letters versed in a wide variety of intellectual discourses. He gave up the pursuit of foundational truths in knowledge and ethics for a more relativist, pragmatist approach, which takes as its goal edifying, useful commentary on culture. In this field, he has published numerous articles and books, most significantly *Philosophy and the Mirror of Nature* (1979) and *Consequences of Pragmatism* (1982), gaining an international reputation as an American philosopher. This pragmatism led Rorty to a deep appreciation of the middle-class democracy of the United States, and in his later writings he promoted a patriotism that separated him from his erstwhile fellow liberals.

Salman Rushdie (*b. 1947*) Rushdie was born and raised in India, but by 1968 he was living in England, first as an actor, then as a freelance writer, finally as a novelist. His second novel, *Midnight's Children*, brought him critical acclaim as a postmodern writer navigating the waters of a multicultural, postcolonial world. His fourth novel, the 1988 *Satanic Verses*, sparked an unprecedented controversy. Sections of the book depict the prophet Muhammad, and these representations were deemed blasphemous by Islamic clerics, especially the Iranian Ayatollah Khomeini, who gave his express approval to anyone who might kill Rushdie. Bounties were offered for Rushdie's death, riots erupted in many Muslim countries, and the writer was forced into hiding. These earlier works and his subsequent novels, all complex intertwinings of various marvelous tales, have established Rushdie as one of the foremost fiction writers of his generation. He has also produced a large body of nonfiction, mostly essays interpreting contemporary culture.

Chief Seattle (*c. 1790–1866*)   Chief of Puget Sound tribes, Seattle ceded Indian lands to white settlers by signing the Port Elliott treaty (1855) and moved his people to a reservation. Grateful for the chief's protection during a period of Indian uprisings (1855–58), local residents named their town after him.

David Sedaris (*b. 1956*)   Sedaris was born in Binghamton, New York, and grew up in Raleigh, North Carolina. He attended Kent State University, though eventually he graduated from the Art Institute of Chicago. Originally, he contemplated a career in the arts, but early on he abandoned that direction to pursue humor. He regularly contributes humorous essays to National Public Radio, including the 1992 series "Santaland Diaries," which told of his experiences as an elf in Macy's department store during the Christmas shopping season. That series launched him into public prominence, and he began publishing his humor, nearly all of it based on his own life, in 1994. He has collaborated with his sister, Amy Sedaris, on a number of plays, continues to broadcast his work on the NPR show, *This American Life*, and now lives in Paris.

Elizabeth Cady Stanton (*1815–1902*)   Born to affluent parents in Johnstown, New York, Stanton was educated at Johnstown Academy and the rigorous Troy Female Seminary before studying law at her father's office, where she learned of legal discrimination against women. She married the abolitionist Henry Stanton in 1840 and that same year met Lucretia Mott at the World Anti-Slavery Convention in London, where several women abolitionists were refused recognition. Her experience in her father's office and in London prompted her to begin speaking publicly about women's rights. Stanton's activism was instrumental in the passage of New York's

1848 Married Women's Property Act. Together with Mott, she organized the first women's rights convention (1848), and she worked closely with Susan B. Anthony (from 1851 on) to liberalize divorce laws, give women greater control over their earnings and their children, and extend the vote to women. She helped found the National Woman Suffrage Association (later the National American Women's Suffrage Association) and was its president from 1869 to 1892. She also wrote the amendment extending the vote to women that was presented to Congress at every session from 1878 until women finally won the franchise in 1920.

Brent Staples (*b. 1951*) Born in Chester, Pennsylvania, Staples grew up in poverty, the eldest of nine children and the son of an alcoholic father. He watched his friends become involved with drugs and crime, but escaped that life through a program that prepared him for college, a scholarship to Widener University, and a Danforth fellowship to the University of Chicago, where he earned a PhD in psychology. He began his journalistic career as a freelance reporter and joined the staff of the Chicago *Sun-Times* in 1983. He now writes editorials for the *New York Times*. He won the Anisfield Wolff Book Award for his 1994 memoir, *Parallel Time: Growing Up in Black America*, in which he discusses both the life he has made for himself and that of his younger brother, who was murdered while selling cocaine.

Jonathan Swift (*1667–1745*) Born in Dublin, Ireland, of English parents, Swift attended Trinity College in Dublin, but fled to England following the Revolution of 1688, the abdication of James II, and the subsequent upheaval in Ireland. From 1689 to 1699, he was secretary to Sir William Temple (a distant relative), took religious orders, and wrote *The Tale of a Tub*, one of his most successful satires. After Sir William's death, Swift returned to Ireland as secretary to the Earl of Berkeley but visited England on extended trips and gained renown for his satiric writings and personal charm. On his visits to England he was drawn into politics, and by 1710 he was the Tories' chief pamphleteer. In 1713, his services were rewarded with the deanship of Saint Patrick's Cathedral in Dublin. When George I took the throne in 1714, however, the Whigs gained ascendance, and Swift returned permanently to Ireland. In this period Swift wrote extensively about the social and economic problems of Ireland, publishing the "Drapier's Letters" (1724–25) and "A Modest Proposal" (anonymously in 1729). His greatest work, *Gulliver's Travels*, was published in 1726.

Amy Tan (*b. 1952*)   Tan was born in Oakland, California, and raised in the Bay Area. Her father, educated in Beijing, emigrated to the United States in 1947; her mother emigrated shortly before the Communists came to power in 1949, leaving behind three daughters from a previous marriage. When Tan was fourteen, both her father and her brother died of brain tumors, and her mother moved the family to Europe briefly. She attended a number of colleges before getting her BA and MA in linguistics from San Jose State University. In 1985, Tan wrote a short story titled "Rules of the Game" for a writing workshop; that story later became part of her extremely successful first book, *The Joy Luck Club* (1989). Tan often writes about the awkward position in which first-generation Americans find themselves, poised between the world of their parents and that of their peers.

Deborah Tannen (*b. 1945*)   Partially deaf from a childhood illness, Tannen, a Brooklyn native, took an early interest in nonverbal signs, which she began to study formally as a student of linguistics. She got her PhD in linguistics from the University of California, Berkeley, and has studied and taught this subject ever since as a fellow at the Center for Advanced Study in the Behavioral Sciences in Stanford, California, at the Institute for Advanced Study at Princeton, and in her current position as University Professor and professor of linguistics at Georgetown University. Her books *You Just Don't Understand! Women and Men in Conversation* (1990) and *You're Wearing That? Understanding Mothers and Daughters in Conversation* (2006) were best-sellers. Tannen also writes poetry, fiction, and personal essays.

Henry David Thoreau (*1817–1862*)   A native of Concord, Massachusetts, Thoreau attended Harvard College and in 1838 founded a progressive school with his brother John. But the death of his brother in 1842 and his friendship with Ralph Waldo Emerson, founder of the Transcendentalist movement, led him to poetry and nature writing, so in 1842 Thoreau moved to New York to cultivate literary society. His failure there, however, pushed him back to Concord in 1843. In 1845 he embarked on a two-year quest for self-sufficiency and a bond with nature that he described in *Walden* (1854). On his return from Walden Pond, he took up surveying and running his family's pencil-making business, and committed himself to the abolition of slavery. He worked on the Underground Railroad, wrote and lectured on the evils of slavery, and adopted John Brown as his ideal. With the failure of Brown's raid on Harpers Ferry in 1859, Thoreau broke down. He died three years later, probably of tuberculosis. While little appreciated in his own lifetime, Thoreau is now recognized as one of the most important members of the Transcendentalist movement and the forerunner of nature writers like Edward Abbey.

James Thurber (*1894–1961*) Born in Columbus, Ohio, Thurber lost an eye as a child when he and his brother were playing William Tell. The injury restricted Thurber's physical activities, and perhaps as a consequence fostered his reflective attitude toward life. After attending The Ohio State University, he worked as a code clerk for the State Department during World War I, traveling to the American embassy in Paris to do so. After the war he took up a career in journalism, which eventually brought him to *The New Yorker*, where his friend, the essayist E. B. White, got him a job in 1927. Thurber was a contributing editor, writing humorous essays and short stories for the magazine and, once his doodles were discovered by White, also cartoons.

Alice Walker (*b. 1944*) Walker was born in Eatonton, Georgia, the eighth child of sharecroppers. At the age of eight, her brother accidentally shot her in the right eye with a BB gun, which caused her to lose the sight in that eye. Because the injury disfigured her face, she had an isolated childhood and spent her time reading, writing, and carefully observing the people around her. In 1961, Walker entered Spelman College, where she joined the civil rights movement. Two years later, she transferred to Sarah Lawrence College and began writing poetry. She published her first book of poems in 1968 and her first novel in 1970. Her most famous work is *The Color Purple*, an epistolary novel that won a National Book Critics Circle Award nomination in 1982 and both the American Book Award and the Pulitzer Prize in 1983. She has been involved with the feminist movement, the antinuclear movement, and the campagn against female genital mutilation. Alice Walker started her own publishing company, Wild Trees Press, in 1984.

Eudora Welty (*1909–2001*)   A novelist and short-story writer, Welty was born in Jackson, Mississippi. She graduated from the University of Wisconsin in 1929 and returned to Mississippi, where she became a photographer for the Works Progress Administration. Her first story was published in 1936, and thereafter she published regularly, at first in small, regional journals, and later in magazines like *The New Yorker* and *Atlantic Monthly.* Her work, both poignant and funny, focuses largely on personal relationships and small-town life in the deep South.

E. B. White (*1899–1985*)   Born in Mount Vernon, New York, White joined the staff of *The New Yorker* magazine in 1927 and remained there throughout his career. (He married Katherine Angell, the magazine's first fiction editor, in 1929.) In addition to his work at *The New Yorker*, White also wrote a column for *Harper's* magazine, but he is probably best known as the author of the children's classics *Stuart Little* (1945), *Charlotte's Web* (1952), and *The Trumpet of the Swan* (1970) and as the reviser of the classic book about writing, *Elements of Style* (1959).

George Will (*b. 1941*)   Will's father was a philosophy professor at the University of Illinois, and his mother was a teacher and education editor. He graduated from Trinity College in Connecticut (1962), attended Oxford University, and earned a PhD in political science from Princeton. In 1960, Will worked to elect John Kennedy president, but by 1967 his admiration for capitalism and the free market led him to conservatism. For a couple of years in the late 1960s he taught at Michigan State University and the University of Toronto, but by the early 1970s he was working in Washington as an aide to the Republican senator Allott of Colorado. He began writing for the conservative *National Review* in 1972, and followed that with a burgeoning career as an opinion columnist for *Newsweek* and the *Washington Post*. He also became a regular "talking head" on the political television show *This Week with David Brinkley*. His close association with Ronald Reagan raised his prominence and earned him some criticism for undermining his journalistic integrity (he coached Reagan for debates with President Jimmy Carter and later commented on those debates as a journalist). Today he is a widely distributed columnist, a recognizable face on television news commentaries, and one of the most respected voices of American conservatism.

Virginia Woolf (*1882–1941*) Woolf was raised in London and educated by her father. After his death, she moved, with her sister Vanessa and her brother Adrian, to Gordon Square, London, where their house became the center of the Bloomsbury group, an intellectual circle that included the economist John Maynard Keynes, the art critics Roger Fry and Clive Bell (who later married Vanessa), and the biographer Lytton Strachey. With her husband, Leonard Woolf, Virginia Woolf founded the Hogarth Press in 1917. While her early work is rather conventional, from *Jacob's Room* (1922) on, Woolf strove to capture the flow of time in both the world and her characters' consciousness and became an icon of Modernist literature. *Mrs. Dalloway* (1925) and *To the Lighthouse* (1927) are generally considered her most successful works. Woolf was also a renowned literary critic, a prolific essayist, and a committed diarist. She suffered from mental illness and drowned herself near her home.

William Zinsser (*b. 1922*) Zinsser was born in New York, earned a degree from Princeton University (1944), and served in Italy and North Africa during World War II. After the war, he took a job as a feature writer for the *New York Herald-Tribune*, eventually working his way up to writing editorials. In 1959, he became a freelance writer, producing nine books before 1976, when he wrote *On Writing Well: An Informal Guide to Writing Nonfiction*. That book came out of his experience as a teacher of writing at Yale University (1970–79) and quickly became a standard in many college writing classes. In the last twenty-five years Zinsser has written or edited another dozen books, among them *Easy to Remember: The Great American Songwriters and Their Songs* (2001) and *Writing About Your Life* (2004).

*

Glossary

accuracy   the quality ascribed to evidence in an inductive argument when it is free from error.

ad hominem   the fallacy in ethical argument of attempting to discredit a logical argument by attacking the character of its author. For example:

> We can't expect this policy to work; the Congressman sponsoring it doesn't even have a college degree.

Logical arguments should be evaluated on their own merits, not on the basis of their author's background or character.

anecdotal evidence   the testimony of a single person or a few individuals, usually conveyed in a brief story.

bandwagon appeal   a fallacy of pathetic argument in which readers are persuaded to adopt a position because that position is popular.

begging the question   the fallacy of trying to support a conclusion with an argument that includes the conclusion as one of its premises. For example:

We all know that government does nothing but get in the way of enterprise, and these new regulations come from the EPA, so they must be harmful to business.

In this case, the conclusion restates the first premise in a disguised form. To make the circularity of the argument clearer, it could be rephrased as "Government (e.g., EPA) regulations are harmful to ('get in the way of') business (another word for 'enterprise').

conclusion   see *deduction, induction.*

deduction   "top-down" reasoning in which one begins with a statement of general applicability (the major premise) and a statement concerning a particular case (the minor premise), and from these draws a conclusion. For example:

> *Major premise:* Cats are smarter than dogs.
> *Minor premises:* Felix is a cat, and Goofy is a dog.
> *Conclusion:* Felix is smarter than Goofy.

(Note that deductive arguments can have many premises.) You consider an argument to be true if you agree with its premises. You consider an argument to be valid if you think the conclusion logically follows from the premises. To be considered sound, an argument must be both true and valid.

either/or fallacy   the fallacy in logical reasoning of excluding all but two choices. For example:

> If this city wants to balance its budget, it's got to raise taxes. The only alternative is to cut services to the bone.

Such arguments are seductive, but they typically depend on oversimplifying the situation.

enthymeme   a deductive argument that suppresses one of its premises. For example:

> The Yankees were the best baseball team in the world in 2000 because they won that year's World Series.

Major premise (unstated): The World Series is a contest between the two best baseball teams in the world.
Minor premise: The Yankees won the World Series in 2000.
Conclusion: The Yankees were the best baseball team in the world in 2000.

ethical argument the methods of self-presentation by which a writer establishes his or her character, and the use of those methods to persuade.

ethical fallacy the way in which ethical arguments can go wrong. See *ad hominem.*

ethos a writer's character as it is perceived by the audience, especially but not limited to his or her moral standing.

fallacies ways in which arguments can go wrong. See *logical fallacies, ethical fallacy,* or *pathetic fallacies.*

falsity the quality ascribed to a deductive argument when one or more of its premises are untrue or to an inductive argument when some or all of the evidence it offers is inaccurate. See *deduction, induction.*

false analogy a fallacy in logical reasoning in which the writer draws conclusions about one case by comparing it to another, dissimilar case. For example:

Puerto Rico is bound to become a state eventually. After all, Alaska did.

Alaska and Puerto Rico are too dissimilar for the history of one to give much insight into the future of the other.

false cause a fallacy in logical reasoning in which one event is presumed to have caused another event merely because the first preceded the second. For example:

The economy of the United States went into a recession because George H. W. Bush was elected president.

hasty generalization a fallacy in logical reasoning in which an inductive conclusion is drawn from insufficient evidence.

induction   "bottom-up" reasoning in which one begins by examining a number of individual cases and from these draws a conclusion—some assertion of general applicability—that governs all similar cases. For example:

> The air war against Germany could not win World War II, the air war against North Vietnam could not win the Vietnam War, and the air war against Iraq could not win the Gulf War. In all of these wars, ground troops were required for victory. Therefore, bombing the enemy will never by itself win a war.

The evidence in an inductive argument must be accurate, sufficient, and representative. The evidence is inaccurate if any of the cases cited are false. It is insufficient if the conclusion is drawn from too small a sample of cases. It is unrepresentative if the cases cited belong to a narrow subgroup of all the cases. Because the example above ignores an important recent case—the war in Kosovo—the argument is faulty because the evidence is unrepresentative.

logical argument   the methods by which we reason; the two types of logical arguments are deductive and inductive.

logical fallacies   ways in which logical arguments can go wrong. See *non sequitur, red herring, false cause, begging the question, either/or fallacy, hasty generalization, false analogy,* and *special pleading.*

major premise   see *deduction.*

minor premise   see *deduction.*

non sequitur   the fallacy in logical argument of trying to support an argument with irrelevant premises. For example:

> Jill is a single mother, so we cannot expect her to have a job.

As marital and parental status are irrelevant to employment status, Jill's being a single mother does nothing to support the conclusion that she is unlikely to be employed.

pathetic argument   the methods by which a writer manipulates the emotions of the audience in order to persuade.

pathetic fallacies ways in which pathetic arguments can go wrong; these are usually exaggerations of responsible pathetic arguments. See *bandwagon, pity,* and *tradition.*

pathos the emotions felt by an audience.

pity, appeal to a fallacy in pathetic argument in which readers are persuaded to adopt a position for reasons of compassion rather than logic.

red herring a deductive argument whose premises are irrelevant to the conclusion and are meant to distract readers. Red herring arguments often pretend to prove the conclusion by proving some other conclusion (which is often unstated). For example, consider this argument from an airline trying to sell seats in December:

> Winter is the best time to go to Italy. Rome, the Eternal City, has more history than you can imagine. You can sample world-renowned pizza in Naples. And from the Alps to the sunny coasts of Sicily, Italy boasts gorgeous landscapes. And if you're like most tourists, you relish history, hearty foods, and great views.

> In this argument, the major premise and minor premises combine to prove that tourists would find what they're looking for in Italy. It does not prove that winter is the best season to travel to Italy.

representative in an inductive argument, a quality ascribed to evidence that considers both cases that support the conclusion and those that do not support it.

rhetoric the art of persuasion, using logical, ethical, and pathetic arguments.

sound argument a deductive argument that has true premises and valid reasoning.

special pleading a fallacy of logical argument in which the writer suppresses evidence that contradicts the conclusion in an inductive argument. For example:

> The food at La Maison is a crime. The cheesecake is runny and warm, the gelato is as tasty as frozen styrofoam, and the eclairs are worse than HoHos.

In this case, the evidence was drawn only from the dessert menu. Most readers would expect some mention of the quality of the appetizers and entrees before they would conclude that this restaurant's food is bad in general.

strong argument   an inductive argument with persuasive evidence.

sufficiency   the quality ascribed to evidence in an inductive argument in which a large enough number of cases has been cited to support the conclusion.

tradition, appeal to   a fallacy in pathetic argument in which readers are persuaded to adopt a position on the basis of their respect for the beliefs and customs of their predecessors.

truth   the quality ascribed to a deductive argument when its premises are factually correct. See *deduction*.

validity   the quality ascribed to a deductive argument when the conclusion follows logically from the premises. See *deduction*.

*

Permissions Acknowledgments

Martin Luther King, Jr., c/o Writers House, Inc., as agent for the proprietor. Copyright © 1963 by Martin Luther King, Jr., copyright renewed 1991 by Coretta Scott King.

Maxine Hong Kingston: "No Name Woman" from *The Woman Warrior* by Maxine Hong Kingston. Reprinted by permission of Alfred K. Knopf, a Division of Random House, Inc.

Jonathan Kozol: "The Human Cost of an Illiterate Society" from *Illiterate America* by Jonathan Kozol. Copyright © 1985 by Jonathan Kozol. Used by permission of Doubleday, a division of Random House, Inc.

Lewis Lapham: "Time Lines" from *Waiting for the Barbarians*. Verso: London and New York, 1997.

Bret Lott: "Atonement" from *Fathers, Sons and Brothers: The Men in My Family*. Copyright © 1997 by Bret Lott. Reprinted by permission of Harcourt, Inc.

Thomas Lynch: "Bodies in Motion and at Rest," from *Bodies in Motion and at Rest* by Thomas Lunch. Copyright © 2000 by Thomas Lynch. Used by permission of W. W. Norton & Company, Inc.

Malcolm X: "A Homemade Education" from *The Autobiography of Malcolm X* by Malcolm X. Copyright © 1964 by Alex Haley and Malcolm X. Copyright © 1965 by Alex Haley and Better Shabazz. Reprinted by permission of Random House, Inc.

N. Scott Momaday: "An American Land Ethic" from *The Man Made of Words* by N. Scott Momaday. Copyright © 1997 by Bedford/St. Martin's. Reproduced by permission of Bedford/St. Martin's.

George Orwell: "Shooting an Elephant" from *Shooting an Elephant and Other Essays* by George Orwell. Copyright © 1950 by Sonia Brownell Orwell and renewed 1978 by Sonia Pitt-Rivers, reprinted by permission of Harcourt, Inc.

Leonard Pitts: "On 9/11: Innocence Was Lost Once Again" from the *Miami Herald* by Leonard Pitts. Copyright © 2006 by the *Miami Herald*. Reproduced with permission of the *Miami Herald* in the format Textbook via Copyright Clearance Center.

Katha Pollitt: "Why Boys Don't Play with Dolls" from *The New York Times Magazine*, October 8, 1995. Reprinted by permission of the New York Times.

Richard Rodriguez: " 'Blaxicans' and Other Reinvented Americans" by Richard Rodriguez. Copyright © 2003 by Richard Rodriguez. (Originally appeared in *The Chronicle of Higher Education*, September 12, 2003.) Reprinted by permission of Georges Borchardt, Inc., on behalf of the author.

Richard Rorty: "The Unpatriotic Academy" from *Philosophy and Social Hope* by Richard Rorty. Copyright © 1999 by Richard Rorty. Reprinted by permission of Penguin U. K.